INEVITABLE REVOLUTIONS

PLEASE READ THE FOLLOWING

1. ALL TEXTBOOKS MUST BE RETURNED BY THE LAST DAY OF FINALS.

2. A FINE OF UP TO ▇▇▇▇ WILL BE CHARGED FOR LATE RETURNS.

3. YOU WILL BE REQUIRED TO PURCHASE THIS TEXTBOOK IF YOU HAVE UNDERLINED, HIGHLIGHTED OR IF THERE ARE VISIBLE SIGNS OF WATER DAMAGE.

4. PLEASE SIGN YOUR NAME BELOW.

NAME   ADDRESS

PLEASE RETURN THIS TEXTBOOK TO:
TEXTBOOK RENTAL SERVICE
EASTERN ILLINOIS UNIVERSITY
CHARLESTON, IL 61920

BY THE SAME AUTHOR

THE AMERICAN AGE: U.S. FOREIGN POLICY AT HOME AND
ABROAD SINCE *1750*

AMERICA, RUSSIA AND THE COLD WAR, *1945–1992*

THE NEW EMPIRE:
AN INTERPRETATION OF AMERICAN EXPANSION, *1860–1898*

THE PANAMA CANAL: THE CRISIS IN HISTORICAL
PERSPECTIVE

AMERICA IN THE COLD WAR:
TWENTY YEARS OF REVOLUTION AND RESPONSE *(ed.)*

CREATION OF THE AMERICAN EMPIRE: U.S. DIPLOMATIC
HISTORY
(2 volumes, with Lloyd C. Gardner and Thomas J. McCormick

THE AMERICAN CENTURY:
A HISTORY OF THE UNITED STATES SINCE THE *1800s*
(with Richard Polenberg and Nancy Woloch)

INEVITABLE REVOLUTIONS

The United States in Central America

2nd Edition

WALTER LaFEBER

W· W· NORTON & COMPANY
New York   London

Library of Congress Cataloging-in-Publication Data
LaFeber, Walter.
Inevitable revolutions : the United States in Central America /
Walter LaFeber.—2nd ed.
p.   cm.
Includes bibliographical references and index.
1. Central America—Foreign relations—United States.
2. United States—Foreign relations—Central America.
3. Revolutions—Central America.   I. Title.
F1436.8.U6L33   1993
327.730728—dc20   92-10349

ISBN 0-393-03434-8 (cl)
ISBN 0-393-30964-9 (pa)

W. W. Norton & Company, Inc.
500 Fifth Avenue, New York, N.Y. 10110
W. W. Norton & Company Ltd.
10 Coptic Street, London WC1A 1PU

This Book is for
MARIE UNDERHILL NOLL

Contents

CHAPTER II: MAINTAINING THE SYSTEM   87

CHAPTER III: UPDATING THE SYSTEM   147

CHAPTER IV: THE COLLAPSE OF THE SYSTEM   197

CHAPTER V: THE REMAINS OF THE SYSTEM   271

CHAPTER VI: REARRANGING THE REMAINS OF THE SYSTEM   325

INEVITABLE REVOLUTIONS

He laughed. "People like to tell you it's the politics of bananas."

"Sure," she said, and her smile changed until it had a bitter turn to it. "It's a banana republic. I'm sure that's in the papers."

"Strategic considerations aside," Holliwell said, "bananas are worth fighting for. Any nutritionist can tell you that."

"Really?"

Holliwell stood up, his eyes on hers. There was clear light there, when the film dissolved. The film of weariness or fear.

"If you don't eat your bananas, you don't get enough potassium. If you don't get your potassium, you experience a sense of existential dread."

"Now I'm a nurse," she said, "and I never heard that."

"You can look it up. One of the symptoms of potassium insufficiency is a sense of existential dread."

"You're the scientist. I'm supposed to believe what you tell me."

"Certainly. And now you know why Tecan is vital to the United States."

"The United States," she told him, "may be in for a spell of existential dread."

From ROBERT STONE, *A Flag for Sunrise*
(Copyright © 1977, 1980, 1981 by Robert Stone.
Reprinted by permission of Alfred A. Knopf, Inc.)

Introduction

■■■■■■■■■■■■■■■■

AN OVERVIEW OF
THE SYSTEM

*Central America is the most important place in the world for the
United States today.*

> U.S. Ambassador to the United Nations
> JEANE KIRKPATRICK, 1981

*What we see in Central America today would not be much different
if Fidel Castro and the Soviet Union did not exist.*

> U.S. Ambassador to Panama
> AMBLER MOSS, 1980

No area in the world is more tightly integrated into the United States
political-economic system, and none—as President Ronald Reagan
warned a joint session of Congress in April 1983—more vital for North
American security, than Central America. Washington, D.C. is closer to
El Salvador than to San Francisco. Nearly two-thirds of all U.S. trade
and the nation's oil imports, as well as many strategic minerals, depend
on the Caribbean sea lanes bordered by the five Central American nations.[1]

North Americans have always treated the region differently from the
remainder of Latin America. The five nations cover only a little more
than one-hundredth of the Western Hemisphere's land area, contain a
mere one-fortieth of its population, stretch only nine hundred miles
north to south and (at the widest points) less than three hundred miles

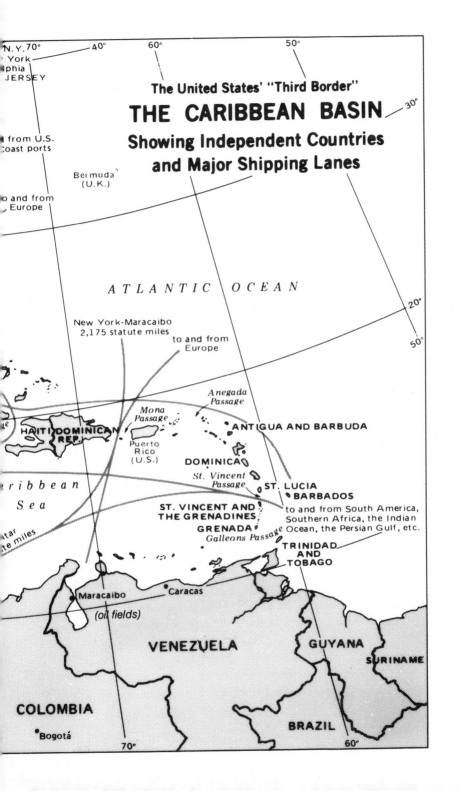

The United States' "Third Border"
THE CARIBBEAN BASIN
Showing Independent Countries and Major Shipping Lanes

from ocean to ocean. But this compact region has been the target of a highly disproportionate amount of North American investment and—especially—military intervention.[2] Every twentieth-century intervention by U.S. troops in the hemisphere has occurred in the Central American-Caribbean region. The unusual history of the area was captured by former Chilean President Eduardo Frei, who observed that the Central American states "to a man from the deep South [of the Americas] seem at times more remote than Europe."[3] Frei's remark also implied that the largest South American nations (Argentina, Chile, Brazil) historically looked east to Europe, while the Central Americans have turned north to the United States.

Few regions in the world have been in greater political and economic turmoil than Central America. And there are few areas about which North Americans are more ignorant. The following is a capsule view of the five nations which, over the past century, have become dependent on the U.S. system. Each is quite different from the other four, but all five share a dependence on the United States that is deeply rooted in history. They also share poverty and inequality that have spawned revolutions in the seventies and eighties.

Guatemala

POPULATION: 9.3 million (most populous in Central America)
AREA: 42,000 square miles (about the size of Kentucky)
ECONOMY: depends on coffee, banana, cotton exports
ILLITERACY: At least 50 percent
PER CAPITA GROSS NATIONAL PRODUCT: U.S. $810
ONE TELEPHONE: per 63 persons

Guatemala has historically been the most economically powerful nation in Central America, but half the population average only $81 income each year. This half are the pure-blooded Indians (descendants of the great Mayans) who are among the poorest and most isolated people in the hemisphere. In the late seventies the Indians suddenly began to form revolutionary bands. They and other exploited Guatemalans became the targets of a 20,000-man army trained and largely supplied by the United States. That army runs the government, and it is a direct descendant of a regime placed in power by a U.S.-planned *golpe* (or coup) in 1954 that overthrew the constitutionally elected, reformist Arbenz government. In 1980 a U.S. official surveyed the spreading revolution, and the government's response of massacres and torture, then observed: "What we'd give to have an Arbenz now."[4]

Honduras

POPULATION: 5.2 million (slightly less than Louisiana's)
AREA: 43,000 square miles (about the size of Louisiana)
ECONOMY: depends on banana and coffee exports, U.S. aid
ILLITERACY: at least 44 percent
PER CAPITA INCOME: U.S. $1000
ONE TELEPHONE: per 79 persons

The original "banana republic," Honduras has become the closest ally of the United States in the region while remaining the poorest and most undeveloped state in the hemisphere other than Haiti. U.S. fruit companies controlled the country after 1900. In the sixties they were joined by New York and California based banks (Citicorp, Chase Manhattan, Bank of America) that took over the financial system. Life expectancy of adults is forty-nine years; more than 20,000 families live on the edge of starvation; and in rural areas families of ten to twelve children are not uncommon, although half die before the age of five. Because it is the only Central American country with boundaries on three of the other four nations, Honduras has traditionally served as a base for revolutionaries and counterrevolutionaries—thus the United States used it as a staging area to overthrow the Guatemalan government in 1954 and to "destabilize" the Nicaraguan government during the eighties. Although civilians sometimes occupied the presidency after 1945, the country has mostly been ruled by military officers trained and equipped by the United States. The country's dire poverty has been caused partly by foreign exploitation, partly by rampant internal corruption, and partly by sterile mountainous terrain. An Honduran legislator once crumpled a sheet of paper, dropped it on his desk, then observed, "That is an outline map of Honduras."

El Salvador

POPULATION: 5.5 million (most densely populated in region)

AREA: 8,236 square miles (the size of Massachusetts)

ECONOMY: depends on coffee exports, U.S. aid, money from Salvadorans in the U.S.

ILLITERACY: at least 50 percent

PER CAPITA INCOME: U.S. $700

ONE TELEPHONE: per 36 persons

Its name is sometimes translated as "Saviour of the World," but its people are among the world's five worst-fed populations. One reason: at least half of all Salvadorans depend on the land for a living, but fewer than 2 percent (the "oligarchs" or "Fourteen Families") control nearly all the fertile soil and 60 percent of all the land. With a 3.5 percent rate of population increase (one of the world's highest), the demands on the soil have become so great that erosion is ruining the land area and extinguishing entire species of indigenous animals and plants. After a 1979 *golpe*, the army—trained and supplied by the United States— seized some of the Fourteen Families' power, but that power was only diminished, not destroyed. Stereotyped as the hardest workers in the region (the "Germans of Central America," the phrase goes), many Salvadorans historically have had to emigrate to survive. Since the revolution accelerated in the late seventies, at least one-tenth of the population, or more than 500,000 people, entered the United States illegally for refuge. They had reasons other than economic for doing so: during 1980 and 1981 the military and right-wing terrorists killed approximately 30,000 civilians to stop spreading revolution. Such a bloodbath (equivalent to killing more than two million of the U.S. population) is not new; fifty years earlier, the military killed a similar number of peasants for similar reasons.

Nicaragua

POPULATION: 3.6 million (most thinly populated in region)
AREA: 57,000 square miles (about the same as North Carolina)
ECONOMY: depends on coffee, sugar, cotton, timber, banana exports
ILLITERACY: 60 to 70 percent before 1979 revolution, 35 percent after
PER CAPITA GROSS NATIONAL PRODUCT: U.S. $610
ONE TELEPHONE: per 77 persons

Modern Nicaragua, dating from the revolution that seized power in mid-1979, was shaped by U.S. military occupation (1911–33), and then the U.S.-created and supported Somoza family dynasty (1934–79). That family seized most of the wealth, including a land area equal to the size of Massachusetts. Meanwhile 200,000 peasants had no land. The major causes of death were gastrointestinal and parasitic diseases, and infant maladies. The country played a pivotal part in Washington's diplomacy because of the Somozas' willingness to act as U.S. instruments, and also because natural waterways made it a possible site for an interoceanic canal. Its significance greatly increased after the Sandinista revolutionaries seized power in 1979. No regime in the world cooperated more fully with the United States than did the Somozas between 1930 and late seventies, and no Central American nation has more directly challenged U.S. policies in the area than the post-1979 Nicaraguan government.

Costa Rica

POPULATION: 3.1 million (one of the most rapidly increasing in the world)
AREA: 20,000 square miles (smaller than Arkansas)
ECONOMY: depends on coffee, banana, sugar exports
ILLITERACY: low, probably less than 8 percent
PER CAPITA INCOME: U.S. $1584
ONE TELEPHONE: per 7 persons

The most democratic, equitable, and literate Central American nation, Costa Rica was oddly blessed by poverty. Christopher Columbus called it "Rich Coast" (Costa Rica) because the Indians wore gold jewelry, but it actually had no minerals and so European adventurers lost interest in it. Instead, industrious Spaniards drove out the Indians, developed farms, and thus established a widely held land base for the strongest and longest-lasting democratic system in Latin America. Unlike the population of the other four countries, Indians are few in number. People of Spanish ancestry control the power centers. After the 1948 revolution, the government outlawed the army, although a U.S.-trained national police of 7,000 efficiently maintains order. Stability and climate made the country a favorite retirement spot for North Americans. But the hemisphere's highest birthrate, combined with oil and price inflation and a steep decline in coffee export prices, caused the most severe crisis in thirty years during the early eighties. Possible cuts in the nation's extensive social welfare system threatened to open Costa Rica to the political upheavals that already ripped apart the other Central American nations.

These five countries are changing before our eyes. Such instability, importance to U.S. security, and North American ignorance about them form a combustible mixture. One explosion has already rocked the hemisphere: the Nicaraguan revolution became the most significant political event in the Caribbean region since 1959 when Fidel Castro seized power in Cuba. Revolutionary movements have since appeared in every other Central American nation except Costa Rica, and even that democracy has not been safe from terrorism.

The United States has countered those revolutions with its military power. Washington's recent policy, this book argues, is historically consistent for two reasons: first, for more than a century (if not since 1790), North Americans have been staunchly antirevolutionary; and second, U.S. power has been the dominant outside (and often inside) force shaping the societies against which Central Americans have rebelled. The reasons for this struggle between the Goliaths and Davids of world power (or what former Guatemalan President Juan José Arévalo called "the Shark and the Sardines")[5] lie deeply embedded in the history of

U.S.–Central American relations. As U.S. Ambassador to Panama Ambler Moss phrased the problem in 1980, "What we see in Central America today would not be much different if Fidel Castro and the Soviet Union did not exist."[6]

These two themes—the U.S. fear of certain kinds of revolution and the way the U.S. system ironically helped cause revolutions in Central America—form the basis of this book. Before that story is told in detail, however, a short overview introduces the two themes.

The Revolutions of the 1970s and 1770s

Washington officials have opposed radical change not because of pressure from public opinion. Throughout the twentieth century, the overwhelming number of North Americans could not have identified each of the five Central American nations on a map, let alone ticked off the region's sins that called for an application of U.S. force.

The United States consistently feared and fought such change because it was a status quo power. It wanted stability, benefited from the on-going system, and was therefore content to work with the military-oligarchy complex that ruled most of Central America from the 1820s to the 1980s. The world's leading revolutionary nation in the eighteenth century became the leading protector of the status quo in the twentieth century. Such protection was defensible when it meant protecting the more equitable societies of Western Europe and Japan, but became questionable when it meant bolstering poverty and inequality in Central America.[7]

How North Americans turned away from revolution toward defense of oligarchs is one of the central questions in U.S. diplomatic history. The process, outlined in Chapter I, no doubt began with the peculiar nature of the revolution in 1776. It was radical in that it proclaimed the ideal of personal freedom. The power of the British mercantilist state, Thomas Jefferson and some of his colleagues declared, had to be more subordinate to individual interest. North Americans, especially if they were white and male, could moreover realize such an ideal in a society that was roughly equitable at its birth, and possessed a tremendous landed frontier containing rich soil and many minerals that could provide food and a steadily growing economy for its people.

Central Americans have expressed similar ideals of freedom, but the historical sources of those ideals—not to mention the geographical circumstances in which they could be realized—have been quite different from the North American. Fidel Castro quoted the Declaration of Independence and compared burning Cuban cane fields in 1958 to the Boston Tea Party of 1773. But his political program for achieving the Declaration's principles flowed from such native Cuban revolutionaries as José Martí, not from Thomas Jefferson.[8]

The need of Cubans and Central Americans to find different means for achieving their version of a just society arose in large part from their long experience with North American capitalism. This capitalism has had a Jekyll and Hyde personality. U.S. citizens see it as having given them the highest standard of living and most open society in the world. Many Central Americans have increasingly associated capitalism with a brutal oligarchy-military complex that has been supported by U.S. policies—and armies. Capitalism, as they see it, has too often threatened the survival of many for the sake of freedom for a few. For example, Latin Americans bitterly observed that when the state moved its people for the sake of national policy (as in Cuba or Nicaragua), the United States condemned it as smacking of Communist tyranny. If, however, an oligarch forced hundreds of peasants off their land for the sake of his own profit, the United States accepted it as simply the way of the real world.[9]

The terrible dilemma that resulted from these two views of capitalism was starkly exposed during a cabinet meeting in 1959. President Dwight D. Eisenhower and his advisers debated how they could choke off the threat that the new Castro government posed to the hemisphere. The U.S. Ambassador to the United Nations, Henry Cabot Lodge, offered one insight. "We should focus on the Declaration of Independence rather than on the Communist Manifesto where [the focus] has been," he told the cabinet, "and in doing so we should not endeavor to sell the specific word 'Capitalism' which is beyond rehabilitation in the minds of the non-white world." Lodge thus outlined why the U.S. and Latin American revolutions differed: both shared a vision of justice for the individual (so why, Lodge demanded, do we keep repeating the terrible error of saying the Latin Americans must have gotten the idea from Marx?), but the newer revolutionaries could not replay the older experience. Latin history told them that capitalism was antirevolutionary. And that, Lodge told the cabinet, was precisely the heart of the problem: "The U.S. can win wars, but the question is can we win revolutions."[10]

From at least the early nineteenth century, Washington officials have believed they had to "win" such revolutions. Otherwise, they feared, an exhausted and unwary revolutionary government might be susceptible to dangerous outside influences. By its nature a revolution is unpredictable. It "can't be bound be th' rules iv th' game," humorist Finley Peter Dunne (alias "Mr. Dooley") tried to tell Theodore Roosevelt's generation, "because it's again' th' rules iv th' game." Resembling loose cannon rolling across the deck on an out-of-control ship, revolutions in an area as sea-tossed as Central America could threaten interests that North Americans have historically considered essential to their safety.

For the United States, capitalism and military security went hand-in-hand. They have, since the nineteenth century, formed two sides of the same policy in Central America. Early on, the enemy was Great Britain. After 1900 it became Germany. Only after World War I were those dangers replaced by a Soviet menace. Fencing out Communists (or British, or Germans) preserved the area for North American strategic interests and profits. That goal was not argued. The problem arose when Washington officials repeatedly had to choose which tactic best preserved power and profits: siding with the status quo for at least the short term, or taking a chance on radical change that might (or might not) lead to long-term stability. Given the political and economic pressures, that choice was predetermined. As former Secretary of State Dean Acheson observed, there is nothing wrong with short-term stability. "When you step on a banana peel you have to keep from falling on your tail, you don't want to be lurching all over the place all the time. Short-term stability is all right, isn't it? Under the circumstances." The "circumstances" Acheson alluded to were the revolutions that began to appear in the newly emerging countries during the 1950s.[11]

When applied to Central America, Acheson's view missed a central tenet of the region's history: revolutions have served the functions of elections in the United States; that is, they became virtually the only method of transferring power and bringing about needed change.[12] Acheson's short-term stability too often turned out to be Washington's method for ensuring that Central American oligarchs did not have to answer to their fellow citizens.

The revolutionaries of the 1770s thus had less and less to say to the revolutionaries of the 1970s and 1980s. The latter were more anticapitalist, pro-statist, and concerned much less with social stability than were the former. These differences appeared as the upheavals increased in number and intensity. "The real issue facing American foreign policy . . ." Hans Morgenthau remarked in the early 1970s, "is not how to preserve stability in the face of revolution, but how to create stability out of revolution."[13] Morgenthau had rephrased Lodge's point. Revolutions in such areas as Central America were inevitable. The only choice was whether North Americans would work with those revolutionaries to achieve a more orderly and equitable society, or whether—as occurred in Guatemala and Nicaragua—Washington officials would try to cap the upheavals until the pressure built again to blow the societies apart with even greater force.

Neodependency: The U.S. System

Central American revolutions have thus not only been different from, but opposed to, most of the U.S. revolutionary tradition. This opposition can be explained historically. For in rebelling against their own governments, Central Americans have necessarily rebelled against the U.S. officials and entrepreneurs who over many decades made Central America a part of their own nation's system. Not that day-to-day control, in Washington's view, was necessary or desirable. Actually governing such racially different and politically turbulent nations as Guatemala or Honduras was one headache that U.S. officials tried to avoid at every turn. They instead sought informal control, and they finally obtained it through a system that can be described as "neodependency."

First outlined in the 1960s, the theory of "dependency" has been elaborated until it stands as the most important and provocative method of interpreting U.S.-Latin American relations. Dependency may be generally defined as a way of looking at Latin American development, not in isolation, but as part of an international system in which the leading powers (and since 1945, the United States in particular), have used their economic strength to make Latin American development dependent on—and subordinate to—the interests of those leading powers. This dependence, the theory runs, has stunted the Latins' economic growth by forcing their economies to rely on one or two main export crops or on minerals that are shipped off to the industrial nations. These few export crops, such as bananas or coffee, make a healthy domestic economy impossible, according to the theory, because their price depends on an international marketplace which the industrial powers, not Central America, can control. Such export crops also blot up land that should be used to grow foodstuffs for local diets. Thus malnutrition, even starvation, grow with the profits of the relatively few producers of the export crops.

Dependency also skews Central American politics. The key export crops are controlled by foreign investors or local elites who depend on foreigners for capital, markets, and often for personal protection. In the words of a Chilean scholar, these foreign influences become a "kind of 'fifth column' " that distorts economic and political development without taking direct political control of the country. Thus dependency theory denies outright a cherished belief of many North Americans: that if they are allowed to invest and trade freely, the result will be a more prosperous and stable Central America. To the contrary, dependency theorists argue, such investment and trade has been pivotal in misshaping those nations' history until revolution appears to be the only instrument that can break the hammerlock held by the local oligarchy and foreign capitalists.[14] Latin American development, in other words, has not been compatible with United States economic and strategic interests.

The first chapter of this book outlines how Central America became dependent on the United States. But as the story unfolds, it becomes clear that the economic aspects of dependency theory are not sufficient to explain how the United States gained such control over the region. Other forms of power, including political and military, accompanied the economic. In Nicaragua from 1909 to 1912, for example, or in Guatemala during the 1954 crisis, or in El Salvador during the eighties, economic leverage proved incapable of reversing trends that North American officials despised and feared. Those officials then used military force to destroy the threats. The United States thus has intervened frequently with troops or covert operations to ensure that ties of dependency remained.

In this respect, U.S. foreign policy has sharply distinguished Central America and the Caribbean nations from the countries in South America. In the latter region, U.S. political threats have been rarer. Direct, overt military intervention has been virtually nonexistent. Central American nations, however, have received special attention. Washington officials relied primarily on their nation's immense economic power to dominate Central America since 1900 (Chapters I and II explain how that power has been wielded), but they also used military force to ensure that control. Hence the term neodependency to define that special relationship.

To return to the original theme of the introduction, no region in the world is more tightly integrated into the United States economic and security system than Central America. That region, however, was ripped apart by revolutions in Nicaragua, El Salvador, and Guatemala, and that threatened Honduras. Even Costa Rica, with the most equitable and democratic system in Central America, is unsettled. As the dominant power in the area for a century, the United States bears considerable responsibility for the conditions that burst into revolution. The U.S. system was not designed accidentally or without well-considered policies. It developed slowly between the 1820s and 1880s, then rapidly, reaching maturity in the 1940s and 1950s. It was based on principles that had worked, indeed on principles that made the United States the globe's greatest power: a confidence in capitalism, a willingness to use military force, a fear of foreign influence, and a dread of revolutionary instability.

The application of those principles to Central America led to a massive revolutionary outbreak. This history of U.S.-Central American relations during the past 150 years attempts to explain why this occurred.

I

![section divider]

SETTING UP THE SYSTEM

From the beginning, North American leaders believed their new republic was fated to be dominant in Spanish-held Mexico, Central America, and, indeed, the regions beyond. Thomas Jefferson, whose interest in Latin America was extraordinary (he once remarked that young empire-builders should first study Spanish), prophesied that United States power would spread on two levels. One would be ideological. "The flames kindled on the fourth of July, 1776, have spread over too much of the globe to be extinguished by the feeble engines of despotism," claimed the man whose writing helped ignite those flames.[1] Certainly the illiberal, corrupt, inefficiently operated Spanish empire could not snuff out the spreading revolutionary fire. It was merely a matter of time.

But Jefferson and other Founders thought the spread of revolution could also open Latin America to more direct North American control. The Virginian's growing concern about expanding U.S. power even led him in the 1780s to decide that it would be better if the Spanish held on to their territory "till our population can be sufficiently advanced to gain it from them peice by peice [sic]." Part of this dream became real in 1803 when, as president, Jefferson acquired the vast former Spanish colony of Louisiana. His confidence that Manifest Destiny required the booming new nation to swoop down over Mexico and Central America was shared by most of the other Founders, including Jefferson's great political rival, Alexander Hamilton.[2]

Thus U.S. leaders became trapped this early in a dilemma that contin-

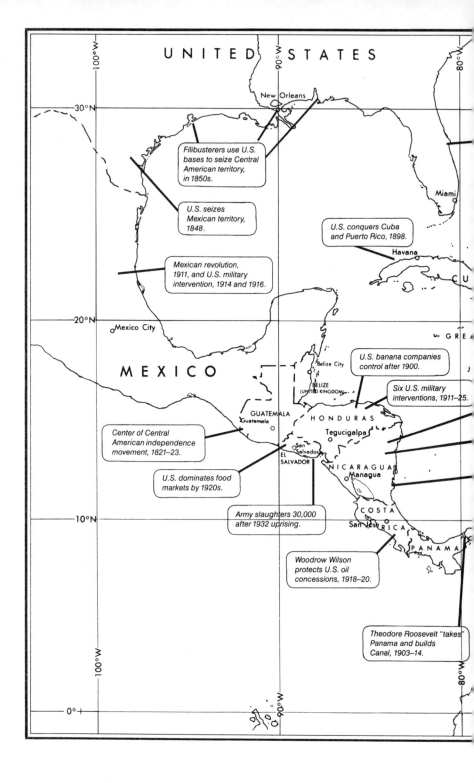

UNITED STATES

New Orleans

Filibusterers use U.S.
bases to seize Central
American territory,
in 1850s.

U.S. seizes
Mexican territory,
1848.

Mexican revolution,
1911, and U.S. military
intervention, 1914 and 1916.

Miami

U.S. conquers Cuba
and Puerto Rico, 1898.

Havana

C U

Mexico City

MEXICO

Belize City

BELIZE
(UNITED KINGDOM)

GUATEMALA
Guatemala

HONDURAS

Tegucigalpa

GRE

U.S. banana companies
control after 1900.

J

Six U.S. military
interventions, 1911–25.

Center of Central
American independence
movement, 1821–23.

San
Salvador
EL
SALVADOR

NICARAGUA
Managua

U.S. dominates food
markets by 1920s.

Army slaughters 30,000
after 1932 uprising.

COSTA

San José R I C A

P A N A M A

Woodrow Wilson
protects U.S. oil
concessions, 1918–20.

Theodore Roosevelt "takes"
Panama and builds
Canal, 1903–14.

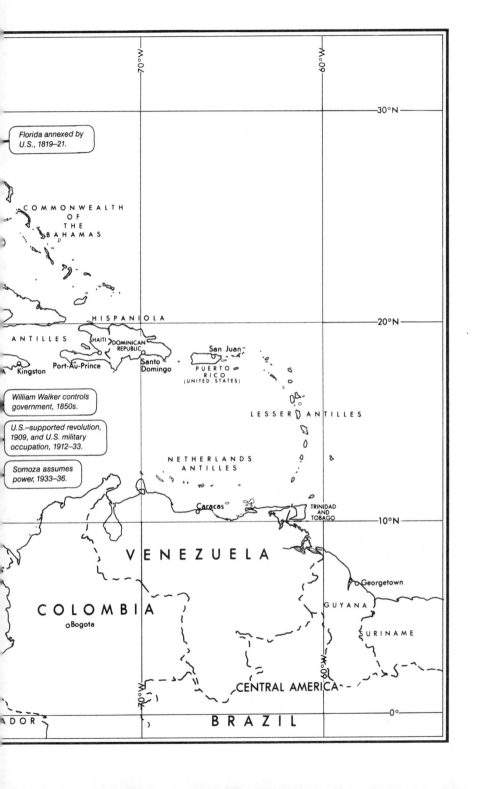

Florida annexed by
U.S., 1819–21.

COMMONWEALTH
OF
THE
BAHAMAS

HISPANIOLA

ANTILLES

HAITI   DOMINICAN
REPUBLIC

San Juan

Kingston   Port-Au-Prince   Santo
Domingo   PUERTO
RICO
(UNITED STATES)

William Walker controls
government, 1850s.

LESSER   ANTILLES

U.S.–supported revolution,
1909, and U.S. military
occupation, 1912–33.

NETHERLANDS
ANTILLES

Somoza assumes
power, 1933–36.

Caracas   TRINIDAD
AND
TOBAGO

VENEZUELA

Georgetown

COLOMBIA   GUYANA

oBogota   SURINAME

CENTRAL AMERICA

ADOR   BRAZIL

30°N

20°N

10°N

0°

70°W

60°W

ues to ensnare their successors two centuries later. On the one hand, the peoples to the south deserved their own war of independence, their full freedom as Jefferson's Laws of Nature and "Nature's God" intended them to have. This, after all, was the first and perhaps the greatest gift bestowed by the United States: providing a case study—including the ideological justification—of how a people can "alter or abolish" any government that no longer derives its "just powers from the consent of the governed," as Jefferson announced to the world in 1776. Within a decade after he penned the Declaration, Jefferson himself recognized that these principles no longer necessarily served U.S. interests. They even contradicted those interests because revolution in Latin America could prevent the "peice by peice" accumulation of a United States-controlled empire. Thus was struck the continuing contradiction in North American policy between the principle of self-determination, whose value has been self-evident to the U.S. mind, and the expansion of their own nation's power, whose value has also been self-evident to North Americans. Nowhere has this historically rooted contradiction been more haunting than in the relationship between the United States and Central America.

The Irrelevant Revolution

Jefferson's faith in the liberating flames of revolution also suffered another less subtle setback. By 1813 the Latin American wars of liberation were underway, but from the mountaintop of his retirement at Monticello, Jefferson could see that liberation did not guarantee freedom. Latin Americans might follow the example of the 1776 Declaration, but they could not soon enjoy the blessings of the 1787 Constitution. "History . . . furnishes no example of a priest-ridden people maintaining a free civil government," he wrote. The Virginian found consolation only in his confidence that "in whatever governments they end, they will be *American* governments, no longer to be involved in the never-ceasing broils of Europe. . . . America has a hemisphere to itself."[3]

Nearly 150 years later, Arthur Schlesinger, Sr., wrote an essay entitled "America's 10 Gifts to Civilization." The first gift, he observed, was the

right of revolution. With a single exception, all of the foreign revolutionary leaders, cited by Schlesinger, who referred to the United States as
their example did so before 1850.[4] By that time, certainly by the end of
the U.S. Civil War in 1865 and the bloody suppression of the Philippine
rebellion by U.S. troops in 1902, the gift had lost a good deal of its 1776
value. U.S. leaders who dealt with the daily complexities and frustrations
of foreign policy had understood this change long before 1865. Jefferson
was one example. Another was John Quincy Adams, probably the greatest of all secretaries of state. Adams's reputation rests, in part, on his
handling of the explosive Latin American revolutionary situation during
his tenure from 1817 to 1825 in the administration of James Monroe.

The president and Adams are remembered for issuing the 1823
Monroe Doctrine in which they warned European colonial powers to
keep hands off the Western Hemisphere. The Doctrine was the public
announcement of Jefferson's private opinion that "America has a hemisphere to itself." By pledging to eliminate the Europeans (over time, of
course—Monroe and Adams were understandably reluctant to challenge
the mighty British fleet), the Doctrine would neatly leave the United
States as the greatest power in the hemisphere.

Adams, however, never concluded that the Doctrine required a U.S.-
Latin American alliance against the considerable European power that
remained in the New World. He did not even want to recognize the
formal independence of the just-born Latin American nations. His reasoning resembled Jefferson's. When Senator Henry Clay of Kentucky
made the mistake of urging Adams to extend his hand to the new nations in 1821, the secretary of state retorted that he knew they must
become free of Spain.

> I wished well to their cause; but I had seen and yet see no prospect
> that they would establish free or liberal institutions of government. . . .
> They have not the first elements of good or free government. Arbi-
> trary power, military and ecclesiastical, was stamped upon their edu-
> cation, upon their habits, and upon all their institutions. Civil dissen-
> sion was infused into all their seminal principles. War and mutual
> destruction was in every member of their organization, moral, politi-
> cal, and physical. I had little expectation of any beneficial result to

this country from any future connection with them, political or commercial.[5]

This outburst, whose intensity grew the longer Adams pondered the nature of the revolutions, stunned Clay, but such arguments did not persuade Monroe. The president forced Adams to begin recognizing the new nations in 1822, preferably before the British gained commercial advantages by doing so.

But Adams refused to alter his belief that the United States must never become closely associated with these different people to the south. Becoming president in 1825, Adams appointed Clay as his secretary of state. Their first foreign policy crisis involved Central America. British influence was growing steadily in the region, particularly around the Nicaraguan area where dreamers were already planning an isthmian canal to link the two great oceans. Latin American leaders met in Panama and invited the coauthor of the Monroe Doctrine to send a delegation. Adams and Congress stalled until it was too late for the two U.S. delegates to attend. Even if they had arrived in time, Adams had placed the two under strict instructions not to join any kind of alliance, not to assume that Latin Americans could ever form a union of states, and not in any way to compromise the right of United States to act unilaterally in the hemisphere when it suited Washington officials.[6]

The newly formed United Provinces of Central America had led the drive that resulted in the Panama Congress. The United Provinces met strong anti-Yankeeism from other delegations, not least from the great revolutionary figure, Simón Bolívar, who outspokenly mistrusted North American imperial ambitions. From their first years of independence, however, Central Americans looked naturally to the United States for protection against the large nations to the south and aggressive Mexico to the north. The most startling turn occurred in 1822 when the threat of a Mexican invasion led El Salvador's Legislative Congress to resolve that its new nation become annexed to the United States. Five leading Salvadorans immediately carried the resolution to Washington. It is interesting to speculate how Secretary of State Adams might have responded had he been asked to allow El Salvador to join his beloved Massachusetts as an equal state in the Union. As it was, the Mexican army quickly settled the issue by conquering the capital of San Salvador.[7]

In 1849, when El Salvador, Nicaragua, and Honduras again faced an invasion, the Nicaraguan Minister in London asked the U.S. Minister whether the three nations might be admitted into the Union. The timing was hardly apt. The slave controversy was heating up in the United States. Northerners held deep and not wholly unjustified suspicions that certain Southerners wanted to annex parts of Central America for new slave territory. Rapidly realizing that nothing could come of his request, the Nicaraguan Minister retreated to his fallback position: would the United States help the three countries defend their territorial integrity?[8]

The Misshaping of Central America

The Central Americans clearly hoped to use the United States as a protector—the "natural protector," as the phrase became used in the 1880s—so the Yankees could be played off against Mexico, Great Britain, or even Guatemala, which dreamed throughout the nineteenth century of conquering the other four Central American countries. Necessity prevented them from following Bolívar's insight that North Americans thought little of most Latin Americans, and that if Washington officials acted at all, they would act on—not for—the five nations.

On their part, Washington officials before the 1840s saw no reason to question Jefferson's and Adams's acute skepticism about the revolutions to the south. Nowhere did this skepticism seem more justified than in the case of Central America. Without the riches of Peru and Mexico, and without the geographical importance of Colombia's Panama isthmus, most of Central America had been the backwater of the Spanish Empire. One and one-quarter million souls inhabited the area when it became independent of Spain in 1822, but half were Indians and most of those lived in isolation and poverty. The relatively few Spaniards dominated the economy and politics.

The region's power center lay in Guatemala. By 1700 its capital was one of the three great cities in Latin America. Its splendor and power lasted until 1773 when an earthquake nearly destroyed the capital, which was then rebuilt as the present Guatemala City. By the 1820s it held 30,000 people, but Guatemala's power was little more than irrelevant during the Latin American revolutions. Although uprisings occurred in El Salvador, Nicaragua, and Honduras during 1811 and 1812, for the next ten years the Central Americans were more disinterested spectators than committed participants. They did not fight for independence or even actively seek it. Central Americans finally moved for a separation only after a Liberal coup in Madrid deposed an absolutist monarchy. Wanting no part of Liberal reforms, Central American conservatives met at Guatemala City in September 1821 to break away from the Spanish regime. Mexico, already independent for the same reason, then tried to conquer the area. A power struggle inside Mexico ended what might have been a vast Mexican empire, and on 1 July 1823, the United Provinces of Central America declared its independence.[9]

The United Provinces constructed a constitution based on the U.S. model. It included guarantees of personal rights and contained the first provision written into a constitution in the hemisphere declaring an end to slavery. But in true federal fashion, it gave each province autonomy in its domestic affairs. That provision turned out to be a self-destruct mechanism. The separate provinces were controlled by local elites who proudly claimed Spanish ancestry and culture. From their vast estates they looked down on other races and any federal governmental interference in their affairs. Fights quickly broke out between these Conservatives, as their party came to be called, and the Liberals who wanted a stronger central government. The smaller provinces also feared the power of the larger, especially the ambitious Guatemalans.

When civil war erupted, Francisco Morazán led the Liberal army to victory. This greatest of all Hondurans became a benevolent ruler who planned an isthmian canal in Nicaragua with Dutch financiers, established habeas corpus and trial by jury, and disbanded monastic orders while working for religious toleration. By 1835, the Church, Conservatives, and other state-oriented interests were determined to cut him down. Morazán moved his capital to El Salvador (then and ever after a hub of unionist sentiment in Central America), while his enemies worked out of Guatemala City. They organized other provincial centers and in 1838 succeeded in breaking up the union. Morazán again tried to put the pieces back together with military force, but this time he was captured and shot in 1842. The union was no more. Morazán remains perhaps the greatest of Central Americans, but his only legacies were a shattered union; a two-party political system of Conservatives and Liberals that characterized the politics of each Central American state (and quickly deteriorated into mere *personalismo*); and Morazán province in El Salvador, that during the 1980s became the stronghold for a growing revolutionary movement.[10]

The five new Central American nations, now on their own, had little experience as separate, workable, political units. In 1776, the North Americans had evolved into politically developed states that were for the most part prepared for independence. In each Central American country, however, a single population group had grown around the provincial capital. Other areas were sparsely settled and virtually cut off by mountains, jungles, or rivers. The urban elites developed local loyalties, then began to cultivate distinct cultures. These new states were in fact so untutored in self-government, so small, and so lacking in apparent natural resources, that a responsible, self-sufficient system would have been a miracle. No miracles occurred. Instead, parochialism and the Conservatives triumphed over Morazán and union, not only by 1839, but during the more than twenty-five other attempts that have been made since 1839 to form a larger economic and political framework.[11]

Localism was victorious over unity, reaction over reform, oligarchies over statesmen. The result would have been less tragic if the five new states had possessed vast open lands for settlement or mineral wealth that guaranteed income—if, that is, these nations enjoyed New York's or Virginia's landed frontier, or Pennsylvania's or Maryland's iron works. But the Central Americans had no such resources. The land and wealth they possessed had long since been locked away by a relatively few oligarchs. New opportunities would need to come from the outside, from foreign investors and traders whose interests, it turned out, had little in common with the national interests of the Central American states. History and nature thus boxed in the five nations.

Nor could the British Empire be shoved aside. Throughout the nineteenth century Britain was the great power in Central America. As an imperial nation, Great Britain, much as the United States did a century

later, used both political pressure and military force to buttress its growing economic influence. (Unlike the United States, however, the British
were seldom troubled by, or felt themselves predestined imperial rulers
because of, Jeffersonian rhetoric.) The empire's commerce and naval
power had been pivotal in helping Latin Americans gain and hold their
freedom from Spain. The British quickly moved to take advantage by
investing heavily in securities and transportation. The first venture
turned out unhappily when the Central American kingdom of Poyais
sold more than a half-million dollars worth of bonds to London investors
in 1822. Both the kingdom and the value of the bonds turned out to be
mythical.

Pounds nevertheless moved into Guatemala, Honduras, and Costa
Rica to finance railroads (never completed) and especially to buy up
government securities.[12] By 1900 the five states were heavily indebted to
Great Britain. The creditors were not reluctant to use force to guarantee
and enlarge their holdings. When the Hondurans refused to honor their
debt in 1872, Her Majesty's warships bombarded an Honduran port
until the government promised to pay both the debt and the damages set
by the British.[13] London officials decided to hold on to Belize, or British
Honduras, and refused to discuss the competing Guatemalan claim. In
Nicaragua, the British seized control of Miskito province, the area that
controlled the eastern entrance to a possible isthmian canal, then virtually made it an independent colony. The United States could proclaim
the Monroe Doctrine, but Britannia's fleet and investors wrote their
own rules.

The Yankee's Appearance

Precisely because of this British expansion, however, the United States
made its first major appearance on the Central American scene. The
premiere produced an historic impact. Between 1845 and 1848 the ram-
pantly aggressive administration of James K. Polk drove westward to
relieve Mexico of one-third of its territory. Part of that territory included
the superb harbors of California. U.S. producers and traders (and adventurers) could now use Texas and Pacific coast ports from which to em-
bark to Latin America. Throughout the remainder of the pre–Civil War

years, moreover, talk never ceased of taking more Mexican territory until North Americans could abut Central America. Interest in the southern areas was great, especially among those, such as Polk, who hated the British, or those, such as the great transportation magnate, Cornelius Vanderbilt, who passionately wished to build an ocean-to-ocean route across the Nicaraguan isthmus.

In 1846 Polk signed a treaty with Colombia that gave the United States the right to build a canal across Panama. In return the President guaranteed equal access for all nations to use the isthmus. Polk had not only beaten the British to the area, but openly defied them by assuring Colombia (which owned the Panama region), that this isthmian area would not suffer the fate of the Miskito province of Nicaragua. Two years later, Polk went much farther. When Great Britain seized part of Nicaragua, he tried to unite the five Central American states under U.S. direction to fight the intruder.[14] Predictably the attempt to coordinate Central American policies failed, but out of Polk's initiative two treaties were born. One, with Honduras, was mainly in friendship and served as a warning to England that the small nation might have a large protector. The other, with Nicaragua, gave the United States rights over the future canal route; in return, Washington guaranteed Nicaragua sovereignty over its territories.[15] There was to be no more British encroachment in Nicaragua—at least according to the paper treaties.

As early as 1850 the United States had thus embarked on a collision course with the British Empire because of Central America. At a time when the Union was under tremendous strain because of the slave controversy, the United States, in its maiden appearance in Central America, established major claims and confronted the world's greatest power. Not for the last time, a crisis in Central America, blamed by Washington officials on ominous foreign influences, formed part of a larger crisis in North American empire-building. But in 1849 a Whig administration under President Zachary Taylor replaced Polk's peripatetic Democrats. The Whig party contained important factions, especially commercial interests in both North and South, who wanted neither war with England nor more of Polk's militant spread-eagleism in Latin America. Instead they wanted calm for profitable dealings with British merchants as well as within the Union.

Faced with growing problems in Europe, the British also sought peace in Central America, although they pointedly refused to buy it by leaving Miskito. England, nevertheless, signed the Clayton-Bulwer Treaty of 1850 in which the British and North Americans agreed to cooperate in the construction of any isthmian canal. By agreeing to the pact, the British shrewdly short-circuited the new U.S. treaties with Honduras and Nicaragua; those agreements never went to the Senate for ratification. In any canal partnership, moreover, England would presumably be the larger partner. But the United States had also gained much. The world's strongest power had recognized Washington's claims to the great Central American canal project. U.S. diplomacy, if not yet Yankee force, proved to be the equal of England's. Suddenly it became clear as a result of Polk's conquests and Whig diplomacy who was the rising power in Central America.

But the next act in the drama was not as pleasant for United States officials. Throughout the 1850s, Central America became the target for "filibusters"—private adventurers who moved out of New Orleans, New York, and Baltimore to conquer the small countries for personal gain, the extension of slave territory, or usually both. The most famous was William Walker, "the grey-eyed man of destiny," who actually ruled Nicaragua between 1855 and 1857. Central American leaders tried to unite to drive Walker out, but their failure was not surprising. Walker even gained diplomatic recognition from the United States. He made the crucial mistake, however, of trying to destroy Vanderbilt's steamship line. That enterprise had become prosperous from carrying goods and travelers across Nicaragua on their way to the promised land of California. Unlike the Washington officials, Vanderbilt refused to recognize Walker. Instead he crushed him financially and then militarily. Neither the Central Americans nor the British had been able to handle the grey-eyed man of destiny, but just as he had been financed by North American capitalists who had set their sights on Central America, so the greatest of the Yankee capitalists destroyed him.[16] As the U.S. Civil War appeared on the horizon, Polk, the Clayton-Bulwer Treaty, and Cornelius Vanderbilt had inexorably shifted northward the balance of power in Central America.

Blaine: Paying the Price of Stability

The Civil War ended the debate over the extension of slave territory. No more were enterprising adventurers or Washington officials to see the five Central American nations as possible new slave states in the Union. The Civil War, however, also accelerated U.S. industrial and financial development. As a result of the vast wartime market and new laws that gave incredible gifts of land and money to railroad builders and steel manufacturers, North Americans emerged in 1865 with a nascent industrial complex which in a mere thirty-five years would make them the world's leading industrial power and, shortly thereafter, turn their country into the globe's financial center.

Those developments had profound effects on Central America. By the 1890s, the primary North American influence in the region was rapidly growing investments in banana and coffee plantations, railroads (to haul the bananas, not people), gold and silver mines, and, a little later, utilities and government securities. Great Britain's financial hold remained secure but while the British bought up government securities or utilities, North Americans built the major productive enterprises on which, by World War I, not only a Central American nation's trade but its very economic survival depended.

United States political power grew with its economic leverage. In 1890, Congress began constructing the Great White Fleet that triumphed in the War of 1898 against Spain. In a critical episode during 1895 and 1896, the British backed down from possible conflict with the United States over a disputed boundary in Venezuela. Then and later, North Americans viewed the retreat as British recognition of—and acquiescence in—U.S. supremacy in the Central American and northern South American areas.[17] Economic, military, and political power coalesced to make the region a North American, not British, sphere.

This change became vivid in the scramble over the isthmian canal. In North American eyes, the canal—whether built in Nicaragua or Panama—was not merely for economic, political, or military purposes. It was to serve all three. When, therefore, a French company began building a canal in Panama during the 1870s, President Rutherford B. Hayes immediately began uttering warnings about the dire consequences if the French refused to stop. A few years later yellow fever was destroying the enterprise, but North American attention remained riveted on plans for a U.S.-owned and operated canal. Under the 1846 treaty with Colombia, which owned Panama, U.S. troops landed in Panama at least six times in the nineteenth century to put down rebellions and ensure that the area remained open.[18] The Clayton-Bulwer treaty was doomed; only a matter of time remained before the power of North Americans would become so potent that they could finally and decisively answer an enraged fellow countryman who asked in 1885 whether they any longer had to "submit to the errors, mistakes and blunders" of the 1850 pact, and "be bound hand and foot by the terms of that . . . covenant of national disgrace."[19]

By the 1880s, Washington officials were concluding that internal Central American squabbles directly threatened U.S. interests in the area. Unless the petty warfare stopped, it might bring about British military intervention. Domestic Central American politics consequently became a topic of increasing concern to the State Department. It did not hesitate to brandish force. When Guatemala invaded El Salvador in 1885 and threatened to cut the cables of the New York-owned Central and South American Telegraph Company, the firm's president, James A. Scrymser, asked Washington for protection. The State Department quickly told Guatemala it would be held "strictly responsible" for any harm done to U.S. citizens or property. To emphasize the point, Washington officials then ordered the USS *Wachusett,* under the command of a middle-aged officer named Alfred Thayer Mahan, to protect North American property in Nicaragua, El Salvador, and Guatemala.[20] The threat quickly blew over, but the point had been made. Five years later Mahan emerged as a world-famous historian and strategist whose self-appointed mission was to prepare the United States for similar military operations wherever the nation's rapidly expanding interests required.

One secretary of state, however, wanted to find nonmilitary solutions in Central America. In doing so he made a lasting impression on U.S.–Latin American relations. James G. Blaine of Maine had become the leader of the Republican party through his skill in the Senate and his understanding of the new industrial complex's requirements. Opponents accused him, not unfairly, of corruption, but such a charge was relative during the Gilded Age when legislators were regularly bought and sold for the betterment of the nation's economy, if not its politics. The "Plumed Knight from Maine" stood apart, however, by virtue of his understanding of that economy's dynamics, and especially of how Latin American markets and raw materials could be profitably integrated into the complex. His approach was simple: political peace and a profitable trade were desired in Latin America, and "to attain the second object the first must be accomplished." If peace could replace the interminable disputes in such volatile areas as Central America, then the United States should "engage in what the younger Pitt so well termed annexation of trade." To assure the Latin Americans, and no doubt to separate himself from the British whom he despised, he pointedly observed, "Our great demand is expansion," but only in trade, for "we are not seeking annexation of territory."[21]

Blaine's words sounded benign until he used this critical distinction between trade and territory to justify U.S. intervention in Central America. When Mexico threatened to invade Guatemala in the 1880s, the Guatemalan Minister to the United States asked for Blaine's help. After all, the minister observed, the United States "is the natural protector of the integrity of the Central American territory." The secretary of state shared that assumption, and he also wanted peace, trade, and a U.S.-operated canal in the area. He consequently warned Mexico to stay out. Blaine justified this move with the wonderful logic that "the now established policy of the . . . United States to refrain from territorial acquisition gives it the right to use its friendly offices in discouragement of any movement on the part of neighboring states which may tend to disturb the balance of power between them."[22] Thus the status quo was to be upheld, if necessary, by the United States because its lack of need for more territory gave it a higher moral standing than other nations could claim.

In 1881 Blaine devised a plan to invite Latin American leaders to Washington so they could work out common grounds for economic and political cooperation. He left the State Department before they could convene, but returned in 1889 to preside over the first truly inter-American conference. The delegates discussed plans for a customs union, common monetary standards, the pacific settlement of disputes, and reciprocity policy in trade so tariff walls could be lowered. But except for a series of reciprocity treaties, which during their several years of life in the 1890s indeed accelerated economic integration between the United States and Central America, only one other concrete result appeared from the meeting. The United States established a Commercial Bureau of the American Republics—the parent of the Pan American Union and Organization of American States—so government and private business could better coordinate their activities in the south. The meager results were understandable. Not only was Blaine far ahead of most North Americans in his plans for tying the hemisphere together, but many Latin Americans harbored deep suspicions about his idea to integrate their economies into the U.S. industrial powerhouse. They saw the entire scheme as little more than a device for allowing the State Department to direct Latin American affairs.[23]

T.R. and Taft: Justifying Intervention

In 1898 an awesome North American force needed fewer than three months to crush the remnants of Spain's New World empire and then establish bases in territory as close as the Caribbean and as distant as the Philippines. In 1901 the United States forced the British to terminate the Clayton-Bulwer treaty so Washington could fully control the building and defense of an isthmian canal. That same year William McKinley was assassinated and Theodore Roosevelt became president of the United States.

The famed Rough Rider, who fought publicly if not brilliantly in Cuba during the 1898 war, believed as much as Blaine that the United States was the "natural protector"—and should be the main beneficiary—of Central American affairs. But Roosevelt's methods were characteristically more direct than Blaine's. Nor was he reluctant to use them on Latin Americans whom he derisively called "Dagoes" because, in his view, they were incapable of either governing themselves or—most important in T.R.'s hierarchy of values—maintaining order.[24]

The U.S. emergence as a world power and Roosevelt's ascendency to the White House were accompanied by a third historic event during the years from 1898 to 1901: the largest export of North American capital until that time. The country remained an international debtor until World War I, but the force of the new U.S. industrial and agricultural complexes was felt many years before. A large-scale capital market centered in New York City allowed further expansion and concentration of those complexes.

England's investments in Central America peaked in 1913 at about $115 million. More than two-thirds of the money, however, was in Costa Rica and Guatemala. U.S. investments in Central America meanwhile climbed rapidly from $21 million in 1897 to $41 million in 1908, and then to $93 million by the eve of World War I. These differed from the British not only in the rapidity of growth, but in the overwhelming amounts (over 90 percent) that went into such direct investments as banana plantations and mining, rather than into government securities (that the British favored), and also in the power—perhaps even a monopoly power—these monies were buying in Honduran and Nicaraguan politics. Not that the two British bastions were invulnerable. In Guatemala, U.S. railroad holdings amounted to $30 million between 1897 and 1914 until they nearly caught up with London's $40 million. U.S. fruit companies alone nearly equalled Great Britain's entire investment in Costa Rica.

Indeed, the British, to Washington's ever-searching eyes, seemed to be on the downhill side of their empire's history. By the early 1900s, U.S. officials considered Germany to be the greater future threat. German enterprise spread through the region (especially in Guatemala and Costa Rica). Equally significant, German ships had been scouting possible naval stations in the region since the late 1860s. Those forays led nervous U.S. officials to warn publicly that they meant to enforce the Monroe Doctrine. The U.S.-German-British race for influence and profits had one other important effect: incorporating ever greater food-producing areas into the world economy helped drive down the price of coffee, bananas, and other Central American exports. The effect locally was quickly felt. Costa Ricans, for example, had to change their agriculture and export more and more coffee and bananas (at lower prices), so they could service debts owed foreign bankers and also maintain their own standard of living. The Costa Ricans, as they turned their lands over to export crops, thus had to import more and more food to feed themselves. Their economy became dislocated and dependent as it was integrated by the new Western powers into the world system and used as a low-cost farm for those industrializing nations.[25]

No one understood these developments and their implications as well as Elihu Root, T.R.'s secretary of state between 1905 and 1909. Root was the nation's premier corporate lawyer, and perhaps his generation's shrewdest analyst of the new corporate America. Returning from a trip through Latin America in 1906, Root told a convention of businessmen that during the past few years three centuries of their nation's history had suddenly closed. The country's indebtedness had given way to a "surplus of capital" that was "increasing with extraordinary rapidity." As this surplus searched throughout the world for markets to conquer and vast projects to build, the mantle of world empire was being passed: "As in their several ways England and France and Germany have stood, so we in our own way are beginning to stand and must continue to stand toward the industrial enterprise of the world."

The northern and southern hemispheres perfectly suited each other, Root observed. People to the south needed North American manufacturers and the latter needed the former's raw materials. Even the personalities complemented each other: "Where we accumulate, they spend. While we have less of the cheerful philosophy" which finds "happiness in the existing conditions of life," as the Latins do, "they have less of the inventive faculty which strives continually to increase the productive power of men." Root closed by putting it all in historical perspective: "Mr. Blaine was in advance of his time. . . . Now, however, the time has come; both North and South America have grown up to Blaine's policy."[26]

In important respects Root's speech of 20 November 1906 resembled Frederick Jackson Turner's famous essay of 1893 on the closing of the North American frontier. Both men understood that three centuries of U.S. development had terminated during their lifetime and that a new phase of the nation's history had begun. Both revealed social and racial views which shaped the new era's policies. Both were highly nationalistic if not chauvinistic. Most important, both used history as a tool to rationalize the present and future: the dynamic new United States necessarily prepared itself to find fresh frontiers abroad to replace the closed frontier at home.

Root and Turner needed only to look around them to confirm their prophecies. For example, Leland Stanford and William Huntington, the builders of the Central Pacific railroad in the United States, began to invest in Guatemalan railways during the 1880s because the North American rail frontier was closing. Other U.S. investors followed the same course in Costa Rica and Nicaragua. In each instance, however, the appearance of powerful foreign capital—and the rivalry that capital invariably caused with equally powerful British, German, or French capital—disoriented the local societies. New indigenous elites, who had closely tied themselves to the foreigners' rising fortunes, began to grow powerful and cause friction in the political arena. Central America did not become integrated into the western industrial economies peacefully. Upheavals, even revolutions, accompanied that transformation. And it was Root's and T.R.'s fate that their plans for the region were directly challenged by the upheavals. The outbreaks and the consequent danger of European intervention posed special problems after 1903. For in that year Roosevelt helped Panama break away from Colombia, and he then began to build the isthmian canal of which several centuries had dreamed. In a private letter of 1905 Root drew the lesson: "The inevitable effect of our building the Canal must be to require us to police the surrounding premises. In the nature of things, trade and control, and the obligation to keep order which go with them, must come our way."[27] The conclusion was unarguable.

It must be noted, however, that one of Root's assumptions was faulty. The Panama Canal was only an additional, if major, reason for injecting U.S. power into Central America. That power had actually begun moving into the region a half-century before. It could claim de facto political and military predominance years before canal construction began. And as Root himself argued in his 1906 speech, United States development, especially in the economic realm, foretold a new relationship with Latin America even if the canal were never built. The Panamanian passageway accelerated the growth of U.S. power in Central America. It also magnificently symbolized that power. But it did not create the power or the new relationship.

For many reasons, therefore—to ensure investments, secure the canal, act as a "natural protector," and, happily, replace the declining presence of the British—Roosevelt announced in 1905 that henceforth the United States would act as the policeman to maintain order in the hemisphere. He focused this Roosevelt Corollary to the Monroe Doctrine on the Caribbean area, where the nation of Santo Domingo was beset by revolutions and foreign creditors, but his declaration had wider meaning: "All that this country desires is that the other republics on this continent shall be happy and prosperous; and they cannot be happy and prosperous unless they maintain order within their boundaries and behave with a just regard for their obligations toward outsiders."[28]

Perhaps Roosevelt's major gift to U.S. statecraft was his formulation of why revolutions were dangerous to his nation's interest, and the justification he then provided to use force, if necessary, to end them. But his Corollary meant more than merely making war for peace. It exemplified North American disdain for people who apparently wanted to wage revolts instead of working solid ten-hour days on the farm. Roosevelt saw such people as "small bandit nests of a wicked and inefficient type," and to U.S. Progressives such as T.R., the only sin greater than inefficiency was instability. A top U.S. naval official called the outbreaks "so-called revolutions" that "are nothing less than struggles between different crews of bandits for the possession of the customs houses—and the loot." A fellow officer agreed that only the civilized Monroe Doctrine held "a large part of this hemisphere in check against cosmic tendencies."[29]

Of course that view completely reversed the meaning of the original Doctrine. Monroe and Adams had originally intended it to protect Latin American revolutions from outside (that is, European) interference. Eighty years later the power balance had shifted to the United States, and the Doctrine itself shifted to mean that Latin Americans should now be controlled by outside (that is, North American) intervention if necessary. Roosevelt justified such intervention as only an exercise of "police" power, but that term actually allowed U.S. presidents to intervene according to any criteria they were imaginative enough to devise. In the end they could talk about "civilization," and "self-determination," but their military and economic power was its own justification.

Roosevelt's successor, William Howard Taft, and Secretary of State

Philander C. Knox hoped that T.R.'s military "Big Stick" could be replaced by the more subtle and constructive dollar. They held to the traditional North American belief in the power of capital for political healing. To bestow such blessings Knox thought it only proper that the United States seize other nations' customs revenues so they could not become the target of "devastating and unprincipled revolutions."[30] To stabilize Central America—and to have U.S. investors do well while doing good—Taft and Knox searched for an all-encompassing legal right for intervention. The president bluntly told a Mexican diplomat that North Americans could "not be content until we have secured some formal right to compel the peace between those Central American Governments," and "have the right to knock their heads together until they should maintain peace between them." Such a general right was never discovered because legal experts in the State Department warned Knox that such a thing did not exist. Taft and Knox fell back on straight dollar diplomacy; that instrument, given their views of Central Americans, then led them to use force in the T.R. manner. As noted below, Knox soon relied upon what he termed "the moral value" of naval power.[31]

To argue, therefore, that the United States intervened in Central America simply to stop revolutions and bestow the blessings of stability tells too little too simply. The motive for Washington's policy in Central America was not to stop upheavals, but to promote U.S. interests. In El Salvador, for example, North Americans—both in the business and the diplomatic community—continually encouraged a revolutionary faction between 1906 and 1913 because they knew the faction was more pro-United States (and anti-European capital) than the actual, legitimate government.[32] Interests and imperial rivalry, not morality and consistency, drove U.S. policies. The Roosevelt Corollary and Taft's dollar diplomacy rested on views of history, the character of foreign peoples, and politics that anticipated attitudes held by North Americans throughout much of the twentieth century. These policies were applied by presidents who acted unilaterally and set historic precedents for the global application of U.S. power in later years.

Double Standards: The United States Destroys a Court

North Americans seldom doubted that they could teach people to the south to act more civilized. The potential of U.S. power seemed unlimited, and as that power grew so did the confidence with which it was wielded. Brooks Adams, the grandson and great-grandson of presidents, and a brilliant eccentric who was a friend and adviser of Roosevelt, studied history deeply, then emerged to declare that the 1898 war was "the turning point in our history. . . . I do believe that we may dominate the world, as no nation has dominated it in recent time." In a personal letter, Adams spoke for his generation when he asserted that the years from 1900 to 1914 would "be looked back upon as the grand time. We shall, likely enough, be greater later, but it is the dawn which is always golden. The first taste of power is always the sweetest."[33]

Adams could have applied his insight directly to U.S.–Central American relations. Between 1906 and 1912 the United States for the first time used its military and economic muscle to stop a widening war and construct a radical new institution for peace in Central America. For their own interest, North Americans then destroyed the institution. And at the end of this period Washington officials, also for the first time, intervened directly to determine the kind of governments that would govern Central America.

For some years, two Latin American men had fought for control over the region. From 1898 until 1920 Manuel Estrada Cabrera, the dictator of Guatemala, flattered the United States and encouraged foreign investment while systematically and violently robbing his own people of both their wealth and personal rights. Estrada Cabrera believed that in extending his blessings throughout Central America he was only carrying out the tradition of Guatemalan supremacy in the area. His mortal enemy was José Santos Zelaya, who had run Nicaragua since 1893. Although sharing Estrada Cabrera's talent for corruption, Zelaya differed by going out of his way to offend North American interests. He also thought a higher manifest destiny—his own—commanded that he and Nicaragua control all of Central America. Few people hated and feared

Zelaya more than Estrada Cabrera, unless it was those who conducted Washington's foreign policy. Caught between the two Central American strongmen was, as usual, Honduras.

Suffering through three different administrations in 1903 alone, Honduras had become a political revolving door even as it was becoming the site of extensive U.S. investments. Zelaya entered the door to demand the allegiance of Honduras, then united with El Salvador and Costa Rica to invade Guatemala. Estrada Cabrera's forces fought back with surprising strength, and by the summer of 1906 Central America was inflamed. Roosevelt finally persuaded dictator Porfirio Díaz of Mexico that they had to stop the war before the area was in chaos. T.R. sent the USS *Marblehead* to act as a display of his naval reach and also as a conference center. Guatemala, Honduras, and El Salvador stopped fighting, but, true to form, Zelaya blasted Roosevelt for butting into an affair that was none of his business. The Nicaraguan refused to stop shooting. He invaded Honduras with a large army. To show his seriousness, the Nicaraguan dictator used the machine gun for the first time in Central American wars. Again Roosevelt and Díaz stepped in, this time more effectively. Now isolated, Zelaya accepted mediation and agreed to meet with the other four states in Washington to work out means for choking off the wars that had suddenly made Theodore Roosevelt his direct competitor in Central American affairs.[34]

The 1907 Washington conference spun a web of agreements that were to make Central Americans more interdependent and—as the North American Progressive theorists of the time believed—more peaceful and cooperative. The meetings established a Central American Court of Justice, planned a railroad network, and worked out a treaty of peace and amity that everyone could sign. Future disputes were to go not to the battlefield, but the Court. The Central American Court quickly became a global symbol for the Progressives' growing faith in legal arbitration for the settlement of disputes. One North American proudly wrote, "To the powers of Europe, to the great powers of the world who struggled with partial success . . . to establish a court of arbitral justice, the young republics of Central America may recall the scriptural phrase, 'A little child shall lead them.' "[35] Retired steel billionaire Andrew Carnegie happily gave $100,000 for a building to house the Court.

It turned out to be one of Carnegie's few bad investments. Within nine years the institution was hollow because twice—in 1912 and 1916—the United States refused to recognize Court decisions that went against its interests in Nicaragua. The North Americans destroyed the Court they had helped create, and in doing so vividly demonstrated how the Progressive faith in legal remedies was worthless when the dominant power in the area placed its own national interests over international legal institutions. A Nicaraguan poet, Ruben Darío, wrote an *Ode to Roosevelt* in which he described T.R.'s "clutching iron claws," and warned that "even though you count on everything,/You still lack one thing: God."[36] Roosevelt and his successors who could now unilaterally determine Central American affairs, however, accepted Napoleon's view: God is on the side of the greatest artillery.

Using the threat of its weaponry, the United States halted the wars between Central American states. There would be no more conflicts on the scale of the struggle between Estrada Cabrera and Zelaya. The 1907 agreement and U.S. arms stopped the conflict, but they could not prevent revolution. Indeed, Honduras and Nicaragua endured the most severe upheavals in their history within five years after the 1907 conference had supposedly established a new order in the region. In the spirit of the Roosevelt Corollary, the United States intervened in both revolutions and helped turn them into long-term disasters.

Determining Who Rules at Home: Honduras

Honduras probably gave the term "banana republic" its negative connotations of dependence on foreigners, a one-crop economy, and all-round corruption. By 1907 Honduras had suffered through seven so-called "revolutions" in fifteen years. The country's foreign debt of $124 million dwarfed its national income (largely from duties on trade) of $1.6 million. Honduras was less a nation than a customs house surrounded by adventurers.

It had been damned from the start. Spain had found a half-million Indians in the area during the early sixteenth century, but when the Spanish finished enslaving and carrying them off for mining operations elsewhere—as well as killing them with European-originated diseases—only 18,000 remained in 1590. The Church and a few individuals took the best land. The nineteenth-century coffee boom missed Honduras, but that turned out to be a blessing in disguise because the land distribution system was not further skewed. This blessing was offset, however, by a railway plan imposed by Englishmen. After a series of highly imaginative frauds and broken promises by the British, the Hondurans found themselves saddled with large debts and a few miles of rails that went nowhere. When the Hondurans defaulted on the loans in the 1870s, the British bombarded a port. As if this foreign attention were not enough, Honduras's pivotal location—the only Central American nation with boundaries adjacent to those of three other countries—made it both a natural refuge for revolutionaries from the other nations, and a natural avenue when, for example, Zelaya or Estrada Cabrera set out to slaughter the other's friends. Honduras was never sufficiently united to fight off such incursions.

The great turn in the country's history occurred between the late 1890s and 1912 when banana companies, led by the Vacarro brothers of New Orleans, appeared on the northern coast. The greatest banana entrepreneur was Samuel Zmuri, who had changed his name to Zemurray but was known in the trade simply as Sam the Banana Man. Zemurray had become interested in the business in 1895. Ten years later he arrived in Honduras, whose people he immediately liked. In 1910 he bought five thousand acres on the Cuyamel River for plantations, then went deeply into debt to buy fifteen thousand. These banana companies bought up lands, built railroads, established their own banking systems, and bribed government officials at a dizzying pace.[37] The northern coast became a foreign-controlled enclave that systematically swung the whole of Honduras into a one-crop economy whose wealth was carried off to New Orleans, New York, and later Boston. The two Honduran political parties, the Conservatives and Liberals, encouraged the development so they could profit from export duties. Their policy made some sense economically but none politically, for the north coast banana plantations were virtually sealed off geographically from the rest of the country. The government's representative in the coastal area became quasi-independent of the Honduran government and easily controlled by the fruit companies. A little-governed country became even less governed.

The power of the Vacarros and Zemurray was unquestioned. Their shipments to the United States accounted for two-thirds of the $3 million of Honduran exports in 1913. North America also provided 80 percent of the country's imports.[38] The banana companies totally controlled the nation's working railroad system. (Even some six decades later Honduras did not have an important railway anywhere but on the northern coast; it did not even have one to its capital city.) By 1900 the Church posed no challenge to foreign domination. Plagued with reactionary, politically ignorant priests, it was stripped by the government until it was desperately poor and held no lands that the fruit companies might have wanted.[39]

The Hondurans had been systematically cut off, first geographically then politically, from their own wealth. Unlike neighboring El Salvador, where a few wealthy families made fortunes in coffee during the nineteenth century then moved to take control of trade and banking, the Hondurans never took that first step of gaining some control over their nation's key product.[40] Instead, the twenty-two or so companies that had initially come in and bought from scattered Honduran banana growers soon melted down to three large companies (United Fruit of Boston came in after the Vacarros and Zemurray were established), that took over the actual growing of the bananas—and the best land as well. All that was left for Hondurans was the customs house receipts, and not even those were certain. A U.S. official reported from the capital: "Occasionally a mule train with money from the coast arrives, but no one knows exactly what becomes of it."[41] This history was never understood by North Americans who wondered why Hondurans continued to be so poor and ungovernable. The companies, of course, were pleased that Hondurans busied themselves fighting over customs receipts; a less dependent government could have caused real trouble.

From 1908 to 1911, however, the situation changed dramatically. A revolution in 1907 overthrew President Manuel Bonilla and brought Miguel Dávila to power. Bonilla had been highly sensitive to Zemurray's every wish, and the North American naturally feared that Dávila might favor other growers. At the same time, the new president came under intense pressure from the British to pay off the nation's debts held in

London. Dávila also became friendly with Zelaya, whose Nicaraguan regime hated the United States. The State Department consequently began to share Zemurray's concern about Dávila, albeit for different reasons. Secretary of State Philander C. Knox moved to replace London's long-held power over the Honduran debt structure with Washington's power. He asked J.P. Morgan and other U.S. bankers to purchase the old bonds at bargain-basement prices. Then Knox made a deal in which Dávila guaranteed the Morgan loan with the customs house receipts and promised not to change any tariff rates without U.S. consent. President Taft was to approve future appointments of the customs collector. In return, the North Americans were to furnish Honduras "the protection which it [the U.S.] judges to be necessary." When Dávila sent the Knox scheme for a U.S. protectorate over Honduras to the Honduran Congress for approval, it was overwhelmingly rejected. Opponents gained an important edge to their argument when mobs invaded the assembly and promised death to anyone who, in their words, made their country "an administrative dependency of the United States." The U.S. Senate also turned down the pact, and Morgan finally pulled out.[42]

That result left the debt problem to the more efficient and ruthless fruit companies. Zemurray's dislike for Dávila was now matched by his fear that if the problem lingered, J.P. Morgan's incredible power might challenge his hold on Honduras. The Banana Man therefore financed his own revolutionary expedition out of New Orleans. It was led by his old friend Bonilla and a soldier of fortune named Lee Christmas, who liked to prove his toughness and intimidate the native people by chewing on glass. The U.S. Navy made several attempts to stop the rebels from reaching Honduras, but when these failed, it set up a neutral territory and forbade any fighting. In reality, the navy's move allowed Bonilla's forces to establish themselves and prevented Dávila's army from attacking. Knox next ordered U.S. Consul Thomas G. Dawson to arbitrate. Dawson asked each side to suggest a temporary president. The consul of the United States then appointed a new acting president of Honduras. Dávila, in no position to take on the U.S. Navy, quietly stepped down. Eight months later, Bonilla won election for the full presidential term. Zemurray again received concessions from the government and in return thoughtfully negotiated a loan from North American bankers so

Bonilla could be reimbursed for his revolution's expenses.

Zemurray had long competed against Minor Keith's powerful United Fruit Company (UFCO) for North American markets, but he was also willing to work with UFCO if the price was right. Zemurray now acted as a front man to gain some acreage and railroad concessions for Keith's operation. (Another group cut in on the deal by Zemurray was an Indianapolis syndicate headed by T.R.'s former vice-president, Charles Fairbanks.) Once its foot was in the door, UFCO began to buy up Honduras. The company's holdings amounted to 14,000 acres in 1918, 61,000 in 1922, and 88,000 in 1924. During 1929 Zemurray finally sold his company to UFCO for about $32 million. The Banana Man soon became UFCO's top official. If Honduras was dependent on the fruit companies before 1912, it was virtually indistinguishable from them after 1912. In 1914 the leading banana firms held nearly a million acres of the most fertile land. Their holdings grew during the 1920s until the Honduran peasants had no hope of access to their nation's good soil. In 1918, U.S. dollars even became legal tender in Honduras.

The Knox-Zemurray policies had succeeded after all. Honduras was free of British pressures and dependent on the United States. But the relationship went beyond economic dependence. North Americans not only controlled the nation's economy but, as a result of direct military and political intervention, the nation itself. It was never a question of whether the North Americans acted for profit or to stop revolutionary instability and British incursions. In Honduras during 1911, Knox and Zemurray considered a little revolution a good thing. U.S. power and profits tended to go hand in hand, and whether they could be best advanced through revolutionary or antirevolutionary activities depended on the circumstances.

Finally, and fittingly, the State Department showed its appreciation for Lee Christmas's talents. He became the U.S. Consul in Honduras. Christmas supposedly suggested the possibilities of his position by observing: "A mule costs more in Honduras than a Congressman."[43]

Determining Who Rules at Home: Nicaragua

The Honduran episode of 1911 and 1912 was historic because the United States government intervened directly to replace British political influence with its own in Central America. Taft and Knox also went through the same process in the largest Central American nation. The operation, however, was not as quick or clean in Nicaragua as in Honduras. Indeed, the events set in motion during 1909 led to twenty years of U.S. armed occupation, a forty-five year dictatorship, and finally an indigenous radical revolution in the 1970s.

Again, the British had been the major foreign power in Nicaraguan affairs through much of the nineteenth century. During the 1840s Polk established the first U.S. foothold, and in 1850 London recognized the new presence by agreeing to the Clayton-Bulwer treaty. During 1894 and 1895, the State Department finally maneuvered the British out of their hold on the Miskito coast. This vital strategic area for a future isthmian canal became a legal part of Nicaragua, although U.S. business interests now predominated in the area.

The power balance was shifting from London to Washington, but after he seized power from Conservatives in 1893, José Santos Zelaya used all of his considerable talents to stop the swing toward the North Americans. His attempts to develop the country with foreign concessions and subsidies to coffee growers were, in the eyes of Roosevelt and Taft, unimportant compared with Zelaya's ambition to unite Central America under his own leadership. He represented the historic Central American Liberal party's aim of creating a union among the five states. Zelaya, however, tended to depend more on rifles than ideology to persuade others, and he stirred up the area at the very moment the North Americans insisted that the region be tranquil. Zelaya's alleged brutality inside Nicaragua also offended North Americans and gave the State Department another public excuse for destroying his power.

The opportunity for U.S. intervention arose in 1909 when Conservatives, led by Emiliano Chamorro and Juan Estrada, wisely chose Bluefields on the Miskito coast to start a revolution. Estrada later bragged that North Americans in Bluefields contributed as much as one million dollars to his cause. The U.S. Consul at Bluefields was sufficiently involved with the revolutionaries to give Washington three days' advance notice of when the outbreak would occur. Two North Americans living in Bluefields actually joined the rebels. Zelaya caught them laying mines in the San Juan River that were intended to blow up ships carrying four hundred of his troops. He promptly executed them despite Washington's cries of outrage. A U.S. official in Nicaragua admitted that at least one of the victims had been involved in previous Latin American revolutions (Zelaya claimed both had been so involved), but that nevertheless the two were shot "not so much because they were revolutionaries but because they were Americans."[44]

Secretary of State Knox bluntly told the Nicaraguan chargé d'affaires in Washington that Zelaya was keeping "Central America in turmoil," constantly violating agreements, and even casting his "baleful influence upon Honduras." Even worse, U.S. officials told each other, was Zelaya's refusal to quit competing with Panama for an isthmian canal, and his willingness to play with French, German, and Japanese capitalists for both Nicaragua's development and the building of a possible canal. Zelaya had to go. He resigned in mid-December 1909 and went into exile with the hope that his departure would forestall U.S. intervention. Such hope underestimated the Taft-Knox objectives. The Nicaraguan Congress elected a distinguished doctor, José Madriz, as president. Knox flatly refused to recognize Madriz because he viewed him as pro-Zelaya, pro-Mexico, and hence anti–United States. The secretary of state also pressured the British not to extend recognition. Madriz bitterly protested: how, he asked Knox, could U.S. actions "be reconciled with the principles of neutrality proclaimed by the law of nations."[45]

By May 1910, Madriz nevertheless had remarkably isolated the Conservative forces and Estrada at Bluefields. The U.S. Consul at Bluefields asked for military help. Two hundred U.S. Marines, transported from the new bases in Panama, landed on May 31. They were led by the colorful Smedley Butler, already renowned for his heroics in the War of 1898, and for leading such Rooseveltian police actions as the 1903 Honduran intervention. The son of a well-connected Philadelphia Quaker family, Butler became the symbol of U.S. militarism in the Caribbean—

Central American region—at least until the early 1930s when he published a tell-all autobiography that damned the interventions he had led for worsening, not improving, the region's societies. In the book he recalled that although the 1910 landing was supposedly a neutral act, in reality he told Madriz's forces that they were free to attack—but without firearms because they might hit North Americans. The Estrada Conservatives, however, were allowed to keep their weapons. The Conservatives then aroused themselves to reclaim power. Knox took no chances. He kept Butler's forces for three more months in what the disgusted Marine leader called "the dull apathy of a third-rate Central American port."[46]

Knox was elated. He had, however, actually walked into political quicksand. Although a hero in New York and Washington, Estrada came under fire from the Salvadorans, Guatemalans, and especially Costa Ricans who bitterly attacked the sellout to the Yankees. The new U.S. Minister to Managua reported in early 1911, "The natural sentiment of the overwhelming majority of Nicaraguans is antagonistic to the United States." Even "with some members of Estrada's Cabinet," the minister added, "I find a decided suspicion if not mistrust, of our motives."[47] In May 1911, Estrada decided to give way to another U.S. selection, Adolfo Díaz.

Two years before, Díaz had earned $1,000 annually from a U.S. mining company in Bluefields, but he somehow came up with $600,000 for the rebels' cause. (He reimbursed himself for this expense after becoming president.) Sensing the situation accurately, the U.S. minister assured Washington that Díaz would become president in any kind of election the United States wanted to be held, but that nevertheless, "A war vessel is necessary for the moral effect," and it should remain "at least until the loan has been put through." Díaz dutifully reopened loan negotiations with the New York bankers rounded up by Knox.[48] (When criticized for using only the large bankers and not dividing the Central American melon with smaller financiers, Knox sharply replied, "When you want to borrow ten millions you don't ask the grocer for it or the boot black; you go to the man who has it.")[49] After the bankers were finished with Díaz, he had their loan and they owned Nicaragua's National Bank, 51 percent of the railroads, and the customs collector.

Discontent spread as the U.S. presence drew the hatred of Liberals and even some Conservatives. The State Department privately described Díaz as isolated. Knox found this out firsthand when he went to Managua on a good-will visit and was greeted by anti-U.S. demonstrations. In mid-1912 Díaz pleaded for Marines to maintain order; in this case order was a euphemism for his own power. Smedley Butler sailed once again from Panama with 350 Marines. This time they met resistance that, in the words of one anti-Díaz journal, condemned "the blond pigs of Pennsylvania advancing on our garden of beauty." Butler did not spare firepower. A generation later Nicaraguan mothers still disciplined their children by saying, "Hush! Major Butler will get you."

Some 2000 lives were lost in the fighting before 2600 U.S. troops snuffed out the rebellion. After losing two of his own troops in one battle, however, Butler wrote his wife, "It is terrible that we should be losing so many men fighting the battles of these d . . . d spigs—all because Brown Bros. [the New York City banking house] have some money down here." Butler reflected intense feeling among the Marines that their code of honor, as well as their lives, was being violated for the sake of profiteering investors. Meanwhile the Central American Court, created with Roosevelt's blessing in 1907–08, condemned the intervention. Knox ignored the ruling. One hundred troops remained behind to guard the U.S. Legation. They marked the start of a twenty-year occupation by U.S. forces. With their help, Díaz held on until 1916. Knox justified all this with a 1911 statement: "We are in the eyes of the world, and because of the Monroe Doctrine, held responsible for the order of Central America, and its proximity to the Canal makes the preservation of peace in that neighborhood particularly necessary."[50]

Those words did not mean that the United States had intervened only for its security interests. The navy had what it needed in the Central American area long before the interventions occurred in Honduras and Nicaragua.[51] The State Department and the bankers pushed for a greater military presence in the area not for strategic reasons, but, as the U.S. Minister to Nicaragua nicely phrased it, for "the moral effect" such force would have on Nicaraguan minds as the United States went about imposing order and replacing British power with North American.

As did Honduras, Nicaragua depended on the dollar. Aside from the bankers' internal control, half the country's exports and nearly 40 percent of its imports involved the United States. But dependence had already gone beyond mere trade. The very structure of Nicaragua was shaped and controlled by North American bankers and soldiers. Díaz's power was determined more in Washington than in Managua. That determination mirrored both the Progressive quest for political stability and the burgeoning U.S. industrial and financial complex's search for profits in an area where its military force now stood supreme.

Wilson's Corollary to the Monroe Doctrine

Taft's successor in the White House, Woodrow Wilson, thought in terms of systems, wrote about systems, and—after becoming president in 1913—based his domestic and foreign policies on certain systems. As a young, distinguished political scientist in the 1890s, Wilson published and lectured extensively on the theme that the U.S. government was not a mere series of random institutions, but a growing network of power structures that after the war of 1898 was prepared to lead the world into a glorious future. As president, his "New Freedom" program of Progressivism rested on his insights into the new industrial society's need for reform from above. Later his League of Nations created an institutional and political process to bring rational order through reform to a western world destroyed by war and threatened with revolution. Wilson obviously did not think small. He understood the U.S. system and its place in the world as well as any president in history.

When these insights became actual policy in Central America they brought disaster after disaster to the region. With his simpler approach, Theodore Roosevelt had cynically referred to "my great and good friends, the Presidents of the various Central American Republics, and the excessively free and independent people over whom they preside."[52] Wilson, however, hoped to treat Latin Americans more equitably. He attacked both Roosevelt's "Big Stick" diplomacy and Taft's dollar diplomacy as simply two sides of the same misbegotten imperialism. The new president agreed with his closest foreign policy adviser, Colonel Edward M. House, who told Wilson: "In wielding the 'big stick' and dominating the two Continents, we had lost the friendship and commerce of South and Central America and the European countries had profited by it."[53] In his search for an alternative policy, however, Wilson—who knew little about Latin America—succeeded only in using the "big stick" more systematically than had the man whom he came to despise.[54]

When hemispheric relations became difficult, Wilson reverted to what he did understand and believe: the virtue of order, the evil of revolution, and the benefits of North American—as opposed to foreign or European—enterprises. Much as he suppressed radicals for the sake of order in the United States during the 1919 "Red Scare," so he suppressed revolutionaries in Central America and the Caribbean. Much as he believed a reformed North American capitalism to be the best tool for rebuilding the post–World War I world, so he earlier urged that it reform Central America. Wilson's policies in Central America proved disastrous because as a Progressive he thought a good system was one that was orderly and slightly reformed—by which he came to mean replacing European concessions with North American—and because, as president of an incomparably successful system, he believed other peoples should enjoy its benefits, by force if necessary. Thus did his anti-imperialistic rhetoric excuse his imperialistic acts.

Within days after moving into the White House, Wilson issued a "Declaration" on Latin America. The new system to the south was to rest on certain fundamentals: "orderly processes of just government based upon law, not upon arbitrary or irregular force"; the "consent of the governed"; and cooperation with "those who act in the interest of peace and honor, who protect private rights." In early 1914 the president focused on the real villains. As he was quoted virtually verbatim in a newspaper interview, "The concessionaries and foreign interests must go. Not that foreign capital must leave Central America, but that it shall cease to be a dominant special interest. . . . Material interests are to be set aside entirely. . . ." Continuing, he asked, "Who commonly seeks the intervention of the United States in Latin American troubles? . . . Always the foreign interests, bondholders or concessionaries. They are the germs of revolution and the cause of instability." As the reporter summarized the president's views, "Dollar diplomacy has been supplanted by diplomatic welfare work."[55]

Wilson wanted to end Central American dependence on all foreign "concessionaries" as much as possible. By September 1914, however, his objectives had sharply narrowed. When Germany indicated it wished to extend investments in Haiti, Wilson warned the Kaiser with a statement of principle: "Certain sorts of concessions granted by governments in America to European financiers and contractors . . . might lead to measures which would imperil the political independence or, at least, the complete political autonomy of the American states involved."[56] Having begun by condemning all "foreign" concessions that treated Latin, and especially the Central, American region unfairly, Wilson had taken an historic leap to excluding only "European financiers and contractors" who, in his view, jeopardized Latin American independence.

This corollary explicitly extended the Monroe Doctrine to European financial as well as political and military intervention. British officials had seen it coming and they understood the implications. But whether Wilson fully understood the British was another question. An emissary from London, Sir W. Tyrrell, talked with the president in late 1913 and reported Wilson's brilliant encapsulation of his Central American policy:

> With the opening of the Panama Canal [Wilson believed] it is becoming increasingly important that the Government of the Central American Republics should improve, as they will become more and more a field for European and American enterprize: bad government may lead to friction. The President is very anxious to provide against such contingencies by insisting that those Republics should have fairly decent rulers.

The British emissary drew the inevitable conclusion:

> The President did not seem to realise that his policy will lead to a "de facto" American protectorate over the Central American Republics; but there are others here [in Washington] who do, and who intend to achieve that object.

Tyrrell noted how the Central American balance of power had only recently gone through a transformation: "It seems to me that we have neither the intention nor the power to oppose this policy."[57] Latin Americans reached the same conclusions but with less equanimity. "Pan-Americanism as applied by Wilson aims at United States domination," ran one Chilean view, "just as Pan-Germanism aims at Prussian control over Germany and even a larger area of Europe."[58]

Nicaragua felt the full effect of Wilson's corollary. By late 1913 Díaz's rule, propped up by U.S. Marines, was both unpopular and economically bankrupt. He needed money and protection. Wilson's secretary of state, William Jennings Bryan, had been more outspokenly anti-imperialist in his long and colorful political career than the president. Bryan never entertained the idea, however, of pulling out of Nicaragua. He instead suggested a novel idea to Wilson: let the U.S. government, not the bankers, give a large loan to Díaz. The government's interest rate would be lower and fairer, Bryan argued, and the Nicaraguans would not have to hand over more of their resources to financiers. He also liked the idea that the deal would give "our country such an increased influence . . . that we could prevent revolutions, promote education, and advance stable and just government." Then, too, an "increase of trade . . . would come from development and from the friendship." The secretary of state wanted to start with Nicaragua and extend the policy to all Central America. He was actually a half-century ahead of his time. By suggesting that U.S. government monies replace private capital to this extent, Bryan had outlined one principle of John F. Kennedy's Alliance for Progress. And that was precisely the problem for Wilson. He rejected the idea as too "novel and radical." The president wanted reform but not this kind of "radical" change. Bryan dutifully told Díaz to return to the bankers. They gave the Nicaraguan a one-million-dollar loan in return for the other 49 percent of his country's railroads.[59]

But Díaz needed more than that to survive. In early 1914 his foreign minister, Emiliano Chamorro, and Bryan worked out a deal whereby the United States received exclusive rights to build and operate an isthmian canal in Nicaragua. In return, and apparently at Díaz's request, Washington was to extend a protectorate over Nicaragua to guarantee stability. "It will give us the right to do that which we might be called upon to do anyhow," Bryan rationalized to Wilson.[60] It also reassured the bankers. The U.S. Senate, however, flatly refused to accept the treaty, then finally ratified it in 1916 only after the protectorate promise had been dropped. Bryan could not understand why the senators and many Central Americans were so up-in-arms. When El Salvador and Costa Rica complained about the growing U.S. presence in their areas, he naively offered them the same protectorate to guarantee their stability, an offer they angrily rejected. The Central American Court then accepted Costa Rica's contention that U.S. claims in Nicaragua infringed on its territorial rights. Wilson and Bryan refused to recognize the decision. That refusal effectively destroyed the Court. In establishing its control over Central America, the United States killed the institution it had helped create to bring Central Americans together.[61]

Meanwhile, World War I culminated the United States' century and-a-half effort to change from a debtor to international creditor. As an historian, Wilson understood the meaning of this process, and indeed had described its workings during the late 1890s and afterwards in his writings. His corollary outlined how the process was to affect Latin America. But mere economic dependence was not enough. Military force and direct political intervention were as necessary for Wilson's policy as for Roosevelt's and Taft's. By the time the United States entered the war in April 1917, Wilson had stationed marines in three Caribbean and Central American nations: Haiti, Nicaragua, and Santo Domingo. The Monroe Doctrine had become a justification for U.S. military and economic intervention.

In June 1916, Wilson sent the draft of a message for Congress to Secretary of State Robert Lansing for perusal. "It shall not lie with American people," the president wrote, "to dictate to another people what their government shall be or what use they shall have or what persons they shall encourage or favor." Lansing wrote on the margin: "Haiti, S. Domingo, Nicaragua, Panama." Wilson never sent the message.[62]

The Power of Non-Recognition: Costa Rica and the Oil Companies

A year later Lansing could have added Costa Rica to his list. That country was at a turning point. Politically it had been ruled in the nineteenth century by a series of dictators who depended on British sufferance as well as their own arms. Coffee had first been planted about 1808 and the nation soon became a classic example of a one-crop economy. Fifty thousand pounds of coffee exports in 1832 multiplied four hundred times by the 1870s. Great Britain almost exclusively controlled the crop by financing the plantings and marketing the beans. The British also owned the nation's leading utility, and their most profitable investment in all Central America was a mortgage company created in 1911 to finance the expansion of Costa Rican coffee, sugar, cacao, and bananas. When the international coffee market sharply declined in 1882 and 1900, the Costa Rican economy sunk just as rapidly. The effect of the coffee economy on the peasants was especially devastating: before 1820 a large majority had small farm plots, but by the 1860s about half were merely wage laborers.[63]

Two decades later the country was rescued from becoming only an economic appendage to England; it became an appendage of both England and the United States. The nation needed railroads to carry coffee beans cheaply to Atlantic ports. British financiers handsomely swindled Costa Rica in negotiations over railway contracts, and when the country tried to sue, it was then swindled by British lawyers. Costa Ricans finally realized about 20 percent of a nearly $12 million British loan that had been intended for the railroad system, but had incurred massive debt payment obligations for the entire $12 million. In 1884 Costa Rica signed a contract with a U.S. builder, Minor Keith, to finish the railroad within three years.

Keith had been building railways in the country since 1871, and as early as 1872 had begun buying up bananas for shipment to the United States. He completed the major railroad after his uncle and three of his own brothers had died while trying to build the transportation system through the jungles. Keith received invaluable help from Costa Rican dictator, Tomás Guardia, and from his own marriage to a former Costa Rican president's daughter. Keith then refinanced the nation's huge debt to the British. In return, Costa Rica gave him a ninety-nine-year lease on the railroad, 800,000 acres of state land, and exemption from import duties on all construction materials. By the 1890s, small banana farmers were giving way to large plantations, and Keith led the pack. In 1899 he merged his firm with Boston Fruit to form the United Fruit Company (UFCO), or "The Octopus," as it soon became known in Central America.

Later described as "an apple-headed little man with the eyes of a fanatic," Keith completed the building of the railways, although at least five thousand men died in the effort. Five years after the merger in 1899, Keith's empire was a virtual independent enclave inside Costa Rica.[64] His economic holdings, his marriage, his talent for swaying an easily influenced government in San José, explained his immunity. In 1911 Keith funded the nation's debt in return for first claim on the country's customs receipts. By 1913 Costa Rica exported slightly more products to the United States than to the United Kingdom (between them they took more than 90 percent of the total exports), but partly due to Keith's import exemption and control over customs, it imported five times more goods from the United States (about $5 million worth) than from Great Britain. Almost single-handedly Keith broke England's hold and brought Costa Rica into the North American system.

As Keith's power rose, the nation's politics quieted, at least temporarily. In 1902 Ascensión Esquivel became president. His tenure initiated a series of constitutional regimes that lasted through three presidential terms and established the pattern that was to be broken only twice in the next seventy-five years. The first break occurred in 1917 when the secretary of war, General Federico Tinoco, overthrew an elected and reform-minded president. Tinoco assumed power and his brother, José Joaquín Tinoco, became secretary of war.

Woodrow Wilson interpreted the coup as a direct challenge to his antirevolutionary policies. He refused to recognize Tinoco's regime. At first Wilson's reasons seemed personal as well as political. Tinoco was close to Keith, whom Wilson mistrusted, and so corrupt that his incredible nepotism entered the country's vocabulary as *tinoquismo.* [65] Tinoco went through the motions of some constitutional procedures to legitimate his power, but Wilson was not moved. Nor was the president persuaded when United Fruit tried to apply pressure on the White House; or when a State Department fact-finding mission (headed by Secretary of State Lansing's bright young nephew, John Foster Dulles), advised Wilson to relent; or when Tinoco offered to do all he could to help the U.S. cause in World War I. In practical terms non-recognition meant that Tinoco was cut off from the U.S. money market, and despite wartime demand, the Costa Rican economy went into a downward spiral. Neighboring Nicaragua, where U.S. power was dominant, threatened invasion. Finally in 1919 Tinoco quit.[66]

Wilson has since been praised for holding obdurately to his political principle in this episode. It is now apparent that more than morality was involved. There was a larger and more important story, and it began in 1913 when U.S. officials discovered an English firm, headed by no less than Richard Lloyd George, son of the great British Liberal leader, seeking oil concessions in Costa Rica. The State Department immediately defined any such concession "to be of unusual interest because of its relation to naval bases and the proximity . . . to the Panama Canal." A U.S. entrepreneur, Dr. Leo J. Gruelich of New York, then entered the race for petroleum. Gruelich turned out to be a front man for the expanding oil holdings of Harry Sinclair. The State Department abided by its traditional policy of playing no favorites among North American concessionaires, but its intervention was also unnecessary because the Gruelich-Sinclair group seemed to have the situation well in hand.

Then came the Tinoco coup. With it came a new oil group led by John M. Amory of New York. The State Department quickly discovered that Amory was a cover for the revived British group, and—much worse—that Tinoco supported it. Washington officials concluded that Tinoco had pulled off the coup in part because the former president, Alfredo Flors, had refused to sign the oil contracts with Amory. The most powerful figure in Costa Rica, Minor Keith, had moreover been working with Amory (and Tinoco) because the Sinclair concession bordered the lands held by United Fruit. Keith did not want Sinclair to drain the oil before UFCO could start drilling.

By July 1918 the State Department had sent a warning to the Tinoco regime: "Department considers it most important that only approved Americans should possess oil concessions in the neighborhood of Panama Canal. Amory concession does not appear to meet these requirements." The Wilson Corollary could not have been more bluntly stated, or the distinction between "bad" European and "good" North American concessionaires more clearly made. The Sinclair group, the Department ordered, was to be protected against Tinoco's attempt to "undermine [the] Company's standing." When the U.S. chargé relayed this message to Tinoco, the President replied "with a shrug of his shoulders, that it was too late," according to the chargé. The Amory concession was already legally accepted. The chargé reported to Washington that nothing could be done to kill the Amory plan and pull Costa Rica "out of its present state of political, financial and economic anarchy and ruin" until "the Tinocos are put out." The State Department stepped up the pressure. Outbreaks erupted in San José. The Nicaraguans, supported by Washington officials, threatened to lead the other Central American countries in breaking off relations with Costa Rica. In August 1919 José Joaquín Tinoco was assassinated. His brother then fled the presidency to live in exile in Paris. When an associate of Tinoco claimed power, the State Department immediately refused to recognize him and set out detailed plans for non-Tinoco candidates to run in new elections. In December 1919 an acceptable regime came to power. It demonstrated its virtue by reopening the oil contracts signed by Tinoco.

The new regime's oil policy not surprisingly brought a strong protest from London. The Costa Rican government needed immediate U.S. help to deal with the British anger, and that help came with diplomatic recognition in August 1920—after the Costa Rican government annulled the Tinoco-Amory contracts. The field was now open for a race between strictly North American companies. By 1924 Sinclair decided the available oil was not worth the race and forfeited his concession. The British, however, were no longer around to pick up Sinclair's discards.[67]

The Wilson administration thus determined not only who was to govern Costa Rica, but who was—and was not—to develop certain of its resources. Washington's policy moved well beyond Roosevelt's simpler antirevolutionary stance. U.S. power in Central America had become so great that it could permit some revolutions if they threw out used-up dictators and promised to stay inside the lines marked out by Washington officials. In Honduras during 1919 and Guatemala a year later, revolutionaries abided by both of these criteria, so the United States allowed the overthrow of two former but now embarrassing friends, Francisco Bertrand in Honduras and Estrada Cabrera in Guatemala. Revolutions in the region could be tolerated as long as they were meaningless for U.S. interests—but, as Tinoco learned, only then.

In 1917, Wilson proposed that "the nations should with one accord adopt the doctrine of President Monroe as the doctrine of the world: that no nation should seek to extend its polity over any other nation or people, but that every people should be left free to determine its own polity, its own way of development, unhindered, unthreatened, unafraid, the little along with the great and powerful." Wilson's words were betrayed by his actions in Central America, especially in Nicaraguan and Costa Rican affairs. At the post-war peace conference in Paris, the Europeans not unnaturally refused to consider Wilson's plea. The most important discussion about the Monroe Doctrine occurred when the U.S. Senate, and then the president himself, insisted that the Doctrine not be open in any way to non-North American interpretation. When Wilson left the White House in 1921, with both his body and dreams broken, his rhetoric of idealism hung dead in the air as North American power tightened its hold on Central America. Wilson's rhetoric had come in part from being the son of a Presbyterian minister. His Central American policies, however, marked him as the diplomatic heir of Theodore Roosevelt.

Tinkering with the System: The 1920s

President Calvin Coolidge's greatest talent was an ability to use few words in touching the core of a foreign policy problem. In April 1925, he sounded the theme for the decade of the 1920s. The president told United Press that North Americans and their property "are a part of the general domain of the nation, even when abroad. . . . There is a distinct and binding obligation on the part of self-respecting governments to afford protection to the persons and property of their citizens, wherever they may be." Coolidge directly related this sweeping power to U.S. citizens in Central America.[68]

Just how far U.S. power had developed became evident in December 1922 when Secretary of State Charles Evans Hughes convened a conference of Central American states in Washington. El Salvador and Guatemala had revived the idea for a federal union in the region. Hughes privately laughed off the thought that Central Americans could get along well enough, long enough, for a union, but a revolution in Guatemala then overthrew the unionist faction and threatened war between the new regime and El Salvador. The secretary of state promptly called the nations to Washington. For the next several months he and his Latin American adviser, Sumner Welles, dictated terms. The occasion was not to be a replay of the 1907 conference, when the Central Americans had come to their own conclusions. Now the United States, with the help of faithful (and marine-occupied) Nicaragua, set the agenda, which included the admonition that no one mention the late, unlamented Central American Court. Nor was such an academic subject as the union to be discussed. As usual the parties promised to support each other's territorial integrity. They then established a new court with virtually no powers and endorsed the so-called Tobar Doctrine: no coups d'état were to be recognized diplomatically unless made legitimate by a free election. After Welles further tightened the wording of the Tobar Doctrine, it was accepted unanimously—by the United States because it promised tranquillity and by the Central American governments because it promised to keep them in power and safe from their own overambitious generals.[69]

With political stability better assured, U.S. power in Central America grew rapidly during the 1920s. The navy, operating out of the Panama Canal Zone and Cuba's Guantanamo Bay, was unchallenged in the hemisphere. Marines could be moved quickly into any trouble spot. The League of Nations, moreover, gave its member states in Central America paper guarantees against outside aggressors, while the North Americans—who refused to join the League and compromise their freedom of action—could act unilaterally to protect their own interests. It was as perfect an arrangement as a great power could wish. By the late 1920s the new frontier of the sky was secured when the Republican administration in Washington dispensed with its loudly professed faith in marketplace competition and gave Pan American Airways a monopoly in Panama. As the State Department explained, "The United States should, in so far as possible, control aviation in the Caribbean region," and especially protect the area from the competition of state-supported German and French airlines.[70]

When critics attacked the State Department for overprotecting Pan American Airways or United Fruit, one experienced officer, Francis Huntington-Wilson, did not bother to deny it. But he privately blasted those who obviously did not know how the system worked.

> Those of our worthy publicists to whom Wall Street is *anathema* have, in the debauchery of their muckraking, been silly enough to insinuate that the Department of State was run by Wall Street. Any student of modern diplomacy knows that in these days of competition, capital, trade, agriculture, labor and statecraft all go hand in hand if a country is to profit.[71]

U.S. economic power in Central America consequently grew enormously during the decade. Between 1913 and 1929 Guatemala's overall exports rose 67 percent, but her exports to the United States shot up over 150 percent. Comparable figures for Honduras were 800 percent and 600 percent, and for Nicaragua 37 percent and 100 percent. El Salvador's and Costa Rica's trade also increased, but not to the extent of the other three countries. By 1929 the United States was by far the leading market for each state except El Salvador, where Germany was in front, and Costa Rica, which sent more of its products to the British. The extent of U.S. power was even more striking as far as imports were concerned. In every country, North Americans at least doubled their markets in Central America between 1913 and 1929. In El Salvador they quadrupled their market. The British and Germans were now a distant second and third even in their former strongholds of Costa Rica and El Salvador.[72]

These small nations were dependent on one or two crops, and those products were in turn largely controlled by North American investors.

The statistics are astounding: of Costa Rica's $18 million of exports in 1929, $12 million came from coffee, $5 million from bananas. Of El Salvador's $18 million of exports, $17 million represented coffee and about one million dollars, sugar. Of Guatemala's $25 million total exports, $19 million was in coffee and $3 million in bananas. Honduras exported $25 million worth of products; bananas accounted for $21 million. Of Nicaragua's $11 million export trade, coffee represented $6 million and bananas $2 million. Clearly if the prices of coffee and bananas suddenly dropped on international markets, all Central America would plunge into disaster.[73]

Many U.S. investors would share in the disaster, for they had become paramount in Central America. Their direct investments in the area more than doubled between 1919 and 1929 to $251 million. In Guatemala they (especially United Fruit) controlled all but a few miles of the railroads, one-fifteenth of the total land area, the leading bank, a number of major industries, and the great utility company (American and Foreign Power owned by General Electric). In Honduras, United Fruit and its subsidiaries controlled the rail system, port facilities, and nearly all the banana and rubber-producing lands. North Americans owned the prosperous silver mine. In Nicaragua, United Fruit and Atlantic Fruit claimed 300,000 acres. North Americans owned and/or managed the leading mines, the railroads, the lumber industry, and banks. El Salvador's bonds were now handled by New York instead of British banks, its most important domestic financial institution was owned by San Francisco interests, and its transportation system depended on North American capital. U.S. investment had nearly caught up with British in Costa Rica, and the dominant company in the nation was unquestionably United Fruit. North Americans controlled railroads, mines, cables, and—thanks to Woodrow Wilson—oil concessions.[74] Behind these dull statistics lay an economic empire of which few (aside, perhaps, from Minor Keith, whose power was matched only by his imagination) had dreamed a mere twenty years before. Always a genius in his timing, Keith died in 1929 just as disaster struck the system.

This economic power was protected, and the politics of several of these small nations largely shaped, by the ever-present military forces of the United States. In Honduras, for example, U.S. troops had intervened six different times by 1925. At that point, North Americans were so dominant that they even fought each other. This embarrassment occurred after Tiburcio Carías Andino (later to be the most skillful of all Honduran dictators) lost a presidential election in 1923 that was obviously fixed by the incumbent Liberal party. Carías had taken care to win the favor of United Fruit, and with the company's support launched a revolt. The imaginative Carías even pioneered the use of aerial bombardment in Central America during the war. U.S. officials, however, had set the ground rules for Honduras in 1911 and 1912, and the Washington treaties of 1923 reaffirmed the rules. So U.S. troops landed in 1924 to protect lives and property, and soon found themselves fighting against United Fruit's presidential nominee. When the conflict spread to areas where foreigners lived, the U.S. forces quickly smashed Carías's dreams of power. The 1923 treaties had been upheld. Sumner Welles then mediated, and a man acceptable to all sides became president. North American power had become so encompassing that U.S. military forces and United Fruit could struggle against each other to see who was to control the Honduran government, then have the argument settled by the U.S. Department of State. But the story ended happily for Carías. In 1929 United Fruit bought out Sam Zemurray's Cuyamel Fruit Company, and since Cuyamel had bought and paid for the Liberal party—Carías's political enemy—the Liberals suddenly found themselves without funds. In 1932 Carías grabbed power over little opposition, and hand-in-hand with United Fruit ruled his country for the next seventeen years.[75]

An ominous reaction to such displays of U.S. force soon appeared. At the Havana Conference of 1928 the Latin American nations resolved that "No state has a right to intervene in the internal affairs of another." The U.S. delegates fought the resolution, but when they offered a weak substitute, only four of the twenty American states (including, of course, Nicaragua) voted with them. The original, damning resolution was put off until the next inter-American meeting, but Laurence Duggan, a top State Department expert on Latin America, later wrote: "It was one of the worst diplomatic defeats ever suffered by the United States at an important international conference."[76] The frequent military interventions and the long occupation of Nicaragua (and Haiti and Santo

Domingo in the Caribbean) by marines drew fire, not only abroad, but at home where liberals objected in principle, and conservatives—dedicated to cutting government budgets and their own personal taxes—objected to the cost.

In 1929 the newly elected president, Herbert Hoover, and his secretary of state, Henry Stimson, set out to create a fresh, non-military policy towards Latin America. Hoover bluntly told one press conference that he had no desire for the United States government to be represented overseas by military forces. Not that the new president welcomed revolutions; having personally experienced the Mexican, Russian, and Chinese upheavals, Hoover concluded in a widely read essay that a modern revolution is "no summer thunderstorm clearing the air," but "a tornado leaving in its path the destroyed homes of millions with their dead women and children."[77] That kind of catastrophe, however, could hardly occur in the socially less organized, U.S.-dominated region of Central America. Internally, as the 1924 Honduran uprising illustrated, the United States could exert full control if necessary. No other nation in the world posed even a faint challenge to North American military and economic power in the Caribbean-Central American region.

Given this context, Hoover and State Department officials realized that military interventions were usually needless. The interventions moreover, never corrected the fundamental problems, usually ended by putting unpopular dictators in power, and caused anti-U.S. outcries at home and abroad.[78] Hoover and Stimson decided that the system could run better on its own without those intermittent, costly military adjustments.

One of the two cornerstones of the system (military superiority was the other) collapsed during 1929 to 1931 when the U.S. economy went into a tailspin. The Central American economies naturally followed in its wake. Costa Rican coffee exports were cut more than half to $4.3 million. In El Salvador the collapse of coffee prices drove down rural wages to half their 1928 levels, and those earlier wages had provided bare subsistence. In Central America, as in Latin America as a whole, revolutions began to break out in greater number than ever before. Stimson agonized over his quandary: "I am getting quite blue over the bad way in which all Latin America is showing up," he wrote during the darkest months of the depression. The southern nations will not keep themselves in order, "and yet if we try to take the lead for them, at once there is a cry against American domination and imperialism."[79]

That sentence defined the problem. But on the other hand, as the secretary of state declared publicly in 1931, the Caribbean region was "the one spot external to our shores which nature has decreed to be most vital to our national safety, not to mention our prosperity."[80] Solutions, preferably short of military intervention, had to be found to keep the system functioning. And they had to be found and applied at a time when the rise of totalitarian states in Europe and Asia absorbed more and more of Washington's attention. The solutions, ultimately worked out in Nicaragua, El Salvador, and Guatemala, proved so effective that they shaped U.S.–Central American relations for nearly the next quarter-century.

Creating the New Nicaragua

The highly unlikely beginning-of-the-end of the U.S. military occupation occurred during the Nicaraguan presidential election in 1924. For a change, North American troops did not supervise the elections, which were won by a coalition that was promptly overthrown by the loser, Emiliano Chamorro, the "Old Lion." A decade before, Chamorro had played the game well by cooperating with William Jennings Bryan's policy of obtaining exclusive rights for a Nicaraguan canal and base system for the United States. But during the 1920s Chamorro unloosed the furies. The State Department, citing the 1923 Washington conference agreement, refused to recognize the regime of its old friend. But then the deposed vice-president, Juan B. Sacasa, reached for power with help from revolutionary Mexico.

Alarm bells went off in Washington, much as they would a generation later whenever word spread of threatened Soviet aid to the Latin Americans. Mexico was going through a revolution considered much too radical by State Department officials, and its appearance in Nicaragua occurred as relations were nearly at a breaking point over Mexico's policy of squeezing North American oil companies. The State Department concluded that the "savages of Mexico" (as the Costa Rican president called them) had "the unquestionable aim of ultimately achieving a Mexican primacy over the Central American countries." Secretary of State Frank Kellogg even told the Senate that Soviet Bolshevism was taking over the region with the help of the Mexican labor movement, a claim leading Senators properly discounted as fantasy.[81]

Coolidge and Kellogg solved the problem in the time-honored fashion: they sent in more marines and accompanied them with Henry Stimson, a tested diplomat as well as a leading New York corporation lawyer. Stimson encountered the usual dilemma: he could use the troops to restore calm, remove any Mexican influence he could find, and mediate between Chamorro and Sacasa, but the U.S. forces would have to remain in Nicaragua a long time to accomplish all of this. Stimson began to feel his way through the dilemma by first forcing Chamorro to step down. The North American made the old reliable politican of 1911 and 1912, Adolfo Díaz, acting president. That transition neutralized Sacasa and his army led by General José Maria Moncada. All of Moncada's officers except Augusto Sandino laid down their arms. Determined to end the U.S. intervention, Sandino fought a bloody battle against the marines in 1927, then disappeared into the rugged mountains along the Honduran border. The United States declared the country pacified. Stimson announced that the U.S. troops could be withdrawn and replaced by a new police force, the *Guardia Nacional*, trained by North American officers.

The United States had hit upon a solution to its traditional dilemma of how to inject force to stop revolutions without having a long-term commitment of U.S. troops. The answer seemed to be to use native, U.S.-trained forces that could both pacify and protect the country. The State Department had begun drilling Latin American police units earlier in the twenties, but the Nicaraguan experiment was exceptional in its size and objectives. The experiment would work, U.S. officials believed, if the National Guard and its commander were properly trained and non-political. Only later—too late—did these officials understand that in Central America such a force would not remain above politics, but single-handedly determine them.

Moncada won the U.S.-supervised election in 1928. His victory, however, was overshadowed by the sudden reappearance of Sandino. By mid-1928, the Coolidge administration had sent in more troops to capture the guerrilla leader. For five years he eluded them and the National Guard. His exploits in fighting the hemisphere's greatest power to a standstill made Sandino one of Latin America's foremost twentieth-century heroes. Thirty-three years old in 1928, Sandino had been raised in a wealthy home and had enjoyed books and classical music. As a young man he worked for Standard Fruit and U.S.-owned mining companies throughout Central America. Those experiences shaped a growing anti-Yankeeism soon fueled by a Joan-of-Arc faith: he was to be the instrument for creating a Nicaragua unpolluted by North American influences. From 1927 to 1933 Sandino became a popular, even charismatic, figure among peasants who, having gotten nothing out of the long U.S. occupation, fed and protected his soldiers from marine-led search parties.

In 1929, President Hoover and his secretary of state, Stimson, decided that the National Guard had developed to the point that it could handle Sandino. Once again the number of U.S. troops was reduced, although officers stayed behind to work with the guard. By 1932 fewer than a thousand North American soldiers and officers remained. But in the minds of Nicaraguans, as well as of the Hondurans who helped supply Sandino, it was the Yankees, not the guard, whom Sandino was fighting. The guerrilla leader proclaimed that he had nothing against the North American people, only the marines who occupied his country.

The Sandinistas fought a war that provided a remarkable preview of the sixties in Vietnam and early eighties in Central America. With the peasants shielding him, the marines could not find Sandino and his followers, but he got close enough to take photographs of marine camps—then sent the pictures to the U.S. headquarters with his compliments. The Sandinistas lived on little and off the countryside; the U.S. troops and the Guard enjoyed far richer diets and found few friends outside the urban areas. The North Americans were especially targeted, and Sandino made most welcome, in the poorest parts of the country where the Managua politicians and their Washington supervisors had built few schools, hospitals, or roads, but had continued to collect taxes. Honduran peasants, who were equally deprived, totally disregarded their government's orders not to shelter the Sandinistas, and their hatred for the North Americans multiplied when U.S. marine planes bombed Honduran villages in searches for the guerrilla. Honduran troops, patrolling the border for five years, captured only one Sandinista—and allowed him to escape.[82]

Sandino triggered the closest thing to a class war that Central America had seen, and the United States was fully involved with the class under siege. The intervention had "proved a calamity for the American coffee planters," one planter wrote Stimson in 1931. "Today we are hated and despised. This feeling has been created by employing the American marines to hunt down and kill Nicaraguans in their own country."[83] Understandably, President Moncada did not want the marines to leave. The troops protected him from his own people.

Stimson nevertheless announced in 1931 that the force would be pulled out. The killing of marines and the high expenses made the occupation politically unpopular in the United States. The depression-plagued Congress refused to spend nearly a million dollars so the marines could be targets for Nicaraguan guerrillas, particularly if the Guard were now available. Then Japan invaded Manchuria in September 1931. Stimson led the anti-Japanese protests in the United States, but he worried that if more U.S. troops went into Latin America, "it would put me in absolute wrong in China, where Japan has done all this monstrous work under the guise of protecting her nationals with a landing force." When U.S. citizens in Nicaragua asked for protection, Stimson told them to leave or be quiet.[84] Just six years before, Coolidge had promised to shield them, but he had not then anticipated the economic crash, the bad example set by the Japanese, or the alternative of a native National Guard.

In 1932, Stimson instructed Moncada to hold an open election. Under the supervision of the remaining 400 marines, Juan Sacasa won the presidency. The troops finally left on 2 January 1933. The two-decade-long occupation of Nicaragua was over. The National Guard moved into the resulting power vacuum.

And as Sandino had promised, once the marines had left he was ready to negotiate. Fully sensitive to the Guard's new authority, he asked that it be disbanded and even offered to protect President Sacasa against it.

After one meeting with Sacasa in 1934, Sandino was driving into Managua when he was seized by soldiers and, along with two of his generals, taken to a nearby field and shot. The Guard's commander, General Anastasio Somoza, admitted issuing the order for execution and claimed he had received approval from the U.S. Minister, Arthur Bliss Lane. The minister had been seen in Somoza's company, including attendance at a baseball game three days before Sandino was executed. Lane vigorously denied involvement in the shooting. Several hours before the murders he had even asked Somoza to give his "word of honor" (in English, so nothing would be lost in the translation) that the guerrilla leader would not be harmed. As Lane later wired Washington with considerable understatement, "I cannot place great confidence in his promises."[85]

Anastasio Somoza nevertheless became the United States' most important and lasting gift to Nicaraguans. Not born to the elite class, he had made his way to Philadelphia where he studied advertising, met the young woman—the daughter of a wealthy Nicaraguan—whom he would marry and who gave him entry to Managua's power elite, and learned English so well that he often preferred it to Spanish. His love for the Phillies and Athletics made baseball a lifelong passion, ranking just below the accumulation of wealth and mistresses. He wormed his way up through Nicaraguan business and political circles until, in 1927, his ability to use English made him invaluable to Henry Stimson's mission. Shrewd, brutal, and unequivocally pro-North American, Somoza became a natural candidate to lead the new National Guard, despite his lack of military training. But then as Sandino's murder demonstrated, power was gravitating to those with the fewest principles, not the most military discipline.

By 1936 Somoza had set his sights on the presidency, even though as commander of the Guard he was (according to the U.S. officials who established the force) supposedly above politics. Sacasa, Chamorro, and Díaz, who had cooperated with the United States beyond the expectations of Washington officials, sent a pathetic letter to Secretary of State Cordell Hull. They had long worried that the U.S.-created Guard "would eventually constitute a threat to peace and order" even when North Americans assured them it would be apolitical. The United States, they concluded, must now protect them from its own creature.

Hull coldly replied that any "special relationship" between the two countries stopped when the marines withdrew. Somoza was thus assured the United States would not interfere. Civil war broke out on 31 May 1936, and within eight days Somoza controlled Nicaragua.[86] For forty-three years he and his two sons ruled the country as a private fiefdom. In 1939, President Franklin D. Roosevelt warmly received the dictator in Washington. Somoza addressed a joint session of Congress and received $2 million in credit from private and governmental banks. U.S. technical advisers and managers moved in to help run banks and railroads in Nicaragua that Somoza quickly tapped for his own profit. A Mexico City newspaper cynically noted in 1939 that F.D.R.'s famed "Good Neighbor doctrine" was "transforming itself into a league of 'mestizo' dictators, with the United States destined to guarantee the slavery of Latin American peoples."[87] Hoover, Stimson, and Roosevelt, however, had found in the National Guard the answer to the perplexing problem of how to maintain an orderly, profitable system without having constantly to send in the marines.

Adapting the Good Neighbor to El Salvador

Another "mestizo dictator" the Mexican newspaper editors may have had in mind was Maximiliano Hernández Martínez, president of El Salvador. He ruled over a nation that had won the reputation as the most industrious, as well as one of the most rapidly multiplying, people in Central America, and who were rewarded for their efforts by being among the poorest, worst-fed, and most exploited laborers in the hemisphere.

The Salvadoran elite (the oligarchy of "Fourteen" or "Forty Families") had managed this exploitation with a minimum of outside help. El Salvador, as Adolfo Gilly emphasized, was not a "banana republic." Among the Central American elites, the Salvadorans enjoyed the highest degree of independence in controlling their internal economy. Foreign ownership was almost nonexistent because as early as 1600, and for the next two hundred years, a small group of people in El Salvador bought up the best land for the growing of the great cash crop of indigo.

In the nineteenth century the coffee boom reshaped the country's economy, as it did Guatemala's and Costa Rica's, but in El Salvador a few families already owned the best land and simply changed over to growing coffee beans. With their monopoly of good soil and the country's great crop, the landholding oligarchy accumulated the capital needed to dominate as well the banking and mercantile systems.[88] By the 1920s, the entire nation was owned and operated by those few families who had possessed the foresight and ruthlessness to control the country's small amount of arable land a century or more earlier. In the nineteenth century they had also controlled the presidency and lesser offices. The 1886 Constitution placed strict civilian rule over the military. But during the twentieth century, as labor and peasant unrest spread, the military and the oligarchy struck a deal: army officers could have the honor of holding political offices (even the presidency) if in return they allowed the oligarchs free economic rein. It seemed to be a natural match.

On the bottom side of Salvadoran society was suffering and exploitation which the people endured with remarkable patience—until 1931. The rapid expansion of the coffee plantations had torn apart Indian villages and their communal lands which provided the food supply. Peasants and Indians became little more than a hungry, wandering labor force to be used at will by the oligarchy. As early as 1900 Salvadorans had sought work in Honduras with United Fruit and other U.S. companies. By the early 1920s they made up as much as 10 percent of the Honduran work force. Their numbers rapidly grew during that decade when lower coffee prices further squeezed out smaller growers and concentrated more power in the oligarchy's hands. As coffee took up more and more territory, the staple foods of maize, beans, and fruit grew scarcer. The only Salvadorans who had enough, not to mention a variety, of food, were the few who could import it from other Central American nations or the United States.

This dependence on food imports explained why during the 1920s North Americans controlled key Salvadoran markets at the same time Germany and Great Britain controlled the country's coffee exports. El Salvador was a seller's market: between 1922 and 1926 the price of maize jumped 100 percent and beans 225 percent. A country that had imported less food than any other Central American nation suddenly needed the United States and its neighbors for subsistence.[89] In 1931 a U.S. Army officer glimpsed the conditions of impending catastrophe when he observed that on the streets of the capital, San Salvador, "There appears to be nothing between these high-priced cars and the oxcart with its barefoot attendant. There is practically no middle class. . . . Thirty or forty families own nearly everything in the country. They live in almost regal style. The rest of the population has practically nothing."[90]

Washington's allegiance lay with the forty families. Financial ties reinforced the trade relationship. London had long acted as the important foreign source for Salvador's capital, but during a short, sharp post–World War I economic decline, El Salvador defaulted on its foreign debt to the British. In 1921 the Salvadorans searched for money to pay back interest and build the remainder of their railway system. The Great War had redrawn the map of international finance. Most roads now led to capital-rich New York instead of to London. A group of U.S. financiers stepped in to give a loan of nearly $20 million in return for control of the railway as collateral, and the appointment of a U.S. fiscal agent to oversee collection of export and import duties from which the loan would be repaid.[91] The proud Salvadorans vowed "never again"—and they indeed managed to avoid such direct U.S. influence until the 1960s when they again began accepting foreign aid. During the intervening decades neither U.S. bankers nor fruit companies enjoyed the power in El Salvador that they had exercised in the other Central American states. But the Salvadoran oligarchs nevertheless remained dependent on North American food and other imports, and did so as the gap widened between the few families and the masses.

One man tried to narrow that gap. Pio Romero Bosque became president in 1927 because he seemed safely conservative and a member of the oligarchy's inner circle. But Romero Bosque opened up the political system for the first time. In 1930, refusing to designate his successor in the presidential elections, he conducted the freest municipal and presidential elections in history. Romero Bosque became known as the "father of Salvadoran democracy." Unfortunately, the child died shortly after birth. For as mass political movements began in the freer air, the oligarchy regrouped. When the Salvadoran Foreign Minister blasted the

United States for occupying Nicaragua, he was fired; oligarchs did not want to alienate North American support as revolution threatened. The coffee planters meanwhile moved away from the government and established a new organization, *Asociación Cafetalera de El Salvador,* in which they could privately run the industry without any interference from elected officials. Modern Salvadoran history began with Romero Bosque's term as president. Lines were being drawn for a series of struggles between the very rich and very poor.[92]

In 1931 Arturo Araujo became president and General Maximiliano Hernández Martínez vice-president in an election that was both close and bitter. Araujo then made the mistake of trying to soften the depression's ravages by passing tax reforms and reducing the military budget. In December of that year, young army officers (whom the U.S. Minister characterized as "little more than half-witted") overthrew the president and placed in power Martínez, who apparently was not involved with the *golpe's* origins. The United States referred to the 1923 treaty arrangements that forbade recognition of governments formed by *golpes* and refused to open relations with Martínez.

Mass uprisings suddenly erupted in the western coffee-growing areas where economic conditions were most horrible. The upheaval was triggered when Martínez allowed the Communist party to run in local elections. After the Communists won victories in several towns, however, the army prevented them from taking office. Material for an explosion was abundant. Indians, who especially suffered after the 1929 economic collapse, had long been ready to rise up against the *ladinos.* But the fuse turned out to be the oligarchy's starving of peasants by taking away their lands for coffee growing, and then paying the dependent peasants practically nothing for their labor. The poor had little more to lose.

Their leader was Augustín Farabundo Martí, whose name would be taken a half-century later by other Salvadoran revolutionaries. A young intellectual from a landowning family, Martí had joined the newly formed Central American Socialist party in Guatemala in 1925. Wearing a red star with Leon Trotsky's face in the center as his lapel pin, he vowed to unite all of Central America under socialism. Martí worked in New York City with groups that opposed U.S. intervention in Latin America, and there he met relatives of Augusto Sandino. When the

New York police began searching for Martí, he fled to Nicaragua and joined Sandino. The two men soon parted company, however. Martí considered Sandino too narrow, nationalistic, and insufficiently revolutionary in his methods. Martí began organizing Salvadoran peasants. He did not lack passion, but as El Salvador's political situation turned chaotic in early 1932, and opportunity seemed to open to the revolutionaries, it turned out that his cause did lack organization.

That lack proved fatal. The Salvadoran Communists were little more than a handful of urban-based ideologues who knew nothing about triggering a revolution in the countryside. They finally backed away from a rebellion at the last moment, but the news of their second thoughts did not reach many peasants. These campesinos, moved not by communism but starvation, met a well-equipped army with only machetes in their hands. Martínez's forces quickly disposed of these peasants and then slaughtered thousands of others in a kind of preemptive strike that set a bloody precedent for later Latin American military dictators who faced mass uprisings. Martí was captured and shot, and as many as 30,000 other Salvadorans were wiped out in a matter of days.[93]

Martínez suddenly became the oligarchy's hero. The bloodbath also changed the mind of Washington officials about the general. Before the slaughter, the State Department had been adamant about non-recognition. Two weeks later it admitted that "the situation . . . is a difficult one. Martínez appears to have strengthened his position . . . as a result of having put down the recent disorders" and winning fresh political support at home.[94] In reality, few of his political opponents remained alive. Large portions of the peasantry had been destroyed precisely in those areas where the oligarchy had been most ruthless and acquisitive. (In the eastern coffee areas, where more land had remained in the hands of peasants, no uprisings occurred.) Indian dress and language virtually disappeared from the country for forty years. Martínez left no doubt that his equivalent of Somoza's guard could maintain order. In a 1932 announcement the U.S. granted Martínez informal recognition.[95] After the British opened formal relations with El Salvador that year, other states followed. In 1934 Roosevelt fully recognized the general. The 1923 policy had breathed its last.

Clearly some priorities ranked higher than non-recognition. And nothing ranked higher for Washington officials than order. Martínez may have had his strange beliefs (he held that it was a worse crime to kill an ant than to kill a man because "a man will be reincarnated after his death while an ant's death is final"),[96] but the general undeniably knew how to keep order. Washington officials preferred military dictatorship to indigenous radicalism. Support for relatively open elections gave way to accepting repression. Of course, such acceptance was easier because the generals repressed their own people. If outside agents had perpetrated the tragedies, the United States could have invoked the Monroe Doctrine, or its various corollaries, and taken action. But the British and other foreign powers posed no danger; they struggled for survival at home. No Soviet military or economic power was in sight or even imagined by calmer types to be possible in the Western Hemisphere. The State Department could consequently conclude that it had no business telling Somoza and Martínez how to keep order at home, just as long as the generals did so.

The Fascist Threat: Guatemala

As the left was suppressed, fascism appeared in Central America. In the eyes of U.S. officials, the latter threat had become equally dangerous by the mid-thirties. Nowhere in the region was the German presence more ominous than in Guatamala, where Jorge Ubico ruled. By 1939, nowhere had the U.S. system better proven its effectiveness and power than in Guatemala.

Ubico was the heir to a long tradition of Guatemalan dictators. The most important had happened to be Ubico's godfather, Justo Ruffino Barrios, who reigned from 1871 to 1885. Barrios built roads, began railways, and succeeded in stimulating the great coffee boom that soon became the powerhouse for the entire economy. The Indians who comprised half the country's population largely continued to live in isolation, but many of the traditional communal land holdings gave way to coffee plantations owned by a new aristocracy. Church power was meanwhile crushed, its property taken, clergy exiled, and education made secular.[97]

With the country dependent on coffee exports, it was, not surprisingly, run by and for the coffee oligarchs. Then United Fruit appeared early in the twentieth century. UFCO soon not only owned two huge plantations and monopolized the banana trade, but also controlled the docks in the nation's ports, ran the railroad, provided its own "Great White Fleet" for Guatemala's merchant shipping, operated the country's communication network, and provided loans to the profligate dictators. The company utilized these facilities for its own purposes, not Guatemala's, although at times—as when UFCO saved nearly bankrupt treasuries and bribed dictators—the two were difficult to distinguish.

Coffee exports went mainly to Germany and the United States. Bananas, however, moved entirely to (and their handling was monopolized by) North Americans. The foreign debt was largely in European hands, but no doubt existed after 1920 that any refinancing, or more credits, would come from New York. For four years the State Department even dictated Guatemala's bank policy. Twice during the twenties the State Department prevented European bankers from penetrating the economy, including once when Minor Keith began to cooperate with German interests to establish a badly needed national bank. A boom in coffee prices finally allowed the Guatemalans to set up the bank with their own capital in 1926.

In 1918 Woodrow Wilson's administration had warned Guatemala, "It is most important that only American oil interests receive concessions." When U.S. oil companies refused to seek concessions unless they were guaranteed reciprocal rights (that is, were recognized as equal in law to Guatemalans themselves), the State Department applied pressure and the Guatemalan government enacted appropriate laws. Then Washington decided it needed an "open door," equal-access rule in Guatemala to establish precedent for its penetration of Middle East oil fields which the British controlled. Guatemalans obediently reversed course and pledged equal access for all comers to the oil. The pledge made little difference commercially. North Americans held all the concessions by that time. The political significance, however, was obvious: key Guatemalan decisions were dictated by Washington officials.[98]

By the thirties the U.S. system was firmly established in Guatemala. Ubico clearly understood the relationship. In his mid-fifties when he came to power in 1931, Ubico was the son of a wealthy coffee growing family. He rose rapidly in the army, meanwhile retaining the family's holdings, and in the twenties organized his own political party. A riding accident had made him impotent, but his military career, dress, and personal belief that he looked (and consequently acted) like Napoleon gave him the *machismo* necessary for political stardom. By 1930 he was the only serious presidential candidate. Then an ill-advised military coup tried to remove a particularly corrupt regime from power. (Supposedly only $27 remained in the national treasury.) Ubico was not involved in the coup, but the lesson that followed was not lost on him. The United States broke the new regime by simply refusing to recognize it, then set up an acting president to supervise a new election. Ubico won the national balloting—unanimously.[99]

The new president's three phobias were intellectuals, Communists, and—until he became dictator—thieves. From 1931 until 1944, Guatemala was his "village." He cared about material things, not ideas, and built the transportation infrastructure (especially a highway system) that for the first time tied the country together and opened new areas for development. It was his greatest accomplishment. It also ultimately destroyed him, for his vast public works produced the nationalism, a new middle class, and the labor movement that threw him out of power in 1944.[100]

During the thirties, however, the State Department saw danger emanating not from a left or liberal nationalism, but from the impressive German population in Guatemala. Since 1900 this community had quietly accumulated wealth by owning large coffee plantations that accounted for perhaps as much as 50 percent of the entire industry. By intermarrying with the Guatemalan elite, it enjoyed social and political status. German interests were deeply entrenched in the country's leading retail stores and owned several of its largest banks. Only in Guatemala did the Germans living in Central America have their own school. The community quickly became a special target for Nazi agents. Ubico personally lauded Italy's Mussolini because of his *machismo* and Spain's Franco because of his military triumphs. The Guatemalan had less use for Hitler, but that did not ease U.S. concern, especially when Ubico became personally close to the German Minister in Guatemala City. After Italy withdrew from the League of Nations in 1936, so did Guatemala, supposedly for economic reasons. As Honduras and El Salvador followed Ubico's example, Washington officials became deeply worried. Secretary of Agriculture Henry Wallace warned Roosevelt in 1936 that the increase of German and Japanese trade throughout Central America was "very striking" and "worth pondering upon at some length."[101] Wallace had sounded a false alarm. Ubico admired Mussolini, but he needed Roosevelt. For Guatemalans, the villain was not the United States but their own Colossus of the North, Mexico, which shared a long boundary with Guatemala and harbored historic ambitions on its territory. For Ubico the danger compounded when Mexico moved sharply to the left in 1937 and 1938. He wanted the United States to act as a counterbalance, and after having watched its performance in the Guatemalan crisis during 1930 and 1931 he clearly appreciated its weight in the region's affairs.

Internally, Ubico turned naturally to North Americans. He asked a U.S. officer to head, for the first time in history, the nation's military academy. In this one move the dictator shrewdly removed the academy from politics (it had been the steppingstone for officers to replace rulers like himself) and allowed Washington to stop worrying about the Guatemalan military being seduced by European fascism. As the officers came under North American care, so did trade. Banana prices rose faster than coffee and thus the U.S. market and United Fruit became even more important to the Guatemalan treasury. In 1936, UFCO gave Ubico a one-million-dollar loan in return for massive tax reductions. Pan American Airways enjoyed exclusive landing rights in key cities. Finally, in the most critical of all economic sectors, U.S. coffee purchases slowly overtook Germany's between 1934 and 1936, and by 1939 outranked the Nazi share 60 percent to 15 percent,[102] totally reversing the 1930 pattern. In Guatemala the United States policy of not examining dictatorial methods too closely seemed to be paying off. As Ubico changed laws to maintain himself in power indefinitely, he also cooperated increasingly with the North Americans. Not that he had a clear choice; they operated his country's transportation, controlled its communications, bought its coffee and bananas, produced its second largest crop, and provided the cash for his government. The country was a case study of how successfully the U.S. system could operate in Central America, and how it had created a neodependent, rather than direct colonial, relationship. As the German danger receded, moreover, it was not replaced by the mass movements that had threatened El Salvador or Nicaragua. By opening parts of the country, Ubico had provided new frontiers for the 75 percent of his people who worked the land.

The danger was to come ultimately not from Germany or the Guatemalan masses, but from the city, whose small middle class began to question the North American system. For Ubico, who disliked ideas and abstractions, that seemed to be no danger at all.

Conclusion: The Good Neighbor

During the half-century between 1890 and World War II, the United States transformed itself from a secondary power to the world's most powerful nation. Its rise to domination in Central America exemplified this rapid process. Unable to challenge the British fleet, North Americans found the Monroe Doctrine to be an empty threat until the 1890s when Great Britain finally recognized the growing economic and military power of the United States in the Caribbean region. Theodore Roosevelt, then William Howard Taft, deployed this new force to mark Santo Domingo, Honduras, and Nicaragua as U.S. protectorates. Woodrow Wilson used his corollary to the Monroe Doctrine to block foreign concessions from Central America.

The 1900 to 1920 quest of U.S. Progressives for order, stability, and profits in Central America mirrored the similar quest at home to restore order and profitability to an economic system threatened by "robber barons" and radical labor movements. In Central America the Progressives had a further purpose: to stop revolutions, particularly before Europeans moved in to protect their interests. Throughout the region, meanwhile, U.S. entrepreneurs, led by Minor Keith's United Fruit Company, pivoted Central American economies until they meshed with the U.S. system. By 1920, the political and economic elites in each of the five countries understood that not only were they increasingly dependent on North Americans, but that the real Colossus of the North was willing and able to reinforce economic dependence with direct military and political intervention. U.S. Marines entered the Caribbean region no fewer than twenty times between 1898 and 1920.[103]

After World War I, Europeans no longer posed a major threat to Central America. By decimating British, French, and German power, the war accelerated the de-Europeanizing process that had begun in the 1890s. The Monroe Doctrine was thus vindicated at the same time it became irrelevant. The fresh U.S. intervention in Nicaragua during 1927 drove home that reality to Washington officials and forced them to reevaluate their traditional policy. Intervention was no longer needed to prevent European penetration; European power was hardly in sight. Nor did U.S. intervention any longer pay other dividends; North Americans already dominated the region's economy. Intervention only brought on anti-Yankee feelings in Latin America and headaches for State Department officials who had more important problems in Asia and Europe. Even the old Marine, Smedley Butler, went public after 1929 to condemn the interventions he had led. Calling himself a "racketeer for capitalism" in 1931, four years later he published his most outspoken attack:

> I helped in the raping of half a dozen Central American republics for the benefit of Wall Street. The record of racketeering is long. I helped purify Nicaragua for the international banking house of Brown Brothers in 1909–12. . . . I helped make Honduras "right" for American fruit companies in 1903. . . . Looking back on it, I feel I might have given Al Capone a few hints. The best *he* could do was to operate his racket in three city districts. We Marines operated on three *continents.*

Butler overemphasized the role of Wall Street and underemphasized that of Washington, but he was correct in implying that it was becoming a debilitating business: the more the United States intervened, the more unpleasant those Central American societies seemed to become. U.S. officials began to see what a distinguished historian of the Monroe Doctrine meant when he observed: "It cannot be stated that the civilizing influence of the United States is an inevitable condition of progress in Latin America."[104] Out of the frustrations in Nicaragua came the conclusion that local police (such as Somoza's Guard) could relieve the marines of maintaining order. The United States held in reserve its right to intervene only if an emergency required it.

This conclusion shaped the Clark Memorandum on the Monroe Doctrine written by State Department officer, Reuben Clark, in 1928 and made public two years later. Clark argued that the Monroe Doctrine had been misunderstood as a mere "cloak" for U.S. intervention. He did not intend to repudiate either the Monroe Doctrine or Roosevelt's Corollary. He did, however, put the U.S. right of intervention on a different basis: the right to preserve North American interests. With that neat turn, Clark downplayed the Doctrine and Corollary (which were now irrelevant because of European weakness and embarrassing because of their association with imperialism in Latin American minds). He instead based any future U.S. intervention on the possible need to preserve North American interests against any threats—including internal dangers that could be more important in the future than external dangers.[105]

Other than the decline of European power, there was another reason why U.S. military intervention had become unnecessary as well as unprofitable: North American influence over the Central Americans was so strong that it could achieve policy objectives by exerting only its enormous political and economic leverage. Thus the objectives did not change as much as did the tactics after 1920. U.S. economic power had become so overwhelming in the region that the State Department could step in and stop North Americans (even Minor Keith) from carrying out projects that the Department considered unproductive. "Wall Street" did not define U.S. policy in Central America. North American investors and traders, however, had created enormous U.S. economic leverage over the region between the 1870s and 1920s, and the State Department worked with them (for example, with the Sinclair group in Costa Rica), to exclude the Europeans and then to develop stable internal regimes (as illustrated by the State Department-banker cooperation in Nicaragua).

In nearly every instance, the interests of the State Department and North American business coincided. When they did not, the business interest usually gave way, as indeed it had to do if a *system* was to be maintained. Washington officials, not the individual, particularistic businessmen, had the best vantage point for understanding all the system's parts and how they meshed (or why they did not). At times, as when Keith dallied with German financiers or New York bankers' wild quest for profits in the 1920s jeopardized Guatemala's stability, the State Department stopped the process to save the investors from themselves.

Between 1933 and 1939, Franklin D. Roosevelt's Good Neighbor policy did not change the Central American policy it inherited, but built on it. The Good Neighbor carried on interventionism in Central America and tightened the system far beyond anything Theodore Roosevelt and Woodrow Wilson probably imagined. The tightening occurred in three steps.

First, Roosevelt, following Hoover's precedents, accepted dictators in Nicaragua, Guatemala, Honduras, and El Salvador. Requiring governments at least to go through the motions of democratic elections (as the 1923 Washington agreements had provided), thus gave way to the higher priority of stability. Adolf Berle, one of F.D.R.'s top advisers on Latin America, spoke for the administration when he said, "I don't like revolutions on principle."[106] As long as the regimes maintained order and protected private property, they were perfectly acceptable. They accomplished for less cost what the Marines had been trying to do for more than thirty years. Deals were easily struck. The United States wanted stability and protection for its economic interests; such rulers as Carías in Honduras, Martínez, Somoza, and Ubico needed U.S. recognition and access to New York money markets. Stability, of course, meant maintaining the status quo: a social-economic system in which 2 percent or less of the population in four of the five Central American nations controlled the land and hence the lives of the other 98 percent. That too was assumed by North Americans as part of the system. The United States thus accepted, and soon welcomed, dictatorships in Central America because it turned out that such rulers could most cheaply uphold order. Dictatorships were not a paradox but a necessity for the system, including the Good Neighbor policy.

The second step occurred when the New Deal radically increased its political leverage by having the government replace the private bankers as a source for funds. The idea was not new. Secretary of State William Jennings Bryan, and then, in the 1920s, Dana Munro (chief of the State

Department's Central American desk) had argued that government contributions could save Central Americans from being constantly at the mercy of the bankers. Their views were dismissed as too radical, but when the bankers were temporarily knocked out by the Great Depression, the New Deal entered the ring. Roosevelt created the Export-Import Bank in 1934 to provide government credit so U.S. exporters could sell more goods overseas. By 1939, the Ex-Im Bank had loaned money for projects in Nicaragua, but with the conditions that a U.S. engineer headed the largest project, that Washington officials had access to Nicaraguan records and approved certain expenditures, that U.S. materials were used, and—of special significance for Nicaragua's development—that Somoza encouraged agricultural and small industrial enterprises that fit into, and would not compete with, North American businesses.[107] The Ex-Im Bank thus not only helped mold Nicaraguan development, but carefully fit it more tightly into the North American system.

In the same manner the State Department negotiated reciprocal trade treaties with the five Central American nations. None of these amounted to much economically because the United States had little left to offer; it had already reduced its tariffs for the region's fruit, coffee, and minerals. But the negotiations had widespread political effects. Each of the four dictators lowered tariff walls to U.S. products (and even offered to discriminate against Japanese goods) in return for the political recognition and approval that the United States offered through the treaties. By importing larger amounts of U.S. agricultural products, moreover, all five nations became more dependent on North America for food. The system was thus tightened at both the political and economic levels.[108]

A third step occurred after 1938 when the New Deal consummated relationships between North and Latin American military officers. In Washington F.D.R. established a new Liaison Committee in which State, Navy, and War Department officers exchanged views and coordinated plans. At nearly 100 meetings in 1939 and 1940, all but a half-dozen had Latin American affairs as the top priority.[109] By 1940, the United States had fully replaced the French and British as suppliers of military equipment and sources of officers for instructing Latin American armies. In Nicaragua, the process had been completed a decade earlier. Now it was completed throughout Central America.

When the United States went to war in December 1941, nearly all the Latin American nations immediately followed. Secretary of State Cordell Hull could proudly claim, "The political lineup followed the economic lineup."[110] It certainly did in Central America, but then it had since at least the twenties. After that point no Central American government fundamentally challenged the system that had been put in place. Nor should any government have done so, for those who cooperated were handsomely rewarded. In return for their internal stability and external friendships, the governments received from the United States much of their food supply, most of the markets needed by their one- or two-crop economies, and nearly all their foreign loans and military supplies.

The system could work as long as the few in Central America dominated the many. And given the developments during World War II and the decade after, the system looked as if it could work forever.

II

![black bar divider]

MAINTAINING THE SYSTEM

For a decade after World War II, Western Europe was as utterly dependent on the United States as Central America had been before the war. With its incredible economy developed in the hothouse of wartime production, its monopoly of the atomic bomb, and its unchallenged supremacy in the air and on the oceans, the United States stood unrivaled as the most powerful nation in history.

During the early postwar years Washington officials were preoccupied with crises in Europe and Asia. Central and South America ranked far down on their priority list. By the late fifties however, Western Europe and Japan had revived until, with startling efficiency, they could challenge even the U.S. economic hegemony. And just as that challenge appeared, the North American system suddenly confronted a series of Central American crises that for the first time threatened the fundamentals of that system.

Double-locking the System

Along with the enormous power came global responsibilities. U.S. officials grabbed those responsibilities with both hands. Many in that generation, including Franklin D. Roosevelt, vividly recalled the missed chance after World War I when Wilson's political errors, Senate opposition, and European obstructionism short-circuited U.S. plans. By 1944,

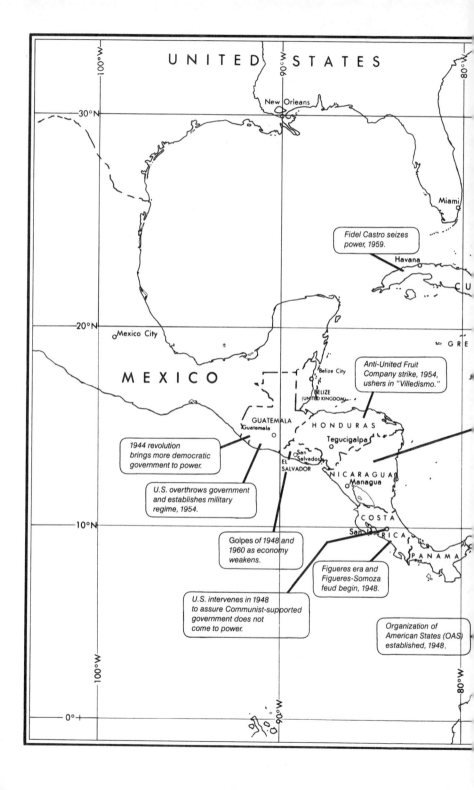

UNITED STATES

New Orleans

Miami

Fidel Castro seizes
power, 1959.

Havana

CU

Mexico City

GRE

MEXICO

Belize City

BELIZE
(UNITED KINGDOM)

Anti-United Fruit
Company strike, 1954,
ushers in "Villedismo."

GUATEMALA
Guatemala

HONDURAS

Tegucigalpa

1944 revolution
brings more democratic
government to power.

San
Salvador

EL
SALVADOR

NICARAGUA
Managua

U.S. overthrows government
and establishes military
regime, 1954.

COSTA

San   RICA

Golpes of 1948 and
1960 as economy
weakens.

PANAMA

Figueres era and
Figueres-Somoza
feud begin, 1948.

U.S. intervenes in 1948
to assure Communist-supported
government does not
come to power.

Organization of
American States (OAS)
established, 1948.

COMMONWEALTH
OF
THE
BAHAMAS

HISPANIOLA

ANTILLES

HAITI   DOMINICAN
        REPUBLIC

Kingston   Port-Au-Prince   Santo
                            Domingo

San Juan

PUERTO
RICO
(UNITED STATES)

*Somoza assassinated,
1956. Sons assume power
in declining economy.*

*Vice-president Nixon
threatened, 1958.*

LESSER ANTILLES

NETHERLANDS
ANTILLES

Caracas

TRINIDAD
AND
TOBAGO

VENEZUELA

Georgetown

COLOMBIA

Bogota

GUYANA

SURINAME

CENTRAL AMERICA

DOR

BRAZIL

70°W   60°W   30°N   20°N   10°N   60°W   70°W   0°

F.D.R. and Congress agreed on the broad outline of a global system built around the principles of the new United Nations organization. England was bankrupt and required Washington's kindness. As the war entered its final year, Secretary of the Treasury Henry Morgenthau told Roosevelt that "England is really broke." According to Morgenthau the president responded only half-jokingly, "This is very interesting. I had no idea that England was broke. I will go over there and make a couple of talks and take over the British Empire."[1] Clearly, any Central American hope of reopening a large trade with the British was quickly dashed. England had little to pay with and not much more to sell.

No nations in the world were more dependent on the United States than the five Central American states. As soon as the war started in 1939, Washington officials worked out a series of agreements to ensure their access to Central American food and raw materials. Even a coffee agreement was negotiated in which the United States accepted purchasing quotas, something it had strongly opposed (and would quickly discard as soon as the war ended). Coffee growers finally enjoyed the semblance of assured markets and stable prices. Dollars poured into Latin America to purchase goods and support U.S. military forces stationed in the area. The raw material producers—partly out of patriotism, partly because of intense U.S. pressure—agreed to sell their goods to North America far below the free market price, but their balance of trade nevertheless turned highly favorable. The dollars they received for their raw materials, however, purchased few U.S. goods; these were going to the war effort. As a result, inflation began to build in the southern parts of the hemisphere.

Latin Americans accepted these conditions, hoping that after the war Washington would show its appreciation with a stream of goods and investment. But they, and especially Central Americans, were doomed to disappointment. The Roosevelt administration moved to develop a postwar policy that was global, not regional, and that pivoted around the United Nations, not the Pan American Union. In practice, this turn meant that South and Central America received little attention politically; their political stability was assumed and accepted, regardless of whether it was enforced by a dictatorship (as in Nicaragua), or a more democratic if corrupt government (as in Costa Rica). It also meant they were to receive little or no economic aid after the war. Available resources went to those nations considered by Washington to be most important for U.S. security and trade: Western Europe and, by 1947, Japan. Early in the war a verbose and optimistic Commerce Department official had bragged: "The Good Neighbor Policy in the hemisphere had been the laboratory in which have been distilled the essences from which a postwar plan can be realistically brewed for the entire world." By 1945, the essences had been so distilled out of the Good Neighbor policy that it was nothing more than vapor.[2]

Not that Latin America no longer remained special for Washington officials. The area continued to hold such a unique place that new categories were constructed for it. State Department officials insisted that after the war the Western Hemisphere be considered exclusively in the U.S. sphere of influence and placed beyond the reach of United Nations authority. The New World had to remain solely under U.S. supervision.

The problem with this position became plain in 1945 when the United States insisted on maintaining Latin America under its own sphere of influence but protested the Soviet Union's creation of its sphere in Eastern Europe. Charles Bohlen, a distinguished State Department expert on Russian affairs, was troubled by the seemingly contradictory position. He finally satisfied himself with this reasoning in a State Department memorandum: "While we do claim the right . . . to have a guiding voice in a certain limited sphere of the foreign relations" of Latin America, "we do not attempt on the basis of that right to dictate their internal national life or to restrict their intercourse with foreign nations except in that limited sphere." Such a "limited sphere" could be, he thought, "roughly defined as the politico-strategic aspect of their foreign relations."[3] Bohlen's broad distinction between the United States and Soviet empires had validity when applied to South America. It was not valid when tested by the specific U.S. policies in Honduras during the years 1911 and 1912, Costa Rica from 1917 to 1920, El Salvador in the twenties, and Nicaragua from 1909 to 1932. Guatemala had not yet joined the list because it had yet to test the boundaries of the system.

By 1945, therefore, the United States insisted that Central America remain in a special relationship politically, but accept a low priority economically. It turned out to be a deadly combination. At the close of the war the Latin Americans had accumulated $3.4 billion by selling their raw materials to the United States. But four nations, none in Central America, held 80 percent of those dollars, and the entire amount rapidly dwindled in real value as postwar inflation drove up the price of North American goods desired by the Latins. By 1949 the wartime nest egg virtually disappeared. The Latin Americans had little or no development to show for it. They had cooperated during the war in the faith that afterwards they would receive their fair share of capital and goods. ("That is a new approach that I am talking about to the South American things," F.D.R. had remarked in 1940. "Give them a share. They think they are just as good as we are, and many of them are.")[4] By the late 1940s the faith could be only that of Saint Paul's: it necessarily rested on things not seen.

In 1950, Assistant Secretary of State for Inter-American Affairs Edward Miller admitted that Latin America unfairly suffered because, during the war, the United States "administered unilaterally" price controls that kept raw material prices down, and then after the war removed the controls and allowed the price of U.S. goods to shoot upward.[5] In other words, Washington fixed the market in its favor not once, but twice: through government controls during the war to keep Latin American raw material prices down, then by resorting to "free market" practices after the war to allow U.S. prices to rise. As they watched their dollars become less valuable, Latin Americans had reasons for believing that such "free market" rhetoric was nothing more than hypocrisy.

Central America emerged from the 1940s further locked into one- or two-crop economies. Of Guatemala's $50 million in exports during 1948, $42 million were in coffee and bananas, $3 million in raw materials and fuels, and virtually none in manufacturing. Percentages for the other four countries were comparable.[6] But the region's import figures were equally striking. Central America perfectly fit into Washington's Cold War policy of rapidly turning raw materials into U.S. goods and capital for the rebuilding and feeding of Western Europe and Japan. In late 1946 Undersecretary of State William Clayton took a longer view when he remarked, "In the past, the emphasis on our foreign trade has been on exports; within the near future it will be on imports. This is true because of our shift from debtor to creditor . . . , the depletion in our natural resources, and . . . the wants of a growing and prosperous population."[7]

Central America became a cog in the system Clayton envisaged. In 1948, $45 million of Guatemala's $50 million in exports went to the United States; the comparable numbers in El Salvador were $35 million out of $46 million; in Honduras, $14 million out of $20 million; in Nicaragua, $20 million out of $27 million, and in Costa Rica, $25 million out of $32 million. The percentage rise of export dependence (when compared with the 1938 figures) was especially dramatic in Guatemala, El Salvador, and Costa Rica—nations that had long found important markets in Europe. As for imports in 1948, the United States supplied 82 percent of Guatemala's (compared with 40 percent in 1938), nearly three-quarters of El Salvador's (it had been 44 percent in 1938), and about 80 percent of Costa Rica's (compared with 46 percent in 1938).

To say, however, that these countries were integrated into the U.S. economic system missed an equally important point: the Central American exports profited only a small group in each country, and only that group had the money to buy many of the imported goods. The State Department's Office of Intelligence Research focused on this problem in 1949 when it asked why "most Latin American countries" were unable to "establish stable and democratic political systems." It then listed the reasons: no clean break with the authoritarianism of the colonial era; the ability of the Church, military, and "landed gentry" to defend their entrenched interests; and the failure to integrate Indian communities into the larger economy. Then in a classic general statement of what would later be known as dependency theory, the State Department's Office of Intelligence Research (OIR) observed that

> the economic development of these countries, adapted to the shifting market of the industrial countries of the northern hemisphere and handicapped by a system of large landed estates, was so unbalanced as to prevent the emergence of an economically strong and politically conscious middle class.[8]

For the next thirty-five years, U.S. foreign policy could be made on the assumption that this "unbalanced" system could never be effectively challenged by the Central Americans. The region's trade was locked up.[9]

The United States built on this solid economic base by constructing a tight military relationship. In 1945 U.S. military officials moved to dominate postwar military planning in the hemisphere by retaining bases in the south acquired in wartime, by continuing to train Latin American officers, and—above all—by standardizing South and Central American equipment along U.S. lines. During the summer of 1945, the U.S. Joint Chiefs of Staff added details that made the policy a textbook example of dependency, but in the military realm. They defined Latin America's importance as being a safe resource base that "foreign" powers could not threaten. The area's raw materials were to be controlled through a Latin American military system that was not primarily geared to fight distant wars, but to preserve and protect the resources that North Americans needed to fight a cold, and perhaps a hot, war. Again, standardization of equipment and a U.S.-dominated command structure provided the leverage.[10]

Pentagon planners, however, encountered strong opposition from the State Department. Its officials argued that a number of Latin American nations could not afford such militarization. They would go bankrupt. In March 1947, the deadlock was passed on to President Harry S. Truman, who worried that if the United States did not sell the arms, "England or Europe" would do so. He instructed the State Department to reconsider and then wrote a note to himself (and no doubt for later historians): "I'm of the opinion that striped pants are trying to run South America. They won't be allowed to do it."[11] In the president's mind, North American Cold War requirements outranked Latin American needs. Six months after Truman made his decision, the JCS policy went into effect when the United States and Latin America (except Uruguay, which refused to attend) signed a military alliance at Rio de Janeiro. The Rio Pact accelerated the integration of Latin America into a U.S.-led alliance system in yet another way: it was the first treaty signed under Articles 51–53 of the United Nations Charter.

Those provisions of the Charter allowed the establishment of regional groups that, in an emergency, could act outside United Nations auspices until the world organization took action. These articles had been included at the insistence of Nelson Rockefeller and members of Congress who were determined that the UN would not be allowed to intervene in the Western Hemisphere. Now the United States delightfully had the best of both worlds: the global organization it had sought since Wilson's era, but also freedom of action under the Monroe Doctrine.

An Omen: The Clash at Bogotá

The Latin Americans were not as delighted. They had gone to Rio hoping that the United States would give economic help in return for their military and political cooperation. No significant aid appeared, however. Washington only agreed to meet at Bogotá, Colombia in 1948 to work out a new network of treaties. The most important turned out to be a charter for an Organization of American States (OAS) that established a new institutional and legal framework for the hemisphere, and a so-called "Economic Agreement."

Once again the United States resorted to UN Charter Articles 51–53 to build a regional organization, the OAS, that could serve as a court of first—and sometimes last—resort in the hemisphere. Americans could run their own affairs far away from the UN Security Council where Soviet veto power might be decisive. Particularly critical in the OAS Charter was Article 15:

> No State or group of States has the right to intervene, directly or indirectly, for any reason whatever, in the internal or external affairs of any other State.

This principle was to apply not only to "armed force," but to "any other form of interference or attempted threat." Then a loophole was written in: "measures" could be "adopted for the maintenance of peace and security in accordance with existing treaties."

With this loophole the United States reserved its right to intervene. In May 1950, Assistant Secretary of State for Inter-American Affairs Edward Miller laid down a "Miller Doctrine" that previewed the U.S. interventions in 1954, 1965, and the eighties. Later updated by President Lyndon Johnson in 1965 when he sent a U.S.-Organization of American States force into the Dominican Republic, the Miller Doctrine is the counterpart of Russia's "Brezhnev Doctrine" of 1968 which justified collective "socialist" intervention to keep the Soviet bloc safe from Western influences.

Miller declared that he regretted the earlier U.S. unilateral interventions, but argued bluntly that they were justified under the Monroe Doctrine. The change since the thirties, he believed, had been the substitution of collective intervention under the Rio Pact and the Organization of American States for the earlier unilateral intervention of the United States. Then came an Orwellian play on words:

> The fact is that the doctrine of nonintervention [under the Good Neighbor] never did proscribe the assumption by the organized community of a legitimate concern with any circumstances that threatened the common welfare. On the contrary it made the possibility of such action imperative. Such a collective undertaking, far from representing intervention, is the alternative to intervention. It is the corollary of nonintervention.

Miller thus argued that collective intervention under the Organization of American States was not a bad thing, but sometimes necessary. He drove home the point by warning of "Communist political aggression against the hemisphere" that "bears directly on the purpose of the Monroe Doctrine, which is as much our national policy today as it ever was." The Rio Pact had become "a Monroe Doctrine of our inter-American community."

The Miller Doctrine of 1950 could be summarized as follows. Monroe's announcement of 1823 still lives but is challenged by communism. The United States does not want to respond to such challenges by intervening unilaterally (which is bad) to defend hemispheric interests as it sees them, so intervention is henceforth to be done collectively (which is good). The Rio Pact and OAS Charter provide the mechanism for upholding the Monroe Doctrine while Washington officials might be preoccupied in Europe and Asia. Since the United States can assume that it controls a majority in the OAS (including four to five Central

American votes), all should go well. If things do not go well, the United States reserves the right to intervene unilaterally just the same.[12]

The hottest arguments at the 1948 Bogotá discussions boiled up over the Economic Agreement. This pact got at the heart of U.S. policy towards the Americas. As Truman's secretary of state from 1949 through 1953, Dean Acheson, neatly phrased it later, "Foreign policy isn't a lot of abstract notions you get up. It's what you do—these business transactions, credit through central banks, food things and their counterpart funds—all this makes foreign policy."[13] The debates over "business transactions" caused acute pain at Bogotá. The Latin Americans wanted economic help or else, they threatened, they would form regional economic blocs that discriminated against U.S. goods. For example, the five Central American states again hoped to build a union so they could pick themselves up by their own economic bootstraps. Such threats caused some fear in Washington among knowledgeable officials who believed that since economic competition easily escalated to political hatreds (as indeed occurred with horrible results in the thirties), such blocs could become "breeding grounds for political strife and uncertainty."[14]

The United States wanted to fumigate such breeding grounds, but not with any large aid programs. In 1948, it began funneling nearly $13 billion through the Marshall Plan to rebuild Western Europe. For the next ten years Latin America received only 2.4 percent of Washington's foreign aid, ranking behind every other region in the world. At Bogotá, as at Rio, U.S. officials declared they would try to increase Export-Import Bank credits for Latin Americans, but otherwise, since such huge funds were moving into Europe, the southern nations had to look to private capital for their needs.

"We intend to turn trade back to private people as quickly as possible," Assistant Secretary of State William Clayton summarized in 1945.[15] But that intention smashed against a different reality in Latin America. The OIR described that reality:

Probably the most striking political development in the other American republics during the past half-century is the wide acceptance of the idea that the government has direct responsibility for the welfare of the people. This has resulted in a phenomenal growth of social and economic legislation designed to protect labor, distribute land more widely . . . and increase opportunities for education.

The OIR noted that, among others, the greatest gains in this direction had been made by Costa Rica and Guatemala.[16] (OIR had neatly isolated the two sorest geographical points of Washington's Central American policy in the years between 1945 and 1960.)

To squash such dangers, the United States opened the debate in 1948 over the Economic Agreement by asking for a pledge to an open door policy: "further access, on equal terms, to the markets, products and productive facilities." The Latin Americans granted the general principle, but then demanded that Washington guarantee equitable prices for their own raw materials, accept restrictions on private investment, and endorse the Latin desire for industrialization through government financing. The South and Central American delegates particularly could not understand why the U.S. group refused to promise basic parity prices for their goods when Washington maintained parity prices, and even import quotas, for its own agricultural produce, lead, zinc, and copper—most of which competed with their own exports. Arguments turned bitter.

In the end the Latin Americans used their majority vote to force three provisions into the Economic Agreement that the United States had opposed: a promise to use government action to smooth out "dislocations" of trade in raw materials; permission for states to form regional "preferential agreements"—deals whose benefits would not be automatically extended to "other countries" (that is, the United States); and a pious wish for "paid annual vacations" and "permanence of tenure to all wage earners" who could not be discharged "without just cause." The last provision particularly upset the United Fruit Company and other U.S. firms that employed large numbers of low-paid workers. The United States finally succeeded in placing general reservations on these clauses, and thus warned the other delegations it would not be automatically bound by the provisions.[17]

It had not been a happy conference for the world's greatest power. The United States had not yet ratified the Pact of Bogotá (that provided for the pacific settlement of disputes) when Truman left office in 1953. Mistrust was rampant, and for its part the United States was in no mood to tailor its exalted status to the specifications of Latin American desires. As for the Economic Charter, it was to be fleshed out at a later conference in Buenos Aires. The State Department showed visible relief when the conference was postponed. And the president wanted to hear no more mass complaints about U.S. economic policy. Indeed, Truman did not agree to another such Inter-American conference during his last five years in office.

He did not have to. Washington's policy was well in place by late 1948. Although the Bogotá Economic Charter laid down principles, the unchallengeable U.S. economic power could largely set the actual conditions of trade and investment. Central America and its oligarchs were more tightly wedged into the North American economic system than ever before. In the Rio Pact, military dependency had been added to the economic. On the political side, the OAS was an instrument with which Washington officials could handle Latin America outside the prying hands of the United Nations, yet do so according to the UN Charter. And if the Latin Americans refused to behave, the Miller Doctrine warned that the United States reserved the right to act in the old way: send in the marines.

For the United States it was a beautifully conceived, balanced, and executed policy. The only ominous cloud was the division at Bogotá over the U.S. insistence on private enterprise as the means for developing the southern hemisphere while the Latins wanted to utilize more state power. That cloud darkened as relatively less private capital moved south than had been the case in the interwar years. The investment that did make the trip went into food and raw-material-producing areas, such as Central America, thus making these nations further dependent on one or two crops and the vagaries of the international market for those crops. But the returns for such ventures could be rich. Between 1950 and 1956, U.S. investments in the food and raw materials of Costa Rica and Honduras brought the highest rate of profit of any Latin American nation except Venezuela, where oil companies flourished.[18] Classic battle lines between private enterprise and state controls were being drawn, even in Costa Rica—and especially in Guatemala.

The Start of the Thirty-one Years War: Figueres vs. Somoza

Riots and revolutions wracked Latin America in the late forties. The dictatorships in Nicaragua and Honduras finally restored order, but a coup brought a military-dominated Revolutionary Council to power in El Salvador. Guatemala's government, which was the most freely elected in the country's history, put down at least a dozen coup attempts in the last years of the decade. Even Costa Rica went through the only major revolution in its post-1840 experience.

The State Department believed it understood the causes of the unrest. "Communism in the Americas is a potential danger, but . . . with a few possible exceptions it is not seriously dangerous at the present time," the Policy Planning Staff of the State Department told Secretary of State George Marshall in mid-1948. The real danger was structural: "Several conditions . . . play into the hands of the Communists. . . . There is poverty that is so widespread that it means a bare subsistence level for large masses of people. There are ignorance and a high degree of illiteracy." Finally, such "anti-Communist forces" as the Roman Catholic Church, the military, and large landowners were so reactionary that they not only created support for Communism, but even resembled Communism in their support of "totalitarian policy state methods." The Policy Planning Staff placed its hope on anti-Communist labor unions and "an increasingly rapid growth of middle classes," although neither the staff nor anyone else in Washington seemed to have any idea where the stimulus for such "rapid growth" could be found.[19]

The great irony in this analysis was that the most explosive outbreak was occurring in the country with the largest and most politically powerful middle class, Costa Rica. But that nation's economy was dominated by United Fruit and other U.S. interests. Costa Rica also had perhaps the most successful Communist party in Latin America. Those two— United Fruit and the Communist party—were not unrelated. The party (the *Bloque de Obreros y Campesinos,* or Workers and Peasants Bloc) was founded in 1931. It made its political fortune in 1934 by leading a massive strike in the banana plantations. A government commission examined the situation and condemned United Fruit for the "inhuman, unhealthful, and careless treatment" suffered by its laborers.[20] For the first time in its history, the company buckled and granted better wages and working conditions. Banana workers became devout party members and provided the reason why, fourteen years later, the State Department viewed Costa Rican labor as one of the most fertile beds for communism in the hemisphere.

Taking advantage of the U.S.-U.S.S.R. wartime alliance, the *Bloque* changed its name to *Vanguardia Popular* and became an unlikely political bedfellow of the Roman Catholic Church in the liberal ruling coalition of President Rafael Calderón Guardia. In 1943, with Church and Communist support, Calderón passed the most extensive social reform program in Central American history: equal pay for men and women, an eight-hour day, Social Security, the right of labor to form unions and strike, labor courts, and collective bargaining. Government controls meanwhile enabled the economy to remain fairly stable during the war. By the late forties the people expected the government to be active, especially as rising inflation and the lack of U.S. economic help caused deepening social and economic problems.[21]

The crucial question became who would direct the government? Calderón had been popular with the masses, but understandably less so with members of the wealthier classes, foreign investors, anti-clericals, anti-Communists, and—above all—some from the middle class who believed that labor and peasants were receiving too much while they received too little. The opposition grew as it became clear that the Calderón government was corrupt and badly administered. Prohibited constitutionally from serving two consecutive terms, Calderón gave way to Teodoro Picado in 1944 and positioned himself to reclaim the presidency in 1948. The opposition also mobilized. A little cold war began as the opposition targeted the *Vanguardia Popular* and accused Calderón of being dominated by the Communists. The allegation was untrue and astounded Calderón; he could not understand how anyone could believe the Communists posed a threat when they had proven to be politically ineffective and intellectually bankrupt—particularly after he had stolen much of their program in the early 1940s. The Costa Rican middle class and a number of peasants nevertheless believed the charges. So did the U.S. Department of State which turned against the Picado-Calderón party. That turn was marked in November 1947 when the pro-Calderón U.S. ambassador was replaced by Nathaniel P. Davis, who had no Latin American experience, but was an expert on communism and had served in Moscow. A new party, the *Partido Unión Nacional,* named newspaperman Otilio Blanco Ulate to oppose Calderón in 1948.

Ulate's candidacy appeared as Calderónista corruption and the country's economy worsened. Costa Rica prided itself on its distribution of wealth, but the equality was remarkable only when compared with the grossly unequal distribution in the rest of Central America. In truth, key sectors of the society were foreign-controlled; the profits from its large amounts of exports rolled out of the country. Housing was in dangerously short supply, malnutrition ravaged peasant children, middle-class earnings could not keep pace with inflation, sanitation in urban areas was horrible, tuberculosis and stomach parasites were common, large areas of the country were controlled by oligarchs who refused either to cultivate their land or allow others to do so, and the rate of population increase approached an astounding 4 percent annually. After witnessing these conditions, a Chilean journalist curtly dismissed Costa Rican bragging about the fair distribution of land and wrote, "What is well distributed in Costa Rica is poverty."[22]

The United States government had not helped the economy by placing wartime ceiling prices on Costa Rican goods, then pressuring the country to send food from an already short supply to U.S. personnel in the Panama Canal Zone. Washington officials also insisted that a section of the Pan American Highway be built so it could better link up with the Canal Zone, although its new location severely hurt Costa Rica's own development plans. Finally, given the country's dependence on North American imports, the U.S. failure to come up with a postwar aid plan was devastating. These problems climaxed with the Calderónistas' most important bit of corruption: through fraud they prevented Ulate from winning the 1948 election. Protests and then riots erupted.

At that point José Figueres Ferrer (or "Don Pepé," as he was nicknamed) stepped to the front of Costa Rican history. He remained there during the next three decades. Figueres had been conceived in Spain and in 1906 was born in Costa Rica. The locations are significant, according to his best biographer, because his parents came from a world of wide ambition that most Costa Ricans envied, and he was born in a nation that put high value on his impeccable Spanish background.[23] Against his father's wishes, he traveled to the United States for a college education, but disliked classrooms so much that he claimed to have spent the entire time reading in the Boston Public Library, which he later called his alma mater. After four years in North America he returned to Costa Rica in 1928 to become a successful farmer. During World War II Figueres emerged as a most outspoken critic of Calderón. Don Pepé indeed so violently denounced him that the president finally deported Figueres to Mexico. He thus became famous as the first Costa Rican exile since Tinoco's regime.

Calderón had committed a blunder of the first magnitude. Figueres quickly formed the Caribbean Legion, a band of other exiles, then plotted to overthrow the San José government. Hoping to use Costa Rica as a base, the Legion planned next to remove the three Central American dictators. Washington officials were not amused. They closely watched the Legion's activities, especially after Figueres carried out a series of terrorist attacks inside Costa Rica during 1945 and 1946 that was supposed to climax in a general strike. But the people did not respond.

Figueres then made a decision that reverberated in Central America for the next thirty years. He turned for help to President Juan José Arévalo of Guatemala. Arévalo had become the leading liberal figure in Central America, indeed in much of Latin America, after assuming power in 1945. But Arévalo not only had high hopes for a new Guatemala. He wanted nothing less than a new Central America in which the Somozas could be destroyed and replaced by a democratic regional union. The Guatemalan had the prestige and the arms to start such a campaign, so Figueres convinced him that the first step must be the overthrow of Picado. In late 1947, Figueres and other Central American exiles signed the Pact of the Caribbean in which they pledged to free the region of dictators. The instrument of removal was to be the Caribbean Legion, supplied largely by Guatemala. With this one step a long chain reaction began. A war to the death started between Figueres and Somoza, a war that finally ended with the destruction of Somoza's rule in 1979.

In March–April 1948, the protests over the election results mushroomed into armed conflict, then into revolution won by Figueres's forces. Arévalo's help proved to be indispensable. As usual, however, the determining force was United States policy. The creators of that policy held little love for Figueres, but they were determined to destroy the *Vanguardia Popular.* Perhaps the Communist party had only seven thousand members, Ambassador Davis reported home, but it could hold the balance of political power in Congress and also constituted "some 70 percent of the police and army." Writing within hours after the Communist overthrow of the Czechoslovak government (an event that severely shook Washington and other Western capitals), Davis warned that Costa Rica's condition was "in many respects similar to that prevailing today in Eastern Europe."[24] When the State Department learned on 17 April 1948 that small Communist groups threatened to take over the capital of San José, U.S. troops were placed on alert in the Canal Zone. Their mission was to move quickly into Costa Rica and stop the revolution before the *Vanguardia Popular* consolidated its power.[25] It was again a false alarm, but it indicated that regardless of any Good Neighbor sentiments, the possibility of unilateral U.S. intervention was no mere abstraction.

Throughout the conflict, Figueres received a steady supply of arms from Arévalo, while Picado's forces were unable to exploit Somoza's desire to help. The United States had ensured Somoza's political impotence. Desperately wanting Nicaraguan help, Picado pleaded with Ambassador Davis to allow what was, after all, the recognized Costa Rican government to obtain help from Nicaragua so it could remain in power. Davis blandly "explained our well-known policy of non-intervention" and then referred to the "obligations of American nations [to] nonintervene." Picado bitterly observed that non-intervention was a fiction; Figueres had received "tons" of supplies from Arévalo, and rumors circulated of aid even from the Panamanian government. Davis ignored the charges. Picado then threatened to take the matter to the United Nations. "The United Nations machinery was cumbersome," the State Department suavely but directly reminded the Costa Rican leader, and "immediate action on the part of the Council [where the United States had a veto and controlled the majority of votes] could probably not be expected."[26] Picado had nothing else to do but surrender. After two thousand deaths, the revolution was over.

By its mobilization in the Canal Zone, constant pressure on Picado, and cutting off Somoza's help, the United States determined the outcome of the revolution in April 1948.[27] The involvement and result are not surprising, given the history of U.S. intervention in Central America, the extent of its power, and its fear of communism. But of at least equal interest was Washington's handling of Somoza. By the late forties the State Department privately castigated the Nicaraguan as controlling an "avaricious dictatorship" that continued the "repressive government characterized by farcical elections, constitutional violations, and negligible consideration of economic and social problems." U.S. officials knew the sordid details of Somoza's personal corruption and greed. They also closely followed the large anti-Somoza rallies that often included businessmen who protested the systematic looting of the National Bank by the Somoza family so that only driblets remained for national development.[28]

The United States, however, refused to help anti-Somoza forces in Nicaragua regardless of the dictator's crimes. One reason for this refusal appeared when Figueres's emissary to Washington suggested in mid-1948 that "it was necessary to eliminate Somoza." The State Department forcefully, if inconsistently, replied that it opposed any invasion of one American state by another.[29] U.S. officials prized stability and peaceful evolution above the removal of even repressive dictatorship, at least as long as the dictatorship did not include active leftist elements.

Another reason appeared during a private meeting of the New York Council on Foreign Relations in early 1949. Attended by such powerful figures as Nelson Rockefeller and Adolf Berle—two men who had constructed much of the U.S. policy towards Latin America during the decade—the meeting called on the State Department to oppose the "establishment of totalitarian regimes in this Hemisphere." How, queried one worried participant, might this rule apply to Somoza? The answer came from Francis Adams Truslow, the chairman of the meeting and a leading New York lawyer and businessman. Truslow sharply distinguished between a dictatorship such as Somoza's, which "involves autocratic rule," and "totalitarianism," which he defined as "autocratic rule, plus total, absolute control of economic life, as, for example, communism. . . . Totalitarianism we refuse to cooperate with," Truslow concluded, but "with dictatorships we will." Somoza therefore had three virtues: he propped Nicaragua open to private capital, allowed minimal state controls, and kept maximum order—even as he ruthlessly looted the country himself. In slightly changed language, Truslow's distinction was to be used much later by the administration of Ronald Reagan, and particularly by his ambassador to the UN, Jeane J. Kirkpatrick, to justify its support of dictatorships in the so-called third world.[30]

In important respects, it seemed that the State Department should have disavowed Somoza and embraced Figueres. The Costa Rican called himself a social democrat, carried out a progressive tax program, proscribed Communists, and voluntarily gave up personal power in 1949 before winning the presidency in an open election during 1953. But Washington officials remained suspicious. Those suspicions revealed tensions in U.S. policy that went beyond the forced, simplistic distinctions between "totalitarianism" and "authoritarianism" drawn by Truslow. For example, Figueres outlawed Communists, but he also nationalized the banks. He did away with the army, but the remnants of the Caribbean Legion worried U.S. officials, even though Figueres had obviously lost interest in the Legion after he gained power. (Indeed it turned out that Don Pepé happily cooperated with North American military plans. After the United States established the School of the Americas in the Panama Canal Zone to train Latin American officers in anti-Communist techniques, more Costa Rican "police" graduated from the School between 1950 and 1965 than did officers of any other hemispheric nation except Nicaragua.)[31] He finally surrendered personal power in 1949 with the words, "The health of democracy in Latin America demands that men who have seized power by force go home when normalcy is restored. We restored normalcy and we went home."[32] Such sentiments in Central America were no more common than economic self-sufficiency.

When Figueres formed the National Liberation Party in 1952, however, U.S. officials feared he intended to institutionalize his power. Those fears grew during the presidential campaign of 1953 when he vigorously attacked the exploitation carried on by United Fruit and other U.S. companies in Costa Rica. All of these fears were misplaced. Don Pepé continued to play by the rules of a functioning two- or three-party system. After winning the election, Figueres never threatened

United Fruit's fundamental position. He instead negotiated a new contract that nearly tripled the country's share of the company's profits in Costa Rica, and United Fruit promised faithfully to obey the nation's minimum wage laws. There was never any threat of expropriation. Figueres, unlike Arévalo in Guatemala, understood the limits of U.S. tolerance.

State Department intelligence reports on Don Pepé were a revelation of the hidebound ideology and anti-Communist preoccupation of Washington officials in the fifties. The problem was that Figueres was neither a fish such as Arévalo nor a fowl such as Somoza. He fit no easy ideological categories. Consequently, the State Department bureaucrats worried. An August 1953 intelligence report illustrated the confusion that resulted when Washington ideologues dealt with social democrats in Central America. Figueres, the report stated, "will not willingly" become a Communist dupe, but "his nationalistic program is, in some respects, similar to Guatemala's and is, therefore, likely to increase Communist capabilities in Costa Rica." Among his apparent sins was the turning of his country into "a haven for exiles from the dictatorships." Don Pepé also threatened to press for "a broader program of economic development and firmer control over foreign investment"—which seemed to be the State Department's accidental admission that the first might require the second. He was anti-Communist, U.S. officials argued, merely because he was politically "opportunistic." The report then focused on a particularly threatening sign: Figueres's reform program was to be financed "preferably by domestic capital," and "does not look with favor upon capital organized beyond the individual or family level. Large private corporations, such as those in the United States, are an anathema in his opinion." A clash threatened because the new President "always" was striving "to increase the bargaining power of the small, underdeveloped countries vis-à-vis the large manufacturing nations."[33]

Figueres therefore was dangerous because he hoped to use government powers to free Costa Rica's internal development as much as possible from foreign control. The intelligence report overstated both Figueres's socialistic tendencies and his power to wring concessions from foreigners. But the themes were clear: Don Pepé set a bad example for other Central American planners. He posed a threat to the Good Neighbor policy's assumption that Latin America could be kept in line merely through economic pressure.

Militarizing the Good Neighbors

How far Washington's Latin American policy had deteriorated by 1950 became dramatically clear when war suddenly erupted in South Korea. Unlike 1941, when Roosevelt and Hull had rallied Latin American nations to the Allied cause, the reaction in 1950 was tepid at best, hostile at worst. A half-dozen nations, including Costa Rica and El Salvador, offered "volunteers," but the number offered was so small that the U.S. Defense Department did not want to bother with the offer. President Truman was deeply disappointed with the hemisphere's response. Officials who were more sensitive to Latin American developments, however, understood the reasons for the lack of support. Thomas Mann, a State Department expert on the area, wrote in late 1952 that the United States spent the forties mobilizing the hemisphere to fight hot and cold wars, but the Latin Americans planned to spend the fifties on reform programs, economic nationalism, and class war. Mann personally could not suggest any remedy except more economic assistance. "Our program of economic aid to Latin America," he pointed out, "is . . . so small, in fact, that it could almost be financed by Export-Import Bank profits from loans to Latin America alone."[34]

Mann's observations were hardly new. Even before Korea erupted in war, U.S. officials had isolated the two central—and related—problems: the rise of left-wing influence and the need to protect the hemisphere's raw materials for future U.S. use. The fear of the left was outlined in several C.I.A. "Review of the World Situation" reports some months before the Korean conflict. The agency warned that Latin America seemed to be coming unglued. Guatemala and Bolivia had moved sharply to the left. Other nations were bitter over the lack of U.S. aid and goods. Communists were "nowhere . . . dominant," a State Department Intelligence Report agreed, but they only hid behind the growing demands of the reformers.[35]

In March 1950, the State Department's expert on Soviet Affairs,

George Kennan, flew to Rio de Janeiro to meet with U.S. ambassadors in South America. After a wide-ranging and often outspoken survey of world events, Kennan outlined how Latin America fit into U.S. policy:

1. The protection of our [*sic*] raw materials;
2. The prevention of military exploitation of Latin America by the enemy; and,
3. The prevention of the psychological mobilization of Latin America against us.

If Europe turned anti-U.S., he observed, "Latin America would be all we would have to fall back on." Unfortunately "our relations with the Latin American countries were not sufficiently good to stand a serious rocking of the boat elsewhere." Under no circumstances, Kennan warned the ambassadors, must Communists be allowed in power.

The final answer might be an unpleasant one, but . . . we should not hesitate before police repression by the local government. This is not shameful since the Communists are essentially traitors. . . . It is better to have a strong regime in power than a liberal government if it is indulgent and relaxed and penetrated by Communists.[36]

Kennan's statement summarized why the United States tolerated Somoza while suspecting Figueres. It also neatly tied together the dual objectives of blocking Communist influences and protecting "our raw materials."

Those raw materials came to be of overriding importance. As the United States began a rapid military buildup (the Defense Department budget quadrupled in less than thirty-six months), demand and inflation drove up the prices of Latin American products. Central America enjoyed a brief burst of prosperity as coffee, cotton, and cocoa prices rose. But as Assistant Secretary of State Miller warned, the flush of better times actually threatened the United States. Cocoa prices rose 40 percent in 1950, coffee nearly 10 percent, and cotton 30 percent. Miller warned that the Latin Americans had to put tight controls on the currency and inflation, even resorting to government controls, if necessary, to keep the prices of products bought by North Americans as low as possible.[37] The Latins, however, had heard that plea not many years earlier. They were not to be seduced again so easily. If there were few Central American offers to help in Korea, there were even fewer government attempts to control rising food and raw material prices.

Frustrated Washington officials then moved to tighten the hemisphere's links with a military wrench. The Good Neighbor became militarized, but in a fashion quite different from the pre-1933 armed interventions. To achieve Kennan's two objectives, the military was to act as carrot as well as stick.

In an historic turn, Congress passed the Military Defense Assistance Act (MDA) in 1951 that created new ties between Washington and Latin American armed forces. The act aimed to build Latin American armies under U.S. direction, but the forces were to be used for country missions (that is, internal security), not for global or even regional operations.[38] (The United States insisted on handling global and regional problems unilaterally.) The military aid proposal encountered strong opposition from major Latin American nations, including three leading democratic governments—Chile, Uruguay, and Mexico—but in late 1951 Congress kicked it off with a first-step $38.5 million appropriation bill. The funding was supplemented with the training of Latin American officers in U.S. methods and equipment at the Panama Canal Zone's School of the Americas. As the School increasingly focused in the 1950s on counterinsurgency warfare, Central American military received a highly disproportionate amount of that training (see Table 1). In 1954–55, Nicaragua, Honduras, and Guatemala became the first Central American nations to sign MDA agreements.

This new approach to Latin America was underway when the Eisenhower administration assumed power in January 1953. Secretary of State John Foster Dulles, however, was not reassured. With Guatemala, and perhaps Costa Rica, in mind, Dulles told Congress that communism was so far advanced

> that the conditions in Latin America are somewhat comparable to conditions as they were in China in the mid-thirties when the Communist movement was getting started. They were beginning to de-

TABLE I The number of military officers from each Central American nation graduated from the U.S. School of the Americas, in the Panama Canal Zone, 1949–64. (Larger South American nations are included for purposes of comparison. Note especially that Nicaragua had more graduates than any other nation in the hemisphere, and that Costa Rica had one of the highest number of graduates although it disbanded its army in 1949 and has only a "police" force.)

Argentina	259	Costa Rica	1,639	Honduras	810
Bolivia	1,124	El Salvador	358	Mexico	178
Brazil	165	Guatemala	958	Nicaragua	2,969

(Source: Willard F. Barber and C. Neale Ronning, *Internal Security and Military Power: Counterinsurgency and Civic Action in Latin America* [Columbus, Ohio, 1966], 145.)

velop the hatred of the American and the Britisher, but we didn't do anything about it. . . . It came to a climax in 1949.

Well, if we don't look out, we will wake up some morning and read in the newspapers that there happened in South America the same kind of thing that happened in China in 1949.[39]

Dulles wanted, as he instructed an aide, "an imaginative program for Latin America, but one that does not cost any money." President Eisenhower, dedicated to severe budget cutting so taxes could be lowered, shared this concern. He described the old policy to his Cabinet: "We put a coin in the tin cup and yet we know the tin cup is still going to be there tomorrow." The tin-cup policy was no longer enough, but the best substitute he could devise was to stress "the need for getting Latin American countries to search out private capital."[40]

Eisenhower and Dulles consequently fell back on the old approach of emphasizing private investment and Export-Import Bank loans, then supplemented this approach with increased military ties. As equipment moved south, so did U.S. military advisers who determined the requirements of recipient countries. If Kennan was correct in preferring a "strong regime" to "indulgent" liberal governments, the policy was amazingly successful, at least in the short run. By the end of 1954, military dictators ruled thirteen of the twenty Latin American nations. This figure marked a new high for the twentieth century.[41] The number included all the Central American nations except Figueres's Costa Rica. The course of U.S. policy seemed clear: economic dependency led inevitably to military dependency. After World War II Washington officials had concluded that access to Latin American food and raw materials, at the lowest possible prices, was essential for the West's security. As radical movements appeared, the United States viewed them as a security as well as an ideological threat. Both dangers—political radicalism and what Kennan called "our raw materials"—were to be dealt with militarily. The Good Neighbor became less a policy of economic growth or reform than of military ties and leverage. And as the United States policy became militarized, it most directly appealed to, and—in a kind of reverse dependence—necessarily counted on Latin American dictators to protect North American interests. In short, the United States did not support the Somozas of Latin America out of ennui or misperception, but out of the clear understanding that given Washington's needs and reliance on military means, the dictators were its best bet to maintain the system.

Thus the suspicions about Figueres. Thus the support for Somoza. Thus a fascinating exchange in Eisenhower's first meeting with his full cabinet, an exchange that moved towards a total separation from reality. Reading his Inaugural Address, Eisenhower declared that Moscow was once the seat of autocracy, but was now the cockpit of "revolution." The representative to the United Nations, Henry Cabot Lodge, wondered aloud whether the president should use that word:

Lots of people won't like to hear that word revolution. . . . A lot of people would like to have a revolution and it might help revolutions in some parts of the world as it is now.

[Eisenhower:] I would like to make that change. In Mexico today they still talk about revolution like the second coming of the Lord. While it hasn't worked too well, nevertheless it is better than what they had.

[Charles Wilson, secretary of defense and former head of General

Motors:] We had a little revolution in our country, a peaceful one.
[Eisenhower:] "Little?"
[Dulles:] We had a violent one.
[Wilson:] I think we are going to have an American renaissance now.[42]

So the new administration avoided the problems of revolution by refusing to use the word. When the problems became unavoidable, these supposed heirs of Thomas Jefferson ended radical change in Central America by allying the C.I.A. with native military dictatorships. Jefferson's older ideals were ground under by the newer system.

Guatemala: Replacing Revolution with Militarism

The first Latin American revolution that the Eisenhower administration confronted ended not in a renaissance but in the overthrow of the constitutionally elected Guatemalan government by U.S.-supplied and directed forces in 1954. This counterrevolutionary operation is becoming one of the best-known and important episodes in Washington's Cold War policies. The details of the countercoup have been well told elsewhere.[43] What requires emphasis here is how the operation fit within a long-developing U.S. policy towards Central America, and how one (and perhaps the most important) result of that policy was to disfigure and disorient Guatemalan society until the country finally stumbled into a more ominous revolutionary crisis in the early eighties.

Between 1931 and 1944 Jorge Ubico's dictatorship made important contributions to Guatemalan life, contributions that also helped lead to his overthrow. These included a massive development of governmental activities (especially the building of infrastructure, such as roads) that created a new, nationalistic middle class and pulled some Indians out of their political isolation. These changes, however, occurred within a system that the State Department later described as a "repressive government characterized by farcical elections, disregard of the constitution, and the negligible implementation of social and economic legislation."[44]

The 1944 revolution, the first and—so far—only one to gain power in Guatemalan history, was a middle-class movement led by university students and young army officers. This new generation had matured in a world shaped by global revolution, Franklin D. Roosevelt's Four Freedoms (which dramatically raised the hopes of Latin American liberals), and a new awareness of the horrible social conditions within the country, especially among the Indians who comprised more than half the population. The young military officers were the determining factor, and their power reassured the United States. The 1944 upheaval marked the first time the Guatemalan military, as a professional force, acted as an *institution* in a political crisis.[45] Guatemala had undergone a fundamental change.

The freest elections in the country's history gave Juan José Arévalo the presidency in late 1944. The forty-year-old author and educator, who had been teaching in an Argentine university, was a kind of mystical figure, determined to restructure Guatemalan society in a way in which no Latin American country had been transformed since the Mexican Revolution. Arévalo described himself as a "spiritual socialist" who simultaneously disavowed Marxism (because it prescribed class struggle and considered people to be economic animals) and individualistic capitalism (because he believed society must be thought of as a collective, an aggregate that was superior to purely individual interests). He quickly discovered, however, that he worked in a political vacuum. As a result of Ubico's oppression, the political party system was in shambles. The mass of Guatemalans had no experience working in an open society. Nor did Arévalo possess a systematic ideology or political tactics to guide his followers.[46] He consequently began a series of ad hoc reforms and grew to depend on left-wing political factions, including communists whose party was officially outlawed.

Arévalo helped the peasants by passing the Law of Forced Rental that obliged oligarchs to lease uncultivated lands at low rates. The government's main concern, urban labor, received support through a legislative program that by 1950 included a social security system, a labor code that allowed strikes and union organizing, and a central bank. This program met bitter resistance from oligarchs and foreign investors. The reaction of the Guatemalan upper class was predictable, as was a 1948 State

Department memorandum which held that the reforms, though not absolute "proof of communism," did not mean that there was "no communist inspiration behind them."[47] The confusion of Arévalo's reforms with communism allowed the Communists to take undeserved credit for correcting centuries of injustice. By 1950, Communist leaders controlled the main labor union, the *Confederación General de Trabajadores* (CGT). Their success was not surprising since they had developed a coherent political program and, in the six years after Ubico's overthrow, had obtained nearly an 80-percent wage increase for workers who had formerly been among the most exploited in the hemisphere. J. Edgar Hoover's Federal Bureau of Investigation, which swarmed over Latin America after 1940 looking for radical activities, quickly ran up warning flags over Guatemala.[48]

In 1949 Arévalo was challenged by a movement led by a popular and powerful army colonel, Francisco Arana, who was variously described as reformist, moderate, or counterrevolutionary, depending on the speaker's politics. In mid-summer of that year, Arana was gunned down by assassins. Their identity was never discovered, a failure that led the suspicious to conclude that Jacabo Arbenz Guzman plotted the murder. Arbenz, minister of war, was also competing for the presidency. At about the same time the government stepped up its harassment of U.S. businessmen, and actually arrested employees of the country's railroad (owned and operated by United Fruit) for trying to destroy the new union.

Even after the killing of Arana and the moves against foreign business, however, the State Department could find no stick to wave except the Good Neighbor. The U.S. Ambassador to Guatemala, Richard C. Patterson, Jr., and the department warned Guatemalans that further unrest would bring a cutoff of economic aid and started a massive publicity campaign so U.S. opinion could focus on Arévalo's activities. But Patterson went too far. He apparently demanded that Arévalo fire seventeen officials whom he, Patterson, considered too radical. The Guatemalans quietly demanded, and obtained, the ambassador's recall to Washington for "medical reasons." There, he became outspoken about the Communist danger to Guatemala, and in speeches around the United States devised the soon-famous "duck test":

Many times it is impossible to prove legally that a certain individual is a communist; but for cases of this sort I recommend a practical method of detection—the "duck test." The duck test works this way: suppose you see a bird walking around in a farm yard. This bird wears no label that says "duck." But the bird certainly looks like a duck. Also he goes to the pond and you notice he swims like a duck. Then he opens his beak and quacks like a duck. Well, by this time you have probably reached the conclusion that the bird is a duck, whether he's wearing a label or not.[49]

When the Korean war began, Arévalo's pledge to support the United States, and even round up all Communists "within twenty-four hours" if a crisis arose, did little to reassure Washington officials about this "duck." They breathed a sigh of relief in late 1950 only after Arbenz ascended to the presidency by winning 65 percent of the vote in an election that was remarkably open and free given the armed outbreaks of previous months. Arbenz might have been involved in Arana's murder, but the U.S. Embassy in Guatemala City called the new president a "realist," rather than an ideologue, and predicted that his government would "veer somewhat toward the center and that the communists will be quietly pushed aside."[50]

Within three months, however, State Department background papers anxiously began following "the ascending curve of Communist influence" under Arbenz. He legalized the Communist party (the Guatemalan Labor party, CTG), and began threatening United Fruit's International Railways of Central America. A State Department memorandum urged a total clampdown on any economic aid from international agencies (which the United States dominated) or bilateral organs such as the Export-Import Bank. More directly, trade could be cut with devastating effect, "since 85% of Guatemala's exports are sold in this country and 85% of their imports come from the United States." The cutoff would have to be done "quietly," Thomas C. Mann told other officials, because it was "in effect a violation of the Non-Intervention agreement, to which we are a party" and which "is a cornerstone of our Latin-American foreign policy. If it became obvious that we were violating this agreement, other Latin American governments would rally to the support of Guatemala." Mann's proposal was approved, but it did not win unanimous consent. Edward M. Martin of the European desk observed that when the same kind of crisis had occurred in Italy during 1948, the United States helped resolve it with aid to reduce unemployment. Mann granted the point, but believed that, if squeezed, the Guatemalan Communists would fight to retain power; then the conservatives, and especially the army (which Mann considered "the key") would "get together and clean their own house."[51]

Mann expressed that hope in 1951. But for nearly the next three years Guatemala continued to challenge the Good Neighbor system. The challenge was being thrown down, moreover, by a government that had been properly voted into office. As Mann complained, it was enough to make one conclude that the United States should "not support all constitutional governments under all circumstances."[52]

As the State Department prepared to tighten the screws, Arbenz dramatically raised the stakes. Campaigning for the presidency he had promised to help the peasants and Indians. In 1952 his program took on a new dimension when he obtained the passage of the Agrarian Reform Law. Rural laborers, as well as urban workers, were to receive governmental protection. The need was obvious. Two percent of the population owned 72 percent of the farm land. At the other end of the spectrum about half the agricultural population owned under 4 percent of the land. These percentages all too drily explained something quite startling: per capita income in rural areas amounted to $89.15 a year, and malnutrition was not only rampant but worsening as banana and coffee plantations spread over areas that once grew such staple diet crops as beans and maize. Since the colonial era, moreover, the rural laborers, especially Indians, had been virtually enslaved to the owners of the large plantations, while the government dutifully passed laws to legalize the slavery.[53]

A major turn had begun in 1950 with the formation of the National Peasant Confederation of Guatemala (CNCG) that unified twenty-five peasant unions in one bloc. Twenty-eight-year-old Leonard Castillo Flores had moved from a teachers' union in 1945 to leadership in the CTG, but then fell away from the growing radicalism of the labor union and its leader, Victor Manuel Guitiérrez, to organize the campesinos.

Guitiérrez and other Communist officials of the CTG fought the new group for two years; to them it was neither sufficiently radical nor did CTG ideology permit revolutions to be made by campesinos as well as the urban proletariat. By 1952, however, the CNCG's strength and Arbenz's commitment to rural reform brought Guitiérrez around to a more cooperative policy. He also began to see that the CNCG could be used to break the oligarchy's power. For their part, Flores and Arbenz needed Guitiérrez. His CTG had the political influence to legislate such a rural reform law and enforce it. The CNCG needed the Communists' organization, as well as Arbenz's power and prestige.

These forces coalesced in the passage of a law in 1952 that aimed to "eliminate all feudal type property . . . especially work-servitude and the remnants of slavery." Land was to be given to "agricultural workers who do not possess such." The purposes were obvious: to break the country's dependence on the oligarchy and foreign investors; to grow more staple food rather than having to import it from the United States; and to free as many rural laborers as possible to work their own plots or become urban laborers. The law had a powerful effect. Economically it expropriated the unused lands of large plantations (estates with lands fully in use were exempted from the law), and paid the former oligarchs with 3 percent, twenty-five-year bonds. Compensation was to be determined by the owners' own tax declarations of 1952, a ploy that raised cries of protest from the owners who had, for tax purposes, always understated their own worth. A campesino was then to receive about forty-two acres. By 1954, 100,000 families had received land as well as bank credit and technical aid for sowing and marketing. Politically the law was equally revolutionary. It was to be administered by peasants at the local and departmental (or province) level, and not run from Guatemala City. The large plantation owners who retained their lands could participate in the program, but they nearly all rejected the invitation and, out of habit formed in those earlier days when they had the ear of Ubico, tried unsuccessfully to influence the president and the congress in Guatemala City.[54]

By most measurements the land reform bill was a success. It aimed in part at putting unused lands into production for export, and Guatemalan exports rose until, by 1954, the nation enjoyed a favorable balance of payments. The experience disproved the common argument that land reform reduced productivity. It also provided campesinos with their own food, even cash from sales, while involving them in the political system for the first time in 400 years.[55]

The CNCG grew rapidly and remained under non-Communist leadership until 1954. Although it necessarily had to cooperate with Guitiérrez to achieve many of its political goals, it never surrendered control over the administration of agrarian reform. The CNCG consequently found itself uncomfortably in the political middle. On one side the radical left demanded greater change. On the other the army grew suspicious and Roman Catholic priests flatly told the peasants they had to choose between Christianity and the CNCG's "Communism." Long an ally of the oligarchs, the Church remained consistent. Some priests even refused to give a mass for the dead because the peasant had belonged to the CNCG.[56]

Washington officials, as usual, concluded that salvation lay with the army and the Church. The U.S. Office of Intelligence Research believed that because the National Agrarian Department administered the program, land reform was open to Communist control. The law, the State Department worried, provided "a basis for the strengthening of political control over the rural population." It also made "the greater part of United Fruit Company holdings . . . subject to expropriation." Compensation was virtually meaningless because of the method of calculation and the low value of the government's bonds on the open market. U.S. officials did admit in 1953 that "thus far, however, agricultural production, which provides the basis of Guatemala's economy, apparently has not been affected."[57] The Wrigley Gum Company was as upset as the State Department. In August 1952 the company announced it would not purchase Guatemalan chicle. Since it had been the sole buyer of the product, the Arbenz government suddenly had to provide a massive aid program for chicle harvesters.[58]

In 1953 Arbenz announced that under the Agrarian Reform Law he was expropriating 234,000 acres of land that United Fruit was not cultivating. Based on tax valuation, the president offered about one million dollars in compensation. UFCO demanded $16 million. It claimed, moreover, that the land was not simply uncultivated, but temporarily fallow to protect it against disease. (A United Fruit executive later noted that at this time only 139,000 of the company's total holdings of 3 million acres were actually planted in bananas. The rest, according to this official, was held by the company to assure, in part, that competition would not be able to utilize the land.)[59] The company could also argue that it was being unjustly targeted because it provided better housing and educational facilities for its employees than could be found anywhere else in the country. Its workers earned more than three times the average individual income.

Arbenz was not moved. UFCO had bribed dictators until it owned 42 percent of the nation's land. It paid minuscule taxes, was virtually exempt from import duties, and had earlier bluntly rejected Arévalo's request that new arrangements be negotiated. The government not only moved to take over UFCO land, but began planning a new electrical generating station that would make the capital city independent of the UFCO-owned utility. Arbenz also drew up blueprints for new roads and railways that threatened to break United Fruit's monopoly on Guatemala's transportation. When workers took steps to strike the UFCO electric company and railroad in 1953, the government took both under control.[60] Neodependence was turning into independence.

But only temporarily. United Fruit launched a massive lobbying campaign for U.S. intervention. It began with enviable connections to the Eisenhower administration. Secretary of State John Foster Dulles and his former New York law firm, Sullivan and Cromwell, had long represented the company. Allen Dulles, head of the CIA, had served on UFCO's board of trustees. Ed Whitman, the company's top public relations officer, was the husband of Ann Whitman, President Eisenhower's private secretary. (Ed Whitman produced a film, "Why the Kremlin Hates Bananas," that pictured UFCO fighting in the front trenches of the cold war.) The fruit firm's success in linking the taking of its lands to the evil of international communism was later described by one UFCO official as "the Disney version of the episode." But the company's efforts paid off. It picked up the expenses of journalists who traveled to Guatemala to learn United Fruit's side of the crisis, and some of the most respected North American publications—including the *New York Times, New York Herald Tribune,* and *New Leader*—ran stories that pleased the company. A UFCO public relations official later observed that his firm helped condition North American readers to accept the State Department's version of the Arbenz regime as Communist-controlled and the U.S.-planned invasion as wholly Guatemalan.[61] On the other hand, John Foster Dulles declared on television that the United Fruit Company's problems had little to do with the growing crisis in Guatemala: "If the United Fruit matter were settled, if they gave a gold piece for every banana, the problem would remain just as it is today as far as the presence of communist infiltration is concerned. That is the problem, not United Fruit."[62] Eisenhower took the same position, as did State Department officials in talks with Guatemalans.

Such a separation oversimplified U.S. policy. As early as 1947, the State Department had believed that Arévalo's restrictions on oligarch property rights smacked of communism. By 1952 the labor and agrarian laws led U.S. officials to conclude that Arévalo and Arbenz had both passed the "duck test." Guatemalan "communism" was dangerous not primarily because it supported the Soviet Union. Although Guatemala City newspapers and the national assembly eulogized Stalin after his death in 1953, the Arbenz government had supported Washington in the United Nations on major issues, including those that required choosing sides in the Cold War.[63] To argue that Guatemala's importation of Soviet bloc weapons in May 1954 prompted the U.S.-supported counter revolution overlooks the previous seven years of growing confrontation that had centered on issues of private property and personnel for the Guatemalan agencies that exercised power over property. Such an argument also misses the State Department's realization, as early as 1950, that U.S. economic power, so essential to the Good Neighbor's effectiveness, was being pecked at by Guatemalans who precisely defined the confrontation as being over the question of who was to determine the future use of their own property.

The United States did not design its military intervention merely to save the property of United Fruit. But Washington officials did view the UFCO problem as another, indeed a critical, piece of evidence that Arbenz was coming under Communist influence. As late as April 1954, that evidence had to rest not on Guatemala's support of international communism—for there was no convincing proof of that—but on its treatment of private property inside the country. Dulles's statement about pieces of gold was therefore accurate: he did not want money from Guatemala for UFCO property. He wanted the company's property restored. If Dulles could force restoration, the Agrarian Reform Law and its multifold implications for Guatemalan development would be dealt a near-fatal blow, the United States economic leverage enhanced, and the Good Neighbor system saved.

Within weeks after the expropriation appeared to be irrevocable, Eisenhower ordered the Central Intelligence Agency to plan a counterrevolution. Volunteers were in abundant supply. In early 1953, Somoza and Guatemalan exiles had tried to plan a coup, but it collapsed amid bickering and the refusal of Honduras (whose strategic location was essential for the operation's success) to cooperate unless the United States signaled its full support. At that point the Eisenhower administration had scarcely settled in office. By late summer, the decision was made. A large operation, costing as much as $7 million, was to train several hundred Guatemalans under C.I.A. direction on a United Fruit Company plantation in Honduras. The C.I.A. chose Colonel Carlos Castillo Armas to lead the attack. Castillo Armas had tried to lead a coup in late 1950, but was severely wounded and then imprisoned before managing to escape.

U.S. policy was carefully orchestrated. In November 1953 a new ambassador, John E. Peurifoy, went to Guatemala City. Peurifoy was a tough, outspoken career Foreign Service Officer who knew little Spanish, but had gained valuable experience in Greece when U.S.-directed forces smashed a left-wing revolt in the late forties. Peurifoy's views appeared unvarnished in his first talk with the Guatemalan Foreign Office. After he complained about the agrarian reform program, the Guatemalan foreign minister tried to make him understand by commenting that before 1944, "farm laborers had been roped together by the Army for delivery to the low-land farms where they were kept in debt slavery." Peurifoy shot back: "Agrarian reform had been instituted in China and . . . China was today a Communist country."[64] Carrying on a dialogue with Peurifoy was clearly going to be difficult.

As the new ambassador pressured the government, Dulles launched a hemisphere-wide offensive. He did this during the same weeks of early

1954 when he and Eisenhower were trying to prevent the surrender of French Indochina to the forces of Ho Chi Minh. In a 14 May 1954 cabinet meeting, the discussion that had begun on Indochina turned to the "possible parallel" with the horrors of the thirties. Dulles wondered aloud how one could now begin "drawing a line" against aggression, "particularly given the differentiation made by foreign nations between overt aggression and internal subversion."[65]

It was precisely that problem that he had encountered at the OAS Meeting in Caracas in March 1954 when he tried to obtain a resolution condemning communism in the hemisphere. But he had had to fight harder and longer than he had planned. The resolution passed only after he finally accepted an amendment that specified "dangers originating outside the hemisphere." (Hence Dulles's concern in the cabinet meeting.) Even the amended resolution was opposed by Guatemala, with Mexico and Argentina abstaining. Costa Rica refused to attend at all. Suspecting that Dulles was trying to obtain a legal excuse for U.S. intervention, these four nations refused to be a party. Other Latin American countries shared the suspicion, but they voted with Dulles, partly out of fear, partly out of the hope that in return for their support the United States would provide badly needed economic help. An hour after the resolution passed, however, Dulles was boarding a flight to Europe. Back at the conference other delegates hurried to explain away their vote with the United States. The Guatemalan Foreign Minister, Guillermo Toriello Garido, condemned the "systematic campaign of defamation that foreign interests, united with native feudalism, have waged against this republic" to "destroy the social advances of the Guatemalan Revolution." Toriello bitterly denied that his country would "permit intervention by any foreign power," including the Soviet Union.[66]

When Dulles finally returned to Washington he told the Senate Foreign Relations Committee that Communist political power in Latin America was "more dangerous than open physical aggression." Then he hedged his bet by associating the multilateral Caracas declaration with "the spirit of the original Monroe Doctrine."[67] The United States had always interpreted the Doctrine unilaterally, most recently with the Miller Doctrine of 1950. Dulles gave fair warning that, as some of the delegates at Caracas had feared, if Latin America did not cooperate, the United States would handle the Guatemalan problem alone. Yet little cooperation appeared. Some weeks after the Guatemalans received two thousand tons of Soviet bloc arms on 15 May 1954, Dulles was still trying to piece together a Latin American coalition for intervening under the Caracas resolution. But no support appeared outside the expected cooperation of two dictators, Somoza in Nicaragua and Rafael Trujillo in the Dominican Republic.

Dulles found himself (and, more importantly, U.S. foreign policy), in a bind. The problem would haunt Washington officials from that time on, although its importance was temporarily hidden after the successful 1954 counterrevolution. The problem could be defined as follows. For more than a century the Monroe Doctrine had rested on the principle that its purpose was to protect the Americas from outside—that is, European or Asian—forces. In conferences during the thirties, for example, the Latin Americans had agreed to cooperate with the United States against Nazi and other outside intervention. The Caracas statement of 1954 was consistent with this history; it focused on "dangers originating outside the hemisphere." But as Dulles understood, the "dangers" in Guatemala were not from outside, but from within the hemisphere: Arbenz had set out to reshape Guatemala economically and politically and aimed to break its dependence on the United States as much as possible. Dulles admitted to Latin American ambassadors that it was "impossible to produce evidence clearly tying the Guatemalan government to Moscow."[68] At the United Nations, as a State Department analysis admitted in 1953, Guatemalan votes differed little from those of other Latin American nations.[69]

The secretary of state encountered problems even after the Soviet bloc arms appeared, because no Communist bloc officials accompanied the shipment and, indeed, the arms were warmly welcomed by the most conservative Guatemalan military officers (whose supplies had been cut off in 1948 by the United States as part of its Good Neighbor economic pressure). In his March 1954 Annual Message, Arbenz refused to drop Communists from his government; perhaps he did not want to appear to be bending to U.S. pressure, or perhaps he simply did not see communism as the critical issue. Only four of the fifty-six members of Guatemala's Congress were Communist. No responsible person (including

U.S. officials) accused Arbenz of being Communist, and the government had never advocated even a program of extensive nationalization. Even greater barriers to a Communist takeover existed outside the government: the Church, the traditions and individualism of the campesino, and the army.[70]

The threat that Dulles perceived was, therefore, both internal and ambiguous. The secretary of state seemed less concerned with outside dangers than with telling Guatemalans how to govern themselves. Toriello emphasized that point in his speech at Caracas. If the United States could interfere with another nation because of that nation's ideas about philosophy and economic theory, the foreign minister argued, "the basis would be laid for the persecution of ideas and discrimination for political reasons." Those political reasons, moreover, would be judged unilaterally by the United States. Toriello was unsubtly comparing Dulles's activities in Central America with the McCarthyite witch-hunt for Communists in the United States.[71]

Thus, Dulles's bind, and thus the significance of the Guatemalan counterrevolution in 1954. The immediate danger to the U.S. system in Central America, in the Eisenhower administration's view, was not (as it had been for more than a century) outside intervention, but the ideas and political practices of Central Americans themselves. That by cutting off bilateral and multilateral funds the United States had left the Guatemalans with few alternatives after 1950 did not seem important in 1954.

As great powers do when they find themselves in such a bind, regardless of principles that are otherwise professed, the United States cut the knot with force. On 18 June 1954, Castillo Armas crossed the Honduran border into Guatemala with 150 men. He was not prepared to fight Arbenz's army, and in the skirmishing that did occur, the counterrevolutionaries did not distinguish themselves. The C.I.A. used radio broadcasts and other propaganda devices to convince Guatemalans that Castillo Armas's forces were driving on the capital; the time had arrived, the broadcasts proclaimed, for the people to overthrow Arbenz. But nothing happened. No uprising occurred, key army officers initially remained loyal, Castillo Armas's troops bogged down, and he lost two-thirds of his three-plane air force.

Eisenhower and Peurifoy then saved the counterrevolution. The president ordered several small aircraft to be sent through third parties (including Somoza) to Castillo Armas. These planes frightened people in Guatemala City merely by dropping sticks of dynamite that loudly exploded, and caused considerable destruction and casualties by bombing and strafing other towns. One plane, piloted by an American with the likely name of "Rip" Robertson, aimed for a ship that the pilot thought was Russian, and instead sank a British freighter. The infuriated insurers, Lloyd's of London, finally persuaded the C.I.A. to pay $1.4 million in damages. (Robertson lost his allure for his C.I.A. superiors, but Somoza immediately made him a business partner.)[72]

Arbenz then made the fatal error of trying to supply a worker-peasant militia with military weapons. The army refused to cooperate in building such a rival force, and the officer corps defected from the president.[73] Arbenz resigned and left the government in the hands of a liberal army colonel. Peurifoy appeared at the colonel's home with a pistol conspicuous in a shoulder holster; power was quickly transferred to Castillo Armas.[74] Dulles then spoke on North American television to abhor "the evil purpose of the Kremlin to destroy the inter-American system," to regret how Arbenz had been "openly manipulated by the leaders of Communism," and to congratulate "the people of Guatemala" because "the situation is being cured by the Guatemalans themselves." Peurifoy meanwhile justifiably bragged that in bringing the counterrevolution to a conclusion, he had been only "forty-five minutes off schedule."[75]

Other aftereffects were not as satisfying. At the United Nations the Soviets cynically acted as the champions of Guatemalan interests, and indeed of the UN itself, by insisting that the world organization fully investigate the U.S. role in the invasion. The United States finally killed this initiative and sent the case to the OAS (where it was quickly buried), but only after putting pressure on its closest allies, Great Britain and France, who had severe doubts about Washington's Central American policies. In Guatemala large numbers of executions occurred. How many fell victim to Castillo Armas's firing squads is unclear, although at least several hundred faced the rifles. Certainly more people were killed immediately after than during the counterrevolution. The leaders of urban and peasant unions became special targets. Those organizations were wiped out for the next decade.[76]

U.S. companies meanwhile moved back in. Castillo Armas signed an investment guarantee arrangement; issued a new petroleum law that, unlike Arbenz's, welcomed foreign companies; erased the post-1945 labor legislation from the books; and wrote a new, conservative constitution in 1956. As for United Fruit, it quickly recaptured a quarter-million acres. In return, UFCO signed a new contract giving the government a 30 percent tax on profits (instead of the pre-1953 10 percent), and surrendered a hundred thousand acres for planned land reforms that were never carried out. The United States injected $80 million of aid between 1954 and 1957 to keep the economy afloat.[77]

Guatemala had fully returned to the system. Its industrial and agricultural diversification stopped. The coffee oligarchy and UFCO were reestablished. Cotton production declined. The auditors of the nation's balance of trade turned from using black to red ink. Dulles liked to compare Latin America in the fifties with China of the thirties "when the Communist movement was getting started." After 1954 he could believe that Central America, at least, was safe. Yet the comparison was stronger than Dulles imagined. In both areas the United States had preferred a moderate middle-of-the-road regime to either extreme, and in the end found itself associated with the most reactionary forces. In both cases that association, and the concomitant military and political alliance that developed, further bipolarized the countries' politics, helped accelerate the revolutions, and totally cut off the United States from the revolutionary forces. These trends were obvious by the late forties in U.S.-China relations. By 1957 they began to appear in Guatemala. Castillo Armas was gunned down by one of his own presidential guard. Eisenhower publicly mourned his death as a "great loss to the entire free world." After a highly fraudulent election, General Miguel Ydígoras Fuentes moved into the presidency. Ydígoras quickly proved to be politically inept. His political failures combined with falling coffee prices to cause mass unrest, especially among students and peasants.

Guatemalan history was being recycled back to 1944, only this time (as with China after 1927), the revolution was to take a more radical and violent turn. In 1954 Eisenhower and Dulles saved the system temporarily, and, ultimately, at tremendous cost.

Nixon and the Wobbling of the System (1954–59)

In late 1954 Dulles referred in part to Central America when he observed to congressional leaders that U.S. strengths were political and military, but "our weakness" was "economic insecurity" and the inability to generate "economic growth in underdeveloped areas."[78] The secretary of state continued his search for an imaginative but cheap Latin American policy. Beset by critical troubles in Indochina and Europe, the administration simply trusted its military policies to maintain stability in Central America. Eisenhower hoped that private investment and the Export-Import Bank would provide grassroots development. But the problem, as the administration admitted in a 1954 report, was that its policy was trapped in an unrelenting cycle: Latin America could develop only if politically stable, but economic underdevelopment brought about *golpes* and instability. Private investors understandably remained leery, unless, of course, they could move into such quickly profitable areas as minerals and agricultural exports. That type of investment created only greater economic imbalance, however, not equitable development. The administration itself was empty of new ideas. At an inter-American meeting of financial ministers in 1954, the United States made the mistake of asking for suggestions. The Latin Americans immediately recommended a regional development bank. U.S. officials devoted the rest of the conference to fighting the idea; they were not about to lose the control they enjoyed through bilateral relationships (the Latins might gang up on them in a regional bank committee), or replace private capital with government sources. The suggestion, the parsimonious secretary of the treasury, George Humphrey, later complained to a sympathetic Eisenhower cabinet, was "overly extensive and most upsetting."[79]

As Richard Nixon was not reluctant to admit, the policy left the United States dependent on Central American dictators. The vice-president returned from a trip through the region in March 1955 to tell the cabinet that affairs were fine in Cuba (where strong-man Fulgencio Batista finally wanted to work "for Cuba rather than himself"), and splendid in Guatemala, where Nixon "saw a great potential for advancement under President Armas who is a middle-of-the-road type and has overwhelming popular support. United States assistance to Armas would make possible more real accomplishment in the next few years than over the past ten." The Salvadoran situation was equally satisfying, for "the President is trying to build up the middle class." Honduras "was a most pleasant surprise," in part because of United Fruit's good work. Nicaragua concerned Nixon only because of Somoza's ongoing "rivalry" with Costa Rica. As for Costa Rica itself, Figueres had "adopted some democratic practices," and "the country has a delightful climate." Nixon could think of nothing more substantive to say about the region's only democracy.

The vice-president's policy proposals were shopworn: more trade and more private investment. His report exemplified the U.S. belief that the Guatemalan intervention had worked so well that nothing new had to be considered. There was, he concluded, the "obvious . . . philosophical question as to what merit there is in dictatorship when efficiency rather than liberty seems most desired." But this question was merely "philosophical." He comfortably concluded that we "must deal with these governments as they are and rely on working over a period of time towards more democracy."[80] Humphrey surely did not find this report "upsetting."

With such reassurances, U.S. direct investment did rise in Central America during the fifties. In Guatemala it went up from $106 million in 1950 to $131 million in 1959; in El Salvador from $18 million to $31 million; in Honduras from $62 million to $110 million; in Nicaragua from $9 million to $18 million. Nearly all of the increase occurred in agriculture-for-export, public utilities, and minerals.[81] The oligarchy-North American relationship became more intimate. United Fruit expanded its holdings not only in bananas, but in sugar, cacao, palm oil, and abaca, as well as in transportation. The "Octopus" had indeed developed such long, powerful tentacles that the U.S. Justice Department finally charged UFCO with being a monopoly that restrained "free competition" in the North American fruit market. The company had accomplished this by dominating the Central American railway system, the Justice Department charged, and by controlling up to 92 percent of the business in the seven banana-producing countries, including Costa Rica,

Guatemala, and Honduras. (In 1958, a U.S. court finally ordered UFCO to set up new companies that would compete with it. The firm entered a rocky era that climaxed with near-bankruptcy in the seventies and the suicide of its chief executive in 1975. These disasters, however, had less to do with the court order than with gross mismanagement inside the company. Its influence over U.S. markets remained important, and its power in Central America remained awesome.)

As Eisenhower prepared to run for a second term in 1956, there was no reason to think that his Latin America policy was in trouble. Central America seemed especially secure. The Soviets, under the new leadership of the flamboyant Nikita Khrushchev, were making their first postwar trade and political arrangements with the Latins, but none of these touched Central America, where the Communists were either outlawed or wisely kept low profiles.[82] The United States meanwhile forged strong links with Central American military forces. By 1957 it had arms agreements with all the countries except Costa Rica and El Salvador. The U.S. Department of Defense, heartened no doubt by the Guatemalan counterrevolution, prepared to go far beyond mere arms sales to keep Latin America on track. In an early 1956 draft, National Security Paper 5613 stated that if ties between the area and the Soviet bloc prejudiced "our vital interests," economic means should be used in response. The Joint Chiefs of Staff wanted the wording changed to: the United States would "be prepared to employ political, military and economic measures, in order to weaken Soviet ties." Eisenhower liked the suggestion, and with slight change, the JCS wording became policy.[83] The Miller Doctrine was thus formally accepted by the National Security Council; henceforth, unilateral U.S. military operations could take precedence over OAS and other multilateral obligations.

Throughout these debates, Eisenhower was of two minds. He knew that threatened military interventions unpleasantly resembled British colonial practices ("Victorian," he called them) and the unproductive policies of Theodore Roosevelt. The president also complained in a cabinet meeting that in his talks with Latin American leaders "only two or three . . . wanted to be called by other than some military title. Moreover, their chests were hung with a great variety of military medals, which were probably struck for their own purposes." This spectacle offended the man who was the most famous general of World War II, but who deeply mistrusted the influence of the military on government. Eisenhower vowed to do nothing "which would encourage any further dependence on the military element in these countries."[84] His heart was in the right place, but his Latin American policies had no place for his heart. They depended increasingly on military leverage. Thus when Costa Ricans proposed in 1957 that the OAS work for a "substantial reduction" in the arms buildup throughout the hemisphere, they met a stone wall of opposition from other nations, including the United States, because the proposal totally contradicted Washington's post-1947 policies.[85]

The Costa Rican initiative was attractive to some because it appeared just as the United States and much of Central America became mired in an economic recession. The downturn and its political consequences finally jolted the Eisenhower administration to reconsider its stolid attitude. Raw material prices dropped sharply. Coffee, which had doubled in worth between 1948 and 1952 and remained at those high levels for several more years, began a long decline that by 1962 slashed prices in half. The blow hurt more because U.S. manufactures, on which Central America depended, remained fairly stable in price despite the recession. Private capital was suddenly rerouted from Latin America to Western Europe as the historic European Common Market opened a vast tariff-free area for investment. Thus in Central America, trade balances turned unfavorable, capital became more scarce, and growth slowed— even as the population increased with one of the highest birthrates in the world.

A special congressional committee issued a report in 1957 warning that the Central Americans were at a critical juncture. The United States, the report observed, obtained 10 percent of its imports and sold 10 percent of its exports to this small group of countries. Their agricultural products, moreover, were almost perfectly complementary (that is, not competitive) with North American goods. The report urged decisive action to preserve this profitable relationship. Unfortunately, Congress had no more new ideas to suggest than did the executive branch.[86]

Central America reflected in miniature the forces that now began to tear away at Latin American stability. In 1956, Somoza was shot by an assassin. The United States provided all help possible to save his life, and even flew the dying dictator to the Canal Zone hospital. (A Nicaraguan doctor observed sardonically that Somoza had never cared much about putting his money into hospitals.) His son, Luis, assumed political power, while another son, Anastasio, Jr., took over command of the National Guard. The younger Somozas did not display the elder's decisiveness. The C.I.A. worried that while Nicaragua was "not likely to degenerate into chaos in the near future," nonetheless a "severe struggle for power" could erupt.[87] Because the country depended on the United States to buy 40 percent of its goods (including large amounts of coffee) and bought nearly 60 percent of its imports from North Americans, the "severe struggle" could be fought out in a dangerously declining economy.

Nicaragua's bitter rival, Costa Rica, fared little better. Figueres's PLN Party surprisingly lost control of the presidency in 1958. This blow to the leader of the democratic left in Central America occurred as the country's economy threatened to go into a tailspin. With each penny drop in coffee prices, Costa Rica lost $6 million. In 1959, moreover, United Fruit announced that the country's coffee crop was the worst in a decade. The government's share of UFCO's profits consequently dropped sharply as the company began a long period of paying little or no income tax.[88]

El Salvador also entered a time of trouble. It had even less fat to live on than Costa Rica.[89] The country's economy depended utterly on coffee and cotton exports to the United States. In all Latin America only Venezuela with its oil was as dependent on the export of a single product as was El Salvador on coffee. When prices fell, Salvadorans became restless. As early as 1948, U.S. Ambassador Albert F. Nufer had warned that valuable lands were being ruined by one-crop dependency, and that expanding coffee, cotton, and sugar production to lands that had once grown corn and beans resulted in rising starvation among the peasants. His next set of prophecies was borne out over the following three decades:

El Salvador's economy, which is based on a single crop, coffee, is necessarily unstable. This, together with the fact that the bulk of the population exists on a bare subsistence level, creates conditions favorable to periodic political disturbance; has at times detracted from the effectiveness of El Salvador's cooperation in international affairs; and affords fertile soil for the seeds of communism.[90]

During the late fifties, however, restless Salvadorans turned less toward communism than toward Honduras. In the thirties about 25,000 had moved across the border to find food and work (especially with United Fruit); by 1949 there were 100,000 and the number began building to more than a quarter-million Salvadorans who tried to scratch out a living in Honduras during the sixties. Throughout much of the postwar era, those who remained behind lived under the military baton of Oscar Osorio, who ruled after a liberal military junta took power in a 1948 coup until a carefully prepared presidential succession was worked out in 1956. José María Lemus held power as the economy began to slide. Lemus visited Washington in 1959 to beg for help in keeping his country's export prices stable. No immediate help arrived. Lemus turned to brutal military oppression in 1960 to maintain order on the streets, and especially on the campuses, of San Salvador. Fearful that Lemus was bipolarizing the country and heading it straight towards the same kind of revolution that had seized Cuba the year before, moderate army officers overthrew him.[91] As the Eisenhower administration had the insight to conclude six years earlier, lack of economic development could indeed lead to political instability.

The break that occurred in Honduran history during the mid-fifties was sharper than anywhere else in the region outside of Guatemala. From 1933 until 1949 the country had been ruled by Tiburcio Carías Andino, perhaps the most significant figure in the nation's twentieth-century life. A 250-pound giant who stood six feet four inches tall, he carefully retained the appropriate constitutional authority even as he ruled dictatorially. It was the longest era of stability in the country's restless history. In a fascinating parallel, Carías's dictatorship prepared the way for a new Honduran liberalism much as Ubico's authoritarianism helped prepare Guatemala for the liberalism of Arévalo and Arbenz. By expanding his National party organization into the isolated, desolate Honduran provinces, Carías perpetuated his own power, but also established a political infrastructure that opened up parts of the country for the first time.

In 1948 Carías preserved the semblance of constitutional procedures by stepping aside and holding an election that ushered in six years of somewhat progressive rule under Dr. Juan Manuel Gálvez. With his political base supposedly secure, the new president presided over a major attempt to modernize the country's economy. The World Bank appeared with financial help and a recommendation to establish an efficient central bank. A *Banco Nacional de Fomento* was established to provide credit to agriculture and industry. The urban elites and U.S. investors continued to control the country, but Honduras became more pluralistic and dynamic than ever before. New political interest groups developed among campesinos and urban laborers. And the army could do little about these changes because it was not yet a self-conscious, professional institution. (That would come after U.S. training raised the military's self-awareness, and North American equipment made it the decisive political force.) Military officers continued to think of themselves as attached to the personalistic politics that fragmented the country, rather than as a member of an elite military institution.

Gálvez did little directly for the new labor movements, but neither did he restrain the pluralism that was beginning to appear. In this different atmosphere an historic event suddenly began on an April Sunday of 1954: laborers refused to load United Fruit Company ships unless they were paid double time. UFCO rejected the demand. Not surprisingly, a court decision upheld the company. But the strike promptly spread through the banana industry until it also paralyzed the other giant U.S.-owned producer, Standard Fruit. Nearly 40,000 workers defied the government and the two companies. This first major labor stoppage in Honduras had occurred spontaneously and without apparent leadership. Indeed, unions were practically nonexistent. The banana workers were simply tired of the low wages and bad working conditions. President Gálvez's actions, moreover, had indicated that he might have some sympathy for the laborers.

The walkout occurred as the Dulles brothers were preparing to move against the Arbenz government in Guatemala. Secretary of State Dulles apparently saw a connection between the strikers and Arbenz. The

Guatemalan officials did encourage the Hondurans to hold out, but Arbenz became involved quite late, and no left-wing influences could be discovered in the initial movement for a strike. The workers finally drifted back to work after Standard offered to raise salaries 4 to 8 percent (quite short of the 50 percent demanded by the workers) and to improve working conditions. Two-week vacations were also granted for the first time.[92]

Thanks, inadvertently, to United Fruit and Standard Fruit, labor unions suddenly became a political force. A new liberalism appeared in the country that was the very model of a "banana republic." It appeared at the same time that similar movements arose in Guatemala and Costa Rica. Clearly, parts of Central America were going through fundamental change. The question was whether the changes could be long-lasting. In Guatemala, the United States made certain they had a short life. In Costa Rica, however, Figueres's ideas prevailed. And in Hondùras, "Villedismo"—the liberalism of Ramón Villeda Morales, who identified himself closely with Figueres—made a lasting impact. Gálvez's successor attempted to seize the presidency by force and was deposed by the army, which then installed Villeda Morales as chief executive in 1957. A new, more liberal constitution appeared that year. Working codes, social security, some agrarian reforms began.

The campesinos experienced nearly as many changes as the wage laborers. After World War II the country's commercial agriculture had boomed, and new transportation networks, including the Pan American Highway, opened important markets for the produce. The coffee area doubled between 1945 and 1959, cotton acreage increased an astounding twenty times to more than 20,000 acres, and the number of cattle doubled. But each of these industries swallowed up land and drove thousands of peasants off their plots. Pressure on the land also intensified as thousands of Salvadorans moved in to search for areas to cultivate.[93] Many Hondurans fled into the few cities, where rapid growth meant horrible slums. Villeda Morales begged Washington for help as the drop in coffee and cotton prices shook Honduras's already strained economy, but no funds or help appeared—except a privately funded survey, conducted by a New York City foundation that recommended the country become yet more dependent on agricultural and raw material exports.[94]

Honduras had made a dramatic turn towards a more pluralistic society in the mid-fifties, but Villeda Morales could not force major changes in the power structure. The oligarchs and foreign investors held on grimly, and the country headed for the troubles of the eighties.

Neighboring Guatemala meanwhile moved inexorably to the right until the old militarism appeared in a more brutal form. Eisenhower did not renege on his commitments. U.S. advisers seemed to be everywhere; Guatemala was to be a model of the good things that befell those who turned away from radicalism. When Roy Rubottom, the head of the State Department's Latin American division, visited a "liberation" celebration in Guatemala City during 1957, one reporter compared it to the Spanish viceroy visiting the colonies 200 years earlier.[95]

But as Rubottom celebrated, a special U.S. congressional report found Guatemala to be an economic basket case. Borrowing limits had been nearly reached. After three years of favorable balance-of-payments under Arbenz, balances were now far to the negative side. Investment turned downward and the country's tiny dollar reserves suffered a disastrous 25 percent drop in 1958 and 1959 of $20 million.[96]

Political fortunes followed the economic, only more precipitously. But unlike the economy, at least some humor could be found in the politics. Castillo Armas had authored the 1956 Constitution which solemnly copied the U.S. Bill of Rights—then gave the president virtually unlimited power to rule the country and ignore all the rights. Castillo's clumsy right-wing successor, Ydígoras Fuentes, astounded even the most cynical Guatemalans with his nepotism. His minister of education was a six-foot, 240-pound female cousin who had never been able to pass beyond the eighth grade. Described by *Time* magazine as a "hulking female transvestite," she had made her mark as a "political goon" for Ubico. The minister unsettled diplomatic functions by arriving in male clothing with her twenty-six-year-old female roommate. More practically, she led street demonstrations for her cousin who lived in the Presidential Palace. She finally resigned when the nation's schools threatened to strike in protest against her presence in the ministry.[97] It was as sad that Guatemalans and North Americans focused on this episode (so that other issues were ignored) as it was that Ydígoras Fuentes appointed her. One frustrated official from Eisenhower's Bureau of the Budget had earlier despaired at the Guatemalans' disorderly political procedures and their penchant for "sitting around and plotting." This official proposed that it was time to "indoctrinate these people with their own indigenous philosophy based on the dignity of the individual, private enterprise, and democracy."[98] It took humorless North American bureaucrats to suggest that native citizens be taught how to be "indigenous."

By 1958, however, few people in Washington saw anything of humor in the growing crisis. A State Department Intelligence Report warned that unless Ydígoras moved away from his right-wing authoritarian image, the left would quickly regain strength. If he failed to invigorate the economy and curb "extreme leftism," then "ambitious officers" would overthrow his regime.[99] The Guatemalans also saw little that was funny. In 1959 a large U.S. technical aid project sent its people home after the minister of agriculture blasted North Americans for "driving fancy cars and throwing money around and [leaving] a bad taste," especially since they were using up gasoline that the country had to buy from U.S. suppliers with its few remaining dollars. This episode occurred as a wave of right-wing-inspired bombings shook the Ydígoras government. Soon leftist groups, looking to the newly established Cuban government of Fidel Castro as their model, launched strikes and terrorist attacks. Ydígoras suspended constitutional guarantees. In 1960, army officers trained by the United States, but now angered at the North American presence and, particularly, at the new Washington plan to use Guatemala as the training base for an invasion of Cuba, nearly succeeded in overthrowing the Ydígoras regime.[100] The political climate was becoming as inviting for the leftists as it had ever been before 1954.

Two North American scholars who knew Guatemala well had anticipated all this in 1956:

> Whatever the full truth may be, we are identified by much of the world as a conspirator in the Guatemalan Revolution of two years ago. If our first "Liberation" is to degenerate into a tawdry poorhouse of quarreling inmates, or another experiment in Communist infiltration, or a reversion to traditional "banana republic" reactionism, many people are going to think that we would do better to remain out of the liberation business.[101]

The Turn in the Cold War and the Eisenhower
Response; or, Condemning the Alliance for Progress

The political turmoil and economic decay in Central America during the late fifties formed a microcosm of conditions that afflicted most of Latin America. Before 1957, Eisenhower thought he could trust in dictators, private investors, and the C.I.A., but the dictators and investors had failed to develop economic and political systems. The C.I.A. had proved only that it could overthrow, not create, an ongoing government.

In May 1958 this policy failure hit Washington with special force. During a "good-will trip" to eight Latin American nations, Vice-President and Mrs. Nixon met a series of anti-U.S. demonstrations. Only in Somoza's Nicaragua had Nixon's reception been all the vice-president could have desired, and he ever after felt a special warmth toward the dictator. These demonstrations climaxed with a Caracas mob stoning the procession and then trying to drag Nixon from his car. Eisenhower ordered U.S. military forces to prepare for a rescue, but before they moved the vice-president had escaped. The Venezuelans were especially irate because the dictator whom they had recently overthrown had once been awarded a medal by Eisenhower for meritorious services, including "sound foreign investment policies." A shaken Nixon suddenly discovered that dealing with dictatorships was not merely a "philosophical" question as he had thought in 1955 (see p. 129).

He announced that henceforth the United States must give "top priority" to Latin America, warmly embrace democratic leaders, and offer only a "formal handshake" to dictators. John Foster Dulles immediately squashed that approach. "If we attempt to adjust our relations according to our appraisal of their government," said the man whose major contribution to Latin American policy had been the overthrowing of the Guatemalan government, "we would become involved in their internal affairs." The vice-president and secretary of state entered into a more revealing exchange in the privacy of a cabinet meeting. Nixon argued that the United States must not create the impression "that it is helping to protect the privileges of a few; instead, we must be dedicated to raising the standard of living of the masses." Dulles agreed, but then "pointed to the difficulty of dealing with it since democracy as we know it will not be instituted by the lower classes as they gain power—rather they will bring in more of a dictatorship of the masses."[102] Nixon made no response. Nor could he, for Dulles had expressed the fear, shabbily dressed-up as political theory, that shaped U.S. foreign policy in Central America and forced North Americans to befriend dictators and endanger vice-presidents.

Nixon received more effective support from the president's brother, Milton Eisenhower. The intellectual of the family (Dwight liked to refer to Milton as the "smart" brother), he also acted as a diplomatic troubleshooter for the president. After one visit to Latin America, Milton had seen no need to change policy, but after the Nixon visit the president dispatched him on a second tour and he returned with a warning that a new set of policies was quickly needed. Central American officials had bitterly complained to him that U.S. merchants bought raw materials at depressed rates, but sold finished manufactured goods to Central Americans at high, fixed prices; and that, in the words of one Latin, "You should not continue your high standard of living at the expense of our well-being and interests." Milton was convinced that the United States had to break with its long tradition and sign commodity-price arrangements.[103] The president was by no means enamored with such recommendations. He believed in the operation of the marketplace (although he continually warned about the need for more enlightened business people to operate it), and—to understate the case—he had a low opinion of most South and Central American military leaders.

Eisenhower, however, no longer presided over the postwar world that he and other North Americans had taken for granted since 1945. A new, more complex, and more dangerous international arena was developing, and it was doing so at the same time that the United States was losing its power to influence events in that arena. The debate that began in Washington during 1957 and 1958 (and climaxed in 1961 and 1962 with Kennedy administration policies, including the Alliance for Progress) marked an historic transition from one Cold War to another, quite different Cold War.

The first cold war of 1945 to the mid-fifties occurred in a "Two-camp" world of communism and capitalism in which the Soviets (as in Czechoslovakia) and the United States (as in Guatemala) had forcefully maintained order in their respective camps. This simpler, bipolar world began to be transformed, however, in 1956 and 1957 with the anti-Russian uprisings in Poland and Hungary; a growing split between the Soviets and Chinese (known to that point in the U.S. press as "the Communist bloc"); the creation of the European Common Market and a new Japanese industrial powerhouse that challenged U.S. economic supremacy; the Soviet launching of a space capsule ("Sputnik") that threatened U.S. military and scientific leadership; and exploding nationalism in such newly emerging areas as Latin America, Africa, and Southeast Asia. Eisenhower started his second term in one postwar world and ended it four years later in a quite different world. A "new Cold War," much discussed in the early eighties, did not begin during 1979 and 1980 with the Soviet invasion of Afghanistan and the crisis in the Persian Gulf area. That perspective is ahistorical. The Cold War made its first and most important turn in the 1956 to 1962 years.

As that turn was taken, the U.S. economy underwent a fundamental change, a change that made it less competitive in the world market. Thus as the Cold War challenges grew more difficult, the power U.S. policymakers possessed to deal with the challenges declined. In just seven years, from 1953 to 1960, the United States suffered three economic recessions. The nation's annual growth rate slowed until it was less than half the 7 percent paraded by the Soviet Union's leadership. Yet despite the recessions, the price of U.S. goods kept climbing until they cost 25 percent more in 1960 than in 1950. That upturn meant they were less competitive with the products of Japan and West Europe. U.S. productivity dropped, its laborers failed to turn out goods at the pace of other industrial nations, and Detroit's automobile industry that had propelled the economy for a half-century began to lose its dynamic effect. Consequently the United States began to suffer unfavorable trade balances that (among other calamities) had to be made-up by shipping out gold and dollars. These, however, were not going to Latin America or other newly emerging areas, but to Japan and Western Europe.[104] The poor were only becoming poorer.

Both camps understood what these changes could mean. Khrushchev explained his interpretation of this new Cold War as early as 1956. Communism, he declared, would triumph over capitalism not by "armed intervention," but because "after seeing for themselves the advantages that Communism holds out, all working men and women on earth will sooner or later take to the road of the struggle to build a Socialist society." C.I.A. Director Allen Dulles gave the U.S. version in a series of significant public statements between 1957 and 1959. Due to Soviet "programs of subversion and economic penetration," Dulles noted in early 1958, "we might win the military race and yet lose great areas of the world that are vital to our own national security." A year later he set down a postulate: "The uses to which economic resources are directed largely determine the measure of national power." Nowhere would these resources be more important than in the newly emerging areas, for as his brother, the secretary of state, lamented in a famous phrase, the United States suddenly faced the "tyranny of the weak"— the increasing power of Latin Americans, Africans, and Southeast Asians to determine the global environment in which North Americans lived.[105]

As Eisenhower listened to his brother and his vice-president calling for a new Latin American policy, the administration began to understand the fundamental changes that were restructuring the postwar world. It is a measure of the crisis the president saw developing that he initiated policy changes even before Fidel Castro came to power in Cuba.[106] Eisenhower's conversion produced two immediate innovations. After having refused for years to join any arrangement to stabilize roller-coaster coffee prices, he decided to join producers in a one-year deal. This agreement was then extended another year. Although it fixed the range of prices at a relatively low level, and thus provided few immediate benefits to Brazil or the Central American producers, the pact offered at least a promise of stability. Later in 1958 the administration also accepted the need for a regional banking institution, the Inter-American Development Bank (IADB) to supplement the inadequate World Bank and Export-Import Bank funds.

The president's acceptance of the IADB signalled a major change in U.S. foreign policy. Before 1958 the United States had staunchly clung to the position that areas such as Central America should look to private investment first and then to such international organizations as the World Bank for developmental help. But according to the administration's own estimates, available private funds were at least 50 percent lower than necessary for Latin American economic progress. If North Americans were prepared to invest overseas, they wanted to do so, and were doing so massively, in the stable, industrialized, richer European Common Market, and not in such impoverished countries as Honduras or Guatemala. As for World Bank funds, the Latin Americans had to compete with nations around the globe for those limited monies. U.S. officials, moreover, had always preferred to work out their economic links with Latin America bilaterally, so they could enjoy the maximum amount of leverage and control, instead of having investment decisions decided by such multilateral bodies as regional banking institutions. But those traditional policies began to disintegrate in the new, post-1956 cold war. It became clear that the United States simply did not have the economic power to stabilize large sections of Latin America while simultaneously spending money and military resources in the far corners of the globe. A regional bank became especially attractive because other Latin Americans could contribute their capital, and all the contributors—not just the long-mistrusted Yankees—would be responsible for ensuring that the funds were used properly. Eisenhower finally supported the IADB because Latin Americans pledged to provide 55 percent of the funds. (He also approved it in part because he wanted a similar institution for the Middle East and discovered that he had to create both if he wanted one.) The bank was initially set up with one billion dollars of capital. The voting system allowed the United States disproportionate power, particularly in the Bank's use of additional, callable funds beyond the one billion dollars. The funds were to be used only for infrastructure projects (and thus not compete against most private business ventures), and strict conditions could be attached to the loans. From Washington's point of view, the IADB had its attractions.[107]

But Eisenhower was reluctant to go any farther in meeting requests for aid. The reasons were spelled out in detail by Thomas Mann, the assistant secretary of state for economic affairs, in a cabinet meeting on 27 February 1959. Perhaps the administration's most experienced and respected official on Latin American affairs, Mann warned that events in the area threatened essential U.S. interests. Fidel Castro had marched into Havana on New Years Day, and Mann now believed that a "shift of power" was occurring that "accelerated . . . the power of governments and labor unions at the expense of the old established order." New regimes threatened to appear that followed neither "sound economic doctrines" (that is, they failed to create the proper climate for private enterprise), nor contained "men of stature and conviction." Equally unfortunate, the Latin Americans were so concerned about their economies that, according to a South American president whom Mann quoted, the southern continent's "future support . . . on Cold War issues in the United Nations was dependent on large-scale grants or soft loans." (If Dulles had not already used the phrase "tyranny of the weak," that would have been the right moment to coin it.) Regarding themselves "more as spectators than participants" in the East-West conflict, the Latin Americans would have to be bought off. Mann believed, however, this should not be done. The Latin Americans wanted the United States to commit 20 to 30 billion dollars over a fixed time to reach a per capita income goal. Such a policy was impossible, he emphasized, because the U.S. Congress, burdened with economic problems at home, would never grant such amounts of money over a long period. He also felt that the governments to the south "would not find it politically possible to ask commensurate sacrifices of their people." And if the promises were made but never realized the peoples would "later feel themselves deceived."[108]

Mann had made a remarkable, even prophetic, presentation. He had identified why the northern and southern continents were on a collision course, indicated that one way to avert the crash was the plan later known as the Alliance for Progress, and then fixed on the exact reasons why John F. Kennedy's Alliance would fail: the competing demands of North American taxpayers, the inability of Latin American oligarchs and military dictators to carry out reforms, and the acid-like disillusionment that would soon eat away the programs. Mann understood a reality that Kennedy's New Frontiersmen learned too late. Under the governmental systems in such areas as Central America, widespread, meaningful reform was impossible, no matter how much money was thrown at the program.

But Castro had conquered Cuba. Disorder did threaten other nations throughout the southern hemisphere. Something had to be done. When the U.S. Ambassador to Cuba, Philip Bonsal, told the Senate Foreign Relations Committee why Castro had been able to seize power, Bonsal could as well have been outlining the U.S. system in Central America:

> [In pre-1959 Cuba] politics was a matter of very small groups. It was a matter of tremendous corruption. . . .
> You had a certain segment of society, not a very large one, living very comfortably and in some cases very graciously. You had rising unemployment which has been estimated . . . [as] quite heavy. . . .
> They felt that the reciprocal tariff arrangements [with the United States] were working very much against them, that the tariff which they had granted us prevented them from protecting their own industries, and from diversifying their own agriculture, all in the interest of our own exports. . . .
> Agrarian reform has been an inspiration . . . for many years. . . . Nothing was done about it. . . .
> It was the degree to which major industries were under foreign control. In the case of sugar 10 years ago we controlled 50 percent of production . . . and it is down now to about 30. We own and manage the two major public utilities, electric power and telephone, and I think we do a good job of it. We own and the British own and manage the oil refineries. . . .
> We have very important mineral interests, some of them acquired under conditions which in many countries have been altered in favor of the country where the mineral resources are owned. All of these things building up . . . are the things which gave Dr. Castro his tremendous support.[109]

The major question now became whether North Americans would learn from their experience in Cuba or merely repeat the tragedy elsewhere in Latin America. For its part, the Eisenhower administration could neither come to terms with history nor devise an escape from Mann's formulation of the dilemma. The administration finally pledged a one-shot, half-billion dollar aid program in early 1960. The gesture was, of course, inadequate. As far as history was concerned, the administration's sense of the past seemed to have stopped with the 1954 invasion of Guatemala. In late 1960 Eisenhower approved C.I.A. plans to train Cuban émigrés for an invasion of Castro's domain. Noting Khrushchev's announcement in 1960 that the Monroe Doctrine's principles were extinct, the State Department retorted that they were "as valid today" as in 1823.[110]

Unlike the problem of 1823, however, the danger emanated not from overseas but from within Latin America itself. Eisenhower could deal with that problem only by plotting to overthrow undesirable regimes. It was now left to the incoming Kennedy administration to find a better answer. In the record of its cabinet meetings, Eisenhower's group left behind two pieces of advice. The first was Mann's warning that a massive, long-term aid program could easily result in false and highly dangerous hopes. The second was the comment, noted above, by Henry Cabot Lodge. "We should focus attention on the Declaration of Independence rather than on the Communist Manifesto where it has been," Lodge told the cabinet in 1959, "and in doing so we should not endeavor to sell the specific word 'Capitalism' which is beyond rehabilitation in the minds of the non-white world." The U.S. "can win wars but the question is can we win revolutions," Lodge wondered.[111] The ambassador to the U.N. had touched the root of the problem.

As they did with most of the advice offered by Eisenhower's advisers, the Kennedy people paid little attention to Mann's and Lodge's warnings. If the New Frontiersmen could make their Alliance for Progress work, a new day lay ahead for U.S.-Central American relations. But the Alliance had to solve the fundamental problems raised by Mann and Lodge. Otherwise, revolutions were inevitable.

III

UPDATING THE SYSTEM

"Latin America," Nikita Khrushchev observed in 1960, "reminds one of an active volcano." Cuba had already exploded. Guatemala began to erupt while the fault lines were clearly shifting in Honduras, El Salvador, and Nicaragua. Attempting to cap these and other Latin American upheavals in 1961, President John F. Kennedy initiated a ten-year Alliance for Progress program. Through the remainder of the decade four Central American nations—Nicaragua, Guatemala, El Salvador, and Costa Rica—ranked in the group with the highest growth rates in the hemisphere. Between 1960 and 1971 they enjoyed an annual real rate of growth of domestic product of 7.1 percent, 5.5 percent, 5.6 percent, and 6.1 percent. Honduras reached the moderate growth cohort with 5.1 percent.[1]

These figures vividly illustrated the paradox, and failure, of the Alliance. Throughout the tumultuous sixties, the first three countries endured the most severe political and social problems. Honduras suffered nearly as many. By the time Kennedy was assassinated in November 1963, the Alliance had only heated up the volcano. Ironically, it became the pivotal, perhaps even the essential, step on Central America's journey to the revolutions of the seventies and eighties.

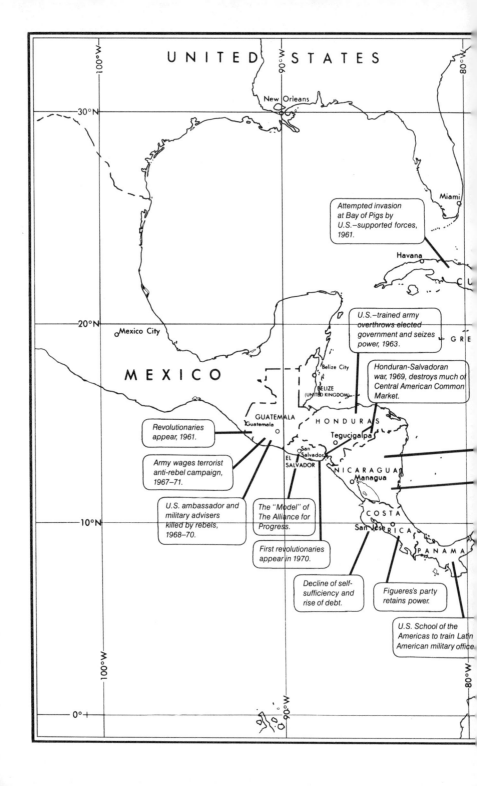

UNITED STATES

New Orleans

30°N

Miami

Attempted invasion
at Bay of Pigs by
U.S.-supported forces,
1961.

Havana

CU

20°N

Mexico City

U.S.-trained army
overthrows elected
government and seizes
power, 1963.

GRE

Belize City

BELIZE
(UNITED KINGDOM)

Honduran-Salvadoran
war, 1969, destroys much of
Central American Common
Market.

MEXICO

GUATEMALA
Guatemala

HONDURAS

Tegucigalpa

Revolutionaries
appear, 1961.

San
Salvador

Army wages terrorist
anti-rebel campaign,
1967–71.

EL
SALVADOR

NICARAGUA
Managua

U.S. ambassador and
military advisers
killed by rebels,
1968–70.

The "Model" of
The Alliance for
Progress.

COSTA

First revolutionaries
appear in 1970.

San José

RICA

10°N

PANAMA

Decline of self-
sufficiency and
rise of debt.

Figueres's party
retains power.

U.S. School of the
Americas to train Latin
American military office

0°

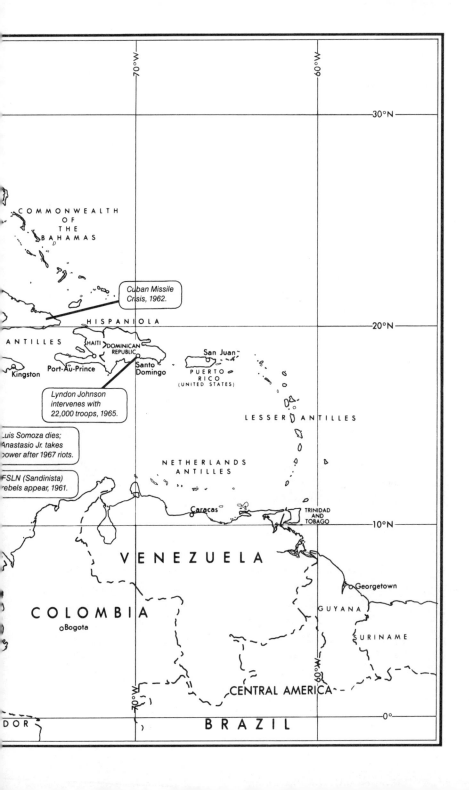

COMMONWEALTH
OF
THE
BAHAMAS

Cuban Missile
Crisis, 1962.

HISPANIOLA

ANTILLES

HAITI DOMINICAN
REPUBLIC

Kingston Port-Au-Prince Santo
Domingo

San Juan

PUERTO
RICO
(UNITED STATES)

LESSER ANTILLES

Lyndon Johnson
intervenes with
22,000 troops, 1965.

Luis Somoza dies;
Anastasio Jr. takes
power after 1967 riots.

FSLN (Sandinista)
rebels appear, 1961.

NETHERLANDS
ANTILLES

Caracas

TRINIDAD
AND
TOBAGO

VENEZUELA

Georgetown

COLOMBIA

Bogota

GUYANA

URINAME

CENTRAL AMERICA

DOR

BRAZIL

30°N

20°N

10°N

0°

The Alliance for Progress and Revolution: Kennedy

John F. Kennedy first outlined a new program for Latin America when he spoke as a contender for the Democratic nomination in December 1958. (The Eisenhower administration began to transform its policies precisely at this time.) In 1960, Kennedy fleshed out his approach in a speech at Tampa and first used the term "Alliance for Progress." Within sixty days after entering the White House, he announced a detailed program for congressional action. Over the next ten years, $100 billion was to be pumped into Latin American development. The United States planned to invest $20 billion, of which about $1.3 billion would be new, private funds. The Latin Americans were to collect and invest the other $80 billion from their own resources, and, equally important, they were to enact tax, land, and other socioeconomic reforms so that the money could be properly used. It was to be a spectacular enterprise. Kennedy aimed at roughly a 5.5 percent annual growth rate in the southern hemisphere's gross national product (GNP), or about a net increase per person of 2.5 percent each year when the extraordinarily high 3 percent population increase was counted. Using characteristic Kennedy rhetoric, the president declared, "Let us again transform the [hemisphere] into a vast crucible of revolutionary ideas and efforts."[2] The key—and highly misleading—word turned out to be "revolutionary."

Kennedy went far beyond Eisenhower's first steps. He made a decade-long pledge, committed government funds in a manner that the Eisenhower administration had found abhorrent, insisted on Latin American reforms, and established a talented bureaucracy to operate the program. The Alliance's origins, however, could also be found in Castro's rise to power, Khrushchev's denial in 1960 that the Monroe Doctrine was still valid, and the Soviet leader's announcement in January 1961—just as Kennedy assumed power—that third-world revolutions were to be the wave of the future. From its inception, the Alliance focused at least as much on antirevolutionary as on developmental activity. Indeed, they were to be two sides of the same policy. When Secretary of State Dean Rusk privately briefed key senators, he emphasized his "most impelling impression . . . that we are in a period of far-reaching and fundamental and rapid change." That change he found especially vivid in the "increased pace in the working out of nationalist revolution." But Kennedy and Rusk believed that their nation, not Khrushchev's, could control such changes. They correctly saw the sixties as the critical test: if third-world demands were not met in "a fairly special period of a few years," Rusk declared, the resulting pressures could lead to war or to violent outbreak in "another decade or two decades."[3]

The administration thus viewed the Alliance as the weapon to fight revolution in Latin America. Demands for revolution were to be met with evolution. The chances for success seemed good. The United States still remained the world's greatest economic and military power. The Alliance seemed worthy of its capacities. In Latin America, leftist democratic forces had been building strength in Costa Rica, Honduras, El Salvador, and a number of South American nations. These Christian Democrat and social democratic groups, Kennedy believed, would act as his main allies in the Alliance. Together, the northern and southern democrats would weaken both dictators and the far left to allow the growth of a stable middle element.

In August 1961 the United States and the southern nations worked out the details of the Alliance at Punte del Este, Uruguay. Kennedy next pushed for a five-year coffee stabilization agreement. Coffee and other commodity prices had dropped so rapidly that about 40 percent of Alliance funds in 1961 and 1962 had to be spent rescuing a number of nations from balance-of-payments crises.[4] Latin American export earnings had to rise if the Alliance were to have any chance to work. The 1962 coffee agreement stabilized prices and thus offered critical help to all five Central American nations, or at least to the elite that grew and sold the beans.

Despite these agreements, the Alliance stumbled at first. A month after Kennedy announced the program in March 1961, U.S.-trained Cuban exiles suffered a humiliating defeat when they tried to invade their homeland. The Kennedy administration had hoped to replay the 1954 Guatemalan operation, but Castro had learned from Arbenz's failure. He kept his army loyal to his government. The Cuban leaders seemed stronger than ever, the United States a blunderer. "Are you gentlemen telling us today," Republican Senator Homer Capehart of Indiana asked C.I.A. and Pentagon officers, "that . . . our high military people who fought in World War I and World War II . . . approved this, what would appear to me to be a Boy Scout operation?"[5] As sensitive about its image as any administration in U.S. history (and believing too often that style was substance), the Kennedy White House set out to reverse its "Boy Scout" image.

The first step was to define the problem. Cuba, said Rusk, was "a part of the powerful offensive" launched by the "Sino-Soviet Bloc [*sic*] . . . around the world to outflank the centers of power in the Free World." Many Latin American nations could not respond properly because "of the degree of penetration which the Communists and Castro-type movement had effected within this hemisphere." C.I.A. Director Allen Dulles agreed that "most of the states of Central America" confronted "the insidious penetration of Cuban communism."[6] In its first six months in office, the administration thus not only announced the Alliance, but, particularly after the Bay of Pigs invasion, began to define Castro—not poverty—as the immediate problem.

The response to the problem came in two parts. The State Department first tried to divide the Cuban regime from the other governments in the hemisphere. At Punte del Este II in 1962, the United States moved to contain Castro by severing diplomatic ties and imposing trade embargoes. Only fourteen of twenty nations voted with the United States, although, under pressure, seventeen finally agreed to stop traffic in arms with the Cubans. After the Missile Crisis in October 1962, the Cuban danger did not diminish. (Few pundits in the press perceived that a failure of U.S. policy had allowed Castro to survive and turn to the Soviets for help; despite, or because of, Kennedy's policies, the Cuban leader had taken the superpowers to the edge of mutual destruction.) Cuba's attempt to aid Venezuelan terrorists in 1963 led to the severing of diplomatic relations and trade by every Latin American nation except Mexico. The president wanted to go farther by issuing a "Kennedy Doctrine" that announced "another Cuba" would not be tolerated. A top State Department expert on the Americas, William Bowdler, privately warned the White House that such unilateral U.S. action would "provoke genuine and deep concern among Latin Americans."[7] The

Doctrine was not issued, but the means to enforce it appeared with a rapid buildup of U.S. conventional and counterinsurgency forces. These forces formed an essential part of the second Kennedy response to radicalism. U.S. officers had long trained Latin police and military for counterinsurgency campaigns. In 1961, Attorney General Robert Kennedy nevertheless passed an F.B.I. report to his brother warning that security in Central America was "extremely deficient."[8] By 1963 a stepped-up military program was well underway. It expanded until security dominated developmental aspects of the Alliance. U.S. military aid to the southern nations increased 50 percent a year over the monies granted under Eisenhower. Guatemala received $5.3 million in military assistance between 1950 and 1963, but $10.9 million from 1964 to 1967. The comparable figures for Honduras and Nicaragua were equally startling: $2.6 million and $4.6 million for the former, and $4.5 million and $7.5 million for the latter.[9]

Military funds inundated small economies, transformed government budgets, and created a large military group trained by U.S. officers in such special schools as the Southern Command's School of the Americas in the Panama Canal Zone. Secretary of Defense Robert McNamara announced in 1963 that the newly trained military leaders' responsibility was not "hemispheric defense," but "internal security." In reality this meant that in Central America the military forcefully maintained the status quo for the oligarchs. The transformation of police forces was notable. Under the Agency for International Development which operated the Alliance program in Washington, these forces learned to use gas guns, helicopters, and other anti-riot equipment. For this newly powerful elite, it proved to be only a short step to controlling dissent through sophisticated methods of torture.

Institutional ties soon cemented U.S. and Central American militaries. In late 1963 Washington officials helped establish the *Consejo de Defensa Centro Americana* (CONDECA, or the Central American Defense Council) for the region's collective security. CONDECA included all the Central American nations except Costa Rica, which repeatedly condemned it. The Council's purposes were strictly internal and largely defined by the United States. By 1968 the military forces had agreed on certain standards: almost all the uniforms and insignias for Central

American soldiers looked exactly like those of the U.S. Army. To the guerrillas, Central American troops protecting oligarchs closely resembled U.S. troops protecting U.S. interests. The Latin militaries no longer pretended political neutrality, but actively helped anti-Communist civilians and engaged in "civic action," a Pentagon term for involving the military deeply in economic and social projects. In the words of one document written by U.S. and Central American military officers, civic action served "as the most effective means of combatting . . . the expansionist plans of Communism." The program also gave the military much-needed "affection and respect of the people."[10]

The program, however, produced quite different results. When a Mexican official learned that the United States planned to give special training to Latin American officers, he said, "Give me the names of those first 60 students, and I'll pick your presidents in Latin America for the next 10 years." Delesseps Morrison, Kennedy's ambassador to the OAS, responded that Latin America would indeed be fortunate if these officers did become the future leaders of their countries. The Mexican official, however, was closer to the truth than Morrison. Between 1961 and 1966, the military overthrew nine Latin American governments, including Guatemala's and Honduras's in 1963. In many cases, civilian conservatives urged the military to act before elections brought undesirable liberals to power, or before planned Alliance programs threatened the oligarchs' interests. The School of the Americas became known as the School of the *Golpes.*[11]

Its own creature helped strangle the Alliance. Kennedy, an enthusiast for counterinsurgency policies, did not know what to do. If he broke relations with the new governments, he also ended Alliance programs and alienated pro-U.S. military leaders. The president believed, moreover, that many officers were not reactionary and were certainly more competent to run Latin American countries than the progressive civilians who winked at disorder and extravagance. The military also wanted to kill revolutionaries. After officers overthrew a more liberal government in El Salvador, President Kennedy approved: "Governments of the civil-military type of El Salvador are the most effective in containing communist penetration in Latin America."[12] On the other hand, if he continued diplomatic relations with the new regimes, the United States became involved with unelected militaristic governments, an involvement that millions of dollars of military aid reinforced. The best Kennedy could do to resolve the dilemma was the unusual idea of establishing a "club" of "democratic presidents." It could meet regularly in Palm Beach and exhibit Kennedy's preference for men who actually won elections. The proposal was quickly dropped. Sporadic meetings of a small group in Palm Beach could hardly match the influence of U.S. military missions and the School of the Americas.[13]

Uncharacteristically, Kennedy became "depressed" by the immense problems in Latin America, although he thought "we ought to keep at it."[14] Some of the problems appeared insoluble. The high birthrate blotted up economic growth and created fast-spreading, slum-ridden cities whose populations threatened to double within fifteen years. Yet when North Americans tried to limit birthrates, they encountered nationalism, the Roman Catholic Church, and the common view that children were both economic assets and security in the parents' old age. Congress also caused Kennedy headaches by threatening to hamstring the Alliance with a series of measures. The most publicized was the Hickenlooper amendment which required suspension of aid to any government that seized U.S. property and did not "take appropriate steps" toward "equitable and speedy compensation" within six months. Rusk vigorously and unsuccessfully fought the act, fearing that it not only set untenable deadlines, but prevented settlement through the usually long negotiations.[15] The Agency for International Development (AID) that administered the Alliance paid large sums to help giant U.S. multinational corporations (including United Fruit, Standard Fruit, and, in Guatemala, International Nickel) conduct pre-investment surveys for roads and port facilities, but often refused to help Central American-owned businesses build facilities that competed with North American-owned plants.[16] Interest groups in Washington, not the needs of Central Americans, shaped too many Alliance projects.

Above all, the pivotal question remained: even if real growth occurred, would the poorer or the richer receive the benefits? As Congress prepared to pass the first funds for the program, Senator Albert Gore (Dem.-Tenn.) warned, "I am not sure that we will not widen the gap between the very rich very few, and the great mass of the majority which, according to Mr. Allen Dulles, contains a majority report for Castro in Cuba."[17] Despite the syntax, Gore was prophetic. Alliance funds in massive amounts went to U.S.-owned firms and to the Central American oligarchs that controlled banks and mercantile businesses, as well as the best tillable land.[18] A United Nations analysis of 1963 feared that the Latin American middle class, on which Kennedy had staked so much of his hope, was turning restless and radical.[19] The Alliance could do little to alleviate such tension. Nor did strong political parties exist through which the tension could be constructively channeled. *Personalismo* (the cult of the strong and usually wealthy leader) and the growing involvement of the military made political parties motorless vehicles for change. Only the tiny Communist parties, and to some extent the new democratic left, offered the needed organization, but they looked feeble beside the oligarchic-military complex. In Central America (outside of Costa Rica), the "center" was little more than the "gap" about which Senator Gore worried.

Revolution, consequently, seemed to be a way of bridging that gap. Ironically, the Kennedy administration also spoke of "revolution." Its use of the term attempted to identify the Alliance with the poor Latin Americans, and perhaps represented an effort to appear tough and realistic—a kind of North American *machismo* not unknown in the Kennedy White House. But the term was dangerously misleading. At Punta del Este I, Secretary of the Treasury Douglas Dillon told the conference that the Alliance "is a revolutionary task, but we are no stranger to revolution." Kennedy significantly modified this claim in 1962: "Those who make peaceful revolution impossible will make violent revolution inevitable."[20] The president only added to the confusion: no Latin American had ever seen a "peaceful revolution." Years later, Thomas Mann, who advised Eisenhower, Kennedy, and Lyndon Johnson from his State Department posts, laid bare the problem:

> I never believed we had an agreed definition of the word revolution, what it meant. To Latin America, I'm convinced that revolution means blood in the streets and shooting. And I think we here in this country refer to nearly everything as a revolution, from the Industrial Revolution on down.[21]

In early 1964, the C.I.A. described how the Alliance was building a powder keg in Latin America. The analysis deserves extensive quotation, for it helps explain how the programs of the 1960s led to revolution in the 1980s.

> The hazards of governing may be increasing rather than lessening in Latin America. The principal reasons: the pressures among organized groups and peoples for positive and radical changes in the inequitable and backward socio-economic structures and for gains in levels of living are mounting steadily. In many areas, inflation has caused a deterioration in levels of living. Moreover, political and popular demands for accomplishments in short periods of time are irrational or unrealistic. Political parties and candidates who attain power by election as well as those rulers who seize power extra-legally have stimulated popular aspirations which are impossible of attainment, even granted unlimited resources and extensive periods of time. In part because of the Latin American paternalistic tradition, the public blames governments for most evils and failures, while both governments and peoples look abroad for convenient scapegoats.[22]

The groups identified in this report began to take seriously the easily used rhetoric about revolution. A further danger, however, appeared; while promising "revolution," the United States trained armies and police to prevent revolutions. The tension built between the two parts of the policy until it helped destroy the Alliance. Mann's fear came to be as prophetic as Senator Gore's. As Gore warned from his liberal perspective that the program threatened to widen the gap between the rich and the masses, Mann, a conservative, feared that the Latin Americans would try to close the gap with truly revolutionary means. By 1964, the C.I.A. worried that Mann's fears were justified.

The Alliance for Progress and Revolution: Johnson

Mann suddenly received the chance to change the policy himself. When Lyndon B. Johnson became president on 22 November 1963, he and

Mann—both Texans—had long been friends. The new president devoutly believed in the almost supernatural results of economic development. He built his political career by using New Deal programs to funnel large amounts of money into his home state, and closed that career by preaching the need for similar development of all Southeast Asia. But he quickly became skeptical about the Alliance, partly because it was a program of the Kennedys (whom Johnson had long feared and envied), partly because he saw how costly the program had become, and partly because he saw how its contradictions were destroying it.

Johnson downgraded the Alliance in one dramatic step. He named Mann to no less than three posts: director of the Alliance, special assistant to the president, and assistant secretary of state for inter-American affairs. The signal could not have been clearer. Mann had been the official who bluntly told the Eisenhower Cabinet why such a program as the Alliance would be disastrous. After 1960 he never shared the Kennedy euphoria about "peaceful revolution." Mann was seldom euphoric about anything. Low-keyed, bureaucratic, skeptical, tough, conservative, deeply experienced in Latin American affairs, he was the perfect choice to dismantle the Alliance at the same time Johnson continued the old Kennedy rhetoric. Harry McPherson, White House aide and speechwriter for L.B.J., later called the president's rhetoric about the Alliance—especially the "passionate terms that seemed to welcome revolution at the same time we were dealing on behalf of our businessmen"—a "lot of crap."[23]

More accurately, half the Kennedy program was dismantled. Economic, but not military support dropped as the needs of the Vietnam war grew. Congress appropriated about $500 million in Alliance funds for fiscal year (FY) 1967, $469 million in FY 1968, and $336 million for FY 1969. As for private investment, the C.I.A. reported in 1964 that "not only had this sector been neglected . . . , but . . . the climate for private enterprise has taken a sharply adverse turn."[24] The danger was subtle but ominous. A Latin American belief in "statism" (the importance of state powers) was, in the C.I.A.'s view, rapidly replacing confidence that private enterprise could develop the continent. The belief struck not only at the Alliance, whose success required large amounts of private investment, but at the U.S. system itself as it had developed over

Central and South America. The C.I.A. targeted Castro as the villain: "Cuba's experiment with almost total state socialism is being watched closely by other nations in the hemisphere," the Agency told the White House in April 1964, "and any appearance of success there could have an extensive impact on the statist trend elsewhere in the area."[25] The two threats, subversion and statism, had to be met. So far, the Alliance seemed to intensify rather than lessen those dangers.

Mann's response came on 18 March 1964. In an off-the-record speech to U.S. officials working in Latin America, he made no mention of the Alliance for Progress. Nor did he stress the need for structural change. Instead Mann announced that the top priorities were economic growth, protection of U.S. investments, nonintervention, and anti-communism. That the third and fourth points might be contradictory passed notice at the time. What was clear was his stress on somehow spurring economic growth while maintaining the sociopolitical status quo. As Mann candidly admitted, this meant quickly recognizing military regimes that overthrew civilian governments.[26] Mann and Johnson thus dropped two of the Alliance's original goals, democratization and structural change, to concentrate on economic development and anti-communism. The administration depended on private capital and the military regimes to accomplish the development. The approach resembled the Eisenhower approach of 1958 through 1960, only now promises had been made, expectations raised—and counterinsurgency units in Central America trained.

In April–May 1965, the Johnson-Mann policy culminated in the president's sending of 22,000 troops into the Dominican Republic. Fearful that an army revolt against a U.S.-supported government created conditions that presented ripe opportunities for leftists, Johnson announced on television that "the American nations . . . will not permit the establishment of another Communist government in the Western Hemisphere." The president had exaggerated the danger of communism in the Dominican Republic. The fundamental point nevertheless remained: "We believe that change comes," the president declared, but "it should come through peaceful process."[27] In the name of anti-communism, Johnson violated the U.S. nonintervention pledge made in 1948 when it signed the OAS Charter, and undermined the respect

North Americans liked to pay to international law. Not that Johnson cared particularly about the Charter. He fervently believed in the Miller Doctrine of U.S. unilateral intervention. As for the OAS itself, Johnson gave the considered opinion that it "couldn't pour piss out of a boot if the instructions were written on the heel."[28]

His message to Central America was equally direct. As a people who had felt the brunt of U.S. military intervention for more than a half-century, the Central Americans suddenly realized that a new era of gunboat diplomacy might be at hand. Given the escalation of violence in Vietnam and the intervention in the Dominican Republic, no one could claim that North Americans reluctantly used military force. Johnson's announcement that "the American nations" would not allow radical change strikingly resembled Leonid Brezhnev's "Doctrine" of 1968. After Soviet troops brutally overthrew the reform government of Communist Czechoslovakia, the Russian ruler declared that the "Socialist" states would never allow one of their members to be corrupted by Western influences. The Caribbean area and Central America occupied the same place in Washington's geopolitical plans that Czechoslovakia did in Moscow's.

That resemblance was not lost on Central American revolutionaries. If they hoped to transform their countries, they had to do it in the face of overwhelming U.S. military power. In practical terms this meant that they had to succeed politically before they could win militarily. Unlike Arbenz in 1954, but as Castro had done in 1961, they first had to develop mass support that could underpin military power. They obviously could not defeat U.S. power in a direct military confrontation. Central Americans learned another lesson after Johnson pushed through the creation of an OAS force that occupied Dominican territory. The army included Costa Rican, Salvadoran, Honduran, and Nicaraguan troops. (Among the larger nations, Argentina, Colombia, and—most notably—Venezuela refused to join because of overwhelming domestic opposition.) When analyses later concluded that Johnson had grossly overestimated the danger, reaction set in among OAS members. Fourteen years later, Jimmy Carter tried to recreate the OAS force to stop the Nicaraguan revolution. The Latin American nations unanimously rejected his plea, in part because of their memories of the 1965 intervention.[29]

Washington's policies in Latin America suffered sharply from the Dominican intervention. Johnson and Mann searched for cheap remedies. After promising a continuation of the Alliance in late 1965, Johnson flew to a summit meeting of the hemisphere's presidents in 1967 and stressed that the Latin Americans must help themselves—especially through regional economic integration—and not look to the United States for help.[30] As Johnson wrote in his memoirs, "The old days, when they had looked to the United States to solve their problems, had ended. We would now be a junior partner in Latin American economic and social development."[31] His listeners, including liberals and revolutionaries in Central America, were about to take Johnson at his word. The trick would be to ensure that the United States remained nothing more than a junior partner, and not militarily involved, when Central Americans began to bring about fundamental change.

By the late sixties, the Alliance's remnants consisted of its most dangerous parts: an emphasis on private investment that worsened the already glaring economic imbalance in Central America; a dependence on the military—trained and supplied by the United States—to maintain order in restless societies; and promises made repeatedly by Kennedy, Johnson, and other U.S. officials that raised hopes and aspirations. The first two were destroying the third. And as revolutionary conditions developed, the United States government stood aside, except for its support of the military. Secretary of State Dean Rusk offered a major insight into hemispheric relations and U.S. priorities when he remarked in 1968, "I get no comfort out of the fact that the defense budget of the United States this year is roughly equal to the gross national product of all of Latin America."[32]

North American critics were outspoken. A small group of Senate liberals led by Gore, Ernest Gruening (Dem.-Alaska), and Wayne Morse (Dem.-Ore.) persistently questioned the Alliance's direction by the mid-1960s.[33] But none was more prophetic than Robert Kennedy, now a senator from New York.

These people [of Latin America] will not accept this kind of existence for the next generation. We would not; they will not. There will be changes. So a revolution is coming—a revolution which will be peaceful if we are wise enough; compassionate if we care enough; successful if we are fortunate enough—but a revolution which is coming whether we will it or not. We can affect its character; we cannot alter its inevitability.[34]

Revolutionary conditions did grow rapidly, even in countries where the Alliance seemed most successful. And the system first self-destructed in Nicaragua, where for a half-century the United States had enjoyed great influence.

Nicaragua: The Alliance and the Origins of the Sandinistas

When a lone gunman killed Anastasio Somoza García in 1956, the dictator left his two sons, Luis and Anastasio, a personal fief called Nicaragua. The elder Somoza had either shot or outmaneuvered all important political opponents. Brave and outspoken men often ended in the dungeon of the Presidential Palace where electrodes of the infamous "Little Machine" were attached to their genitals for long sessions of torture. Somoza destroyed any hope that peaceful change could occur. He buttressed his authority with the neat balancing act of loudly championing Nicaraguan nationalism while doing everything the United States asked. Fittingly, the U.S. Embassy was next to the president's residence. The U.S. Ambassador ranked as the second most powerful man in the country, and, at times, as the most powerful. The Somoza family, however, did not devote all of its time to tiresome politics. Just before his death, Somoza held as much as 15 percent of all the land in Nicaragua. When he remarked that "Nicaragua es mi finca" (Nicaragua is my farm), he only stated a fact.[35] *Familism,* or showing strong loyalty to kinsmen, is accepted in Nicaragua as a traditional, proper, and appropriate method for protecting oneself in business and politics. Somoza's greed, however, added an entirely new dimension to *familism.*

In 1957 Luis replaced his father in the Presidential Palace. Anastasio, Jr., ("Tachito") remained in control of the National Guard. His father had thought this son a better soldier than politician since he loved personal gain too much even for a Somoza. (Luis, therefore, went to Louisiana State University for his education, but Tachito attended West Point.) In 1963 Luis ostensibly stepped aside and obeyed constitutional requirements by allowing his father's former foreign minister, René Schick, to become president. The Somozas wielded the real power. In 1966 Schick suddenly died. Anastasio won election in a stormy, bloody campaign. During one anti-Somoza protest the National Guard fired into the crowd, killing forty people. Shortly after, Luis died of a massive heart attack. Having brutally restored order, Tachito ruled Nicaragua with the power his father had once employed.

Thus the Alliance for Progress could move into a nation that appeared to be as politically stable as any in Latin America. The Alliance also could work in an economy undergoing little structural change. It was overwhelmingly dependent on exports of coffee and cotton, and on the U.S. market which took 40 percent of the country's exports in 1962. The United States meanwhile supplied half of Nicaragua's imports. (By the end of the sixties, Japan became Somoza's best customer as the country's cotton exports soared.) These export crops came from giant *latifundia:* these 2 percent of the farms occupied nearly half the tillable land. Rigid class distinctions shaped nearly every part of the nation's life. The rich lived in Managua; that city had 8 percent of the country's population but 74 percent of the sanitary sewers. Only 8 percent of the other Nicaraguans had access to any sewage service. Only 2 percent of those living in rural areas had access to potable water. A particularly striking statistic showed that the agricultural population had shrunk from 67 percent in 1950 to 60 percent in 1963. The decline resulted from increased mechanization on the *latifundia.* Some of the displaced moved into towns and cities, only to discover that Nicaragua's small industry offered few jobs. Others, however, remained behind to claim land for subsistence farming so they at least had a chance to eat. By the mid-sixties, squatters occupied nearly 20 percent of all farmland.[36] Without land titles, they were a target for the oligarchy. Without hope, they soon became an opportunity for the left.

The Alliance moved into this tinderbox with confidence. After all, political stability seemed assured. On that foundation a more equitable economy could be constructed. Between 1961 and 1967, the Alliance authorized nineteen loans totaling $50 million. The Inter-American Development Bank injected another $50 million. Private enterprise did its part, as U.S. direct investment rose from $18 million in 1960 to $75 million ten years later. That investment rose faster in Nicaragua during the 1960s than in any other Central American country and by the end of the decade accounted for 8 percent of the country's gross national product. The result seemed spectacular. The country's GNP rose a dramatic 6.2 percent annually between 1960 and 1970, the third best in all Latin America. Nicaraguans meanwhile formulated plans for tax and land reform. Those plans, however, were stillborn.[37] Nor did the Somozas have to pump them back to life, for as Alliance funds poured in and agricultural exports streamed out, no one—including Washington officials—wanted to threaten progress by trying to make its results equitable.

Alliance dollars disappeared in agricultural projects that almost solely benefited the oligarchy. Exports rose 20 percent annually between 1960 and 1965, yet imports rose so much faster that the country began to pile up a large foreign debt. Its currency, the cordoba, weakened for the first time in decades. The Alliance had aimed at diversifying the economy, but the oligarchy interpreted that to mean the building up of cotton instead of coffee production. It was, according to a U.S. government-sponsored analysis, only "diversification without [a] difference." Cotton stood as highly exposed to roller-coaster world market prices as coffee—and more so in that it could be replaced by synthetic fibers. The cotton boom not only evicted small farmers from their grain-producing lands, but made their labor less necessary when mechanical cotton pickers appeared. Most ominously, as cotton replaced grain in many areas, the country turned from being a net exporter to net importer of this staple food. The Alliance was inadvertently helping the Nicaraguans lose the capacity to feed themselves.[38]

In 1966 and 1967, economic progress, such as it was, virtually stopped. Drought and insects ravaged crops, thus also ravaging the one major source of export earnings. As imports remained high, the balance of payments rapidly worsened. Unemployment spread. In the midst of the crisis Tachito ran for the presidency. This time the opposition united behind one candidate, Conservative Fernando Agüero, who promised land reforms and had once even threatened to divide Somoza's landed empire. As opposition rallies grew in number, the government closed down the major opposition newspaper, *La Prensa*, and jailed its owner, Pedro Joaquín Chamorro, one of the more distinguished and courageous editors in Latin America. Agüero flew to Washington and asked the OAS to supervise the election. The organization replied it could intervene only if Somoza and the United States approved. Neither, of course, had any intention of doing so.[39] As Washington officials sided with Somoza, Tachito won a victory by a three-to-one margin. He had, however, paid a price.

The most dangerous threat in 1967 could not be eliminated by Somoza. A new guerrilla organization, the National Sandinista Liberation Front (FSLN), had begun operations. Founded in Havana and Nicaragua during 1961 and 1962, it took the name of the most famous Nicaraguan nationalist (and the victim of Anastasio, Sr.'s, bloody double cross in 1934) before beginning urban terrorist campaigns in 1966. Its real strength, however, lay in the rural areas where Sandino had been most popular. As late as 1964, the C.I.A. did not consider the FSLN "to be a serious threat to the government." It was, according to the Agency, a "Cuban-supported and Communist-infiltrated subversive group," but it remained apart from the small, innocuous, and illegal Communist party. The C.I.A. believed the five-thousand-man National Guard could handle the problem. Washington officials then tried to ensure that the prediction came true. By 1967, twenty-five U.S. military advisers resided in Nicaragua. The Pentagon supplied over $1.2 million, or 13 percent of Somoza's annual defense budget. U.S. military relations with Nicaragua's forces were perhaps the closest in the hemisphere. Somoza required all of his officers to spend one year at the School of the Americas in the Canal Zone. The School trained more Nicaraguans during the fifties and sixties than officers of any other Latin American nation.[40] The FSLN nevertheless continued to grow.

The Alliance accelerated Nicaragua's revolution. The program raised hopes, but it did little or nothing for peasants and laborers who were displaced by machines, forced to subsist as squatters, or searched for survival in the cities. Unlike Honduras, where many peasants could scratch out a living on small plots of land, only a relatively few Nicaraguans could find land to farm. The country possessed many virtues: a relatively homogeneous population compared with other Central American countries, a developed monetary economy, and a rising gross national product that met and exceeded Alliance targets. It also finally led Central America in coming under the control of revolutionaries.

Guatemala: "5,000 Little Dictators"—and Revolutionaries

During the sixties, U.S. officials feared that Guatemala, not Nicaragua (or El Salvador) might be the first state in the region to fall to revolutionaries. By 1967 it held top rank on the State Department's list of Latin American nations threatened by insurgents. As in Nicaragua, the upheaval that accelerated in 1966 and 1967 occurred after several years of promising political stability, and despite nearly $50 million that the Alliance had poured in to invigorate Guatemalan productivity.

The country was not blessed with talented leadership, but the military and U.S. officials cooperated to build a façade of stability. Ydígoras Fuentes, who had replaced the 1954 counterrevolutionary leader, Castillo Armas, after the latter's assassination in 1957, continued to govern—barely. In early 1960 he bragged too soon that the country was becoming more liberal. The Ubico-type dictatorships had seen their day, he told a U.S. reporter, "as your days of the Wild West when sheriffs carried two guns and a star" had passed into history. Ydígoras added, when "you have one big dictator in the country you automatically have 5,000 little dictators and we don't want to go back to that."[41] He was wrong on both counts.

In late 1960, Ydígoras agreed to Eisenhower's request that Guatemala serve as the training base for an invasion of Cuba. The Cuban exiles who arrived were wealthy and reckless. "I'm sure that more were killed [in their cars] on the roads of Guatemala than were killed at the Bay of Pigs," U.S. Ambassador John Muccio recalled. The North American-controlled invasion and the flaunting of wealth by the exiles angered liberal members of the Guatemalan army who were not overawed by Ydígoras's abilities as a leader. In November, one-third of the army revolted. Ydígoras immediately filled a transport plane with Cubans to fight his own army. That strange confrontation was stopped by Muccio, who ordered the Guatemalan President to return the Cubans and settle the revolt with native forces. Ydígoras dutifully obeyed the order.[42] The rebellion fizzled, but the president had publicly demonstrated both his ineptness and his dependence on the United States. He appeased the army by naming career officers to nine of his ten cabinet posts. That move, however, failed to stop a revolt in 1962 by the air force, which was then virtually destroyed by the army.

In 1963 the hapless Ydígoras allowed Juan Arévalo to return to campaign for the December presidential elections. For showing such bad judgment the military leaders overthrew Ydígoras. Arévalo went back to Mexico. The United States soon recognized the new dictator, Colonel Enrique Peralta. Washington's quick reaction was notable. Evidence later surfaced that U.S. officials had encouraged the *golpe* to keep Arévalo out of power.[43] Relative peace reigned for three years, as Alliance experts moved to lift Guatemala up to the program's targets for economic growth.

In 1966, Peralta presided over a surprisingly free and open election. At last the U.S. investment in the Guatemalan military seemed to be paying off. The election indeed proved to be pivotal in the country's history, but not as North Americans had hoped. The winner, Julio César Méndez Montenegro, was a distinguished lawyer who led a party that identified with the Arévalo-Arbenz revolution of 1944 to 1954. Méndez's victory did little to reassure the hardline military-conservative coalition of public support. Its candidate received only 24 percent of the vote. A left-right split along party lines came into the open. Méndez appreciated how close his administration was to falling into the widening gap. During inaugural ceremonies, and amidst rumors of a military coup, he announced one overriding objective for the next four years: his own survival. That objective was achieved. He became only the second elected president in Guatemalan history to serve a full term. The nation, however, was to pay a terrible price.

Superficially the economic figures seemed auspicious for Méndez's success. Between 1954 and 1970 the United States pumped more dollars into Guatemala than into any other Central American nation. Nearly

$50 million arrived from 1962 to 1966, and after a slow start, U.S. private direct investment jumped from $131 million in 1960 to $186 million in 1970. Over one hundred Peace Corps volunteers also worked in the country. Alliance officials still hoped to prove that the 1954 counterrevolution could create a happier Guatemala. But a 3.2 percent population growth (or a doubling of the population every twenty-two years), kept the critical figure of aid per person to the lowest in Central America.[44]

Conditions were worse for those working on the land, that is, for 80 percent of all laborers. Using U.S. dollars and experts, the government made a pass at land reform between 1955 and 1962, but it did not chalk up even a near miss. The territory distributed to about four thousand families came out of government-owned, undeveloped, inaccessible jungle land. Nine of ten rural families (about two-thirds of the entire population) lived on subsistence farms that they tilled with machetes, hoes, and pointed sticks. One U.S. agricultural economist who worked in Guatemala concluded, "The life of the subsistence farm family is one of poverty, malnutrition, sickness, superstition, and illiteracy." The illiteracy rate rose from 72 percent in 1950 to 74.5 percent a decade later. On the other hand, half the country's land—the best half—was exploited by eleven hundred families.[45] When Méndez tried to meet Alliance demands by passing a minuscule tax reform program, the oligarchs recoiled in such horror that his finance minister who urged the program went into exile overseas.

The Guatemalan rich did not have to face the consequences of paying few taxes. The Alliance saved them by funneling dollars into the country. As large sums flowed into agrarian programs, Guatemala streamlined its banking system to handle the aid. The benefits were negligible, other than, in the words of a critical U.S. Senate staff report, providing profits for the oligarchs and a bureaucratic job "for somebody's wife's second cousin."[46] The government did try to open up Petán, an enormous northeastern jungle area comprising nearly one-third of the country. The results were predictable. Because economic growth depended on exports, and because exports came from large commercial farms, a U.S.-supported plan for Petán turned much of the newly opened area into huge cattle ranches and plantations of 62,000 acres each. Only the peasants lost.[47]

In all, the Alliance provided little progress for Guatemala. As a U.S. Senate study concluded, President Méndez's government "appears to be standing still" on agrarian reform, but "perhaps he has no choice if he wishes to remain in office." When population pressure finally forced peasants into squalid urban areas, they found industrialization developing so slowly that new workers outnumbered available jobs by thirty or forty to one.[48] Capitalists became reluctant to invest because of political uncertainty, oligarchic corruption, unstable currency, and the small size of the market. Foreign investment that did enter went into a few large firms that concentrated on exports, not on developing the small internal market. Foreign-owned firms dominated the country's export trade. Taking control farther out of Guatemalan hands, they further skewed an already lopsided economy.[49] Labor unions were impotent. They either had been destroyed after 1954, or were taken over by the Inter-American Regional Organization of Workers (ORIT), that was U.S.-dominated and aimed at creating a cooperative, nonmilitant movement that caused no problems for investors or oligarchs.

Instead of redistributing wealth, the Alliance funds initially worsened the disparity between rich and poor.[50] U.S. dollars paid for programs the rich should have financed themselves. But even after a decade of dollar inflow, 80 percent of rural children received no schooling, the literacy rate ranked as the lowest in the entire hemisphere outside of Haiti, and the average Guatemalan received one-third the requirements needed for a proper diet. The percentage of the Guatemalan government budget devoted to social services ranked among the lowest of the five Central American nations in 1966. The percentage spent on the military was the highest. The country had money to spend: between 1950 and the mid-sixties its trade balances and gross national product improved. Sixty-six percent of the people, however, actually dropped in average per capita income from $87 a year to $83. The rural population, according to one investigator, was "as wretched and backward as anywhere in Latin America."[51]

These statistics explain why after six years of the Alliance Guatemala ranked first on the State Department's list of hemisphere countries threatened by revolution. The insurgency, erupting initially against Ydígoras in 1960 and 1961, had been led by two army lieutenants, Marco Antonio Yon Sosa and Luis R. Turcios Lima. The United States had trained both at Fort Benning, one reason why the rebels fought the U.S.-trained Guatemalan army to a draw in 1961 and 1962. Between 1963 and 1965, the two leaders separated over ideological differences. Yon Sosa turned to a Castro-type program of allying peasants, workers, and students. He named his group MR-13 (the Revolutionary Movement of November 13, the date of the 1960 coup attempt). Turcios moved into a more conservative coalition with the Guatemalan Communist party. The Communist ideology was so outdated and moribund that it actually planned to work with a "progressive bourgeoisie" to gain power. In Guatemala such a bourgeoisie hardly existed. The urban middle class that did exist enjoyed profitable economic and familial ties with the oligarchs.[52]

Turcios died in a 1966 automobile accident. Yon Sosa suffered setbacks until his movement seemed paralyzed in 1966. His mere existence, however, worried Washington officials and the oligarchs. Insurgencies occurred mostly in the southern and eastern parts of the country where *ladinos* (of Spanish culture) predominated; if Yon Sosa's influence spread to the Indian-populated north and west, the revolution would take a radical turn (as it indeed did when the Indians began to organize a decade later). Yon Sosa's copying of Castro's model did not mean that Cubans controlled the movement. A U.S.-Senate investigation in 1968 found no Cuban connection, other than the borrowing of Castro's political model.[53] For oligarchs and conservative military officers, however, Méndez's election in 1966 and his failure to eradicate Yon Sosa signaled a warning. The president seemed overly cautious, too liberal, and insufficiently pro-military. Right-wing groups decided to take action.

The U.S. military provided help of an unusual but essential kind: it developed the Guatemalan army into an institutional force that could use modern North American weapons. The process had begun in the mid-fifties when U.S. advisers took a rag-tag force and through reorganization, the teaching of political as well as military tactics, and the development of a centralized communications and transport system, created a mobile, more efficient army that had growing institutional pride and allegiance. This transformation explains why the military stood ready to govern the country in 1963, and why the United States accepted its rule.

The transformation further explains why the military demonstrated some ingenuity in trying to crush Yon Sosa's guerrillas after 1967. By that time the Guatemalan officers wanted only supplies, not advice, from the United States. They were determined to fight their own war their own way, including using counterterrorism and deputized vigilantes (little more than heavily armed gunmen) who worked at the village level. The vigilantes, deputized or not, worked for the highest bidder, who usually turned out to be the local oligarch. The army thus created a band of terrorists to kill or otherwise force villagers into compliance with government wishes. A military whose officers before 1954 had been attached to individual politicians became by the sixties an institutional force dedicated to its own preservation and prosperity. Its political tentacles reached down to the village level. From this point through at least the early eighties, Washington officials expressed severe reservations about the tactics and ambitions of the Guatemalan army, but they could do less and less about it.[54] They were losing control of their own monster.

The Guatemalan leaders reacted on two levels. Officially the army launched an all-out, terrorist offensive. The commander, Carlos Arana Osorio, received advice from U.S. Military Attaché Colonel John Webber and nearly a thousand U.S. Green Beret Special Forces.[55] The Pentagon spent more than $12 million annually during the late sixties to develop Arana's six-thousand-man force. (At one point in the mid-sixties, Yon Sosa had about forty regular troops.) Arana contained but failed to destroy the revolutionaries, although he killed as many as 8,000 peasants in his pacification program.

On a less official level, the repression was even more brutal. With President Méndez's consent, and despite constitutional prohibitions, private right-wing groups formed their own units to murder students, Indians, and labor leaders suspected of sympathizing with the rebels. At least twenty so-called anti-Communist armies appeared; the most notorious were *Mano Blanca* (the White Hand), and *Ojo por Ojo* (Eye for an Eye). These groups included off-duty police and retired military men. They soon moved beyond killing suspected revolutionaries to murdering leading members of Méndez's own party. The leftist forces responded in kind, although more selectively and without the torture used by the conservatives. Twenty-eight U.S. soldiers were killed. That figure, lost amidst the casualty lists coming in from Vietnam, indicated how deeply the Johnson administration had become involved. In January 1968, guerrillas killed two high U.S. advisers, Colonel Webber and Lieutenant Commander Ernest A. Munro. In August, terrorists murdered U.S. Ambassador John Gordon Mein. In 1970 the West German Ambassador was kidnapped, then shot, when the government refused to release political prisoners. Violence was so common that when the archbishop of Guatemala fell victim to kidnappers, few people seemed to care. "It was like athlete's foot in a leper colony," said one observer. "One hardly noticed it."[56]

North Americans certainly paid little attention to the horrors. In 1968, however, their attention briefly focused on Guatemala, not only because of the three U.S. officials' deaths, but because several Maryknoll priests and a nun publicly defended the guerrillas. Headquartered in Ossining, New York, the Maryknoll Fathers supported more than one thousand missionaries in Latin America. Unlike other parts of the Church, the organization worked at the grass-roots level. The three young workers were nonrevolutionaries when they went to Guatemala. The poverty and its new bedfellow, violence, changed them rapidly. When ordered home, one priest and a nun refused, married each other, and joined the guerrillas. The other missionary, Blase Bonpane, came home but then told reporters that "Violence is institutionalized in Guatemala." He had seen "a pre-Vietnam. I see napalm. I see Green Berets." Bonpane wanted the United States to leave the country. "Then we'd see what a real people's revolution is. We have intervened too many places, too many times."[57]

By 1968, U.S. policies had collided with the problem that caused so much trouble in the seventies and eighties: the Guatemalan army and the conservative class, whom the North Americans thought they were protecting, turned on their protectors. Filling the vacuum left by the disintegrated political parties, the army developed interests that diverged from the Alliance's programs. Becoming major landholders themselves, Guatemalan military officers formed closer relationships with the more reactionary economic factions. They set out to overturn Méndez's regime. The president saved himself by giving the army total freedom to attack its enemies (hence the bloodbath of 1967 through

1970), and fired his British-trained finance minister, Alberto Fuentes Mohr, whose tax reform programs Alliance officials had welcomed. The Alliance's blessing turned out to be the kiss of death. Fuentes Mohr observed that the conservatives could not decide "whether my tax proposals have originated in Washington or Moscow." When Ambassador Mein was gunned down, observers could not be certain who had killed him, the right or left, until the guerrillas boasted about the assassination. One North American critic wrote, "Such is the bankruptcy of [U.S.] policy in Guatemala that we are hated with equal intensity by both sides."[58] The dilemma of the eighties had emerged in the late sixties.

Guatemala was moving out of control. Arana, the new hero of the oligarchs, won the presidency in 1970. Division among the left-liberal parties (which received a majority of the votes) allowed the triumph of a right-wing that a C.I.A. study had called "the most extreme and unyielding in the Hemisphere."[59] Arana promised no new taxes, then launched a counterterrorist campaign that claimed hundreds of lives. A U.S. Senate study in 1971 summarized the quandary of North American policies in Guatemala between 1954 and 1970: the country is a textbook case "of the wisdom of the adage that it's easier to get into a bear trap than to get out of it." The report noted the ignorance of North Americans, including some of the U.S. citizens in the field:

> In response to a question as to what he conceived his job to be, a member of the U.S. Military Group in Guatemala replied instantly that it was to make the Guatemalan Armed Forces as efficient as possible. The next question as to why this was in the interest of the United States was followed by a long silence while he reflected on a point which had apparently never occurred to him.[60]

El Salvador: The Alliance's Proud "Model"

Immediately to the south, El Salvador seemed to offer a quite different story. The country became the pride of the Alliance. Kennedy and Johnson ensured that it received more Alliance funds ($63 million between 1962 and 1965) than any other Central American country. In 1964 the

C.I.A. called it "one of the hemisphere's most stable, progressive republics."[61] By 1980, however, the country was devastated by a revolution that had claimed thousands of civilian victims and drew ever deeper U.S. involvement. A terrible change had occurred in those sixteen years. The taproot of that change developed with the Alliance programs of the sixties.

As in Nicaragua, Guatemala, and Honduras, the plan for El Salvador was carried out by military regimes close to the oligarchs. The governments guaranteed stable, if not always peaceful, political institutions. As late as 1967 a U.S. Senate-sponsored analysis concluded that El Salvador, Nicaragua, and Honduras ranked among the most militaristic governments in the hemisphere, but "the 20th-century popular revolutionary stirrings by which most of the rest of Latin America has been deeply affected have been felt" in these countries "hardly at all."[62] Military force apparently equaled political peace.

After a 1948 coup, military strongmen had ruled El Salvador through the fifties. In 1960, President José María Lemus, who had made a political career of pointing out Communist threats (even though the party was outlawed), declared a thirty-day state of seige after allegedly uncovering a "wide-spread Communist plot." His evidence consisted of a student protest against his outlawing of political parties. Military officers jailed the students, then invaded the sanctity of the university to tear it apart, rape female students, and kill a librarian. The student protests grew. Lemus ordered the army to open fire. At that point moderate military officers overthrew the president before he could cause a full-scale revolution. The new junta promised to implement the mild reforms promised during 1948 through 1950 by relatively liberal generals, and to hold elections in 1962.

Eisenhower found the promises insufficient. He withheld recognition, apparently because the U.S. Ambassador in San Salvador, Thorsten Kalijarvi, believed several junta members admired Castro. U.S. nonrecognition condemned the moderate reformers (very moderate) to political oblivion, and in late January the right-wing officers overthrew the junta. They pledged to take tough actions against the students, cut relations with Castro, and warmly welcome foreign investment. The U.S. military mission apparently encouraged the countercoup. Kennedy recognized the new regime, which then perpetuated itself by establishing its own political party and choosing Colonel Julio A. Rivera as president in a corrupt election. Rivera maintained order for five years until handpicking his successor, Colonel Fidel Sánchez Hernández, whom the oligarchs also found acceptable and who consequently became president in 1967.[63]

Not only did U.S. monetary aid, fifty-five Peace Corps volunteers, and a million dollars per year of military assistance enter the small country during the sixties. North American investment also increased until its $34 million represented 65 percent of all foreign investment and strongly influenced such infrastructure sectors as transportation, oil refining, and electric power. Until this time, the Salvadoran oligarchs had been little more than lukewarm to foreign capitalists who wanted to operate in the country. The oligarchs generated enough capital to control their own banking and mercantile systems, and besides they recalled bad experiences with foreigners—even North Americans—during the post–World War I era. But the Alliance changed that: half of all foreign investment since 1900 was made during the sixties. The Salvadorans responded with new tax laws, promises of land reform, and one of the highest economic growth rates in the hemisphere—a rate that touched an extraordinary 12 percent in 1964 and 1965. Hundreds of new industries (especially in food processing, textiles, and chemicals) sprang up until, by the mid-sixties, the country possessed the largest number of any Central American nation. El Salvador, the Johnson administration proudly announced, was "a model for the other Alliance countries."[64]

But as with Nicaragua and Guatemala, the Alliance's figures disguised ugly reality, including a jammed-in population of three million living in Central America's smallest country and growing at a high rate of 3.2 percent. Another reality was that the reforms did not touch the oligarchs. The reforms did redistribute the new wealth in the country more equitably than in most other Latin American nations, but there was a good deal more to distribute. The power and wealth of the oligarchs burgeoned with the Alliance. (Ironically, the oligarchs had so hated the plan at first, that they had bought television time to claim that it was "Communist inspired.") Under U.S. pressure the government set minimum wages (one dollar per day) and established health centers which so infuriated the oligarchs that they protested directly to U.S. Ambassador Murat Williams. A former State Department official, now representing U.S. corporations, flew to San Salvador and, in Williams's words, "quite rudely told me I should go to the Casa Presidencial to bang on the desk and tell the President to slow down the reforms." North American leverage on the government was taken for granted by both sides.[65]

But the oligarchs quickly learned how to turn the Alliance to their profit. Their wealth multiplied as they moved into the new industrial-mercantile businesses that the program helped build. Certain family names appeared repeatedly: the Alvarez wealth came from coffee *fincas*, coffee-exporting businesses, a commercial bank, and new factories including one making auto parts; the Regalados made their money from an automobile agency, an investment company, a soluble coffee plant, sugar refineries, and a commercial bank, as well as from coffee and sugar growing; the Quiñónez family discovered large profits in a brewery and plants for making bags, container caps, and materials for tire recapping as well as in the traditional areas of coffee and sugar growing.[66] For the most part, the new industries remained in a few, tightly clasped family hands, as did the coffee and sugar plantations, regardless of the influx of foreign capital. When a C.I.A. analysis reported the oligarchs' sudden interest in the Alliance, it should have noted also that their interest focused on new investments that further concentrated Salvadoran wealth and power.[67]

When the country attempted to diversify its export base, and rely less on coffee, disastrous results occurred. Throughout the twentieth century, land under cultivation had actually increased, yet staple food supplies for the poor had become smaller. This paradoxical trend accelerated in the fifties and sixties until, amidst a booming agricultural economy, Salvadorans ranked among the world's five most malnourished peoples. The reason for the paradox, of course, was oligarchic control of land on which to grow export crops of coffee and—in a fit of diversification—sugar and cotton for the North American and Japanese markets.

Salvadorans did not need to be hungry. The oligarchy's interests and the needs of the international marketplace, nevertheless, dictated a hungry peasantry. That hunger grew as sugar exports jumped over 1,000 percent during the sixties. The oligarchs drove peasants and tenant farmers off their plots to obtain new land. Only when cotton and coffee prices fell, and some lands temporarily returned to staple production, did Salvadorans have more food available. But that did not mean the bulk of the poor possessed money to buy the food. When cotton prices declined, for example, and land was turned back to grain, the grain did not necessarily go to peasants. Rice and other grain crops were exported while poor Salvadorans lacked money to buy the food—particularly since government-imposed price supports kept food prices high.[68]

By 1969, 300,000 Salvadorans—one in every eight citizens—had fled this "model" Alliance nation to find food and work in neighboring Honduras. During June of that year, however, the Hondurans began expelling the immigrants. In July, war broke out between the two nations. It lasted less than a week, but several thousand people on both sides were killed, and 100,000 left homeless. It also threatened the destruction of the decade-old Central American Common Market under whose auspices El Salvador and Guatemala particularly had found markets in neighboring states. (The growing economic imbalance within CACM, in El Salvador's favor, had already undermined the group.) About 130,000 Salvadorans returned home to put enormous pressure on the land.[69] President (and Colonel) Fidel Sánchez Hernández immediately pledged agrarian reforms, but as usual nothing happened. (The colonel had made the same pledge during his 1967 campaign, but once in office declared candidly he would not touch the estates: "We simply cannot afford to divide up the only wealth this country possesses.")[70] The oligarchy was in no mood for a share-the-wealth program.

In 1964, the C.I.A. had discounted the "little guerrilla activity in the country," and added that "most organized political elements are opposed to subversion and violence."[71] After six years of spectacular economic growth, however, the first important armed rebels appeared in 1970.[72] The oligarchs and U.S. officials naturally turned for help to the Salvadoran army. That force had long been recruited from villages that were mere annexes to coffee plantations. Many officers had advanced as the protégés of coffee oligarchs. Those origins, as well as the lack of education (Chilean army officers, for example, had twelve to sixteen years of schooling, Salvadoran six to ten), made the army the oligarchs' personal enforcer. Besides training Salvadoran officers at the Canal

Zone's School of the Americas, the United States posted twenty-two military advisers in El Salvador in 1968. At times, North American pressure verged on the absurd. Ambassador Murat Williams complained to the State Department in 1963 and 1964 that more U.S. officers worked with the embassy's air force mission than there were aviators in the entire Salvadoran Air Force. A deputy of Secretary of State Dean Rusk replied that he sympathized with criticism of such overkill, "but we can't do anything. You have annoyed the Pentagon by making the suggestion" of withdrawing some of the officers.[73]

The decade of the Alliance ended in El Salvador as the decade of revolution began. The country that Johnson believed to be the "model" for the Alliance became a model for violent Central American revolutions.

Honduras: The Transformation of a Banana Republic

In 1950 Honduras lagged behind the other Central American nations in economic development and (except for Costa Rica) in revolutionary activities, but by 1970 it had closed the gap in both categories. Long considered a mere "banana republic," Honduras turned into one of the most fascinating and quickly changing countries in the hemisphere. In almost every respect, the nation revealed how a relatively simple land could become more complex, restless, and, by 1969, involved in a class war that expanded into regional conflict. The effect of the Alliance was determining.

Some aspects of Honduran life, of course, never changed. They served as the constant background against which the new drama unfolded. President Ramón Villeda Morales declared that his was "the country of the 70's—70 percent illiteracy, 70 percent illegitimacy, 70 percent rural populations, 70 percent avoidable deaths." During the middle of the Alliance decade a visitor traveling through isolated Indian villages learned that the inhabitants "had not heard of World War II, much less of the first—or the possibility of a third."[74] The country's 2.2 million population continued to grow at a rate slightly over 3 percent a year, or nearly as fast as El Salvador's. The nation possessed large unsettled areas, but only one-quarter of the land was worth farming. Poverty and primitivism pervaded, especially in rural sections where only one in four peasants farmed with a plow, infant mortality was among the highest in the world, and half the couples who lived together had not been blessed in marriage. Expenses ran too high, or priests and civilian authorities were too scarce, or personal mobility seemed too threatened for formal vows. The government recognized this unchangeable part of life by giving the children of such informal unions the same rights as those produced by legal marriages.

In 1954, however, the entire country had reverberated with sudden change. The banana workers conducted an astonishingly successful strike against United Fruit. It marked a historic turn. The society loosened and even began to liberalize as certain workers' rights were recognized for the first time. The liberalization became known as "Villedismo," after Dr. Villeda Morales who emerged as president in 1957 in the wake of a series of coups and countercoups that rippled out from the 1954 strike. By sponsoring a labor code, social security, and even agrarian reform, he changed sociopolitical relationships. He wanted to do more, for he saw himself in the liberal tradition of Arbenz in Guatemala and Figueres of Costa Rica. Unfortunately, Villeda Morales had neither Arbenz's intellectual drive nor Figueres's political sense. By the early sixties, the Honduran slowed change to preserve the interests of both the small middle class that provided key support, and the United States whose citizens controlled 95 percent of all foreign investment, including the country's infrastructure and vital exports.

His values (liberal reforms but an acute sensitivity to private property rights) seemed to make him a natural for the Alliance. The U.S. Ambassador in Tegucigalpa, Charles R. Burrows, suggested that Villeda Morales set the example for other Alliance partners by breaking off relations with Castro. "It might lead to something happening in Cuba. Who knows?" Burrows observed. Villeda Morales organized a large anti-Castro demonstration, then told the press that because the people obviously demanded it, he must cut Cuban ties. "Really he was rather acute about the whole thing," Burrows recalled.[75]

But Villeda Morales became too acute about the Alliance's objectives. At the 1961 Punta del Este meeting, he took the Kennedy administration's rhetoric so seriously that he drafted an agrarian reform law which threatened the massive uncultivated lands owned by United Fruit and Standard Fruit. Burrows quickly told the Honduran president not to allow the law to pass until the State Department gave its approval, an interesting demand to be made by one sovereign country to another. The president, however, signed the legislation before Washington gave its signal. Standard Fruit said it could live with the law, but United Fruit retaliated. It stopped expanding its operations. Jobs were lost and, as Burrows later remarked, "people by that time realized what the company meant to Honduras." Villeda Morales was then summoned to Miami, where he and UFCO worked out a deal that sharply cut back the law's effect. United Fruit had forced the Honduran president to retreat after the U.S. Ambassador failed.[76]

Burrows encountered other troubles as well. He and Villeda Morales wanted Washington to sponsor low-cost housing and sanitation projects; they were willing to accept any improvement over the dirt floors common to peasants' shelters. But Alliance planners, Burrows recalled, "always had to add on these aluminum spouts and copper fitting and make sure the ceiling was regulation height."[77] Costs became so high that few could afford the improvements. The Alliance also ran into patriotism. Perhaps because they did not care to be known as citizens of a banana republic, Hondurans fought back when the Alliance tried to standardize textbooks and teaching methods throughout Central America. The government finally passed laws that texts must be highly patriotic and all teachers native-born Hondurans. In the end, the Alliance's books became only supplementary reading.[78]

By 1963 changes were occurring rapidly enough so that Villeda Morales's days in power were numbered. Alliance officials, the small middle class, the banana companies, and the U.S. Ambassador all had growing doubts about an Honduran president raising such issues as agrarian reform and patriotic textbooks. The army had even sharper doubts, especially since the president had formed his own 2,500-man Civil Guard to keep the army a safe distance from the presidential residence. Villeda Morales could not constitutionally succeed himself. He played by the rules when he supported another candidate, then began to disarm his Civil Guard. The decision to disarm turned out to be an error, especially after his candidate in the Liberal party took anti-military positions. Fearing a Liberal victory, the army struck ten days before the election, "slaughtered" many of the Civil Guard "in half an hour or hour," as Burrows remembered, and named the army commander, Oswaldo López, as the new president.[79]

The effect on Washington of this coup in an out-of-the-way Central American country was electric. John Kennedy and Alliance officials became furious; the Honduran coup was the last in a series—Peru, Guatemala, the Dominican Republic had preceded it—in which the military had overthrown elected governments in 1962 and 1963. Oswaldo López promised new elections, even a new constitution, but Kennedy was not moved. He condemned military *golpes* as "self-defeating and defeating for the hemisphere," warned that "of course dictatorships are the seedbeds from which communism ultimately springs up," and broke relations with the Honduran regime. López was to be made an example for overly ambitious military officers. Kennedy cut off the Honduran while working with military dictatorships in Vietnam and South Korea, Arthur Schlesinger wrote later, because "the United States had special obligations within the western hemisphere" to consolidate "within the framework of democratic institutions . . . a system of individual liberty and social justice."[80] The Honduran conservatives had heard this before. "You'll be back in six months," they told the departing Burrows. "And we *were* back, of course," the ambassador recalled, "and nothing much was accomplished."[81]

U.S. officials had no choice, really. For along with the banana-workers' strike, another event in the fifties had changed Honduran society: the first political involvement by a professionalized army. Until that decade, the military had largely been a series of guerrilla bands who, if they gained power, gave their officers civilian jobs. World War II and the advent of U.S. military training changed the guerrilla leaders to professional soldiers. A trained, institutionalized fighting force appeared, moreover, at the same time the rapid decline of the traditional political parties—the Liberal and National—left a political vacuum. The new army intervened for the first time in national politics during the crises in 1954 and 1957 when, uncertain of its own power, it helped Villeda Morales gain the presidency. The military, however, exacted a price.

The new 1957 Constitution required that presidential orders to the military were to be obeyed only if they were issued by the chief of the armed forces. The military could constitutionally disobey civilian commands it considered unconstitutional. The president also lost power over military appointments and assignments. By 1963, the army was confident it could govern and refused to be neutralized by the president's Civil Guard.

General (and in 1965, President) Oswaldo López took control of the government. In an underdeveloped country, the military had become the most developed political institution.[82] The United States played a vital role in fashioning that army. In the 1954 agreement that established the military relationship, the United States promised military aid and in return Honduras promised to open for U.S. exploitation any "raw and semi-processed materials required by the United States of America as a result of deficiencies or potential deficiencies in its own resources."[83] (That provision and other parts of the treaty resembled clauses in the 1903 pact in which the United States made a virtual colony out of Panama.) Both sides obviously stood to gain from the deal, especially when the Honduran side consisted primarily of military officers. Consequently, in 1963 Washington officials had no choice but to recognize this U.S. creation, for without the army the Alliance had no chance to succeed in Honduras.

The post-1963 Alliance assumed a different form in Honduras. Resembling the larger change in Latin American policy when Johnson replaced Kennedy, increased amounts of U.S. private capital appeared in Honduras as the López regime rolled back the Villeda Morales labor and welfare programs and provided inviting opportunities for foreign investors. The government paid special attention to the labor unions. When one union tried to strike in 1968 because the government imposed a 20 percent tax on consumer goods, López locked up the labor leaders and declared a thirty-day state of seige to "combat subversion." When newspapers tried to report these activities, the president closed some down and imprisoned leading editors.[84]

U.S. direct investment declined in Honduras during 1960 and 1961, rose during 1962 and 1963, and then doubled between 1963 and 1971 to well over $200 million (in book value). Despite this inflow, U.S. companies took more out of Honduras after 1963 than they put in: in 1968 the outflow reached $22.4 million and in 1969, $17.7 million. The country exported more goods than it imported, yet its current account balance swam ever deeper in red ink until it threatened to drown amidst the benefits of the Alliance for Progress.[85] The United States continued to control the banana industry, the largest mining companies, and key parts of the infrastructure including the two most important railroads.

The two largest commercial banks, *Atlantide* and Bank of Honduras, came under the respective control of Chase Manhattan in 1967 and National City Bank of New York in 1965. In an essay for *Foreign Affairs* in 1966, David Rockefeller, chairman of Chase Manhattan Bank, applauded the post-1963 "change" in the Alliance that placed less stress on "rapid and revolutionary social change and on strictly government-to-government assistance." Rockefeller strongly approved of the Johnson-Mann emphasis on private investment. He believed that "a more favorable business climate" would bring about "more meaningful social reform" and a "rising standard of living."[86] Rockefeller's thesis was contradicted by events in Honduras. The post-1963 changes led to a stripping of the nation's wealth by foreign investors, the Hondurans' increased loss of control over their own banking and productive system, and major defeats for Honduran liberals. If the symbol of "Villedismo" was the failed agrarian reform law, the symbol of the López regime was, as Ambassador Burrows recalled, the president of Standard Fruit and the vice-president of United Fruit sitting in the places of honor when Oswaldo López took the presidential oath. Foreign dignitaries and the diplomatic corps settled for the less prestigious seats. "Gosh, we're going to hear about this," Burrows thought at the time. But nothing happened.[87] U.S. power was taken for granted. Nor did many bother to dress up that power with the rationales offered by Rockefeller.

By 1968 such rationales were bankrupt. A crisis in the Honduran economy infected politics and the society. The investment boom in commercial agriculture (especially in cattle and cotton) had led to an illegal expansion of large haciendas over peasant-tilled lands. The oligarchs' agents simply strung barbed wire around the area they wanted, then expelled any families found inside the barbed-wire compound. Peasants who tried to take wood from these areas to cook food were jailed on order of the new owner. The peasants were trapped on four sides: their own lands disappeared, the U.S.-owned fruit companies controlled much of the remaining soil, few jobs existed in the towns, and the Salvadorans—squeezed out of their own country—streamed into Honduras to compete for the little decent land that remained. Contrary to Rockefeller's assurances, moreover, the new investment failed to raise the per capita gross national product figures to Alliance targets. Even if it had, the distribution of the wealth had grown so uneven that the 60 percent of the labor force dependent on agriculture would have received precious little of that wealth. Unemployment rose 25 percent between 1961 and 1967, not counting the 150,000 coffee workers who earned wages only during the harvest. Most could not compete for better-paying and more complex jobs because 90 percent of the labor force had never finished primary school. The military regime did nothing effective to lower that astonishing figure. A labor movement, AIFLD, tried to keep workers quiet, especially those on banana plantations. AIFLD, the American Institute for Free Labor Development, had been created by the Alliance for Progress and the North American AFL-CIO in 1962. It received sponsorship from North American investors led by Peter Grace whose family's Grace Lines had a century of Latin American experience. He was joined by Exxon, Shell, ITT, IBM, United Fruit and eighty-five other large corporations. But economic conditions in Honduras became too difficult for even AIFLD's supporters to handle.[88]

Two events triggered the crisis. First, in 1968 the government decided to impose higher sales and consumption taxes that were nonprogressive (thus favoring the oligarchy), and added as much as 20 percent to the prices of some goods. A skidding government budget required new income, and this device troubled the rich least. As noted, the president used force to quell the strikes and riots that resulted from the new tax.

Second, national campesino movements emerged to fight barbed-wire and other incursions by the oligarchy. The new groups reoccupied land in force. The landowners promptly organized FENAGH (National Federation of Agriculturalists and Cattle Ranchers of Honduras) to discipline the peasants. FENAGH focused on attempts to turn poor Hondurans against the incoming poor Salvadorans. This tactic should have been effective since the latter took jobs and land from the former. But it failed. In a surprising turn, the campesinos banded together to protect each other. In one of many defiant gestures, the peasants moved back into their former lands in Choluteca, announcing that the enemy was not Salvadoran, but their own country's system. "Hunger obliges us to act," they declared, "since we have children to feed and women who do not even have anything to clothe themselves."[89]

The battle lines formed between rich and poor. The rich ordered large numbers of the 300,000 Salvadorans back to their own country. This order formed the context in which the "soccer war" of mid-1969 erupted. When a soccer match between El Salvador and Honduras ended in a bloody riot, López's government seized the opportunity to expel all Salvadorans. War broke out between the two nations. It ended after both sides suffered heavy casualties and the Central American Common Market began to break down. But FENAGH achieved its objectives. Ruthlessly expanding its export-crop operations into land long held by peasants, FENAGH finally succeeded in destroying united peasant opposition during the war against El Salvador.

FENAGH, however, had to share the benefits with the already autonomous and virtually supreme Honduran army. The Alliance had set out to develop Honduran society, but ended by creating a highly efficient military force. The Alliance helped make such a force necessary, for the program's failure to diversify the Honduran economy led to an expansion of an export economy. That expansion in turn took lands from campesinos and set the class war in motion. The Alliance's post-1963 emphasis on private investment worsened the growing crisis, for it increased the nation's indebtedness, lessened Honduras's control over its own economy, paradoxically pulled wealth from the country while doubling U.S. investment, and—in all—helped create conditions that could lead to revolution.[90] In 1970, Villeda Morales's Liberal party, on which the Kennedy administration had placed such high hopes nearly a decade before, divided. Younger, more radical members drove the party's old guard out of power.

Costa Rica: Degradation of a Democracy

The model for the Alliance for Progress should have been Costa Rica, not El Salvador. Nowhere in Central America was political democracy healthier. In building the nation after 1948, José Figueres ("Don Pepé") and his *Partido Liberacíon Nacional* (PLN) exemplified the kind of liberalism the Kennedy administration hoped Latin Americans would emulate. Costa Ricans unabashedly expressed pro-U.S. feelings. In neighboring Panama only one-third of the elite high school students admitted to liking North Americans, but in the San José area the figure ran as high as two-thirds, and virtually no one disliked Yankees (the remainder were "indifferent"). Three-quarters of the Costa Ricans polled even believed "the United Fruit Company is beneficial" for their country; the same number agreed that Castro's revolution "is a bad example for Latin America."[91] For beleaguered Washington officials, Costa Rica seemed almost too good to be true.

By the late sixties, however, the nation's government found itself immersed in problems. The threat appeared more subtle in that it did not involve revolutionary insurgent movements, but was equally fundamental because it weakened the political economy's foundations. The United States was again deeply involved in the process. U.S. power in Costa Rican affairs was awesome, as Kennedy learned during 1961 and 1962. The president publicly said a few nice words about the then-retired Figueres, and the San José government, controlled by an anti-Figueres party, became deeply angry. In late 1961, U.S. Ambassador Raymond Tolles feared that Figueres might pull a *golpe* if his PLN lost the 1962 presidential election. Tolles wanted U.S. ships to sit off the coast as a warning to Figueres that gunboat diplomacy still lived. The State Department shared Tolles's concern, but believed such heavy-handedness was unnecessary. Non-recognition could whip Figueres back into line, the Department told the ambassador, then it bragged that "El Salvador provides a recent example that these pressures [nonrecognition as a means of removing an unwanted regime] do work in Central America."[92] T.R. and Wilson had long since disappeared, but the system still functioned: a mere State Department paper on recognition could bring down Central American governments.

In this case the paper never had to be written because Figueres's candidate, Francisco José Orlich Bolmarcich, won the election. Orlich continued expanding the nation's vast welfare system (with U.S. emergency help), and led the country in overcoming several natural calamities. A calamity that Orlich could not master was the 4.5 percent annual population growth, perhaps the world's highest. Nor, even with welfare programs, could he reduce an infant mortality rate (eighty-six per thousand births) that ranked among the worst in the hemisphere.[93] Early in Orlich's term, the economy soured as coffee and sugar prices dropped. A major cause of the drop was the enormous U.S. influence over Costa Rica. Kennedy had inadvertently caused problems when he vastly increased the country's share of the rich U.S. sugar market. The president had clearly stated that the quota would last only for one year, but the Costa Ricans multiplied their sugar production, lost the U.S. market in 1962, and panicked. Kennedy nevertheless refused to continue the higher quota.[94]

With the Alliance's help, and with the possibility of selling within the newly established Central American Common Market, Orlich's government did try to diversify by building light industry (especially food processing and textiles), a large fertilizer plant, and—with French aid—an oil refinery. These industries and the rise of coffee and banana prices put a glow on the country's economic system between 1962 and 1966. By the late sixties, however, an ominous sign appeared: the expansion of staple export crops was fundamentally changing the landholding and production system, the system that had long undergirded the nation's democracy as well as its prosperity. Coffee lands became so consolidated that fewer than 2 percent of the growers produced half the crop. Large estates in the coffee highlands resembled those that had distorted Guatemala's and Nicaragua's society. The banana plantation area tripled between 1963 and 1967 to over 40,000 acres. The expansion was healthy in that it involved small farmers who could sell their crop to United Fruit or another major distributor. But it posed dangers in that the farms grew more bananas and less corn. As this staple of the diet began to disappear, the country had to import two-and-one-half times more grain in 1968 than it did at the start of the decade. The Costa Rican trade balance suffered severely, particularly when banana prices—over which the growers had no control—slumped.[95]

Many Costa Ricans had no choice at all. Nearly three-quarters of the peasants were little more than landless laborers. By 1967 squatters so threatened private landholders that the government tried to move the poor into nationally held land. When that failed because the territory was so inaccessible, San José authorities tried to act as referees between the rich and poor. But the squatter problem grew in the seventies. Nor did organized unions make important advances under the Alliance. During the forties, Costa Rica had the most active union movement in the region. As Figueres consolidated his party's power after 1949, he outlawed the most radical union group and co-opted the moderates into his PLN. Workers won minimum wage laws and other benefits, but they lost every collective-bargaining contract except one that covered a single group of banana workers. Minimum wage laws were not enforced. By the sixties, "it was almost as if the entire labor movement had ceased to exist," in the words of one observer.[96]

Costa Rica was living beyond its means, and peasants and union workers were beginning to pay a price. The country's high literacy rate, for example, was attained by devoting half the national budget to education. That budget rose with the birthrate, and as the economy slowed in the late sixties the country ran up the highest national debt in Central America. A deepening financial crisis in 1968, continuing into 1969, prevented government workers from receiving paychecks and prisoners from being regularly fed. Washington officials expressed growing displeasure. They had given Costa Rica special favors, including the largest of all Central American foreign loan authorizations in 1961, but after 1965 they saw their former Alliance showcase displaying shoddy goods. U.S. policy-makers cut back loans and demanded fiscal restraint. Thus the hemisphere watched the spectacle of North Americans pouring millions of dollars into Nicaragua because Somoza imposed, by brute force, a conservative fiscal policy on his people, while the Costa Rican government was publicly disciplined by Washington for educating and providing large-scale welfare programs for its people. The Alliance had not been designed to produce such irony.[97]

With the economic crisis inevitably came a political counterpart. Figueres's PLN split in 1968 when younger members declared, "We aspire to have Socialism as an organizing economic and social system . . . without renouncing the use of violence if it be necessary." The words were quite different from those recorded by the pollster who had talked with the elite high school students in the early sixties. Younger Costa Ricans had become frustrated with an economy that was uncontrollable and increasingly dominated by an elite, while their leading political parties were personalistic and did little to explore alternative ideologies or programs.[98] Figueres controlled the rebellion by threatening to quit the PLN and establish a new party to support his run for the presidency in 1970. Enough younger PLN members obeyed his wishes so that Don Pepé won a third term.

But not even Figueres could deal with the fundamental economic challenges that appeared. He tried to make the best of them, and in 1972 completed a large coffee deal with the Soviet Union. The Alliance for Progress had not been established to produce that result either.

The Central American Common Market: A Last Chance

Figueres merely followed a hallowed economic postulate: when existing markets cannot absorb your glut of goods, find new markets. A remarkable variation of that view developed during the sixties when Central Americans pioneered the creation of a common market for newly emerging nations. Most western conventional wisdom held that when capitalism in small areas became unstable, it could be saved by extending the area in which the capitalists operated. The United States had accomplished this, somewhat miraculously, in 1787 by outlawing state tariffs and creating a huge common market in which goods, capital, and labor could cross state borders without suffering discrimination. The West European Common Market of the nineteen-fifties repeated that miracle. But the process had yet to be tried in such a poverty-stricken, class-stratified society as Central America.

During the fifties, economists led by Raul Prebisch and W. Arthur Lewis argued that Latin America could break through its dependency and poverty by using "industrialization by invitation"—that is, creating a large tariff-free zone (bounded by a common tariff to keep out certain competitive goods) to attract investment and thus diversify the one- or two-crop economies. Such a policy would also replace expensive imports with the zone's own goods. This economic cooperation could lead to political cooperation, perhaps even integration. It was a beautiful theory.[99]

The Central Americans first discussed such ideas in July 1950. They made detailed studies, resulting in a 1960 agreement, the Managua Treaty, in which four of the nations pledged to remove tariffs on nearly all goods produced in the region, and to create a common tariff for goods brought into Central America. Besides the customs union, the nations planned a more radical and interesting idea: an Integration of Industries Plan in which governments—not the marketplace—would help determine placement of industry and ensure that the benefits were spread as evenly as possible to all the countries. Costa Rica remained apart from the Managua agreements, but within two years even it joined the Central American Common Market (CACM). The great experiment had begun. If successful it would reduce the region's dependence on foreign trade, allow the vast number of landless unemployed laborers to find work in manufacturing, and bring in fresh capital and new technology from industrialized nations.

The planning phase received no help from U.S. officials during most of the fifties, not because they thought the idea would fail, but because they feared it would succeed. Since becoming a great economic power at the turn of the century, the United States has consistently questioned any regional bloc threatening to discriminate against North American traders. Only after the shock of the Nixon visit in 1958, the economic recessions, and Castro's victory did U.S. policy-makers change their view. Even then support was half-hearted until the Kennedy administration concluded that CACM fit naturally into the Alliance's objectives. During the sixties, Washington loaned the Central American Bank for Integration over $180 million and gave nearly another $20 million for CACM projects.[100] By the mid-sixties, the Johnson administration had reduced its policy in the hemisphere to military assistance, the encouragement of private investment, and regional integration (CACM and the Latin American Free Trade Association in South America). As the Alliance died and Vietnam turned inordinately expensive, the common market approach attracted Johnson because it was cheap. It also threatened no important interests, particularly after Johnson accepted the advice of those such as David Rockefeller and began stressing private rather than government involvement. Common markets seemed ideally designed for North American multinational industries and banks that searched for new frontiers.

CACM thus got off to roaring start. Trade among the five countries jumped from $32 million in 1960 to $136 million in 1965 to $260 million in 1969. Import substitution (that is, producing needed goods in the country instead of importing them) stimulated the economies. By 1965, however, the roaring start slowed to a cautious walk, and by 1970 CACM had collapsed. Import substitution dwindled in importance because the poor—that is, the overwhelming majority—lacked the money to buy the goods. Intraregional trade, moreover, notably enriched Guatemala and El Salvador, which possessed the necessary skills and capital; it drained Honduras and Costa Rica of considerable amounts of money. Hondurans particularly resented providing not only a captive market, but even subsidies to build Salvadoran industry—and doing so at the very time Salvador's government solved its terrible labor problems by pushing 300,000 of its citizens into Honduras. El Salvador might have gained fame as the "Ruhr of Central America" because of its industrialization, but to Hondurans the Salvadoran oligarchs were the most parasitic people in the region.

At this point, according to the CACM plan, the Integrated Industries scheme should have stepped into the breach, used government powers to even out industrial development, and thus helped Hondurans, Costa Ricans, and Nicaraguans. It never happened. At the critical moment, the oligarchs who controlled wealth and political power prevented government intervention.[101] It reminded an historian of the 1820s and 1830s when conservatives in the newly independent cities stopped Central American integration because of their own parochial interests. The dream of Central American development clashed head-on with the reality of Central American class structure. The oligarchs (or, in countries such as El Salvador, Honduras, and Guatemala, an oligarch-military complex) seemed to be in no danger of losing such a conflict.

Meanwhile, throughout the sixties North American investors made Central America an ever more tightly integrated part of their own system, without in any significant way transforming the region's economy so it could be more equitable. Between 1961 and 1965 about $200 million of net private foreign capital went into CACM-induced operations. A remarkable turnabout thus occurred. U.S. investment in the hemisphere had historically gone mostly into the larger South American countries. With CACM in operation, investment suddenly moved northward. In 1955 South America had accounted for about 45 percent of the total book value of U.S. direct involvement in Latin America, Venezuela for 25 percent (mostly because of its rich oil reserves), Middle America (excluding Cuba and Panamanian shipping interests) 30 percent. In 1965, however, the figures for the three areas were 35 percent, 25 percent, and 40 percent respectively.[102]

Much of the foreign capital bought out existing manufacturing plants and banks. This money did not produce many new facilities or redistribute the wealth of the old, although it certainly added to that wealth. By 1965, foreign, and especially the North American, presence had grown until the economic ministers of the five CACM countries issued a joint statement warning that the foreign capital should be made part of joint ventures with Central Americans. The statement had been forced by an odd coalition of left-wing nationals, who attacked U.S. influence, and local business people who feared North American competition for credit and trade. They especially expressed concern for their banking sector which New York and California institutions were taking over. But the call of the five ministers ran directly against U.S. determination to allow the marketplace, not government agencies, to determine winners and losers. To make this point abundantly clear, the Johnson administration exercised its power in the Inter-American Development Bank, and its tremendous leverage through the granting of foreign aid funds, to stop money from being spent in CACM for the Integrated Industries plan. United States policy-makers thus found themselves trapped again: if they continued to push traditional marketplace principles, they would offend many CACM officials who believed in the need for government intervention. But if the North Americans changed policy to allow the redistribution of investment through government planning, U.S. corporations and other private investors would strenuously object, if not reduce their interest in CACM. Simply continuing the old policy seemed the easiest path to follow.[103]

These growing problems endangered CACM even before the "soccer war" broke out between Honduras and El Salvador. That conflict was a result, not a cause, of long-festering problems between the two nations. Honduras had been searching for a way out of its unprofitable role in CACM, and in the conflict got to vent its frustration on the Salvadorans who had been, in Honduran minds, insensitive exploiters. Honduras quit CACM in 1971. Never was the Integrated Industries scheme brought into play.

CACM had succeeded until 1965 because it increased trade without troubling either the political elites or the avowed U.S. belief in marketplace competition. After 1965 the imbalances, contradictions, and power of foreign capital that had been implicit in the CACM plan became explicit. The fundamental question, as one expert phrased it during 1965 and 1966, was "Central American economic integration for whom?"[104] Integration certainly did not benefit agricultural laborers who were losing their land and wages so oligarchs could use machines to grow more coffee, cotton, bananas, and cocoa for foreign markets. Urban laborers benefited little; the best study of CACM cautiously concludes that the industrialization process discriminated against labor in order to use new technology and—most strikingly—that by stressing capital-intensive industry instead of labor-intensive agriculture, "integration might have *reduced* employment by about three percent of the labor force."[105] The plan certainly did not break the region's dependence on U.S. capital and markets. It intensified that dependence. It did not weaken the power of the oligarchs to exploit and control the large majority of Central America. It confirmed that power.[106] It did little to lessen the region's bondage to one or two crops. It tightened the bondage. And it did little to distribute more equitably the food and wealth of Central America.[107] With CACM's failure and the larger problems of the Alliance, other means now had to be found to bring about change.

Conclusion: Fall of the Alliance and the Rise of "Romantic Revolutionaries"

CACM was the last hope of the Alliance for Progress in Central America. When the common market collapsed, the most visible parts of the area's political landscape became the extremes: the rising revolutionary movements (in every country except Costa Rica) and the oligarch-military complex supported by U.S. arms and advisers. The Alliance failed to deal with the root problems of the poverty. United Nations figures showed that of one hundred dollars per capita increase in wealth that Latin Americans gained during the sixties, only two dollars reached the poorest 20 percent of the population. The cause of this statistic was not economic but political. The Alliance officials had assumed that economic growth could be achieved without radical political change. In Central America, at least, that proved to be a tragic illusion. In 1968 Professor Ernest Halperin described the illusion by using an analogy from U.S. history:

> As an instrument for insuring democracy and stability, the Alliance for Progress is therefore bound to fail. Examining its long-range aims, one finds that the Alliance is the modern version of an old American dream: That the happiness of other nations can be insured by persuading them to adopt the triple formula of private enterprise, grassroots democracy, and the family farm. This is ideology, not practical politics. . . . It is not ridiculous, like William Jennings Bryan's vision: "Our Nation will lead the world in the great crusade which will drive intoxicating liquor from the globe." But it is no more realistic than that.[108]

The one slight hope the Alliance (or CACM) had for a major success rested upon large-scale land reform. Congressional legislation, however, expressly prohibited the use of U.S. funds to purchase agricultural land. Any agrarian reform had to be paid by Central American funds, and since the oligarchs had no desire to tax themselves so the revenue could be used to seize their own lands, reform was out of the question.[109] In 1968 a frustrated Alliance official in the State Department publicly emphasized the need for land reform accompanied by new government credits. His superior, Assistant Secretary of State for Inter-American Affairs Covey T. Oliver, immediately added a caveat: only in "some cases" could the United States support "redistribution of land to the landless, or colonization opportunities."[110] Officials apparently had great difficulty finding such cases.

But they found frequent opportunity to send U.S. aid to Central American armed forces. In the eyes of Washington officials, such aid produced benefits. Military units in Vietnam, Latin America, and elsewhere in the free world were finally forcing the "romantic revolutionaries," who had long disturbed world order, to face reality and put down their arms. Or so declared Walt Whitman Rostow, President Johnson's assistant for National Security Affairs, in a 1967 speech. The "romantic revolutionaries" (the term implied that unfortunate idealism led them astray) were to be replaced by "pragmatism and moderation." If the Vietnam War turned out well, Rostow argued, evolution would replace revolution in other parts of the newly emerging world as well.[111] Rostow, a well-known economist while working at the Massachusetts Institute of Technology, had even mapped out the evolutionary path with his "stages of growth" theory that applied European, and especially North American experiences, to third-world areas. Those experiences, and Rostow's theories, turned out to be largely irrelevant for emerging nations. Vietnam, moreover, had no relationship to the local, fundamental problems that pulled apart Central America. The causes for revolution in Central America had existed long before the United States became involved in Southeast Asia.

Nor was communism the problem in Central America. The people in the region admired Castro more for his nationalism and successful defiance of the United States than for his ties to the Soviet bloc. Communist parties existed in some form in all five Central American nations, but without exception they were small, illegal, had much of their leadership in exile, and their members were under close surveillance.[112] Instead the effective revolutionaries came from middle-class, nationalist, non-Communist, and often military backgrounds.

Washington officials had learned little from their long experience in Central American affairs. In early 1968, Professor Richard Adams of the University of Texas nicely summarized the reasons North Americans should have confronted certain historical lessons:

> Latin America has, for over a hundred years, been the mercantile hinterland of the industrial west. Since the Second World War, the United States has been its biggest buyer of raw materials and agricultural export crops and the largest supplier of imported goods. Within Latin America, a dualistic society provides the basically cheap labor that is a requisite to keeping prices on export items low. The U.S. housewife pays under a dollar for a pound of coffee: this means that the Latin American laborer working in coffee gets around 50 cents a day. . . . Yet the United States operates within a system that helps keep these wages at that level. There is no getting around this simple relationship, and no amount of diplomatic good will can alter the basic structural relationship that keeps Latin America in a subordinate position. . . .[113]

The United States, however, continued to refuse to confront either the economic or political results of its system in Central America. Commemorating the tenth anniversary of the Alliance for Progress, former President Eduardo Frei of Chile—a moderate reformer and strong friend of the United States—sadly concluded that when Kennedy launched the Alliance, "it was stated that unless a peaceful revolution was implemented, a violent revolution would take place. If we are not actually witnessing one now, its imminence should be obvious even to the blind." Frei concluded, "And that is why there is no time for the injection of classical solutions; they simply can no longer work."[114] The Chilean leader thus provided an epitaph for the sixties and an introduction to the seventies and beyond.

IV

THE COLLAPSE OF
THE SYSTEM

For Richard Nixon, to be a world statesman was to open China to the U.S. and negotiate treaties with the Soviet Union. He stayed far from the embarrassing passions and intractable problems of Latin America. This is not surprising. Nixon clearly harbored glaring memories of the southern nations, particularly of being spat upon and nearly pummeled by Venezuelan mobs in 1958. It must have seemed to him that Eisenhower—whose respect and affection for Nixon were limited—sent him on such missions only to get him out of Washington. To Nixon, Latin America was a diplomatic and political dead end. Indeed, it had also long been so considered by ambitious foreign service officers—one reason why assistant secretaries of state for inter-American affairs seemed to go in and out of office during the post-1945 years as if through a revolving door. Soon after his election victory in 1968, the new president captured the spirit of his Latin American policy. Posing for the obligatory photo session with an ambassador he had appointed to a southern nation, Nixon blurted out to his new appointee, "Don't trust them, you can't trust them. They're all a bunch of kooks."[1]

During his first four years in the White House, Nixon actually needed to pay little attention to Central America. Those years, in retrospect, were the calm after the storms from the Alliance in the sixties, and before the terrors of revolution in the late seventies. By 1971 the Guatemalan military apparently had stamped out the guerrillas. El Salvador seemed prosperous. Its high growth rates had survived the virtual

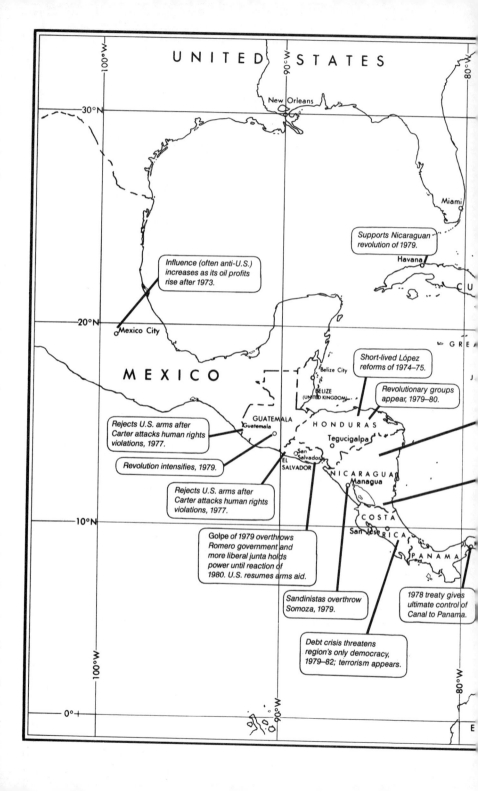

UNITED STATES

New Orleans

Miami

Supports Nicaraguan
revolution of 1979.

Havana

Influence (often anti-U.S.)
increases as its oil profits
rise after 1973.

CU

Mexico City

GRE

MEXICO

Belize City

Short-lived López
reforms of 1974–75.

BELIZE
(UNITED KINGDOM)

Revolutionary groups
appear, 1979–80.

GUATEMALA
Guatemala

HONDURAS

Rejects U.S. arms after
Carter attacks human rights
violations, 1977.

Tegucigalpa

Revolution intensifies, 1979.

San
Salvador

EL
SALVADOR

NICARAGUA
Managua

Rejects U.S. arms after
Carter attacks human rights
violations, 1977.

COSTA

Golpe of 1979 overthrows
Romero government and
more liberal junta holds
power until reaction of
1980. U.S. resumes arms aid.

San José
RICA

PANAMA

Sandinistas overthrow
Somoza, 1979.

1978 treaty gives
ultimate control of
Canal to Panama.

Debt crisis threatens
region's only democracy,
1979–82; terrorism appears.

E

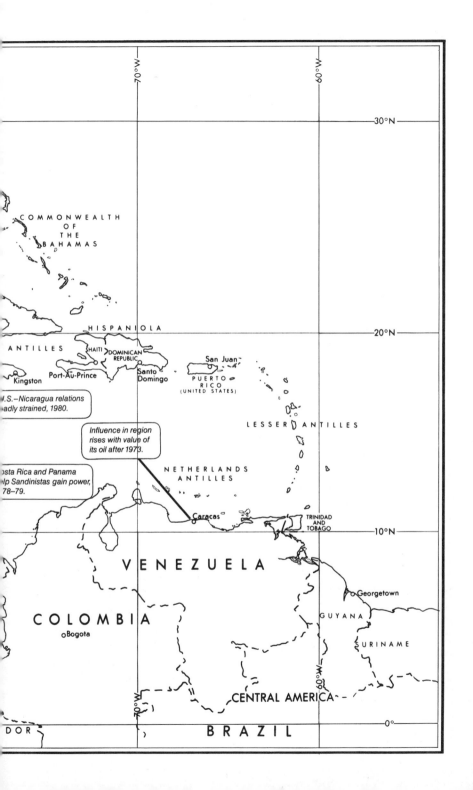

COMMONWEALTH
OF
THE
BAHAMAS

HISPANIOLA

ANTILLES

HAITI   DOMINICAN
              REPUBLIC

Kingston   Port-Au-Prince   Santo
                                        Domingo

San Juan

PUERTO
RICO
(UNITED STATES)

LESSER ANTILLES

U.S.–Nicaragua relations
badly strained, 1980.

Influence in region
rises with value of
its oil after 1973.

Costa Rica and Panama
help Sandinistas gain power,
1978–79.

NETHERLANDS
ANTILLES

Caracas

TRINIDAD
AND
TOBAGO

V E N E Z U E L A

Georgetown

C O L O M B I A

GUYANA

Bogota

SURINAME

CENTRAL AMERICA

DOR

B R A Z I L

30°N

20°N

10°N

0°

70°W

60°W

destruction of the Central American Common Market and—miracle of miracles—it was developing a workable party system featuring the moderately reformist Christian Democrats. Honduran unions were restless as usual, but the army held firm control. The Somoza dynasty appeared entrenched in Nicaragua for generations to come despite many rumors that the dictator's son and heir-apparent was of small intelligence. Costa Rica enjoyed its reputation as the region's most democratic nation. True, throughout the area problems of hunger and illiteracy remained severe. But progress seemed likely.

Danger from the Soviet Union, or even Cuba, appeared unlikely. Throughout the mid-sixties, the Soviets and Cubans fought bitterly over policies for Latin America. Chastened by the Missile Crisis of 1962, and dealing with the effects of Khrushchev's ouster by Leonid Brezhnev in late 1964, the Soviets advised Communist parties to go slowly and not support armed revolution in the Western Hemisphere until at least a larger "proletariat" appeared. To suspicious third-world revolutionaries, this approach smelled like a superpower deal: the Kremlin only watched when the United States smashed revolts in the Dominican Republic or left-wing governments in Chile, and White House officials stood aside as Russian tanks crushed Czech liberalism in 1968. Nixon and Henry Kissinger (national security advisor from 1969 to 1973 and secretary of state between 1973 and 1977) paid little attention to such areas as Latin America and Africa because they believed that the Soviets implicitly recognized specific spheres of influence in return for access to U.S. wheat and technology which the Russians desperately needed. Soviet trade with Latin America (other than Cuba) amounted to less than $250 million annually. Moscow's diplomatic representation in Central America was almost nonexistent.[2]

Cuba pursued a different approach. As Brezhnev counseled restraint, Castro urged the creation of "two, three" even "four or five more Vietnams" in the hemisphere. The Communist parties in Central America, however, were inconsequential in size, illegal, and impotent. Tied closely to Moscow, they infuriated Castro by refusing to join armed insurrections. The Cuban leader consequently worked with guerrillas in Guatemala and Nicaragua who had broken with the Communists. This strategy worked for him until he had to moderate his policies after Ernesto

"Che" Guevara was killed while trying to ignite rebellion in Bolivia, and after guerrillas in Guatemala, Venezuela, and Colombia were virtually wiped out. As early as July 1969, Assistant Secretary of State for Inter-American Affairs Charles A. Meyer told Congress: "Communist insurgencies are currently at a relatively low ebb," and "a significant increase in insurgency movements is not likely at this time."[3]

The United States had a breathing space. How would the supposedly imaginative Nixon-Kissinger diplomacy take advantage of it?

Nixon and Rockefeller: Using the Military to Avoid 1776

The public rationale for Nixon's Latin American policy was provided by Nelson Rockefeller, governor of New York and Nixon's long-time Republican party rival. Since the thirties, Rockefeller had been a businessman with family interests in the southern continent ranging from retail stores to Venezuelan petroleum. Involved in the area as a State Department official as early as the New Deal, Rockefeller probably knew Latin America better than any other major political figure of his era. It was, however, perhaps a measure of Nixon's lack of interest in the hemisphere (and his feelings for the New Yorker) that he sent Rockefeller to Latin America. Nixon obviously knew that no one more epitomized "Yankee imperialism" to the Latin Americans than did Nelson Rockefeller.

The president instructed the governor to meet with officials in the southern countries and give him a full report with recommendations. Rockefeller made four journeys to Latin America in 1969, but they were bumpy trips indeed. He was unable to enter Peru, where a left-wing military regime shocked Washington by nationalizing a U.S.-controlled oil company. A jaunt to Honduras climaxed with anti-Yankee riots in which a student was killed—and quickly became a martyr. Chile and even Venezuela canceled the governor's visit.

In reporting to Congress, Rockefeller identified the central problem when discussing the need to pay fair prices for Latin American raw materials:

I think they find themselves very much in the position which we did at the period of the Continental Congress in 1776, and if you have been to see that play in New York, *1776*, you will feel, as I did, that what we rose up in arms against the British about, we are now doing to the other Western Hemisphere nations.

When a congressman asked about the taxation-without-representation issue of 1776, the governor was equally blunt: "That is the only one we don't have, but we do that indirectly." He then emphasized: "I think we are moving rapidly into a period of revolution."[4]

Unfortunately, Rockefeller's major recommendations did not reflect this insight. Shying from a restructuring of the economic and political relationships, he recommended instead a military response. When the British had tried that same response in 1776, it had driven the colonials to a separation, but Rockefeller gave no sign of having learned that lesson from either history or the theater. Acknowledging that U.S. military missions in Latin America "too often have constituted an overly large and visible United States presence," he asked Congress to remove the $75 million limit placed on military assistance to Latin America in 1967 legislation.

His reasoning was simple. Since 1961 when the Alliance began, "There have been seventeen coups d'état in the other American republics, much more than in any comparable period in the history of the Western Hemisphere." Nearly all had been caused by military factions, so Rockefeller might have denounced such coups, but he drew the opposite conclusion: "Without some framework for order, no progress can be achieved." A U.S. policy to provide training and equipment for the police and military "will bring about the best long-term hope for the . . . improvement in the quality of life for the people." Rockefeller did have some economic recommendations, but his main message was unequivocal: "The essential force of constructive social change" was the military.[5] It was as if the U.S. military policies of the twenties, fifties, and sixties had never happened.

In a speech of 31 October 1969, Nixon laid out his new policy. U.S. foreign aid to Latin America, he announced to the Inter-American Press Association, would no longer have to be spent on North American goods. This was an important concession; the United States had started to suffer from massive balance-of-trade deficits, and Nixon could have eased the problem by forcing Latin America to buy more U.S. goods. He then surprised his audience by declaring: "We must deal realistically with governments in the inter-American system as they are." This could only mean that the president would deal with any military regime, no matter how dictatorial, for "realistically" the army held power in every Central American country except Costa Rica.[6]

This approach fit well into the widely trumpeted Nixon Doctrine of 1969: that, in the wake of the Vietnam War, the United States could no longer act as sheriff in the world, but would work closely with—and arm heavily—selected allies who could act as policemen. The cops included the Shah of Iran on the Middle East beat, the Brazilian generals on the South American, and the military regimes on the Central American. Somoza turned out to be a special favorite; he had always treated the president obsequiously even during Nixon's dark years of political exile in the early sixties.

The Central American military enjoyed the best of both worlds: its direct assistance levels remained relatively high, and since the U.S. Treasury provided liberal credit, arms sales for cash steadily rose. In 1972, Guatemala, whose Indians averaged $83 a year income, bought $6.5 million of military goods from North America, much of it on credit. Nixon (and Rockefeller) liked the idea that the recipients participated in the well-publicized civic action programs. The Alliance had designed these programs to improve the military's image by involving soldiers in building schools and roads. Civic action, however, did little for economic balance and democracy. The program turned civilian jobs over to government troops even as unemployment was rampant. It promoted militarism and gave the generals an increased voice in economic and social policies. And it publicly allied the United States with the Central American military at the grass-roots level, even as revolutions picked up momentum in the towns and villages.[7] Other side effects appeared. The number-three man in the Salvadoran military was convicted in New York City during 1976 for attempting to sell 10,000 machine guns— apparently Salvadoran surplus—to East Coast mobsters.[8]

The U.S. military's Southern Command meanwhile pressured Central Americans to reform CONDECA (the Central American Defense group), a United States creation of the early sixties. CONDECA had fragmented after the 1969 "soccer war." The Nixon administration now sought to revive it. U.S. generals even tried to push the Costa Ricans to develop a military force and join a revitalized CONDECA. The San José government, however, wanted nothing to do with such plans. Its foreign minister declared that he did not know why CONDECA even existed. Central American generals meanwhile cared more about internal opportunities than external cooperation. CONDECA had finally ceased to function by the mid-seventies.[9]

North American arms aid and sales nevertheless continued in amounts that threatened to engulf some of the small nations' budgets. Not that the Nixon administration cared. Arms sales formed its Latin American policy, a policy that fit the administration's values and global principles. The approach worked in a few larger South American nations. In 1973, Salvador Allende, the Chilean reformer who had won the presidency fairly and constitutionally, died while being overthrown by a Chilean army that received support from Kissinger and the U.S. military and was well supplied with North American arms.[10] Brazil's military dictators moved closer to Washington's policies. The forces of democratic Colombia and Venezuela also received advanced weapons, including supersonic jet fighters. But in every Central American nation except Costa Rica, few democratic groups existed to check the military. And as U.S. aid came in, military debt piled up until the countries began to bend under the burden.

Triple Threat: The Crises of 1973 and 1974

In 1973 the diplomatic world turned upside down for Nixon and Kissinger. Until the autumn of that year, the president had been preoccupied with affairs among the great powers. Then Egypt and Israel went to war in October. When the United States helped the Israelis, Arab producers retaliated by embargoing their petroleum exports to the United States and some of its allies, then quadrupled oil prices in a matter of months. Funds gushed out of Western (and Central American) pocketbooks into Arab bank accounts. As energy prices jumped, inflation rates followed. In a 1971 speech, Nixon had talked confidently of manipulating a five-power world made up of the United States, the Soviet Union, China, Western Europe, and Japan. Two years later observers only half-joked that the five powers had suddenly become the United States, the Soviet Union, Saudi Arabia, and the oil sheikdoms of Bahrain and Abu Dhabi.

The United States sank into an economic recession. Unemployment and inflation seemed beyond control. The nation was losing resources needed to fight the old cold war. These new realities explain why Nixon looked to other "policemen" to help him guard the "free world." This background also explains why the oil embargo was so shocking: it struck an already weakened economy, and it revealed—glaringly—how vulnerable U.S. power had become.

A second crisis also threatened. Since 1947, when Harry Truman mobilized North Americans with his Truman Doctrine to fight communism in distant places, a broad public consensus had undergirded strong presidential initiatives in foreign policy. Every U.S. chief executive since Truman had single-handedly committed his country to historic acts (as armed intervention in Korea or diplomatic deals with Russia or Vietnam) without gaining approval from Congress or other political factions. The U.S. consensus broke, however, in 1974 when the once imperial president resigned in disgrace following exposure in the Watergate scandal. The remainder of the seventies was presided over by presidents who wielded power not as had Truman or the early Nixon, but with the indecision of Gerald Ford (the only unnominated as well as unelected president in the country's history) and Jimmy Carter.

These dual crises of authority in the economy and in foreign policy struck just as Central America entered a revolutionary era in the mid-seventies. Washington had to deal with upheavals in a world of different power centers, and with diminished economic and political capabilities. Gone was the Good Neighbor's power of persuasion.

For example, rising petroleum prices had a devastating effect on Central America. Between 1973 and early 1980, the region's annual cost of oil imports leaped from $189 million to $1½ billion. The catastrophe struck economies already at the breaking point because of rising military expenses and the enormous debts incurred in the sixties to pay for the Alliance for Progress programs. As money drained out of these small economies, they soon lacked the means to pay for U.S. food and industrial goods. A sharp decline in the current account balance of their foreign trade dispassionately portrays the dilemma:[11]

(In millions of dollars)	1972	1973	1974	1975
Costa Rica	−100	−112	−251	−217
El Salvador	+12	−44	−134	−104
Guatemala	−12	+8	−103	−112
Honduras	−9	−36	−107	−135
Nicaragua	−6	−37	−257	−108

Internal changes also shook Central America. Before the fifties, the masses of the region had been fairly inactive politically and therefore unimportant to Washington. North Americans dealt easily with a few elite urban officials. But the Central American Common Market and outside investment had created a larger urban proletariat who could be mobilized by charismatic leaders. The rapid expansion of mechanized, export-oriented agriculture fit perfectly into the U.S. system because large agribusiness needed both foreign capital for expansion and North Americans for markets. The system, however, also created ever larger numbers of landless peasants, who were replaced by machines. Peasants, urban labor, and the small middle class were peculiarly vulnerable to the post-1973 economic disasters that struck Central America.[12]

The revolutions that threatened to uproot the Central American system in the eighties emerged from these domestic crises. As they grew, the United States did little, partly because North Americans were confused about what was happening (blaming the Soviet Union, for example, for starving Salvadorans did not clarify the situation), and partly because the U.S. faced economic and leadership problems of its own.

Testing the System: The Banana War

Central American leaders did understand the dangers in the post-1973 crisis. They searched desperately for ways to reduce the dangers without restructuring the system—a system on which their power rested. These elites attempted to reach outside U.S.-dominated trade areas for deals with Japan, Argentina, and Europe. Central Americans especially looked to Mexico and Venezuela, whose oil fields had conjured up sudden riches. When Brazilian coffee growers held back their huge crop to drive up world prices, Central American producers skillfully, if uncooperatively, sold their own beans for large profits. The post-1973 years were not the best times for maintaining the integrity of gentlemen's agreements.

Central Americans learned this the hard way when they tried to fix banana prices at higher levels. In early 1974, Costa Rica, Guatemala, Honduras, Nicaragua, Panama, and two South American producers (Colombia and Ecuador) agreed to establish a growers' cartel—the Union of Banana Exporting Countries, or UPEB—that demanded an immediate increase in their income from bananas. The idea obviously was stimulated by OPEC's startling success in raising oil prices. Banana prices, moreover, had gone up little in twenty years while Central American producers bought U.S. goods whose prices rose steadily. A U.N. study concluded that no more than seventeen cents of each dollar spent by North Americans on bananas went to the producing countries. UPEB initially hoped to collect an export tax of one dollar on each forty-pound crate of bananas.

Bananas, the largest fruit business in the world, were monopolized by three U.S.-controlled companies: United Brands (formerly United Fruit), Standard Fruit, and the Del Monte Corporation. All flatly refused to negotiate a price-fixing plan with UPEB. They claimed it might open them to antitrust charges in the United States. Of equal importance, the companies wanted to go on dealing with small, individual growers, not with a government-supported cartel patterned on OPEC. Faced with these giants' refusal to agree on the one dollar figure, Ecuador broke ranks and declared it would not impose the new tax. The companies next focused on Costa Rica, whose costly welfare programs made it peculiarly vulnerable to the economic crisis. José Figueres bluntly declared that Standard Fruit's holdings should be nationalized if the firms refused to pay the tax. Standard quickly told the new president, Daniel Oduber, that in response to any more such talk Standard would close its Costa Rican operation. Costa Rica dropped its demand to twenty-five cents a crate. UPEB was on the ropes.

The final blow fell when Honduras suddenly reduced its tax to twenty-five cents. Then, in early 1975, Eli Black, president of United Brands, smashed the window of his office on the forty-fourth floor of the Pan American building in New York City and jumped to his death. Investigators discovered mismanagement inside the company, including the payment of a $1.25 million bribe to the president of Honduras and to other officials. Another $1.25 million had also been promised, apparently to ensure that the bought-off Hondurans remained bought. For all the recent change, Honduras continued to be a "banana republic" in many ways. President Oswaldo López, the country's strongman since 1963, had to resign. A shocked Costa Rica threatened to return to the one dollar tax, and cries arose for the nationalization of all three companies' holdings. But Ecuador firmly refused to change its mind; Guatemala and Nicaragua joined it. The cartel collapsed. The three companies resumed normal business. They raised prices for U.S. consumers, but UPEB by no means shared proportionately in the profit. Not until 1981, after several years of rampant inflation, was one nation—Costa Rica—finally able to collect the one dollar tax. Having challenged the rules of the North American system, the cartel had lost despite the corruption of an affair that came to be known as "bananagate."[13]

United States interests could control their affairs in Central America, or at least they could if Central America continued to rely on discussions and marketplace demands. Revolution and political restructuring, however, would change the rules of the game.

The Carter Approach

Some economic links actually strengthened during the seventies. Central America continued to depend on North American food and manufactures. But particularly striking was an increased dependence on U.S. markets for its new industrial complex, as well as for its traditional exports of coffee and bananas. From 1970 to 1976, El Salvador's exports of manufactured goods to North America leaped from $1 million to $67 million. During the same years, Costa Rica's increased from $3.6 to $27.2 million, Nicaragua's from $.4 to $10.6 million, Guatamala's from $1.7 to $9.4 million, and Honduras's from $1.5 to $8.4 million. Well over half of Central America's total exports went to the United States, despite attempts by North American vegetable and fruit growers, and shoe and textile producers, to keep these goods out.[14]

The more Central Americans tried to solve their problems through industrialization, the more they seemed to depend on the United States. When Jimmy Carter entered the White House in 1977, the U.S. economy continued to stumble. The government's reputation remained under the dark cloud left by Nixon. But the new president apparently had little reason to worry about the nation's "backyard" of the Caribbean and Central America. At least such was the assumption based on superficial indicators—the end of the banana wars, the flourishing of bilateral trade, the apparent solidity of the military regimes. Overburdened presidents and media glutted with information seldom looked beyond the superficial.

The new president proceeded in Central America as he did at home. Carter wanted pragmatic, conservative reform. He emphasized the spiritual over the structural. In the United States, that approach at least stood a chance of political success. North Americans, as French writer Alexis de Tocqueville pointed out in the 1830s, love change, but they dread revolution.[15] After the turmoil of the sixties and early seventies, many North Americans even dreaded change. But the Carter approach threatened disaster in Central America. Spiritual improvement offered too little to malnourished people (as Roman Catholic priests were discovering). Few Central Americans wanted to return to the fifties. In Nicaragua, Guatemala, and El Salvador, pragmatism meant the continuation of conservative, increasingly oppressive, military regimes. And quite unlike their neighbors to the north, many Central Americans dreaded not revolution but growing poverty and torture. Carter's Latin American policy never offered an acceptable alternative.

The president received foreign policy advice from his National Security Council adviser, Zbigniew Brzezinski, born in Poland and steeped in the intricacies of Soviet bloc affairs. Brzezinski tended to view crises in such third-world areas as Cambodia, Angola, or Central America as challenges thrown down by the Soviet bloc. Carter's other source of advice was the State Department, where Secretary of State Cyrus Vance and U.S. Ambassador to the United Nations Andrew Young argued that the major problems in the third world were indigenous and had to be resolved internally, not through the Soviets or their allies. As Central American revolutions picked up speed, Carter increasingly accepted the simpler, more politically attractive explanation offered by Brzezinski.[16] In 1979 Nicaragua fell to the Sandinista revolutionaries, and radical Moslems who had driven out the Shah of Iran seized North American hostages. Soviet armies invaded Afghanistan. Carter's policies remained confused, but the internal debate was over. Young, then Vance, left the administration. Negotiations with Castro for more normal relations ended. U.S.-Cuban relations worsened as the Central American revolutions heated up.[17] In four years the Carter administration was not able to develop a consistent policy on North-South problems.

The inability is exemplified in the president's policy on human rights. That policy was to be a touchstone for dealing with such areas as Central America. The nation's "commitment to human rights" must be "absolute" and "a fundamental tenet of our foreign policy," Carter announced. "Our moral sense dictates a clear-cut preference for those societies which share with us an abiding respect for individual human rights," the president proclaimed in his Inaugural Address. Such a view did not mean conducting "our foreign policy by rigid moral maxims," and he realized "fully the limits of moral suasion." But Carter believed the United States should lead in protecting "the individual from the arbitrary power of the state."[18]

By viewing human rights as a diplomatic tool, Carter chose a most complicated instrument. Congressional legislation instructed the State Department to report annually on the status of human rights in countries around the world. If nations violated those rights and made no effort to correct the violations, U.S. aid could be cut off. The drawing up of the final report in the State Department was not a simple process. It produced bureaucratic warfare at its worst. Conflicting moral values are never easily compromised, and the stake—hemisphere security and hundreds of millions of dollars in aid—was great.

The procedure started with U.S. officials in a foreign country sending information on the human rights situation in that nation to Washington. The State Department's Human Rights bureau, led by an able and outspoken lawyer, Patricia Derian, judged the material with high seriousness. But the information also went to the desk officers responsible for dealing day-to-day with the foreign government in question. The desk officers, effective and self-confident professionals, often wanted to play down the publicity on human rights violations, were reluctant to cut off aid for the violators, and believed they could use aid to bring the violators into line. In other cases, as when dealing with the People's Republic of China, strategic interests clearly outweighed the moral, even though Chinese jails held political prisoners. Carter's human rights policies were thus whipsawed between moral and strategic considerations, as well as between different parts of the bureaucracy. But Latin America, and particularly Central America, felt the full force of the administration's human rights offensive.

The Central Americans did not occupy the delicate strategic position of, say, China or Iran which shared long borders with the Soviets. Within the State Department, moreover, Latin American desk officers had less clout than other geographical desks to deal with Derian's bureau. Finally, no one could dispute that military figures ruled four of the five Central American governments, or that these regimes treated their people badly. The countries also contained activist Roman Catholic and other groups that kept careful records of human rights violations.

Central America thus became a public laboratory for Carter's human rights experiment. The experiment went badly in its first year. In 1977 the State Department's reports targeted El Salvador, Guatemala, Brazil, Argentina, and Uruguay as gross violators of their citizens' rights. A cut-off of U.S. military aid should have followed, but before that occurred, the five countries told the United States they did not want its aid. The Guatemalan and Salvadoran military followed Argentina and Brazil by purchasing weapons from West European and Israeli suppliers. The dependence of these small nations on U.S. military arms and advisers began to change.[19] In addition, the Carter policy struck at the legitimacy of the two governments. The Guatemalan and Salvadoran generals subsequently attacked domestic groups, however moderate, which threatened to reduce the regimes' power and legitimacy further.

Carter's human rights policy made sense only if he were willing to take the heat of the consequences: the growing isolation and brutality of military regimes, political polarization, spreading revolution fed by ever greater repression. This process did occur in three Central American nations while Carter occupied the White House. The president seemed surprised. He had naively sought to change the status quo without upsetting it, without revolution.

It followed that the president's human rights policy became the moral equivalent of Kennedy's Alliance for Progress. Both men talked about revolution when they meant painfully slow evolution. Both desired more democratic societies in Central America as rapidly as possible, but without the radical changes those desires entailed. Both wanted the military-oligarch elites, long nourished by and dependent upon the United States, to share power and distribute their wealth more equitably, but neither wanted to lose U.S. power and influence that had always worked through those elites. Both men wanted change in Central America, but they dreaded revolution. In the end when they realized that one was not possible without the other, both presidents backed away from the consequences.

Another Carter administration contradiction was its approach to restructuring economic systems in the third world. The problem was captured in testimony given to Congress by Richard Cooper, undersecretary of state for economic affairs, in 1980. The United States understood and sympathized with the developing nations that wanted "a new international economic order" aimed at "a more equitable distribution of the world's wealth," Cooper declared.

> However, we also have an enormous stake in the continuing smooth functioning of the economic system. We are the world's largest exporter and importer of both raw materials and manufactured goods, the largest overseas investor, and the largest international debtor as well as the largest creditor. Major changes in the system can thus have important implications for our own welfare.[20]

The administration wanted, somehow, both "a more equitable distribution of wealth" in such areas as Central America, and "major changes in the system" necessary for such a redistribution kept to a minimum. That circle proved to be impossible to square.

To bring about moderate change required almost complete control, much as one governs the speed of a car by use of the accelerator and brake. The contradictions in Carter's policies precluded such control. He could not use military aid as leverage for reducing human rights violations when the violations led to cutting off aid. Other new developments also impinged on his (and later Ronald Reagan's) ability to control change. Two of the new factors were external. One was internal. Together they changed the politics of the Central American region.

Outside Alternatives: Mexico and Venezuela

Throughout the seventies, Mexico caused major headaches for Washington officials. When they tried to isolate Cuba from hemisphere affairs, Mexico went out of its way to include Castro in those affairs. When Washington tried to destroy the radical left in Nicaragua and El Salvador, Mexico supported those leftist forces. When U.S. officials wielded their economic power to pressure Central American regimes, Mexico spent its oil wealth to ease the pressure. Jimmy Carter did not improve relations between the two countries when during a visit to Mexico he made a bad joke about "Montezuma's Revenge" suffered by tourists in that country. His hosts felt deeply insulted. But Carter's gaffe only reflected the deeper misunderstandings between the two countries, including the right way to deal with Central American revolutions.

Those misunderstandings go far back in history. Mexico's two-thousand-mile border with the United States created an understandable fear of North Americans, especially after they removed one-third of Mexico and attached it to their country in 1848. When Theodore Roosevelt and Woodrow Wilson began intervening regularly in the Caribbean region, Mexico twice suffered the invasion of U.S. troops. As a consequence, it went to one international conference after another to fight any right of United States intervention, regardless of cause. Relations reached their nadir after the Mexicans launched their own revolution in 1911 and then, in the twenties and thirties, fulfilled one objective of the revolution by nationalizing the oil industry that was dominated by U.S. capital. The North Americans needed years to recover from that shock.

Fearful of U.S. power, but highly dependent on it, the Mexicans walked a tightrope to maintain both their economic balance and their political independence. Their country became a prime target for U.S. investment, but they refused to join the U.S.-sponsored General Agreements on Tariffs and Trade (GATT) because of their determination to control their own commercial policy. (That same determination led to their refusal to join OPEC, although Mexico followed the oil cartel's general pricing policies.) The Mexicans sought more independence from the North American economy, but they also insisted that millions of Mexicans—the number cannot be fixed because so many enter illegally—be allowed to cross the border to find jobs in the United States. Inside Mexico, a high birthrate, sluggish economic growth, and one of the highest foreign debts in the world created enormous political pressures. If the mass of emigrants returned home, an explosion could occur. Equally sensitive was the role of the country's military. The Mexican government had carefully kept its forces subordinate and closely watched.[21]

The famous Mexican explanation for their problems is that they are "so far from God and so close to the United States." An equally useful explanation, especially for understanding critical differences over Central American affairs, might be that they are too close to the United States but too far from completing their own revolution. The distribution of Mexico's wealth in the seventies ranked as one of the most inequitable in the hemisphere. The country contained important left-wing groups, and it held regular democratic elections. But the politics were controlled by one party—the *Partido Revolucionario Institucional* (PRI)—which was sufficiently authoritarian so that it had never lost a presidential election. Presidents, however, could not succeed themselves. "Mexicans avoid personal dictatorship," was one saying, "by retiring their dictators every six years."

Mexico's policy in Central America must be understood in this historical context: the country coexists with an unfinished revolution and a restless military while living between a giant neighbor and tumultuous

Central Americans. PRI continually sought negotiated solutions for Caribbean revolutions—and continually opposed the knee-jerk reaction of many U.S. presidents to handle the revolutions with armed force. Mexico needed peace and normal relations with others to resolve its own internal problems. More specifically, no Mexican government followed Washington's belligerent antirevolutionary policy in Central America because such a policy would have pitted the government against Mexico's left. Mexicans believed that their own revolutionary experiences gave them the ability to handle Central American radicalism. They did not have the North American dread of revolutionaries. They saw little reason why Central American, or Cuban, radicalism could not be channeled into more democratic politics—as was their own revolution.[22] The Mexicans also viewed Castro as an ally in containing U.S. power. In the late sixties and early seventies, Castro had responded by refusing to support the small guerrilla movements that appeared in Mexico.

In 1973, Mexico's fortunes improved spectacularly. The surge in petroleum prices occurred simultaneously with discoveries of new fields that pushed the country's proven reserves to nearly sixty billion barrels. It ranked now as one of the top six oil powers in the world, and as one of the top four producers.[23] The next two presidents, Luis Echeverría Alvarez and José López Portillo, manipulated the new power as they pursued well-publicized diplomatic initiatives with third-world nations. Most important was the decision by Mexico and Venezuela to ease the crushing burden of oil costs by selling the product to small Caribbean nations at favored prices, then loaning back some of the income for development projects. That stroke partially neutralized the political power of U.S. aid.[24]

Mexico and the United States especially worked at cross-purposes in Guatemala and Nicaragua. The Guatemalans tried throughout the seventies to lessen their dependence on Washington, and found Mexico willing to help. If the Mexicans disapproved of the repressive Guatemalan military junta, they cared less for either increased U.S. military interference and/or guerrilla warfare in a country that abutted their richest oil fields. In Nicaragua, Mexico opposed the tottering Somoza dictatorship, then stepped up its aid to the victorious Sandinista government even as the United States criticized the Sandinistas as too radical. By early 1981, Mexico and the revolutionaries had agreed on a $200 million aid plan that countered Reagan's attempts to isolate Nicaragua.[25]

But Mexico's ability to neutralize the United States was limited. Washington could cause a political crisis in Mexico by cutting back the movement of migrant workers. The Mexican economy depended on U.S. oil markets, technology (especially for the $15 billion development program for PEMEX, Mexico's national oil company), and investments that controlled key segments of the nation's production. Foreign debt rose so high that observers doubted Mexico's ability to handle the payments.

Internal problems also worsened. Government corruption, unfair taxation, and inadequate food supplies marked much of Mexican life. As many as 40 percent of the population suffered unemployment or underemployment. Inflation raced towards 30 percent yearly. The military began demanding its share of the oil wealth. As it did so, the Pentagon was ready to oblige by sending weapons, including F-5 fighter planes. Washington officials, not those in Mexico City, seemed more willing to build up the Mexican military—and to have it used along the southern border where Guatemalan guerrillas gained strength.[26] Mexican civilian officials needed time and wanted negotiations, not fighting.

Mexican economic power, therefore, could be overrated. But the country's internal political requirements generated aggressive foreign initiatives that gave Central American governments alternatives and Washington officials problems. U.S. policymakers expected such problems given the course of history and Mexican politics. They did not, however, expect difficulties with Venezuela.

Since the twenties, Venezuela had been virtually a subsidiary of U.S.-owned oil companies. North American presidents got along famously with Venezuelan dictators. When the country's democratic forces seized power in the late fifties, they moved into the vanguard of the Alliance for Progress. But the Venezuelans opposed U.S. intervention in the Dominican Republic during 1965, and at the end of the decade grew disillusioned with the Alliance.[27]

By 1973 Venezuela was the healthiest democracy in South America. Its economy enjoyed equal vigor, but depended on North Americans who helped run its oil fields and bought one-third of its petroleum exports. Caracas was appropriately called "Miami Beach South." The oil relationship, of course, could be turned around: the United States obtained 53 percent of its imported oil in 1973 from Venezuela. When OPEC multiplied its price, Venezuela—the third largest exporter of oil in the world—seemed to discover the secret of King Midas. Oil income that had amounted to $3.5 billion in 1972 rose to nearly $15 billion in 1974. Venezuela did not have Mexico's unfinished revolution or high inflation rate to hold it back, although its problems with unemployment and urban slums remained severe.[28] In 1973, Carlos Andrés Perez positioned himself on the moderate left of the country's political spectrum as the presidential candidate of *Acción Democratica* (AD) and won a stunning victory.

Armed with oil riches and AD's liberal philosophy, Venezuela assumed a new and more powerful role in hemisphere affairs—just as U.S. power became vulnerable and Central American revolutions accelerated. Andrés Perez took steps toward independence from the United States. First, he nationalized the iron and steel industry and then, in May 1974, dropped the bombshell: oil was to be taken over by the government. Once the greatest depository of U.S. investment in Latin America, Venezuela constructed a tough policy to regulate foreign capital. The U.S. Congress retaliated by removing trade preferences from OPEC nations. That blow hit Venezuelans directly, and they protested bitterly. Andrés Perez resumed diplomatic relations with Cuba. He shocked U.S. officials by agreeing to supply fuel to Castro, thus removing a burden from the Soviet Union. This move was aimed not only at the U.S. Andrés Perez—and his Mexican friends—wanted to bring Cuba back into the hemisphere's relationships and separate it from the Communist bloc.[29]

The Caracas government concentrated on the Central American region. Large bilateral credits went to Costa Rica and Honduras for development projects. Venezuela set aside a special fund for countries dependent on its oil. As one observer noted, if any Latin American country had become as economically involved in Central American development a decade before, Washington officials would have proclaimed a triumph for the Alliance for Progress. But conditions and power relationships had changed. The United States watched the Venezuelan and Mexican initiatives suspiciously. When Venezuela lent Honduras $103 million for a huge pulp and paper mill, U.S. power in Honduras suffered. When top Caracas officials met with Castro, or cooperated in overthrowing Somoza, or publicly called North American control of the Panama Canal "a humiliation . . . to all of Latin America," they directly challenged Washington's policies.[30]

By the end of Jimmy Carter's term, a new, moderate Christian Democrat president held power in Venezuela. President Luis Herrera Campíns cooperated with Carter in trying to help the government of El Salvador (also led officially by a Christian Democrat) with its struggle against revolutionaries, and to curtail the leftist programs of the Sandinista government in Nicaragua. But the fundamentals did not change. The 1973 events in the Middle East revealed a vulnerability in U.S. power and created wealth in Mexico and Venezuela that opened economic and political alternatives for Central America just as it burst into revolution. As it had throughout its history, Central America continued to depend on the kindness of foreigners, but after 1973, at least, several were close neighbors who spoke the same language.[31]

Internal Alternative: Bases for Christ and Other Revolutionaries

External changes in the Central American region were accompanied by an internal transformation. The Roman Catholic Church, whose main mission in Central America for centuries had been to comfort the rich, bless the military, and Christianize (but not disturb) the peasants, dramatically became an engine for revolution. Not since the sixteenth century had the Church made such a massive effort to change the lives of so many people.

The beginnings of the transformation went back to at least 1891 when Pope Leo XIII's encyclical, *Rerum Novarum,* officially stated the Church's position that capitalism as well as socialism could dangerously distort social and religious values. For the next half-century, however, priests in Latin America devoted their time to fighting socialism (as in post-1959 Cuba), not capitalism. A small breakthrough did occur in Chile, where the Church (trying to find an alternative to Castroism), worked with the Christian Democrat party to put Eduardo Frei into power in 1964. Frei's success and the onrush of Alliance for Progress funds raised hopes for a moderate reform movement that might provide a model for the continent. These hopes were dashed by 1968. Both Frei and the Alliance failed, especially in the critical area of land reform.[32] Salvador Allende replaced Frei; the Alliance gave way to Nixon-Kissinger militarization. And the Church began a fundamental reexamination of its role in a hemisphere where Castro had succeeded and Kennedy had failed.

The reexamination had begun with Pope John XXIII's extraordinary encyclicals of 1961 and 1963 that stressed the need to honor human rights and create decent standards of living for all peoples. Otherwise, Pope John warned, revolution was probable. He then opened Vatican Council II (1963–65) that studied anew the relationship between the Church and the world. The Church defined its members as a "Pilgrim People of God," that is, a changing people making their way through changing historical circumstances. The Church thus became concerned about development, and specifically how social science could help explain the changes that wracked such areas as Latin America. This in turn opened the clergy to ideas about "dependency" and the effect dependency had on the "Pilgrim People."[33]

The impact of the debate on Latin American churches was profound. Not only had the Church failed politically by opposing Castro and supporting Frei. Membership and attendance had dropped steadily, and recruits for the clergy grew scarce. The working class and peasants, who had venerated priests, refused to defer to them. The gap between the poor and the rich also separated the poor and the priests.[34] Concern in the hierarchy heightened until Pope Paul VI decided to speak personally to the Second General Conference of Latin American Bishops held at Medellín, Colombia, in 1968. The Medellín conference helped trigger the religious revolution that swept the Church into Central America's secular revolutions, and also proved crucial in formalizing liberation theology.

Pope Paul condemned violence as non-Christian, but the bishops turned his view around to argue for the existence of different kinds of violence. One of the worst and most prevalent, they concluded, was "institutionalized violence." The phrase (perhaps the most famous to come out of the meeting) referred to the social and structural conditions of poverty that starved the poor. This approach shifted the problem of sin from individuals to societies. Attention switched from personal conversion to social change, a change that could end "institutionalized violence." The Church thus focused on the poor, not the rich.

At this point in the argument, several other terms appeared that would haunt oligarchs during the seventies. Through a process of consciousness raising, or *conscientización*, the poor themselves were to change their conditions. The idea of the masses becoming the catalyst for their own freedom became known as "liberation theology." During the late sixties, as the rhetoric of the Alliance became hollow, Medellín's documents placed a premium on acts: "It has not ceased to be the hour of speech," one document entitled "Justice" stated, "but it has come to be, with an even more dramatic urgency, the hour for action."[35] Action was to reshape entire societies. To understand how that could be accomplished the bishops returned to dependency theory—the view that international capitalism had through a long process exploited Latin America and institutionalized poverty by making the continent dependent on foreign-controlled trade and investment.

The consensus view was captured by Marcos McGrath, Archbishop of Panama. McGrath belonged to the moderate group at Medellín, but shortly after the conference he stood in the forefront of Panama's fight to gain control of the Canal, and he also aligned himself with Central American revolutionaries. In 1973, as these struggles intensified, McGrath explained his position in the influential journal, *Foreign Affairs:*

The liberal capitalist system and the temptation of the Marxist system appear as the only alternatives in our continent for the transformation of economic structures. Both these systems are affronts to the dignity of the human person. The first takes as a premise the primacy of capital, its power, and the discriminating use of capital in the pursuit of gain. The other, although ideologically it may pretend to be humanist, looks rather to collective man, and in practice converts itself into a totalitarian concentration of state power. It is our obligation to denounce this situation in which Latin America finds itself caught between these two options and remains dependent upon one or other of the centers of power which control its economy.[36]

Neither McGrath nor the other clergy knew where that third option might be. The Medellín documents, however, agreed that a starting point for the search was to work with the poor to change the status quo. That decision had special meaning for priests and especially nuns and laywomen who lived and worked with the poor. By 1970 trouble stirred in Nicaragua, Guatemala, and El Salvador, among other Latin American areas, but the revolutionaries seemed confined mostly to the bourgeois class. Conditions changed after the failure of the Alliance and the 1973 economic crisis. They also changed as priests and nuns began to work in villages to transform not just isolated individuals, but a system.

The Church, it turned out, was superbly structured for such activities. At the local level it established *communidades de base*, or base communities, in which the clergy worked with peasants at a smaller and more informal level than the Church parish. In the base communities, all issues could be discussed—political, human, doctrinal, and religious. The bases became a more radical counterpart of the black people's churches in the United States during the civil rights drive.[37] The base communities, moreover, could be protected by the Church's top hierarchy that continued to have close relations with high government officials, and by Roman Catholic international organizations that channeled funds into, and provided publicity for, the grass-roots operation. The military-oligarchy complex could chop down political opponents, but the Church's voice continued to be heard.

El Salvador became the first testing, and killing, ground in Central America. Shortly after Medellín, the Salvador Conference of Bishops split into conservative and liberal factions, but all, nevertheless, urged the government to divide some idle cotton and coffee plantations into small plots for campesinos. Oligarchs pronounced the bishops to be "Communist and Catholic leaders." Elderly Archbishop Luis Chavéz y González refused to back down. He sent a delegate to the nation's first congress called to debate agrarian reform. Right-wing vigilantes kidnapped the delegate; when later found he had been pumped full of drugs and was delirious. In January 1972 police arrested a parish priest who had been ministering to peasants. The next day passersby found his body dismembered.[38]

Repression deepened as revolution spread in the mid-seventies. Priests in the base communities lost heart when a moderate, Oscar Romero, became archbishop in 1977. But then a close Jesuit friend of Romero's, Rutilio Grande, was murdered because of his work in the villages. Father Alfonso Navarro declared that Grande had been correct in believing that peasants, priests, and oligarchs were equal. Navarro and a fifteen-year-old boy who was in the priest's home were killed by right-wing groups armed with government rifles. One vigilante group, the White Warriors, threatened to kill the remaining forty-seven Jesuits in El Salvador. Pamphlets appeared: "Be a patriot! Kill a priest!"[39] Once hesitant, Archbishop Romero became outspoken in condemning government and vigilante terrorism. The Church did not retreat. Priests continued to work with campesino groups. But the Church also publicly condemned the guerrillas' murder of the Salvadoran Foreign Minister who belonged to the dominant Fourteen Families.

Of most importance, many priests and nuns at the local level changed dramatically. They had begun the seventies ministering to the poor and obeying the instructions of their bishops. They soon learned that neither their commitment to the campesinos nor the principles of Medellín could be carried out without political action. When peaceful attempts to obtain food, land, and other rights ended without change or in repression, the clerics moved to nonviolent opposition, then to supporting violence. A religious commitment to ameliorate poverty could end in a political, even an armed, commitment to oppose the government. The system that enveloped Central America seemed to leave no other alternative.

A different Church met in 1979 at Puebla, Mexico, for the Third Council of Latin American Bishops. At the local levels, priests and nuns were radicalized. But atop the hierarchy a new pope, John Paul II, appeared to declare that while the Church had to be committed to the poor and to evangelization, it had to be committed only in the religious, not the political, sense. Priests were to be involved in "community," not partisan, causes. Unlike the 1968 conference, conservative lay experts and clerics controlled the agenda and the position papers. But debate at Puebla occurred in a limited ideological area. The Church had experienced too much to return to the fifties. As one scholar observed, the bishops worked within an intellectual consensus in which no one sounded like a true Marxist on the one side, or like a Latin American dictator on the other.[40] The bishops could not change events in the base communities. Regardless of how they feared the animal, Church leaders now rode a tiger.

The bishops therefore condemned both capitalism and Marxism, both "terrorist and guerrilla violence." They warned that Catholics must not confuse "gospel values with a particular ideology." (That phrase brought the most revealing quip of the conference from a Peruvian bishop: "Let him who is without ideology throw the first stone.") The Puebla group then reconfirmed the central tenets of Medellín. Poverty had become worse among "our indians, peasants, women, marginal people of the city, and especially the women in these social sectors." The groups picked for attention were significant because they provided the support for revolutions in Nicaragua, El Salvador, and Guatemala. The conference denounced selfish multinational corporations that cared little about "the host country's welfare." It noted the "declining value of our raw materials in relation to the prices of the manufactured goods we buy."

The bishops explicitly condemned the "stages of growth" theory advanced by U.S. economists during the fifties and sixties: "Poverty is not a transitory state; but it is the product of economic, social, and political situations and structures." The key word was "structures," for it signalled the need to redesign the system and not wait for slow—and often illusory—transitions. The conference listed specific human rights and declared them to be an "indispensable part" of the Church's mission. But the bishops went beyond Jimmy Carter's political and civil rights; these were inadequate—even a trap—because they provided restricted democracy, not a remedy for poverty. Conservative Catholic leaders might have prepared the conference agenda, but as one participant observed, "The visiting team managed a tie."[41]

That judgment understated the meaning of Puebla for the more liberal and radical clergy. In Nicaragua, priests were instrumental in the revolution. At a critical moment they played the major role in transforming a narrow Marxist movement into a more moderate, broad-based, and powerful force. In El Salvador, Archbishop Romero became highly critical of government-supported vigilante groups and the atrocities committed by the military. One group of Jesuits led the first strike in history in a large sugar mill and worked closely with a peasant union that supplied soldiers and supplies for a guerrilla unit. As repression increased, Archbishop Romero found himself in a minority among the leaders of the Church. He heard the voice of disapproval directly from Pope John Paul II in the Vatican. On his return to San Salvador, a right-wing political group murdered Romero while he said mass.[42]

Later in 1980 the bodies of three nuns and a Catholic lay person, all U.S. citizens, were found in a shallow grave. At least three of the women had been sexually assaulted before being shot. With these atrocities, support for the revolution spread, even in the United States.[43] One of the murdered women, Maryknoll Sister Ita Ford, said just before her death that "the Christian base communities are the greatest threat to military dictatorship throughout Latin America." One reporter, Clifford Krauss, visited such a group in El Salvador's Chalatenango province—a rebel stronghold—in early 1982. He wrote that midway into the afternoon thirty-five guerrillas and peasants stopped working to read from the New Testament Gospels about the evil of egotism and selfishness. The lay minister then observed, "The Word of God is for us to put into action, to develop our mission. God came to earth to liberate man. If we want to create a new society, we have to sacrifice, we have to suffer."[44]

The best account of the Latin American Church in the seventies estimated the suffering of Roman Catholics who followed the Medellín principles: 850 priests, nuns, and bishops were tortured, murdered, expelled, or arrested between 1968 and the Puebla conference of 1979.[45] In Guatemala, the reaction took several forms. Priests who worked with Indian communities were driven away or murdered. But by the early 1980s they confronted a different challenge. Fundamentalist Protestant sects spread through the country, preaching individual conversion, the glories of military and political authority, the virtues of capitalism, and the value of inequality.

One sect was the Christian Church of the Word, associated with Global Outreach of Eureka, California. That group helped Guatemalans rebuild after the 1976 earthquake. Among the sect's missionary conquests was General Efraín Ríos Montt, who seized dictatorial power in 1982. His Church of the Word, not surprisingly, aligned itself with the Guatemalan military that defined priests and nuns as the enemy. Three priests were killed within a thirty-six-month period in just one province—an area in which rebel strength nevertheless grew. According to one Guatemalan army officer, General Ríos Montt's word for the Indians and peasants was simple: "If you are with us, we'll feed you, if not, we'll kill you."[46] The Roman Catholic priests meanwhile warned that if the sects succeeded in spreading their doctrine of individualism, the village communities would be fragmented and the last hope of the Indians destroyed.

Little more than a decade after the Medellín meeting, the Roman Catholic Church literally stood on the firing line in Central America. The transformation had been historic, the kind of history measured in a half-millenium, not just a decade or a century. The post-Medellín years also turned out to be historic for the Central American nations: one fell to revolution, another was on the edge of doing so, and two others stumbled towards the edge. A guerrilla movement even appeared in Costa Rica. In the first four countries, the revolutions derived much power and direction from the priests and nuns who had not intended to become revolutionaries when they began searching for the alternatives to the poverty and disease which enshrouded their work.

Nicaragua: The System Overthrown

Revolution triumphed first in Nicaragua. With the exception of Costa Rica, no Central American nation in 1970 had seemed more safe from upheaval. Anastasio Somoza and his National Guard controlled the country. In 1969 the Guard trapped and killed five leaders of the Sandinista revolutionaries. Somoza pronounced the Sandinista Front (the FSLN) dead. The dictator, moreover, enjoyed total support from Washington. His relations with President Nixon were so close that he paid a state visit to the White House during Nixon's first term and allegedly dispatched his mother to Washington with $1,000,000 in her handbag for Nixon's reelection campaign.[47] Nicaragua, Somoza proclaimed in 1974, did not belong to any third-world nonaligned group, but was "totally aligned with the United States and the Western world."[48]

During the new cold war, as nationalist, third-world leaders chipped away at U.S. power, Somoza was a welcome relief: he did as he was told. He consequently did well. In 1972, Nixon performed a much appreciated symbolic act by terminating the 1916 Bryan-Chamorro treaty that had given the United States monopoly rights to build an isthmian canal in Nicaragua. More concretely, North American aid and private investment flooded into Nicaragua. Much of this money directly enriched the Somoza family and the Guard officers. Nicaragua was blessed with a highly favorable person-to-land ratio, but after the Guard officers and Somozas took what they wanted, 200,000 peasants had no land at all. (The officers and the family also monopolized the high profit industries: prostitution, gambling, construction kickbacks, taxation.) Nicaragua enjoyed the highest annual increase in agricultural production (5 percent) between 1950 and 1977 of any Central American nation. By the end of that era, however, the landless rural labor force in some areas was more than 1,000 percent larger than during the fifties.[49]

As late as 1976 the country boasted a $46 million trade surplus, inflation dropped to 3 percent, and the gross national product grew 8 percent. But such aggregate figures had little meaning for most Nicaraguans. Within three years, Somoza and the Guard had to flee the country. One reason for their disappearance after decades of extraordinary economic growth was offered by a leading Nicaraguan banker after the revolution had triumphed: "It was an ingenious thing. For 45 years the Somoza family ran this country like their own private enterprise. The country was only a mechanism to invest abroad."[50]

Without exception, U.S. Presidents did not care. Nixon's administration never flagged in its support. It sent bilateral aid and urged large contributions to Nicaragua from international lending agencies.[51] A Nixon friend, Turner B. Shelton, arrived in Managua as ambassador. Shelton had been only a run-of-the-mill foreign service officer, but in his travels had come to know Bebe Rebozo, a Florida wheeler-dealer who was perhaps Nixon's closest friend, and multibillionaire Howard

Hughes, who contributed to Nixon's campaign. For a brief time Hughes even found refuge in Managua when Shelton was ambassador. The new appointee did not know Spanish, but, as *Time* correspondent Bernard Diederich phrased it, he "had a special way of bowing when he clasped [Somoza's] outstretched hand."[52] Knowing his man, the dictator soon made decisions after consulting no one in Managua but Shelton.

But the end was near. When an earthquake destroyed much of the capital and leveled many villages in 1972, Nixon sprang to the rescue, sending $32 million for reconstruction. Even so, the National Guard proved to be incapable of keeping order in the devastated areas; Shelton therefore ordered 600 U.S. troops to fly in from the Panama Canal Zone so Somoza could maintain control.

The earthquake had started a chain of events that climaxed in the success of the Sandinistas. They and others watched with surprise as the National Guard, even Somoza's personal elite guard, faded into the chaos. Discipline collapsed as soldiers deserted to find their families or join in the looting. Those officers who did not loot publicly did so privately when they and the Somozas handled all the U.S. funds and medical supplies. Of the $32 million sent by Nixon, the Nicaraguan Treasury finally accounted for about $16 million.[53] The Guard sold relief supplies for its own profit. When reconstruction began, Somoza and his fellow officers drove out other businessmen to control construction funds. Managua was never totally rebuilt, but a new area rose on the outskirts of town where Somoza's friends made a fortune in land speculation and building. The business class never forgave the dictator. As a leading U.S. businessman in Nicaragua recalled in 1979: "He robbed us blind. He was not at all interested in us, except for what we could give, and we gave him plenty. . . . Right now it is showing up in a backfire."[54]

Somoza then made another mistake. With Shelton's help, he had swung a political deal that guaranteed him no opposition and a lifetime in power. As the 1974 election approached, his greed outpaced itself. He filed criminal charges against those who urged a boycott of the voting, then declared nine parties illegal. The Roman Catholic bishops issued a pastoral letter that denounced attempts to force people to vote, and indeed denounced the entire campaign. (Later the bishops refused to attend the inauguration.) The small liberal press, led by Pedro Joaquín

Chamorro's *La Prensa*, published stories about the post-earthquake corruption and urged a boycott of the election. Chamorro was among those whom Somoza arrested and tried in the courts. Somoza won by a margin of twenty to one, leaving nothing to chance: his henchmen bribed voters with money, food, and rum. He had, however, stirred powerful enemies.[55]

The election results meant little. They impressed only those who believed that statistics generated by voting in an authoritarian Central American country were somehow blows struck on behalf of the free world. The Church and Chamorro were actually signalling that Somoza was becoming vulnerable. Just how vulnerable became clear in late 1974 when a faction of the FSLN seized a number of Nicaraguan and foreign officials at a dinner party (Shelton had left only minutes earlier), and held them until Somoza promised to release political prisoners, pay $5 million—which he obtained without delay in New York City—and allow the thirteen guerrillas to fly out of the country. As the guerrillas traveled to the airport, crowds cheered them. Somoza retaliated by launching terrorist campaigns against areas suspected of harboring the Sandinistas.[56]

For a time, Somoza's forces scored significant victories in the field. They killed several FSLN leaders, and the movement broke into three sections: the Proletarian Tendency, which urged urban warfare; the Prolonged Popular War (PPW), which argued for mobilizing campesinos to fight a long-term conflict; and the Third-World Tendency *(Terceristas)*, which was the most open and pluralistic (although it did oppose the Communist party), and advocated war in both the cities and villages. But the factionalism did not entirely benefit Somoza. The *Terceristas'* pluralism and moderate rhetoric won over conservative businessmen who had given up on the regime. The *Terceristas* built a broad ideological umbrella under which all anti-Somoza forces could organize. The revolution thus gained momentum despite the Guard's victories. Anti-Somoza feeling also spread in the United States during 1975 and 1976 when priests testified before Congress about Guard atrocities. The torture included not only the usual rape and electric shocks, but more imaginative devices, such as forcing a prisoner to swallow a button on a string while a Somoza official kept tugging it up.[57]

When Jimmy Carter became president and dedicated himself to upholding human rights, Nicaraguan Archbishop Miguel Obando y Bravo issued a pastoral letter condemning the National Guard's atrocities. The White House made no significant response. But a group on Capitol Hill led by Representative Edward Koch (Dem.-N.Y.) and Senator Edward Kennedy (Dem.-Mass.) moved to stop all military aid to Nicaragua. After a bitter fight, the so-called "Somoza lobby" defeated the move. Congressman John Murphy (Dem.-N.Y.) led the pro-Somoza forces; he had been a classmate of the dictator at LaSalle Academy and remained a close friend. Murphy received help from high-powered lobbyists, including the former legal counsel of the Republican party, William Cramer, who received at least $50,000 from Somoza. Koch and Kennedy, however, forced the Carter administration to take a stand. Human rights had to be improved or, according to congressional legislation and the president's campaign rhetoric, aid would be severed. Neither side, the State Department or Somoza, wanted a cutoff to occur.[58]

As every president after Hoover knew, Somozas did as they were told. The National Guard eased up on its victims. Freedom of the press reappeared. From the dictator's point of view, however, requests by Carter ("that Baptist," as Somoza disgustedly called him) to deal more gently with his enemies turned out to be useless advice. The rebellion spread. A group of professional people, later known as "the twelve," publicly condemned Somoza and demanded that he resign. The growing chaos was partly due to his absence during the summer of 1977. (He had suffered a heart attack while at the villa of his mistress, Dinorah Sampson, and his doctors rushed him to Miami for treatment. Hospitals in Nicaragua were apparently little better than when his father had suddenly needed a good one in 1956.) The disorder also resulted from growing concern over a sudden decline in the economy, a decline forced by ever-higher military spending, the fleeing of capital to New York and Switzerland, and guerrilla attacks on large farms and power plants.[59]

But the crisis soon testified to the contradictions of Carter's human rights policy. As long as the United States stressed opening up the political process and limiting Guard violence, while at the same time doing nothing to redistribute wealth or opportunity, Carter's policy was a recipe for disaster. His administration moved from the assumption that by changing political methods Somoza could weaken the revolution. The assumption had no basis in reality. Modifying the political process did little to ameliorate the economic maldistribution and built-in corruption that initially gave the revolution its life.

North American conservatives later condemned Carter's policy as a primary reason for Somoza's fall.[60] Their condemnation had little basis in fact. The problem was that Carter and his predecessors never pushed Somoza far enough, early enough, so that either he or another Nicaraguan leader could begin to remove the socioeconomic causes of the revolution. Neither Carter nor his critics can escape that judgment by answering that the United States should have interfered only so far, or not at all, in Nicaraguan affairs: the Somoza dynasty had been a subsidiary of the United States since 1936.

Another contradiction also plagued Carter's policy. He valued human rights, but he preferred Somoza to the FSLN. Consequently when the dictator eased his repression, the United States sent in $2.5 million in arms in late 1977 (while continuing to hold back economic aid). The Carter administration forgot its commitment to human rights, and looked away from the massacres and the rapes, to send the arms just before the legislative authority to do so expired. The military supplies arrived just as the rebels launched a major offensive during "Sandinista October," as it came to be known. After months of silence, the revolutionaries demonstrated their considerable military power. On 10 January 1978, the humane and distinguished Joaquín Chamorro of *La Prensa* was murdered by pro-Somoza gunmen. The killing launched the first mass uprising against the regime, and for the first time people from the urban slums joined the rebellion. The National Guard met the uprising with renewed repression.[61]

Carter was trapped. He wanted both to send aid and to force Somoza toward reform. The president, moreover, came under much pressure from the Somoza lobby on Capitol Hill. One member, Representative Charles Wilson (Dem.-Tex.), threatened to hold up all foreign aid appropriations until Nicaragua received its millions. Somoza bragged that he had more friends in the U.S. Congress than did Carter. State Department officials argued at length whether to send arms secretly, but finally decided to do it publicly because secrecy was impossible in Nicaraguan affairs, and any revelation could only further embarrass the Carter administration.[62] Somoza complained loudly that Carter's human rights policy interfered in Nicaragua's internal affairs, but the dictator played the game: he gave amnesty to some political prisoners and allowed an OAS team to investigate human rights violations. The situation had grown too serious for either Carter or Somoza to stand on principle. As the *Washington Post* editorialized in early August, the central question no longer revolved around human rights violations, because the United States "is really dealing with . . . a revolution. . . . A 'second Cuba' in Central America? It is not out of the question."[63]

As Somoza's regime tottered, a major debate broke out within the Carter inner circle. Zbigniew Brzezinski and the National Security Council began to play a more active role. An initial result of the debate was a secret letter in which Carter congratulated Somoza for improving his human rights record. The State Department's original evaluation proved true: little remained secret in U.S.-Nicaraguan relations. News of the letter leaked, probably through a State Department official. The media interpreted it as indicating Carter's strong support for the dictator's regime. But the message was not that simple. The State Department, which had fought against sending the letter, had finally succeeded in adding language that politely ordered Somoza to open up his political system.[64]

Within a month, the importance of the human-rights debate all but disappeared. Led by Edén Pastora ("Commandante Zero" as he became known), twenty-five FSLN guerrillas dramatically seized the National Legislative Palace, kidnapping nearly all of Somoza's congress and several of his relatives in what Pastora called "Operation Pigpen." Pastora extracted a string of concessions from the humiliated ruler before leaving via the Nicaraguan airport. Again, crowds lined the streets to cheer, and they were particularly enthusiastic along the airport road that passed through some of Managua's worst slums. Another general strike and urban uprising followed the incident. The FSLN army multiplied ten times to 7,000 members.

Somoza retaliated by turning the Guard loose in September 1978. It levelled parts of towns and massacred thousands of people. One survivor later testified, "I could see what they did to my Mother after they killed her—they slit her stomach open with a bayonet. They cut off the genitals of my brother-in-law and stuffed them in his mouth." Amnesty International declared that in some areas all males over fourteen years of age were murdered systematically. At this moment, the OAS human rights investigating team arrived and recorded the atrocities.[65]

Anti-Somoza uprisings occurred spontaneously and without FSLN direction. Venezuela, Mexico, Costa Rica, and Panama sensed the kill. They moved supplies to the revolutionaries while the Costa Ricans— José Figueres and his countrymen had long memories—allowed the FSLN to establish its government-in-exile in San José. The Costa Ricans did not care for the radicalism of some FSLN leaders and programs, but understanding that the revolution had moved into its final phase, they worked to make its results as acceptable as possible. The Costa Ricans received help in this task during February 1979: the three FSLN factions merged under *Tercerista* leadership into the Government for National Reconstruction (GRN). More moderate, less doctrinaire revolutionaries gained considerable political control, but all the groups agreed on the primary objective of totally removing Somoza and the guard.

Only the United States refused to accept the inevitable. As they have done almost automatically since Woodrow Wilson's dealings with Mexican, Chinese, and Russian revolutionaries, U.S. officials began the search once again for an acceptable (and now nonexistent) middle. For eleven months (September 1978 to July 1979), Washington teams tried to split moderates away from the FSLN coalition, and to keep Somoza— or at least the Guard—in business until the scheduled 1981 elections.

But nothing worked. No middle could be found because to U.S. officials this meant Somoza's National Guard ruling without Somoza—and such a "middle" way would be opposed by Nicaraguans to the death. The United States turned to other tactics. These were described by Alfonso Robelo, probably the most important moderate and pro-North American figure in the FSLN movement:

First, the U.S. came and told everyone they would put pressure on Somoza to go. They created false expectations. When Somoza's reaction was to say, "Come and [remove me] physically," they backed down. They actually downplayed the process and at the end put little pressure on Somoza and gave him valuable time to build up his National Guard.[66]

In early 1979 Carter tried to pressure Somoza by cutting off military and economic aid, while sharply reducing U.S. diplomatic personnel in Nicaragua. That move also turned out to be unproductive. It publicly announced that Somoza no longer enjoyed the unwavering support of the White House, but it did not reduce his military effectiveness. The United States had already trained his Guard. As North American supply lines dried up, the Israelis and Argentines sold Somoza arms and ammunition during his last months.[67] The purchases drained more money out of Nicaragua. Facing huge debts, Somoza asked the International Monetary Fund for emergency help. As late as May 1979, two months before Somoza fled, the United States supported his request for a $66 million loan from the IMF. U.S. officials somehow hoped to prop up the Somoza regime, but not prop up Somoza.

On 29 May 1979, the FSLN troops moved out of their Costa Rican bases to launch a "final offensive." For its part Mexico conducted a diplomatic offensive by breaking relations with Somoza and then, to Washington's anger, sent missions urging other nations to follow suit. Suffering a series of military defeats, the National Guard retaliated by rocket-bombing the slums (that supplied increasing numbers of FSLN fighters) and killing thousands of women and children. Most of the men had already departed to fight.

U.S. officials understood this was their last opportunity. Policy-making was concentrated in the White House where Carter, Brzezinski, and C.I.A. and Pentagon officials could overbalance the State Department's growing reluctance to support the Guard. A White House spokesman even declared the Guard had to be kept to "preserve order"; at that moment Somoza's troops were dive-bombing slums, murdering unarmed people in the streets, and looting the cities.[68] Carter and Brzezinski reverted to tactics that had worked before: they called an emergency OAS meeting to urge an inter-American force that could move into Nicaragua, stop the fighting, and establish an acceptable regime. A propaganda campaign was launched emphasizing Cuba's role. The FSLN soon seemed to many North Americans little more than a puppet controlled by Castro and the Kremlin.

Nothing worked. The U.S. proposal for an OAS "peacekeeping force" ran into united opposition from the other states in the hemisphere. The Mexican delegation led the fight against Washington's idea. Carter suffered a humiliating defeat. For the first time since its origins in 1948, the OAS had rejected a U.S. proposal to intervene in an American state.

In seeking to replay Johnson's exercise of 1965 in the Dominican Republic, Carter discovered that the two situations were not similar. The Dominican episode had involved not a mass revolution but two army-supported factions opposing each other in a small strip of territory. Nor was U.S. influence the same as in 1965. The ghosts of past U.S. interventions could not be laid to rest; if North Americans had poor memories the Latin Americans did not. Assistant Secretary of State Viron P. Vaky accurately observed that the OAS rejection "reflected how deeply the American states were sensitized by the Dominican intervention of 1965, and how deeply they fear physical intervention."[69]

Carter had no more luck convincing other governments that Castro pulled the strings controlling the FSLN. Cuba had supported the revolutionaries since 1961, although the extent of the support varied greatly over the years. During the final climactic months of war, at least four other Latin American nations provided considerable support and political guidance. During the final offensive of April through June of 1979, however, Castro cooperated with Costa Rica and sent in at least one hundred and fifty tons of munitions on planes flown by Costa Rican and Panamanian pilots. They used northern Costa Rica as a supply base for the Sandinistas. Assistant Secretary of State Viron Vaky nevertheless declared that Cuba was "not the only or even the most important" supporter of the Sandinistas.[70]

On 20 June 1979 most other North Americans witnessed a horror that pushed Castro out of their minds. National Guard soldiers took an ABC-TV newsman, Bill Stewart, out of his car, made him kneel in the middle of a street, and shot him through the head. Unknown to the killers, Stewart's camera crew caught every moment of the murder on film.

Within hours after Stewart's death, North American television viewers saw for themselves the senseless brutality that Nicaraguans had suffered at Somoza's hands for years. Confronted with total failure, U.S. officials scrambled to make the best possible deal with the revolutionary Government for National Reconstruction (GRN). Since late 1978, State Department official William Bowdler had led the mediation attempts. Bowdler came with an interesting background. He helped create a new regime in the Dominican Republic in 1965 after the U.S. military intervention. Carter now dispatched Lawrence Pezzullo to join Bowdler. Pezzullo had a decade of experience in Latin American affairs. Carter ordered him to demand Somoza's resignation then use it as bait to obtain FSLN agreement for a moderate post-Somoza regime. (At their first meeting, Pezzullo found Congressman John Murphy sitting next to the dictator as an adviser.) After some dallying, Somoza gave his resignation to the ambassador. Pezzullo and Bowdler then asked the GRN to enlarge its five-person governing junta (Sergio Ramírez, Alfonso Robelo, Violeta Barrios de Chamorro, Moises Hassan, and Daniel Ortega) to at least seven members by adding two or more "moderates." A *New York Times* correspondent watched the bargaining and reported from Managua that "the United States seems to be assuming its traditional role as final arbiter of Nicaragua's political destiny."[71]

Traditions, however, were changing in Central America. The junta rejected key parts of Carter's proposal. The first U.S. demand—that no mass executions be held after the FSLN victory—caused no problems. The revolutionaries had long promised to allow no mass killings, even of the hated Guard officers, and the junta made good that promise. (Some *Somocistas* were even allowed to leave for neighboring Honduras or the United States, where they began scheming to overthrow the new government.) Nor was the U.S. Embassy or any North Americans ever threatened by revolutionary mobs. A second demand—that the junta be enlarged—was rejected. The junta argued that it already represented a broad-based group. Carter turned to Venezuela and Mexico for help. Wanting to ensure post-victory moderation, these two nations leaned on the junta to be more flexible. The revolutionaries complied by appointing an eighteen-member "Cabinet" with only one Sandinista representative; the remainder were businessmen and professionals. But the five-member junta was not enlarged.[72]

On the third U.S. demand, that elements of a "purged" National Guard be preserved and brought into the government, no compromise was possible. Nicaraguans hated the Guard. They were appalled that Carter tried to maintain some of its power. In his Sunday message issued during the negotiations, Archbishop Obando y Bravo declared, "We lament the ambiguity of those governments who have thought or continue to think of their own political interests before the common good of the Nicaraguan people."[73] The Guard was an empty, rotted shell. It delighted in its reputation of toughness, but its officers had grown fat and lazy from corruption. The Guard's toughness, moreover, had been proved by the murder and brutalizing of women, children, and unarmed men. That turned out to be insufficient preparation for fighting armed, dedicated revolutionaries. Since 1979 U.S. conservatives have tried to rewrite the history of the Nicaraguan revolution's last days to make it appear that the Guard never lost—or lost because of the U.S. arms cutoff. Somoza's troops, however, had been given all the arms they should have needed; between 1975 and 1978 the United States alone provided $14 million of arms for the 8,000-man Guard. As for the actual result, a foreign mercenary fighting for Somoza disgustedly described the Guard towards the end: "There was nothing gutsy about those guys. . . . They ran like rats."[74]

As the Guard disintegrated, so did U.S. policy. Somoza finally fled on 17 July 1979. After several intermediate stops, he and his mistress (his U.S.-born wife had long since moved to London) settled in a fortress in Paraguay, a gray, stifling dictatorship that Somoza had once described as "the last place on earth for the worst people in the world."[75] In 1980, bazooka shells shredded Somoza, his armor-plated Mercedes, and a U.S. businessman riding with him.

Debate meanwhile erupted in the United States, just as the 1980 presidential campaign began, over whether Carter "lost" Nicaragua. Henry Kissinger accused the president of "actively working to overthrow Somoza without having any idea [of] what to replace him [with]. . . . I think we should have been prepared simultaneously to put in in his place a moderate alternative."[76] Kissinger's view became a common criticism. It was also an irony. Carter had worked to replace Somoza with the most "moderate alternative" possible: Somoza's National Guard. But the president could not have maintained the Guard's authority, it turned out, unless he had been willing to land U.S. troops unilaterally—no other OAS nation would join the operation—then use those troops not only to fight revolutionaries that were supported by all the major regional powers, but to put down spontaneous uprisings in Nicaraguan towns and villages. No other alternative appeared. And no knowledgeable observer, including Kissinger, suggested sending in marines in July 1979.

The United States now had to live with a revolutionary government whose authority it had fought to the end. Both sides clearly wanted to avoid repeating the disaster during the years 1959 through 1961 when U.S.-Cuban differences pushed Castro into the Soviet camp.[77] Long before their victory, the Sandinistas repeatedly declared their intention to become economically dependent on no one and to follow a "non-aligned" foreign policy. The Sandinistas, however, had the misfortune to gain power just as the Soviets invaded Afghanistan, the U.S. Congress rejected the SALT-II agreements to limit the arms race with Russia, and North American conservatives gathered strength for the 1980 elections.

In this charged atmosphere few acts could be non-aligned. Within a week after taking Managua the top Sandinista leaders flew to Havana where Castro celebrated them as heroes. Nicaragua next joined the "Movement of Non-Aligned Countries" and openly criticized U.S. assistance to El Salvador's military regime. Most notably, the Sandinistas supported self-determination in Afghanistan, but joined major non-aligned countries (such as India) in refusing to vote for a U.S.-sponsored U.N. resolution that condemned the Soviet invasion. The Nicaraguans publicly defended all of these policies. They feared the U.N. resolution could lead to increased U.S. involvement in Southwest Asia and perhaps create a major East-West conflict. Neither the new regime nor most other emerging nations wanted to be trapped in that kind of struggle between the two superpowers.

Discussing the touchy issue of El Salvador, the Nicaraguan Ambassador to the United Nations worried that U.S. intervention "could turn all of Central American into Vietnam" and spread "counterrevolutionary intervention" into his own country. He also argued that Cuban-Sandinista relations had always been close, and that Castro's help—especially in the health and educational areas—was critical as well as without strings. (Or at least without visible strings. Castro must have realized that by involving thousands of Cubans in the most fundamental grass-roots organizations, he had considerable influence in a new Nicaragua.) The Cuban leader had warned the Sandinistas not to copy his model, but to maintain a large private business sector and retain as many ties as possible to United States funds. The Sandinistas intended to follow that advice.[78] They had excellent reasons for their foreign policy strategy: self-preservation and maintenance of maximum freedom of action. This kind of behavior, however, was not what North Americans had experienced historically with Central Americans—especially Nicaraguans.

For all their searching, the Sandinistas needed immediate U.S. help on an emergency basis. The country had lost 40,000 to 50,000 people in the war (the equivalent of 4 million U.S. deaths). One-fifth of the population was homeless, 40,000 children were orphaned. Somoza and the Guard officers had plundered the economy. They left behind only a $1.5 billion debt. (Somoza personally made off with a fortune estimated at upwards of $100 million.) At the end, the dictator's Guard had turned industrial plants into rubble.[79] The country was little more than a ruin.

The United States responded in mid-1979 by sending in nearly $20 million in aid. North American businessmen reentered the country to be welcomed by the revolutionaries. When radical union organizers tried to foment a strike against Coca-Cola and other U.S. companies, Commander Daniel Ortega, emerging as the junta's strongman, expelled the organizers from the country. United Brands and Standard Fruit resumed operations. As it had promised, the junta did create a huge public sector simply by nationalizing Somoza's former properties. The banks (looted by the dictator) were also nationalized and turned over to respected bankers to operate. Nationalization went no farther. One experienced U.S. businessman in Nicaragua told a congressional committee that the Sandinista "economic team" was of high quality: "Communists are not in control, and unless we democratic and private types concede the issue by default, the chances are against Communism in Nicaragua."[80]

Ambassador Pezzullo had no illusions after bargaining with the junta. He told Congress much the same:

> It is very much a Nicaraguan phenomenon. There is no question about that. Sandinismo, whatever its opportunities ought to be, is a Nicaraguan, home-grown movement. Sandino predates Castro. He was a man; he lived. So there is no reason to believe they are going out and borrow from elsewhere when they really have something at home. The nature of this thing is such that you have to see it take its own form, rather than make prejudgments about it.[81]

The autumn of 1979 was the high-water mark of U.S.-Sandinista relations. Decline quickly set in. The Sandinistas gave the relationship a severe jolt when they delayed long-promised national elections. From Washington's point of view, the delay meant that the revolutionaries intended to impose a Communist-style regime. From the Nicaraguan perspective, however, the announcement meant that the Sandinistas were splitting into factions; any election campaign could turn into a struggle that would fragment and even destroy the revolution. That possibility could not be risked. In mid-1980, Defense Minister Humberto Ortega formally announced that elections would not be held until 1985.[82] Another such jolt and good relations could be impossible.

Important U.S. congressional leaders had already reached that conclusion. In September 1979 Carter asked Congress for an $80 million aid package for Central America, $75 million of which was to go to Nicaragua. Nearly one-third of the amount was for the U.S. training of Sandinista soldiers. The State Department declared that prompt approval would be an "important symbol" to show that the United States could respond positively to revolutionary change in Latin America. But Carter had lost most of his influence over Congress. The legislature itself was burdened by too little discipline and too many old-style Somoza lobbyists. Congress did not debate the request until January 1980. The House then added sixteen conditions, including one that required 60 percent of the aid to go to the private business sector, another insisting that no funds could go to projects using Cuban personnel (that provision effectively cut out aid to health and educational facilities), and yet another making aid conditional on the Sandinistas following high human rights standards and holding elections in a "reasonable period of time." The Nicaraguans bridled at these conditions (20,000 marched in one anti-Yankee protest). But the junta realized that more was at stake than $75 million: unless the measure passed to indicate Washington's confidence in the regime, international banks would be reluctant to make loans. The Nicaraguans consequently continued to ask for the money, even after the House added another clause requiring some of the money to be used for propaganda that told the recipients how much the United States was helping them. By March, the House and Senate had still not reached agreement. The Sandinistas were desperate. Their Treasury was virtually empty, and the spiraling oil prices created a new economic crisis.[83]

Then Nicaragua opened expanded diplomatic relations with the Soviet Union. A series of trade agreements with the Soviet bloc followed. Amounting to $100 million in value, they provided help in agriculture, power generating, transportation, and communications. This shock was not the last. The Sandinista government (and others, including Mexico), channeled aid to revolutionaries who stepped up campaigns in El Salvador. The Nicaraguans meanwhile began building their own army and tightening internal controls.[84] They feared, justifiably, that Somoza's forces were preparing a counterrevolution. Finally, the two leading moderates, Violeta Chamorro and Alfonso Robelo, resigned from the junta in May 1980. For them, the government had moved too far to the left. At the same time they also urged U.S. non-interference, and Robelo particularly defended his country's non-aligned foreign policy. The two wanted the arguments kept within the revolutionary regime. Two of the most respected members of the Managua establishment—Rafael Cordova Rivas of the Supreme Court, and Arturo Cruz, head of the Central Bank—joined the junta.

Lines hardened while Congress dawdled, but it finally passed the aid measure in June 1980, eight months after Carter had submitted it. The reasons for the final passage after the traumas of the spring are varied: a desire to maintain leverage on the Sandinistas; an attempt to counter the Soviet-bloc aid; the fear that without such help the Sandinistas—as had Castro in 1960 and 1961—would move sharply to the left; Carter's acceptance of Congress's provisions requiring support for El Salvador's military regime, and no use of the funds for land reform. But another critical reason was the desire by 120 of the largest North American, European, and Japanese banks to avoid a Nicaraguan default on the country's $1.5 billion debt. After long, tough negotiations (at one point the largest creditor, Citibank of New York City, tried to push for debt-service payments that would hand over to the bankers nearly one-third of the country's entire export revenue in 1980), a deal was struck in September 1980. The junta agreed to reschedule nearly $600 million of debt—piled up by Somoza, not the revolutionaries—for payment over the next twelve years. Assuming the debt meant assuming also an austerity program to pay it off; the traditional year-end bonuses for workers, for example, had to be sharply cut in 1980. But the Nicaraguans had few alternatives. If they were to stay out of the Soviet bloc they had little choice but to tie themselves to the international bankers and lending agencies. Nicaraguan bankers wanted the United States government involved. They lobbied hard in Congress for the $75 million aid package during the spring. Once these steps were taken, a third would follow: the Nicaraguans could obtain over $200 million in long-term loans from the IADB, World Bank, and other lending agencies. The importance of this series of deals, all interrelated, could not be overestimated. As former Assistant Secretary of State Viron Vaky observed, the debt arrangements with the banks "locked Nicaragua into the private money market, and Nicaragua's willingness to do so was a significant move toward a pragmatic, pluralistic course."[85]

Yet no sooner were these deals completed than the United States and Nicaraguan governments resumed their collision course. On July 19, 1979, the day of the FSLN triumph, the C.I.A. began to help reorganize Somoza's officers. By late 1980, Carter told the C.I.A. to fund anti-Sandinista press, labor unions, and political parties. Mistrust increased. Nicaragua's economy deteriorated despite the agreement with the bankers. Disillusion spread within the country. After Reagan's victory in November, the Sandinistas tightened their control. They prohibited opposition political rallies and increased censorship. The junta arrested members of the private sector for allegedly plotting to overthrow the government, and one private sector leader was killed by Sandinista troops who claimed they caught him running guns.[86]

Both sides, Nicaraguan and North American, had vowed to learn from history, not be trapped by it. But half a century of U.S. intimacy with Somoza held sway; neither could avoid the path taken by U.S.-Cuban relations between 1959 and 1961. The North American system was unable to tolerate revolutionaries. And vice versa.

El Salvador: Oligarchs Fall, Colonels Rise, Revolution Spreads

Until the sixties, U.S. involvement in El Salvador never matched that in Nicaragua or the other three Central American nations. The oligarchy controlled El Salvador, even when it did not control the international coffee price so critical to the economy. During the sixties, however, North American investment and aid poured in. U.S. military aid more than doubled during the Alliance decade. But the North Americans arrived at a bad time. Already enduring one of the world's widest gaps between the rich and poor, El Salvador was about to explode in bloodshed. Washington officials were caught in the middle of that explosion.

The 1969 "soccer war" had ended in a glorious victory over Honduras. Ardent nationalists and pleased oligarchs cheered the military government. But troubles soon appeared. Honduras forced hundreds of thousands of Salvadorans to return home. Already suffering from the worst people-to-land ratio in the hemisphere, the country came under tremendous economic pressure. Then the Central American Common Market collapsed. El Salvador, perhaps the prime beneficiary of CACM's trade, suddenly found that the war brought vicarious pleasure militarily but instant disaster economically. Between 1970 and 1974 per capita income dropped more than 2.5 percent each year. By 1971 the number of landless families had more than tripled since the Alliance's promises had been made in 1961; this change occurred in a nation where 60 percent of the people depended on the land.[87]

The political economy systematically starved the poor. Almost half the land on the larger farms (those over 100 acres) was used for pasture or kept fallow. The campesino meanwhile tilled his small plot until it eroded. Thus as cattle prospered, production of the two staples for the peasant diet—beans and pork—declined. Sorghum, which grew on the poorest soil, replaced beans. It became human as well as cattle feed. As one expert phrased it, "Land is a scarce resource [in El Salvador] only for the small [land] holders."[88]

The first major challenge to the oligarch-military complex, however, came not from the countryside but from urban areas. During the sixties, the cities and towns had multiplied in population and wealth along with the industrialization generated by the Alliance and Common Market. The oligarchs siphoned off the wealth: in 1974 the top 1 percent of the families in San Salvador, the capital, received more income than the top 50 percent of the poorest.[89] The inhabitants in the urban areas, however, developed a weapon the peasants lacked: the Christian Democratic Party (PDC).

Along with other moderate liberal parties in Latin America, PDC support burgeoned during the sixties under the joint encouragement of the Alliance and the Church. The Salvadoran party received able leadership from José Napoleon Duarte, a Notre Dame University-trained engineer who urged that reforms be enacted before the system blew up. His support concentrated in San Salvador, where he served as mayor. Duarte's party never displayed great dedication to campesino interests, but by 1968—just eight years after its founding—it became the dominant nationwide party by gaining control of hundreds of cities, towns, and villages. Shocked oligarchs and military leaders retaliated in the 1970 elections by reducing PDC control to eight municipalities.[90] But Duarte had become the most popular politician in the country. In 1972, he and his running mate, Guillermo Ungo, headed a coalition in a heated national campaign that raised a new Salvadoran political consciousness. An uncommonly hopeful, democratic era seemed to dawn.

The results, however, never even began to meet these expectations. The army-controlled government chose Colonel Arturo Molina to oppose Duarte in the 1972 elections. As expected, the PDC swept urban areas, but when the countryside also began swinging to Duarte, the national radio suddenly went dead. When broadcasting resumed, Molina was ahead. The fraud was so blatant the junior army officers—more liberal than their superiors as well as jealous of their superiors' privileges—revolted, seized the outgoing president, and tried to put Duarte in power. After skirmishes in which more than 300 people were killed or injured, the senior military command put down the coup attempt, but only after receiving help from forces in CONDECA. To no one's surprise, Somoza's National Guard and Guatemalan forces led the mission. U.S. military advisers also participated. Molina's supporters arrested Duarte—who had been brutally beaten—and put him on a plane for Guatemala. Evidence suggests that Molina wanted the Guatemalan military to kill Duarte when he landed, but the PDC leader escaped to live in Venezuela for the next seven years.[91]

The army then set out to destroy the PDC. Molina's troops occupied the National University to purge anyone suspected of liberal sympathies. PDC leaders dispersed. But as in the past, the military only succeeded in further bipolarizing the country and driving the opposition to violence. Left-wing kidnappers seized members of oligarch families. In the next decade these crimes produced more than $50 million in ransoms, with the money spent on arms. (In the words of one reporter, however, "moonlighting military officers" also carried out and profited from the kidnappings.)[92] The repercussions of the 1973 oil embargo added to the crisis. An inflation rate of 60 percent in 1973 and 1974 led desperate Salvadorans to join guerrilla groups that robbed banks and carried out bombings.

Economic pressure mounted. The remaining Christian Democrats could no longer hold the middle together. On one side of the widening gap a number of revolutionary bands appeared. The most important was the Farabundo Martí Popular Liberation Forces (FPL) led by Cayetano Carpio. Known as the "Ho Chi Minh of Central America," he ranked as one of the oldest (born in 1920) and most experienced revolutionaries. Raised by nuns, Cayetano Carpio had been a seminarian and labor organizer before heading the Communist party. Latin American Communists had usually allied with middle-class parties while opposing armed revolution. But Cayetano Carpio knew by 1970 that El Salvador could not be changed through the political system. He left the party and concentrated on organizing rural areas, where priests and the base communities provided natural allies. A second group, the People's Revolutionary Army (ERP) had arrived at the same dour conclusion in 1972 and split from Duarte's Christian Democrats. After ERP leaders executed one of their own officials (poet Roque Dalton, accused of being a "Soviet-Cuban-C.I.A." agent) yet another faction sprang up calling itself the Armed Forces of National Resistance (FARN). It was later led by Fermán Cienfuegos.[93]

These three groups had their differences—whether to concentrate on urban or rural areas, whether to plan for short- or long-term conflict—but they posed a common threat to the power structure. Consequently thousands of peasants who joined unions disappeared or their bodies turned up along back roads. Students who moved into the countryside to help organize campesinos became special targets. When they marched to protest government spending of more than three million dollars on the Miss Universe spectacular in 1975, the army fired into the marchers, killing and wounding as many as fifty people; several dozen others were arrested and simply disappeared. Between 1972 and 1977, 150 teachers suspected of union activities vanished, three dozen others were killed, and the head of one teacher was placed in front of a school as a lesson for would-be reformers. Parish priests suffered execution and expulsion. Terrorist groups such as ORDEN (a Spanish acronym meaning "order") committed many of these murders. Organized by General José Alberto Medrano in the late sixties as a counterinsurgency force, ORDEN became a dreaded, uncontrollable power a decade later. Throughout, the United States assisted the Salvadoran army through military missions, military training at the School of the Americas, and large amounts of aid. Between 1974 and 1976, assistance included four Bell helicopters and three Douglas C-47 transport aircraft that gave the Salvadorans greater mobility in their search for guerrillas, peasants, and priests.[94]

General Carlos Humberto Romero ordered many of those manhunts. In 1977 he won the presidency in an election so fraudulent that North Americans living in the country tape-recorded military police and national guard command posts giving radio orders to units who were to rig ballot boxes.[95] A protest in San Salvador climaxed with the army gunning down more than ninety people. Jimmy Carter could not cut off military aid; it had already been stopped in 1976 when U.S. authorities caught Salvadoran officers selling surplus weapons to North American gangsters. Romero then announced he did not want Washington's military goods anyway. The Yankees were obviously undependable suppliers. He turned to West European and Israeli arms merchants.[96]

An impassioned debate began in the United States. One part of the debate centered in the Roman Catholic Church. Father Timothy S. Healy, president of Georgetown University, had gone to El Salvador in early 1977 and learned the extent of the atrocities. Back home he spoke about "an agricultural people who starve to death on rich land while they farm it," and "of distant and absentee landlords who suck the land dry, return nothing to it or the people, and live a safe and protected distance" away. Healy, Father Theodore Hesburgh (president of Notre Dame University), and Father Robert Drinan (a Democratic congressman from Massachusetts) expressed their concern to top State Department officials.[97]

For awhile, U.S. policy moved in their direction. Older Latin American hands in the State Department had wanted to use continued aid as leverage to civilize Romero and keep him close to the United States. They especially favored supporting loans for a huge San Lorenzo dam project. But human rights officials in the Department opposed both aid and loans. After a bitter debate, the human rights advocates won. Romero did ease the repression; students were allowed to demonstrate, and he permitted an Inter-American Human Rights Committee to investigate reported atrocities. But the Carter administration then became worried: leftist forces grew and pro-Romero voices warned that if the Europeans built the dam the United States would lose its influence. Priorities therefore changed. Assistant Secretary of State for Inter-American Affairs Terence Todman laid out new priorities in 1978: "Terror and subversion are the major problems" in Latin America—not human rights—and he then congratulated the police for cracking down against rioters. A new U.S. Ambassador, Frank Devine, traveled to San Salvador. Devine had fought for support of the San Lorenzo dam loan, and after arriving at his new post became close to the Romero regime; he hoped to use carrots instead of sticks to correct the abuse. Todman succeeded in reversing the dam decision. A small U.S. military mission worked closely with Salvadoran forces, and $10 million in economic aid flowed southward. The Carter administration had radically changed course.[98]

So, consequently, did Romero. Human rights violations increased. The general set out to destroy the left and the Church's base communities. He succeeded mainly in mobilizing the peasants and unions, turning the Church (even the new, moderate archbishop, Oscar Romero, who was no relation) against him, and ruining the economy. The left retaliated by kidnapping two U.S. businessmen in 1979, then releasing the pair after receiving a large ransom. One U.S. company consequently closed down and El Salvador lost 600 jobs. After the rise of oil prices in 1979, unemployment shot up, but badly needed money could not be borrowed from international banks. Romero's policies proved to be disastrous.

Then the Somoza regime fell in July 1979. New talk of a "domino" effect appeared, now applied to Central America instead of Southeast Asia. Carter responded to the Salvadoran crisis as he had in Nicaragua. Decision-making moved to the White House, where Brzezinski's National Security Council defined the problem in an East-West framework and argued for the resumption of military aid. William Bowdler and Assistant Secretary of State Vaky flew to San Salvador and asked Romero for at least cosmetic human rights reforms so Carter could resume sending assistance. As in Nicaragua, the president championed human rights principles until a revolution—caused in part by the very absence of human rights—threatened the government. Then he reversed direction. Romero, however, could not move fast enough. The army began to divide under U.S. pressure. On 15 October, junior officers overthrew Romero and seized power.[99]

The evidence strongly suggests that the United States encouraged the coup. Romero had proved reluctant to take advice. The younger army leaders, however, seemed heaven-sent. They opposed senior officers closely associated with ORDEN and the oligarchs, sympathized with moderate reforms that could safely redistribute some wealth, wanted a close relationship—that is, counterinsurgency weapons—with the United States, and possessed the power to fight against the guerrillas while buying off moderates with the promise of reforms.[100] Carter had apparently found the solution in El Salvador that had eluded him in Nicaragua.

The 15 October 1979 coup, however, marked the beginning of deep

U.S. involvement in the revolution. The rise and fall of the military reformers also turned into the historical turning-point of the revolution itself. At first all appeared well. Two officers, Colonel Jaime Gutiérrez and Colonel Adolfo Majano, led the junta, but they agreed to accept three civilians to form the ruling five-person junta: Román Mayorga of Catholic University; Guillermo Ungo, who represented a number of centrist and moderate socialist groups (and who had run with Duarte for the presidency in 1972); and Mario Andino, the manager of the subsidiary of the huge U.S. multinational copper corporation, Phelps Dodge.

Optimism reigned. The junta moved to disband ORDEN. It vowed to find and free political prisoners, nationalize the coffee exporting business, establish minimum wages, and—most significantly—initiate a land reform program. That agenda, however, immediately shook the army leadership. A number of officers had been deeply implicated in corruption and the atrocities.[101] Arguments erupted over whether the junta should place its priority on reform or rooting out the guerrillas. For some officers, idealism about land reform easily gave way to seizing the land for personal profit. The major question concerned the military itself: could the younger officers undertake their reform program without destroying both the army as an institution and the loyalty of men below them to that institution? For Gutiérrez and, to a much lesser extent, Majano, the immediate issue turned out to be not the revolution, but the protection of their own profession and power base.

On that issue the reform movement collapsed. The liberalization process slowed as Andino (whose firm had close ties to the military) repeatedly voted with the two colonels and against the civilians. Political prisoners could not be found. Military members of ORDEN simply joined other armed bands and engaged in "generalized violence," as an OAS report called it, without government response. Terrorism and violence rose as the junior army officers could not control other members of the military. As early as the first week of the junta's existence, 160 people died at the hands of police. The left charged that the government had become "Romeroism without Romero." The leftist guerrillas meanwhile stepped up their own attacks, at first out of fear that the junta's reforms might actually destroy the left's political base, and then out of a realization that the army had chosen repression over reform. In late

October, guerrillas attacked the U.S. Embassy, wounding two marines. On his way to San Salvador in 1977, Frank Devine had been warned by a Latin American friend, "El Salvador is replete with problems—and they are all insoluble!"[102]

The Carter administration discovered this truth on its own. It was trapped by the government it had helped create in October 1979. Much to Devine's disgust, some U.S. officials and Salvadoran conservatives tried to escape the trap by calling for "free elections." (Washington, Devine later complained, is a place where many people believe "elections are always good.") The Church and the moderate left understood that elections could only reaffirm the status quo; with the ambassador's help they finally pigeonholed the idea. But beneath the election ploy lay a U.S. strategy to isolate the radical left. Carter apparently wanted no political agreements with that left even though Ungo urged such a settlement as an alternative to the escalating bloodshed. Dedicated to not moving backward, fearful of moving forward, the junta was being ground down by the pressure of internal army politics and the inability of U.S. officials—particularly after the fall of Nicaragua and just before a U.S. presidential campaign—to accept Ungo's political solution.[103]

The junior officers finally admitted defeat. In January the three civilian members of the junta resigned, and within months five of the leading military reformers who had staged the October 15 coup fled the country. One narrowly escaped when his jeep was machine-gunned. A right-wing coup was barely averted. Gutiérrez and hardline Defense Minister Colonel José Guillermo García assumed power. With frantic U.S. help, the military tried to restore appearances by bringing in two Christian Democrats to join the junta. Since 1972, when Duarte and Ungo should have won the presidential elections, the PDC had moved to the right. Church leaders deserted it and the Left ignored it. Now the party only lent undeserved respectability to the military regime.[104]

The State Department quickly moved to consolidate its ties with the military. U.S. diplomat James Cheek promised thirty-six military advisers so the Salvadorans could wage what Cheek liked to call a "clean counterinsurgency." One of the Christian Democrats immediately resigned from the junta and was replaced by Duarte, who had recently returned from his seven-year exile in Venezuela. As a result of his absence, Duarte was more isolated, less potent politically, and hence more acceptable to the military than any other PDC leader. No longer possessing his magic of the sixties, Duarte represented a rump part of a faction-torn party. But the military soon made him president and ostensible head of the junta. Duarte, the officers knew, was fine for dealing with North Americans.[105] Aided by the media, U.S. diplomats immediately portrayed Duarte as the great moderate hope. The extent of his weakness was exposed when the 1982 elections pushed him out of power—much to the surprise of North Americans.

Bipolarization accelerated as violence escalated. The army chased peasants to the Honduran border then, with the help of Honduran troops, slaughtered 600 people. The government made no comment. A priest who walked out of the area to tell the story said, "There were so many vultures picking at the bodies in the water that it looked like a black carpet."[106] After Ungo and Mayorga left the junta, Archbishop Romero declared, "The real power is in the hands of the most repressive sector of the armed forces." He called on government leaders to stop the killings by those whose "hands are red with blood." In his final sermon, the archbishop announced, "No soldier is obliged to obey an order contrary to the law of God." The army officers interpreted this as an appeal for their men to lay down their arms.[107]

On 24 March 1980, as he said mass in the chapel of a cancer hospital where he lived and worked, a single shot in the heart killed Romero. The OAS Human Rights Commission reported that evidence implicated General Medrano (the founder of ORDEN) and Major Roberto D'Aubuisson. The judge who named these two men was himself shot, but recovered. D'Aubuisson had served as a top intelligence official after training at the International Police Academy in Washington, D.C. He was then cashiered from the army in late 1979 with others after the October *golpe*. The major had made his reputation as the founder of the White Warriors, a death squad of former military members who seemed to specialize in killing priests. A moderate Salvadoran newspaper called D'Aubuisson a "psychopathic killer." After Romero's murder, the major circulated through army posts a speech on cassette in which he applauded the archbishop's death and asked officers to join him in overthrowing the junta. No coup occurred, however.[108]

The murder of the archbishop did not slow U.S. aid. In early 1980, Carter asked Congress for $5.7 million of military supplies to "help strengthen the army's key role in reforms." Congress bought this cynical explanation of U.S. policy—a policy that aimed at maximum military stabilization with, necessarily, a minimum of reform. (At this same time, Congress had been debating economic help for Nicaragua nearly eight months.) When Murat Williams, former U.S. Ambassador to El Salvador, prepared to testify against Carter's request, he received a call from Robert Pastor, Brzezinski's aide on Latin America, who urged Williams to change his view. Williams noted Archbishop Romero's objections even to "non-lethal" aid for the military. Pastor responded, "Archbishop Romero is naive."[109]

While pushing military supplies south, Carter also pressured the newly conservative junta to undertake a massive land reform program. Announced with much publicity, the program became the centerpiece of the U.S.-Salvadoran strategy for winning the revolution. Important authors of the plan were the American Institute for Free Labor Development (AIFLD), an anti-Communist group established by the U.S. American Federation of Labor and a number of U.S. multinational corporations; and Roy L. Prosterman, a University of Washington professor who had devised the successful land reforms in Japan and Korea in the forties, as well as the considerably less successful scheme in Vietnam. The Salvadoran contribution to planning its own reform program was not great.

As finally announced in March–April 1980, three stages were envisioned: Phase I, in which the government purchased estates larger than 1,250 acres and distributed land to peasants and cooperatives; Phase II when the government repeated the process with farms between 250 and 1,250 acres; and Phase III, or "land-to-the-tiller," when sharecroppers, with government help, could become owners of small pieces of land they had rented. Carter's new ambassador to El Salvador, Robert White, captured the intent of the program: "Washington wants something to the right of Nicaragua."[110]

Specifically, that meant the land reforms aimed at destroying the oligarchs' power on the far right, while creating mass peasant support for the military-controlled junta. Phase I partly accomplished the first objective, but at tremendous cost. As the largest estates divided, some oligarchs moved to Miami after they maneuvered the government into paying grossly inflated prices for the land; the money, along with the remainder of the oligarchs' wealth, then disappeared into Miami or Swiss bank accounts. Other landowners simply subdivided their estates into subplots and passed them out to family members. Still others hired former ORDEN members or D'Aubuisson's killers to eliminate peasant groups that tried to take the land. Between January and August 1980, peasant deaths accounted for more than half of all civilians murdered. The death rate ran highest in areas where land reformers were most active.[111]

In January 1981, three top reform officials—two North Americans from AIFLD and José Viera, the Salvadoran leader of the program— were shot to death in the coffee shop of San Salvador's Sheraton Hotel. Duarte, now president, accused two men closely tied to the oligarchy (and to U.S. multinational corporations in El Salvador) as the killers. The FBI arrested the two men in Miami, but Salvadoran judges soon released them. New evidence then pointed in a different direction: Viera had strongly attacked army leaders for corruption and threatened to resign as head of the land reform program. The army, speculation ran, had killed all three to protect itself and its new wealth, then blamed the oligarchs. That the murders occurred in the usually secure Sheraton Hotel lent credence to the theory, as did the government's inability to find the killers.[112]

The land reform program was also not what it seemed. If Phase I cost many lives and produced fewer results than hoped, Phase II and Phase III never began at all. The second stage struck directly at the coffee plantations. Neither Salvadoran politics nor economics could stand that jolt. As it was, rising violence and the mere threat of reforms threw the economy into a tailspin. Between 1978 and 1981, according to one informed estimate, as much as $5 billion of private capital fled the country.[113] No one in Washington ever dreamed of making up that loss with U.S. aid.

A fatal contradiction thus appeared in Carter's policies. Reforms without revolution meant alienating the very wealth needed to carry out the reforms. Faced with that impossible problem, the administration tried to finesse its predicament by playing for time. It publicized the intent of the agrarian reforms, downplayed the violence, and tried to educate conservative and corrupt Salvadoran army officers about their democratic duties.

Then the clock ran out on Carter. After years of brutal infighting, in April 1980 the revolutionary groups agreed to cooperate and coordinate their actions. The timing was not accidental. United States involvement grew daily. With the rise of Reagan's popularity the Left faced the possibility of confronting ever greater firepower as time passed. Archbishop Romero's death and the splintering of the junta opened new areas of support. The promise of land reform posed a political threat and increased army violence.

Two coordinating groups consequently appeared. The Revolutionary Democratic Front (FDR) brought together sixteen organizations into the political arm of the revolution. Even the small, ineffectual Communist party gave up trying to work with the bourgeois class and joined the Front. The FDR recognized the various guerrilla bands as its military ally. After prolonged negotiations over the correct strategy for waging the conflict, in October five guerrilla groups formed the Farabundo Martí National Liberation Front (FMLN) as the military counterpart to the FDR. The FDR leadership, headed by Ungo, Enrique Alvarez Córdoba, and Rubén Zamora, arose out of the moderate Social Democrat and Christian Democrat movements of the early seventies. Enrique Alvarez, the FDR president, had been a landowner. The FMLN, on the other hand, developed out of Marxist groups and guerrilla fighting. The two organizations differed in origins and ideology. But they united in their determination to remove the oligarchical, and more recently, military rule, and replace the old system with massive land reforms and nationalization programs.

Washington officials worried that if revolutionaries seized power, the more moderate Ungo group could never restrain the more radical military organization. The truth of that generalization depended on many circumstances, however, including the course of U.S. policy. In late summer 1980, Carter tried to split the FDR by convincing the moderate left to join the military in a coalition. A success would have re-created, in effect, the October 1979 junta. But it was too late. Neither side trusted the other. "The State Department contradicts its own words," said FDR leader Rubén Zamora. "On the one hand they tell us we are so weak that some alleged madman on the left will eat us alive. On the other hand, they urge us to go in with the junta so that it can rely on our strength to break the oligarchy."[114] Carter could not take the one essential step: force the army to share power with the Left so the Left could survive. That point was driven home in November 1980 when the government security forces assassinated the first head of the FDR, Enrique Alvarez. (Ungo replaced Alvarez at the top.)

Alvarez's murder occurred in an important context. During the same month that Ronald Reagan won the presidential election, six FDR leaders, including Alvarez, met in a Jesuit High School several blocks from the U.S. Embassy in San Salvador to discuss strategy. One report said they were preparing to explore talks with President Duarte. Security forces seized the FDR officials. Their six bodies were found the next day. Duarte privately admitted to Ambassador White the military's responsibility for the killings, and implicitly admitted that neither he nor any other civilian could control the forces.[115] A month later, the bodies of the three North American nuns and a lay worker were found in a shallow grave outside San Salvador. They had suffered one of the most brutal murders in a conflict characterized by sadism. Carter demanded a full investigation, threatening otherwise to stop all U.S. economic aid (he had already delayed military assistance).

But U.S. officials now found themselves too deeply involved to demand very much. In late December, the guerrillas' military organization, the FMLN, announced the launching of a "final offensive" so Reagan would "find an irreversible situation in El Salvador" when he entered the White House. The rebels claimed a force of 10,000; U.S. military sources estimated the number at 2,500. Given the chaos and the opportunities, however, the FMLN posed a danger to the junta regardless of numbers. The Carter administration that had entered office pledging "absolute" commitment to human rights now held quite different views. The slaughter of the nuns, or the other thousands killed by security and right-wing vigilantes in 1979 and 1980, became less important than the danger of an FDR-FMLN victory. "El Salvador," reporters Karen DeYoung and Jim Hoagland noted later, "was the stage on which Jimmy

Carter would give perhaps his most anguished version of Hamlet as played by a policymaker." The president rapidly recommended sending large amounts of military aid to the junta.[116]

As Reagan took the presidential oath, the FMLN offensive had stalled. The army contained attacks on the towns. More important, the peasants failed to join the revolutionaries in a mass uprising. The rebels controlled several of the northernmost provinces, but elsewhere the government had quieted the campesinos with promises of land reform or threats of terrorism. The threats were not empty. The Church counted nearly 10,000 political murders during 1980, the overwhelming majority committed by the government or right-wing vigilante groups. Meanwhile, Carter had tied the United States to the Salvadoran military. Following a policy known as KISSSS ("Keep it simple, sustainable, small, and Salvadoran"), Carter sent the first U.S. military trainers in late 1980.[117]

Since the sixties, United States economic and military assistance had reshaped the Salvadoran political landscape. The massive aid program, followed by the economic shocks administered by the "soccer war," energy inflation of 1973 and 1974, and a new round of price rises in 1979, had disoriented every segment of the society. When peasants and students, often joined by priests, tried to limit their suffering by demanding reform, the oligarchs and military responded with death squads to restore the order of the fifties. As the Salvadoran government swung more sharply to the right, hundreds of people continued to be murdered each month. The land reform program stopped. North Americans could not figure out why. Nor could many understand why the guerrillas continued to fight—unless, of course, Cubans (or Russians, or Mexicans) controlled them.

Guatemala: Turning a Country into a Cemetery

Compared with their experiences in Nicaragua and El Salvador, North Americans suffered few illusions about Guatemala. The military regime in control of that country since 1954 made little pretense about its liberalism or concern for human rights. "I wish the Americans would just leave us alone," one Guatemalan declared. "If we want to kill each other off it's our business. The United States has no right to interfere."[118]

The advice came too late. The natural political descendant of the U.S.-sponsored coup in 1954 presided over the slaughter. U.S.-trained and equipped army personnel carried out most of the killing. The force became so efficient and disciplined that after the newly professionalized Guatemalan officer corps seized power in 1963, it effectively controlled the country for the next eighteen years without the kinds of public arguments that bedevilled the Salvadoran officers. With a single voice it told the United States to provide supplies and training but no advice, as its troops killed thousands of peasants and political opponents in the name of "counterinsurgency." Washington officials largely complied. In keeping with Nixon's policy, military supplies replaced Alliance for Progress programs. Between 1967 and 1976, the United States acted as virtually the sole supplier; it delivered $35 million in aid to the Guatemalan military. During the height of one particularly bloody repression in 1971, twenty-five U.S. officers and seven former U.S. policemen worked with that military.

The stakes, after all, were large. Since colonial days Guatemala had acted as bellwether for the region. The direction it traveled politically often anticipated the politics of the other four Central American states. It was the most populous country, and had the greatest amount of U.S. investment in Central America. The investments and the military aid indicated how much the United States cared about Guatemala. With those signs of support, Colonel Carlos Arana Osorio, selected by the army to win the 1970 presidential elections, swore to eliminate all guerrillas even "if it is necessary to turn the country into a cemetery." After declaring martial law, Arana's troops, and such right-wing vigilante groups as MANO, began to make good his pledge. They raided the National University, assassinated three law professors, arrested 1,600, and murdered as many as 1,000 people in twelve weeks. Guerrillas retaliated, shooting about thirty army and government officials. Arana climaxed the campaign by killing guerrilla leader Yon Sosa.[119]

The country enjoyed relative quiet until the 1974 presidential campaign began with the murder by right-wing groups of a dozen Christian

Democratic Party officials.[120] As in Nicaragua and El Salvador, the army was not content merely to kill those on the Left; it wanted to eliminate everyone between itself and the Left as well. Important civilian politicians understandably lost interest in the 1974 campaign. General Efraín Ríos Montt ran as the most moderate of three military candidates. He even discussed the need to redistribute some wealth. The army, which held increasing amounts of that wealth, countered with its own candidate, General Kjell Laugerud. Ríos Montt doubtless won the election, but in a fraudulent recount conducted by the army, Laugerud became president. Ríos Montt protested, but played the game and did nothing more. The military's unity held.

Throughout the killing (50,000 died violently between 1966 and 1976) and militarization of Guatemala, Presidents Nixon and Gerald Ford kept military supplies flowing. Washington officials stopped aid only once: when, in 1975, the generals threatened to invade neighboring British Honduras—a British-controlled colony that Guatemala had long claimed as its territory of Belize. Ford held back the delivery of several transport planes. The generals bought comparable aircraft through the Israelis, but did not invade the disputed area.[121]

On 4 February 1976 a mighty earthquake destroyed large parts of the country in perhaps the worst natural disaster in Guatemalan history. Over 22,000 died and another one million were made homeless (out of a total population of 5½ million). The tragedy marked a sharp turn in Guatemala's history, much as the 1972 earthquake affected Somoza's Nicaragua—but not for the exact same reasons. Unlike Somoza, the Guatemalan government was not blatantly corrupt in dispersing more than $60 million of U.S. and IADB relief.

The Indians, however, had suffered most. They made up half the country's population and averaged less than $85 per year income. In one area of 22,000 people, an Austrian development team discovered that the average cash income per month for a nine-member family amounted to $3.40, and that only three families even had an outhouse. Many Indians wanted only to be left alone in their villages, where they lived in a world of strong family ties; distinctive dialects, costumes, and patron saints; and total loyalty to village life. That life, however, had been destroyed in many areas before 1976, as the oligarch-military group seized Indian lands that seemed fertile for the new mass industry of cattle exporting or a likely spot to drill for oil. The army also brutally regimented villages in anti-guerrilla campaigns. In its rapacity, the government had thus not only opened up the Indian communities, but also had made them enemies. The failure of the government to rebuild the villages after the 1976 earthquake only added to already great misery.[122]

But the Indians had begun to organize. International relief agencies appeared on the scene after the earthquake to do what the government refused to do, subjecting many villages to new political influences. Local priests provided leadership in the spirit of the Medellín pronouncements. For the first time in centuries, the Indians began to organize. The country's political wars no longer involved merely one army faction against another. Mass uprising threatened. The triggering event can be specified: a massacre in the northern town of Panzós on 29 May 1978. During the 1950s the valley around Panzós was filled with poor Indians whose small plots enabled them to survive. In the 1960s, however, the Alliance for Progress and other foreign-supplied funds encouraged wealthy Guatemalans to turn the area into ranches so beef could become a profitable export. On 29 May 1978 a group of Kekchi Indians met on the town square to ask authorities for help in protecting their land. Instead the Indians were met by Guatemalan military who opened fire. The army claimed that 34 died. Other observers put the toll in the hundreds. One rancher bragged that the government had "authorized" the killings. Indians who had been passive for centuries became revolutionaries.[123]

The economic crisis of the late seventies sharpened the conflict. Coffee and sugar earnings dropped more than 45 percent. Tourism, a large money-maker, fell as fighting spread. But prices of such vital imports as food and energy soared. The poor not only became poorer, they also lost their land. Oil companies, led by Shenandoah Oil, had started major exploration efforts in the early seventies. By 1980 the firms found as much as three to four billion barrels; in April 1980 the country exported petroleum for the first time. The oil discoveries set off a scramble for land in northern areas—precisely the region where revolutionaries grew in number. Mining of tungsten, nickel, and other minerals also focused on territory long held by Indians and other campesinos. Multinational corporations, in league with the Guatemalan military, forced people off land they had possessed for centuries. In early 1980 some campesinos asked for help from foreign officials in Guatemala City, then sought sanctuary in the Spanish Embassy. The military overran the embassy and machine-gunned thirty-nine people to death, including seven Spanish employees.[124] The search for quick wealth—and relief from the worldwide economic squeeze—had led to yet another slaughter.

Urban laborers received similar treatment. Between 1970 and 1980 their already paltry buying power dropped one-third. Labor militance and government brutality grew simultaneously. In 1977 a leading labor lawyer and educator was murdered outside his home. When laborers at the largest Coca-Cola franchise in Guatemala City tried to form a union (to raise their daily base pay of $2.50 for twelve hours work), they first encountered bribery, then force. The owner had been deeply involved in right-wing politics and anti-union activities since the sixties. After negotiations broke down, he brought in scabs to break the strike. The workers then occupied the building, only to have military police break in and beat up the workers. Leaders of the union began to be gunned down. One leader escaped to the United States and pleaded with Coca-Cola stockholders for support. The U.S. company, however, refused to assume responsibility. It claimed in a highly doubtful argument that the parent company had little influence over this supposedly independent franchise. Other Coca-Cola plants in Guatemala and Central America were unionized, but the owner of this one, convinced that he was fighting a Communist conspiracy, refused to give way.[125]

Clearly, American interests and Guatemalan oligarchs needed protection. By 1978 guerrilla activities had spread through a number of provinces, including Indian-populated provinces where guerrillas had never been seen before, and claimed the lives of right-wing landowners and military officers. The fall of Somoza and the acceleration of the Salvadoran revolution further shocked the country's elite. General Romeo Lucas García, the army-annointed president in the 1977 election, ordered all-out war on the guerrillas. Army brutalities grew until in 1980 the country's civilian vice-president resigned in protest. "There are no political prisoners in Guatemala," he remarked, "just political assassinations." The military killed over 3,000 people in 1979 to mid-1980, twenty-seven labor leaders "disappeared," eighteen faculty of San Carlos University lost their lives to machine guns, and fifteen questioning journalists were gunned down. Yet the revolution continued to spread.[126]

Not only liberals and leftists died in increasing numbers. So did the elite. As the economic crisis grew, competition for the country's land and mineral wealth increased. Military officers allied with certain business cliques warred on opposing military-business groups. A former mayor of Guatemala City described the violence as comparable to "shoot-outs between rival mafias." The "mafias," he said, divided along functional lines: agricultural exporters versus importers, monopoly industrial sectors versus bankers, for example.[127] That the Guatemalan elite had started killing one another should not have occasioned surprise given the elite's post-1954 history of savagery. But the split in the army did surprise. Greed had overcome professionalism. By 1982 these fissures reached the top of the government as generals, resembling little more than chieftains of rival mobs, fought each other publicly for power and plunder.

Washington officials were not pleased with their own creation in Guatemala, but—much as one hesitates to stop feeding a pet boa constrictor—they were reluctant to cut off aid and face the consequences. Throughout these bloody, bleak years, they tried to resolve the irresolvable: extend U.S. military and economic aid so the army could fight the growing revolution, but threaten to cut off aid if the "rival mafias" did not stop murdering Indians, labor leaders, educators, lawyers, and each other.

During his last months in office, Secretary of State Kissinger tried to excuse Guatemala's horrible human rights record so aid could continue. After the 1976 earthquake, and as the search for oil and mineral wealth led to the massive killing of Indians, such excuses no longer worked well. The Carter administration condemned President Lucas García's death-squads after 1977. Guatemalan officials then rejected U.S. aid on the grounds that Carter interfered in Guatemala's internal affairs. By 1980, the guerrillas and the military had only one point of agreement: both despised the United States. (The military did so even though U.S. economic aid flowed, and the Pentagon continued to train Guatemalan troops.)

The hatred had its ironical side. The United States had handed power in Guatemala to this army in 1954. By 1980 the post-1954 system approached its climax as the Carter administration could no longer control the U.S. creation, and the incoming Reagan administration desperately searched for ways to reopen aid to the murderous regime. A U.S. official who had a sense of the past declared in 1980, "What we'd give to have an Arbenz now."[128] Most North Americans, ignorant of that past, solved the problem by looking the other way.

Honduras: Main Girder in the Bridge

One bright spot nevertheless remained. Honduras became less of a mere banana republic and more of a U.S. military redoubt. Its people endured the lowest per capita annual income in the region, but—with a few exceptions—they knew their place in the system. Those who did not received instruction from a professional and politically astute military, which in turn had received its instruction from the United States. As rewards for its proven ability and unflagging cooperation, the Honduran command soon possessed the strongest air force in Central America, vast quantities of supplies, the assistance of as many as 100 to 200 U.S. military advisers (the largest group in the area), and complete support from Washington in governing the country or—as in 1972—in overthrowing elected civilian governments. In Honduras, at least, the old system still worked.

But it worked mostly for the military. In their hope of finding a dependable ally, North Americans overlooked that ally's condition. It had started changing rapidly in the fifties and sixties into a more industrialized and pluralistic country, particularly as the U.S.-owned banana companies diversified into new areas of enterprise. As the country became the most important ally of the United States in Central America, it thus also hinted of danger: incredibly poor, Honduras was a rapidly—and unpredictably—changing country. It was therefore not the most stable base on which to build a policy for the entire region. By the end of the seventies, however, Washington officials tried to do exactly that kind of construction.

The United States certainly had locked Honduras tightly into its economic system, tighter than any other nation in Latin America. North Americans ate 75 percent of the country's bananas, drank half its coffee, sent nearly two-thirds of its imports, and provided 85 percent of all foreign investment (about a quarter-billion dollars). When companies moved to kill the Central American attempt to raise banana prices through an OPEC-like arrangement in 1974 and 1975, they not unnaturally focused on the two links in the cartel that snapped easiest under U.S. pressure: Honduras and Nicaragua.[129]

The military relationship, however, best exemplified how one part of the system continued to work. After 1954 the United States professionalized the Honduran army until by 1963 its commander, General Oswaldo López, could overthrow a liberal government and run the country for the next dozen years through an efficient institutional network. The army's power grew from its own discipline, but it developed for other reasons as well. With the disappearance of an always weak political party structure and the proliferation of economic interest groups during the sixties, only the military possessed the order and power to mediate among these groups and keep the country functioning. The army acted as the glue for an impoverished yet rapidly changing society.

It also acted as a tough policeman. López's hand-picked civilian government won the 1971 presidential election, but quickly made economic and political misjudgments. With the approval of nearly all the key civilian sectors, López disavowed his own creation and, on behalf of the military, seized the presidency for himself in 1972. The policeman immediately surprised Central America, and Washington officials, by demonstrating an awareness of the new political forces sweeping the region—an awareness that eluded the more highly publicized pro-U.S. regimes in Nicaragua and Guatemala. López understood the growing dissatisfaction of the peasant and labor organizations that resulted from losses in the "soccer war" and the post-1973 economic squeeze. (Honduran unions were the most politically potent in all Central America.) A faction within the army itself astutely hoped to undercut revolutionary movements by copying Peru's military, which had moved sharply to the left and carried out a major reform program. López consequently announced a series of labor laws that guaranteed collective bargaining, provided minimum wages, and placed controls on foreign-owned mining companies. The government joined the banana producers cartel. Most important, López responded to a march of 20,000 peasants on the capital by proposing a major land-reform program and nationalizing the rich, foreign-controlled timber industry.[130] U.S. military officers could point with pride to their creation in Honduras that, unlike Somoza's guard or Guatemala's torturers, blended force with the promise of real reform.

By 1975 the promise was dead. It fell victim to groups that traditionally crushed hints of meaningful change. The large landowners' association (FENAGH) and the right-wing Council of Private Business (COHEP) condemned the reforms for, of all things, attacking "the democratic system, liberty, and individuality." These two groups received help from some U.S. officials and the large fruit companies. Their opportunity for retaliation occurred suddenly in September 1974 when Hurricane Fifi blasted into the country, killing 8,000, leaving 300,000 homeless, and tearing apart the nation's most productive agricultural-industrial areas. López needed immediate help from Washington and the major foreign investors. But U.S. officials showed much less interest in helping him than Nixon had demonstrated in aiding Somoza after the 1972 Nicaraguan earthquake.

The message got through. The regime slowed land redistribution. The army helped Standard Fruit reclaim territory abandoned in 1973 and 1974. Foreign investors received reassurance instead of eviction notices. Honduran officials suddenly lost interest in fighting for the banana producers cartel. One reason for that change turned up in mid-1975: López and other top officials had taken $1.25 million in bribes from United Brands. López resigned. The short-lived reform era was over.[131]

Some peasants did not understand that it had ended. They invaded a number of haciendas to take the land. The army drove them off. In Olancho province, nine bodies of campesino leaders were found on the estate of a rich landowner. That massacre produced new outbursts from the peasants. They received support from Church leaders who condemned the wealthy elite and the multinational corporations for the "exploitation and oppression of the vast majority of the Honduran people." López's successor in the presidency rode out growing violence until a conservative army faction led by General Policarpo Paz García seized power in August 1978. The Paz García group had been the target of stories linking it to U.S. drug traffic. The new president used his freshly acquired prestige to squash the investigations.[132]

But he could not stop the growing unrest, especially as it was fueled by the worldwide economic downturn of 1979 and 1980 and the termination of the López reforms. As newspaper headlines warned that "We are on the brink of widespread hunger," revolutionary groups formed. One of those groups, the Morazan Honduran Liberation Front, fired shots at the U.S. Embassy in Tegucigalpa on 30 October 1980. Paz García did conduct a peaceful election for the National Assembly in 1980, just as Jimmy Carter urged him to do. An opposition party surprisingly won the largest number of seats, but the victory was meaningless. The army ruled regardless of who sat in the National Assembly. The editor of a leading Honduran independent paper encapsulated the result: "People voted for a change, but nothing has changed."[133]

As the military pulled the country to the right, Jimmy Carter, and then Ronald Reagan, viewed Honduras as the U.S. surrogate in Central America. Carter sent a U.S. Major General to tell the Hondurans in mid-1980 that they were now to assume Somoza's old role as "a bulwark of anti-communism against the pressures of popular revolt." Military aid amounting to more than $3.5 million, including at least ten U.S. helicopters, easily gained congressional approval. Much of the aid specifically gave the Honduran military the capability to patrol border areas— that is, to have the U.S.-trained and directed force confronting the Nicaraguan Sandinistas and helping the Salvadoran military regime if necessary. In late 1979 Assistant Secretary of State Vaky noted "that geography gives Honduras a central role in the prevention of regional conflict" between "Nicaragua and its conservative northern neighbors." Vaky concluded, "Honduras is thus central to the 'bridge building' process we hope will emerge in Central America."[134]

The pivotal question became whether an impoverished nation could carry out such sophisticated military and geopolitical responsibilities. Honduras ranked very low among Latin American nations in literacy, industrialization, and life expectancy. It ranked near the top only in such categories as poverty, disease, and banana exports. Washington officials, however, now needed friends to maintain a collapsing system in Central

America. Since reform programs in the sixties produced so much radicalism in the seventies, dependable underdevelopment was to be preferred over unstable development. The United States stood solidly with the poor—and with the regimes who wanted to keep them that way.

Costa Rica: From Democracy to Debtor

That generalization, of course, did not completely explain North American friendship for Costa Rica, but then that friendship amounted to much less than the United States support for military regimes in the other four Central American nations. As the cold war intensified after 1975, the State Department found San José governments to be troublemakers: they aided Nicaraguan revolutionaries, strongly opposed U.S.-supported intervention schemes, refused to join CONDECA and other pet projects of the Pentagon planners, and generally irritated the region's military regimes that the White House viewed with favor.

Costa Rica's ability to cause trouble, however, declined with its economy, especially in the wake of the post-1979 recession. By late 1981, a well-informed reporter in San José wrote, "Technically, the Costa Rican government is already bankrupt."[135]

The problems that developed in the seventies threw a glaring light on the nation's fundamental weaknesses that most of its people had long preferred to ignore. José Figueres, however, could not ignore them after voters returned him to the presidency in 1970. The termination of Alliance funds, as well as the collapse of the Central American Common Market, threatened to cripple the country's economy until Don Pepé discovered a new market by selling 30,000 tons of coffee to the Soviet Union in 1972. Costa Rica then became the only Central American nation to establish diplomatic relations with Moscow. The World Bank and International Monetary Fund also delivered millions of dollars to keep the economy afloat.[136] Figueres's chosen successor, Daniel Oduber, carried out an even more intense search for alternatives to the U.S. system. In the wake of the post-1973 oil shocks, he turned to Venezuela to obtain lower energy prices and closer trade relationships. Oduber changed tax and customs legislation to regulate foreign investors and restrict the privileges and tax advantages of the more than 10,000 North American *pensionados* who had retired to Costa Rica. "Ticos" (native Costa Ricans) blamed many of their higher prices on the North Americans' willingness and ability to pay more for goods, especially houses and land. As farmland converted to residences, peasants lost jobs and the nation's food production dropped. Foreign investment began to shy away from the country's "chillier clime," as the *Wall Street Journal* described the business atmosphere.[137]

Rising coffee exports helped reinflate the economy during the middle seventies. The economy, however, was fundamentally unsound. The country's large welfare programs increased with its birthrate, which ranked among the highest in the world. Even in 1977, a trade deficit of nearly $100 million occurred despite the historically high coffee exports. Then the worldwide 1979 economic crisis struck. Coffee exports remained at record levels, but energy and food imports soared in price. When coffee sales suddenly dropped by one-quarter in 1980, Ticos spent one-third of a billion dollars more abroad than they received for their exports. Their national debt tripled in just three years.[138]

The most common explanation offered for this rapidly growing disaster was the country's extensive and costly welfare system. Ticos lived beyond their means. Deeper structural problems, however, deserved greater attention. Resembling every other Central American nation, Costa Rica for more than a century had been dependent on international markets, and—consequently—was less sufficient in food and less able to provide land for its peasants. A 1974 census showed Costa Rica to have the sixth most unequal land distribution system of fifty-four nations studied. Oduber had tried to correct this with new settlement projects, and even expropriated 40,000 acres owned by United Brands. But rural unrest spread faster than San José authorities could deal with it. Violence and illegal squatters became more common. The root causes were deep; they had been apparent to observant travelers in the twenties.[139] The seventies were suddenly and radically different, however, because of the oil price spirals, the rapid population increase, and Costa Rica's attempts to become freer of outside control. Those attempts understandably cooled investor interest.

By 1980, Costa Rica had twice defied the system that encased Honduras, El Salvador, and Guatemala: by providing educational and other social services to a relatively large and democratic middle class, and then by trying to break somewhat free of the century-long control held by North American groups. It consequently began to pay a price for its policies. Many Ticos blamed President Rodrigo Carazo, who won office in 1978, for being incompetent. Others, however, looked more deeply. A guerrilla movement appeared. Costa Ricans began to buy weapons for private use in record numbers. The elite class, many of whose members came from a few families that have dominated the nation's economy and politics since the nineteenth century, felt the ground shift under its feet. This class could no longer appease the middle-income Ticos, or buy off the peasants, with an expanding economy and ever larger social programs.[140]

The United States meanwhile did little to help the Costa Ricans. The San José government's symbolic attempts to regulate foreign investors, and its public aid to the Sandinistas, won few friends in Washington. Nixon preferred Somoza. Carter focused on Nicaragua and El Salvador while turning the Honduran military into his closet ally in the region. Not even Costa Rica's unblemished human rights record, a record light-years ahead of any other in Latin America, won any special favors. Central America's lone democracy was too anti-military, too anti-dictatorial, to fit U.S. policy. In their own way, and for their own good reasons, the Ticos tried to defy the system in the seventies. They would pay for that defiance in the eighties.

Conclusion: The Turning Point

The seventies began with the failure of the Alliance for Progress and the collapse of the Central American Common Market. These setbacks triggered a political chain reaction. The Roman Catholic Church reexamined its role and emerged as a leader of the poor masses who began to organize for self-protection. Richard Nixon and Nelson Rockefeller reexamined U.S. Latin American policy and decided that stability—militarily imposed—must have top priority. Thus the Church and the masses on the one hand, and the U.S. government on the other, began moving on a collision course.

Internally, the shocks of the Common Market and Alliance failures were worsened by the post-1973 oil price rise. As Central American military forces bought more arms from Washington (or Bonn, Paris, and Jerusalem), their governments found themselves trapped between rapidly increasing energy costs and steady or declining prices for the one or two export crops that kept their economies alive. In every country except Costa Rica, political party systems crumpled; the military assumed undisguised control. Urban labor and especially campesinos—who were driven off land in increasing numbers by the oligarch-military complex's feverish attempts to accelerate production of export crops—organized, often with the Church's help, to define themselves in this new political universe. In Costa Rica and Honduras the governments sporadically responded to their demands and an uncertain stability continued. In Nicaragua, Guatemala, and El Salvador, the regimes met the demands with violence. Revolutions resulted. For the first time in the twentieth century—that is, since the North American system had been imposed—the entire area, including Costa Rica and Honduras, faced the possibility of regional war arising out of the mass-based revolutionary movements.

Washington's only consistent objective throughout the decade was to arm and support the military forces which, in three of the countries, oppressed and frequently slaughtered their own people. U.S. officials were trapped by history and circumstance. Historically they had played the pivotal role in the post-1900 development of the system now under attack. They lacked both the imagination and perspective to understand how they less resembled the defenders of a free world than those who defended the late Roman Empire or the British Empire in Egypt. But, for good or ill, they also fell victim to circumstance: the 1973 and 1979 oil price shocks wounded the U.S. economy and pulled attention inward (or towards the Middle East) while simultaneously creating new regional forces in Mexico and Venezuela. The United States of course remained indisputably the greatest power in the region, but after 1973 the Central Americans—governments and revolutionaries alike—had alternatives to dealing with that power, although the alternatives were limited.

Jimmy Carter entered the White House just as the system collapsed in Nicaragua and El Salvador and came under tremendous stress in the other three nations. To blame him for the fall of Somoza or to give him credit for the collapse of the Salvadoran oligarchy would be equally foolish. The causes go back to the sixties and beyond. His human rights principles, which were to be the rudder for his hemispheric policy, assuaged North American consciences and—considerably more important—saved Latin American lives. But the principles helped undermine his policies in Central America. By stressing individual political and civil rights, they did not—as the Roman Catholic clergy quickly realized—touch the inequitable property system that produced revolutionaries and atrocities.

Carter, moreover, wanted it both ways: decrease governmental coercion and publicly attack (and hence de-legitimate) the military regimes, while at the same time urging those regimes to fight the revolutions. U.S. officials acted as if they were dealing with governments, like their own, that had other kinds of legitimacy (such as the respect of their people or fair election mandates). In reality they dealt with Central American rulers who maintained order through fear and oppression. Once the fear and oppression were reduced, so were the rulers' chances for survival. As the Carter administration realized the trap it had laid for itself, it tried to reverse course in 1979 and 1980. Carter sought to keep Somoza in power until the 1981 elections (then attempted to maintain the National Guard's blood-splattered authority); or poured arms into El Salvador at the last minute to help the military junta, a junta whose security forces slaughtered the large majority of the 30,000 civilians who died in 1980 and 1981, and who had murdered North American nuns just weeks before Carter dispatched the aid.

The nearly century-old system was collapsing, pushed by the contradictions in Washington's policy and victimized by historical North American views of property relationships and revolutions. As large parts of Central America flashed into class conflict, the United States easily blamed the crises on Communists and other outside influences. That explanation ignored more than a century of history.

During one of the bad moments in his presidency, Jimmy Carter was asked what he was doing differently from what he had been doing before entering the White House. The former engineer replied that he had read more history since 1976 than he had in all the earlier years.[141] It would be more helpful if presidents read history before they entered office to make life-and-death decisions, and—given the fundamental change occurring in their "backyard"—if some of that history included Central America. For the old saying had it wrong; it was ignorance that had long bred contempt for Central Americans. By 1980 ignorance had also bred failure.

V

———————

THE REMAINS OF THE SYSTEM

Recent U.S. Presidents have won office less for proven talent in governing than for an ability to soothe. These presidents have resembled the clergyman welcomed by a tragedy-stricken family. Jimmy Carter's non-Washington background seemed a welcome relief after the chicanery of Watergate and the Nixon pardon. Ronald Reagan offered both congeniality (a welcome contrast to Carter's up-tight insecurity) and a soothing traditionalism that promised the triumph of the nation's past over its future complexities.

In no foreign policy area was Reagan's traditionalism more apparent than in Central America. And no area needed more attention. His ambassador to the United Nations, Jeane Kirkpatrick, warned in early 1981, "Central America is the most important place in the world for the United States today." A secret National Security Council paper of April 1982 spelled out the endangered U.S. interests: "We have an interest in creating and supporting democratic states in Central America" that can act "free from outside interference" (a reference presumably to the Soviet Union). "Strategically," Washington must prevent "the proliferation of Cuba-modeled states which would provide platforms for subversion, compromise vital sea lanes and pose a direct military threat at or near our borders. This would undercut us globally and create economic dislocation and a resultant influx to the U.S. of illegal immigrants." A U.S. Army analyst noted as well the need to ensure "continued access to strategic raw materials, mainly oil and natural gas in Venezuela and

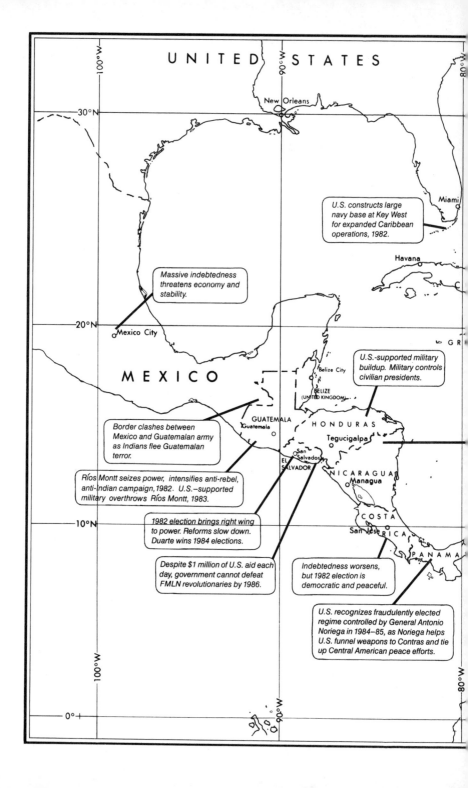

UNITED STATES

New Orleans

30°N

Miami

U.S. constructs large
navy base at Key West
for expanded Caribbean
operations, 1982.

Havana

Massive indebtedness
threatens economy and
stability.

20°N

Mexico City

GR

U.S.-supported military
buildup. Military controls
civilian presidents.

MEXICO

Belize City

BELIZE
(UNITED KINGDOM)

Border clashes between
Mexico and Guatemalan army
as Indians flee Guatemalan
terror.

GUATEMALA

Guatemala

HONDURAS

Tegucigalpa

Ríos Montt seizes power, intensifies anti-rebel,
anti-Indian campaign, 1982. U.S.–supported
military overthrows Ríos Montt, 1983.

San
Salvador

EL
SALVADOR

NICARAGUA

Managua

1982 election brings right wing
to power. Reforms slow down.
Duarte wins 1984 elections.

COSTA

10°N

San José RICA

Despite $1 million of U.S. aid each
day, government cannot defeat
FMLN revolutionaries by 1986.

PANAMA

Indebtedness worsens,
but 1982 election is
democratic and peaceful.

U.S. recognizes fraudulently elected
regime controlled by General Antonio
Noriega in 1984–85, as Noriega helps
U.S. funnel weapons to Contras and tie
up Central American peace efforts.

0°

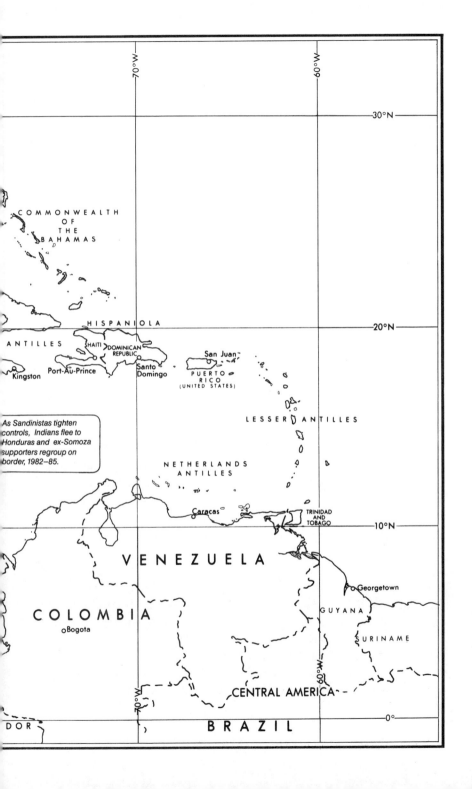

70°W

60°W

30°N

COMMONWEALTH
OF
THE
BAHAMAS

HISPANIOLA

20°N

ANTILLES

HAITI DOMINICAN
REPUBLIC

San Juan

Kingston Port-Au-Prince Santo
Domingo PUERTO
RICO
(UNITED STATES)

As Sandinistas tighten
controls, Indians flee to
Honduras and ex-Somoza
supporters regroup on
border, 1982–85.

LESSER ANTILLES

NETHERLANDS
ANTILLES

Caracas

TRINIDAD
AND
TOBAGO

10°N

V E N E Z U E L A

Georgetown

C O L O M B I A

GUYANA

oBogota

SURINAME

60°W

70°W

CENTRAL AMERICA

0°

DOR

B R A Z I L

Mexico." To a respected Latin American observer, Adolfo Gilly, U.S. policy was motivated by a crisis of "capitalism" and danger to the historic North American "domination" of the Central American region.[1] To the N.S.C., "interests" did not explicitly include U.S. multinational corporations, although sixty-seven of the top 100 corporations in the United States did business in Central America. These included sixteen of the largest food and beverage firms and nine of the ten biggest petroleum companies. Such agribusinesses as Hershey and United Brands were deeply involved, along with such banks as Citicorp and Bank of America. Perhaps the N.S.C. overlooked an estimated $5 billion of direct U.S. investment in the region because many of the most visible, including IBM and Exxon, were highly skilled at making deals with whichever government held power (whether reactionaries in Guatemala or revolutionaries in Nicaragua), and were less worked up about Marxism than were U.S. officials. An IBM official observed privately that whether governments were capitalist or socialist, "they need us."[2]

The 1980 Republican platform nevertheless vowed to protect these interests by reversing the "precipitous decline" in U.S.-Latin American relations caused by "the Carter Administration's economic and diplomatic sanctions linked to its undifferentiated charges of human rights violations." Identifying the rebel movements in Central America as "Marxist," the platform declared that "we will support the efforts of the Nicaraguan people to establish a free and independent government."[3] Reagan announced during the campaign that the Caribbean was "rapidly becoming a Communist lake in what should be an American pond." Richard Allen, soon to be the new president's national security adviser, added a fascinating interpretation of the past century of U.S. interventions: "U.S. military power has always been the basis for the development of a just and humane foreign policy." He and Reagan played to a large number of North Americans who felt, in one irate citizen's words, that "What we need is another Teddy Roosevelt."[4] That need was stated in more detail by the Council for Inter-American Security's "Santa Fe Commission Report." Written largely by conservative military officers and academics, it flatly demanded a vast program to support the Salvadoran military and remove the Sandinistas.[5] Three of the Commission's authors moved into State Department and N.S.C. jobs in

1981. The halcyon days of empire building could be recaptured, if only North Americans thought positively, acted militarily, and rewrote history.

Assumptions: Reagan and the Militarization of Policy

Rewriting history was of special importance. After the horrors of Vietnam, many North Americans were reluctant to become involved in another indigenous revolution. Reagan tried to circumvent that problem by declaring that the Vietnam conflict was "a noble cause" and—more important—the problems in Central America were not indigenous but caused by Castro and the Soviets.

Anyone who disagreed with that view of history, or who thought the problems could be dealt with politically rather than militarily, were purged. Four key Foreign Service Officers in Carter's Bureau of Inter-American Affairs were fired. The new Assistant Secretary for Inter-American Affairs was Thomas Enders, who had little experience in Latin America, but had established his military credentials by helping to conduct the massive, secret air bombings of Southeast Asia during the Nixon years. Secretary of State Alexander Haig, a General and former Commander of the North Atlantic Treaty Organization's forces, also brought in career military officers, including General Vernon Walters (a former C.I.A. deputy director), and Robert McFarlane (a former Marine Corps officer who later became Reagan's N.S.C. adviser.) At the Pentagon, top policy posts were held by Nestor Sanchez, a career C.I.A. operator who had been the Agency's deputy chief in Guatemala when the C.I.A. overthrew Arbenz in 1954; and Fred Iklé, undersecretary of defense for policy, an expert on the military dimension of foreign policy, and ironically nicknamed "Dr. Warmth." Control of Central American policy was a payoff to militant conservatives for their support of Reagan. "Haig and Enders realized they had to throw a bone to the right-wingers," a conservative Senate staff member observed. "They can't have the Soviet Union or the Middle East or Western Europe. All are too important. So they've given them Central America."[6]

Assumptions: Kirkpatrick and the "Authoritarians"

Besides viewing Central America through the prism of a militarized cold war, the administration formulated another theory about revolutions. It had appeared before, in the forties, to support the elder Somoza's dictatorship (see p. 105). It resurfaced in a 1979 essay by Jeane J. Kirkpatrick. She had been a political science professor at Georgetown University in Washington, D.C., before this essay caught Reagan's eye and he appointed her U.S. Ambassador to the U.N. in 1981.

Kirkpatrick based her argument on a sharp distinction between "authoritarian" and "totalitarian" governments. Authoritarians sought to preserve "traditional" societies, she argued, and maintained open capitalist economies. Totalitarians, however, sought to control every part of the society, including the economy. Good authoritarians included Somoza and the Shah of Iran. Bad totalitarians were exemplified by Stalin and Hitler. Focusing on Latin America, Kirkpatrick attacked Carter for opposing authoritarian governments merely because they violated human rights. Somoza, she believed, had established little more than "an efficient, urban political regime."

Certain conclusions followed. Human rights plummeted in importance. A government's degree of anti-communism and its warmth towards foreign investment became the major measuring sticks in any U.S. decision to help or hinder that regime. In a major speech of 31 March, 1981, Secretary of State Haig adopted Kirkpatrick's view. He announced a preference for authoritarians because they "are more likely to change than their totalitarian counterparts." Kirkpatrick's reading of history was triumphant, at least in Reagan's Washington.[7]

Some doubted Kirkpatrick's history. True, authoritarian societies had changed, but sometimes for the worse—as when the Czar of Russia gave way to the Communist Party. Authoritarians in Latin America (and the Middle East), moreover, did not always preserve traditional societies. Somoza, the Salvadoran oligarchs, and Guatemalan generals destroyed the bonds that held their societies together. If authoritarians had been as beneficent and flexible as Kirkpatrick claimed, the professional elite and the Catholic Church (certainly the most "traditional" Latin American institution), would not have become radicalized. Authoritarians had exploited and divided their societies until revolution became the last hope of the masses and the middle class.

Authoritarians did not even turn out to be good anti-communists. Both Kirkpatrick and Haig focused on the Argentine military regime as a linchpin of anti-communism in the hemisphere. In early 1982, however, Argentina went to war with Great Britain over the Falkland (Malvinas) Islands. The United States supported the British. Deeply angered, the Argentine military quit training anti-Sandinista forces, immediately moved closer to the Soviet Union (to whom they annually sold vast amounts of wheat), and lined up with Castro on third-world issues.[8]

Within a year after the Reagan administration adopted the authoritarian-totalitarian distinction, the policy was paralyzed. The authoritarians could not handle modernization. They responded to change with violence. Kirkpatrick's thesis failed even to offer a coherent criticism of Carter. She had labeled his policies, especially in the human rights area, as largely responsible for Somoza's defeat. Actually, Carter had supported Somoza and then the Guard until nearly the moment of Sandinista victory. Finally, her history ignored the revolution's causes. More accurate was a National Guard officer's reading of history as Somoza fled for his life: "I'm going too. There is no way we can defend ourselves against the people. It's not the guerrillas I'm afraid of but the people. I know they hate us and they could overwhelm us."[9]

Kirkpatrick's formulation actually put U.S. interests at risk instead of protecting them. Authoritarian violence against Salvadoran civilians forced nearly one of every four (or about 1 million) to flee, many to the United States where they crowded in inner cities. Kirkpatrick and her supporters also found themselves on the wrong side of human rights issues closer to home. In discussing the brutal 1980 murders of the nuns and church woman in El Salvador, Kirkpatrick seemed to justify the slayings by claiming, "The nuns were not just nuns," but "political activists" for the FMLN. Those charges were untrue. Haig told a congressional committee that "perhaps the vehicle the nuns were riding in may have tried to run a roadblock." He even referred to them inaccurately as "pistol-packing nuns." But the final judgment on Kirkpatrick's theory occurred in Eastern Europe and the Soviet Union after 1988 when totalitarian communist regimes fell from power and were replaced by elected governments. Ironically, Kirkpatrick's assumptions had resembled the Marxist-Leninists': both vastly overestimated the political and ideological power of Marxist-Leninists.[10] That refutation of her theory, however, occurred too late to save U.S. Central American policy from making fatal false assumptions about history and social change.

Assumptions: "Domination by Force Eliminates a Lot of Ticklish Problems of Cultural Understanding"

Within a month after taking office, Haig warned NATO delegates that "a well-orchestrated Communist campaign designed to transform the Salvadoran crisis from the internal conflict to an increasingly internationalized confrontation is underway." Vietnam's mistakes would not be repeated; instead of trying to resolve the problem within only Central America, the administration intended to "go to the source" of the problem. The phrase meant a possible attack on Cuba, since Castro's regime, in Enders's words, "is a Soviet surrogate."[11]

Reagan then raised tensions with Cuba to the highest pitch since the 1962 missile crisis. (In late 1991, Enders told a Senate committee that "military contingency plans for use against both Cuba and Nicaragua had been drawn up [in 1981], but not yet approved as policy.") Some officials demurred. The top U.S. official in Havana, Wayne Smith, told the State Department that Castro's aid to the revolutionaries had been overestimated, and that the Cuban leader wanted to negotiate with, not confront, the United States. Enders was correct in claiming that Cuban arms had helped the Sandinistas. He neglected to add, however, that they received large amounts of weapons from other sources, including Venezuela and the U.S. mafia.[12]

The major administration effort to sell its version of Central American history came in mid-February 1981 when the State Department issued a long "White Paper" on Cuban and Soviet involvement in El Salvador. Within four months, the White Paper came under scathing attacks from correspondent John Dinges of the *Los Angeles Times* and Latin

American expert James Petras in *The Nation*. In June they were joined by the usually pro-administration *Wall Street Journal*. These attacks shredded the White Paper's claim that Cuban and Soviet officials guided the revolutionaries, and that large Soviet-bloc arms shipments enabled the rebels to expand their control. No serious observer doubted that Castro and Soviet officials were deeply interested in, and supportive of, the revolutions. But few outside the administration believed that the Communist bloc provided most of the arms, or that international communism rather than nationalism fueled the revolutions.[13] By late March 1981, Reagan's policy was already in trouble. Public opinion polls showed North Americans overwhelmingly opposed to any U.S. military involvement in Central America.[14]

The president became bitter. Asked on March 27 about his foreign policy problems, he blamed them on a worldwide conspiracy: "We have to recognize that the campaign against what we're doing, the helping of El Salvador, is a pretty concerted and well-orchestrated thing." He claimed the conspiracy was obvious because the same slogans were used in European and U.S. demonstrations. Reagan's words closely resembled the "paranoid style," as historian Richard Hofstadter had noted during the sixties, that frequently afflicted North Americans when they were confronted with sudden change. But the administration kept at it. The *Latin American Weekly Report* of London finally concluded that "the administration has been grossly inept, misusing, manipulating, and inventing evidence. This has meant that even when it does have a case, few believe it."[15]

In view of such failures, why did the Reagan administration persist in following its Central American policies? First, the President did not want simply to contain, but to destroy, the Sandinistas and FMLN. His hardline advisers, such as Kirkpatrick, White House Counselor Edwin Meese, and William Clark, Haig's top deputy, also wanted to use force, although none seemed certain how it was to be done. But a commitment to force was nevertheless made. As Major General Fred Woerner of the U.S. Southern Command observed, "If there is a certain vacuum" in decision-making, "there is a sucking-along effect." In this administration, moreover, it was not politically healthy to be open to attacks from the militant right.[16]

Second, Central America seemed to be a perfect place to demonstrate that the new administration's hand (supposedly unlike Carter's), did not become palsied when force had to be used. Employing military force would reestablish U.S. "credibility," a term notoriously hard to define, but whose use nevertheless stopped arguments over whether force was to be employed. It also would blot out Vietnam memories. In 1984, Assistant Secretary of State for Inter-American Affairs, Langhorne Motley, defined the problem for which Reagan and his advisers never found a solution: "There are two things the American people do not want. . . . [A]nother Cuba on the mainland of Central America," and "another Vietnam . . . which translates into the ground use of U.S. troops in Central America." Haig understood this. He reassured Reagan, "Mr. President, this is one you can win." No Southeast Asian-type jungles, porous borders, or Ho Chi Minh supply trails could frustrate U.S. military might in the small, vulnerable Central American nations. From Haig in 1981 to Lt. Colonel Oliver North in 1984–87, Vietnam veterans in the administration swore that their nightmares could now be exorcised by giving this Central American story a happy ending.[17]

Others, however, were not as ready to kick the "Vietnam syndrome." Top U.S. Army officers, having suffered nightmares after Vietnam had turned the military into a public enemy on North American streets during the 1960s, feared that the Sandinistas were too well entrenched. Supporting discredited Somoza officers or right-wing Salvadorans, while Reagan could give no guarantees about the length or cost of the commitment, reminded these U.S. officers of Vietnam. One Reagan aide admitted in late 1981 that the administration "did not appreciate how rapidly El Salvador would take off in the minds of the press as a Vietnam." The problem was not the policy itself, another official believed, but "the packaging of the activity. It wasn't well staged or sequenced."

So Haig was told to quiet down. Undersecretary of State Walter Stoessel asked the Senate for $25 million of military aid for El Salvador, but assured his touchy listeners that Reagan did not intend to repeat "what happened in Vietnam," and—more notably—"we do not see the necessity for increases" of this amount. (By 1984, Reagan was sending $196 million of military aid to the Salvadorans.) The White House tried to divert attention by focusing on the president's tax-cut proposal. Reagan flatly asserted that "there are no plans to send American combat troops into action anyplace in the world."[18]

By 1982, however, Reagan had secretly ordered the C.I.A. to undermine the Sandinistas and block the flow of arms from Cuba and Nicaragua into El Salvador. C.I.A. Director William Casey devised and oversaw these operations. A World War II veteran of the Office of Strategic Services (the C.I.A.'s parent), Casey fondly recalled dropping saboteurs behind Nazi lines as a romantic highlight of a full life. A lawyer and investor, Casey often moved in the shadows of the business world, but in 1980 chaired Reagan's election committee. Few accused Casey of sharing his thoughts with the public or even his closest advisers. If he believed a blow could be struck at what he considered communism, Casey moved quickly, secretly, and with little concern for consultation.[19]

The C.I.A. plan, National Security Decision Directive 17 (NSDD 17), allotted $19 million as a first payment for the Agency to create an anti-Sandinista, or Contra, force of about 500 men to oppose the Nicaraguan government and isolate the FMLN in El Salvador. Reagan signed the directive on 11 November, 1981. Haig strongly opposed NSDD 17. He wanted to deal with Soviet-Cuban influence directly, not merely through its surrogate in Managua. He was too late. The C.I.A. had begun operations months before in Honduras, although only in December did Casey privately inform the two congressional committees that oversaw the Agency's activities. Congress had no significant response to an enterprise aimed at overthrowing another government, although the general outlines of Casey's policy were obvious by late 1981. Nor did Congress respond after the *New York Times* and other respected publications revealed that the administration was using anti-Castro Cubans to give paramilitary training to Latin American exiles in Florida, California, and New Jersey for the purpose of overthrowing the "leftist regimes in Nicaragua, Cuba, and Panama," to use the *New York Times*'s words. The 1794 Neutrality Act provided for prosecution of anyone who helped such an "enterprise" aimed at a government with which "the United States is at peace." Washington had also solemnly voted for a 1970 U.N. resolution that condemned such training. Enders dismissed such legislation. A leader of one private army was more direct: "Under the Carter and Nixon administrations, what we were doing was a crime, [but] with the Reagan administration no one has bothered us for ten months."[20]

In April 1982, Reagan's top advisers who formed his National Security Planning Group on Latin America agreed in a secret memorandum that the military crisis had improved. (The Group included Vice President George Bush, Haig, Secretary of Defense Caspar Weinberger, Casey, Meese, and White House Chief of Staff James A. Baker, but, notably, no uniformed military official.) The foundations of the U.S.-Central American system, however, continued to wash away: "The regional economic situation continues to deteriorate, causing social and political dislocations which impede our efforts to stabilize the situation." The Group could only suggest putting $1 billion into the region and hope for a "gradual upturn in the world economy" to produce miracles. Neither happened, in part because as the Group recognized in El Salvador and Guatemala, the "political consensus" was so weak that it "could lead to political disintegration." Moreover, "We continue to have serious difficulties with the U.S. public and congressional opinion which jeopardizes our ability to stay the course." The Group concluded that military training and C.I.A. covert activities had to expand rapidly.[21]

In early May 1984, Reagan, running for reelection, looked back and declared, "As soon as I took office, we attempted to show friendship to the Sandinistas. . . . It did no good." Another assessment of 1981–82 was anticipated by Louis Hartz when he wrote in a widely read 1955 book: "Domination by force eliminates a lot of ticklish problems of cultural understanding."[22]

Assumptions: Unilateralism—or the Monroe Doctrine

Reagan's advisory Group worried that "Mexico and Social Democrats in Europe" were becoming troublemakers by interfering in Central America. Washington moved ruthlessly to squeeze out unwanted foreigners while bringing in others who would train the region's right-wing armies.

Problems began in May 1981 when François Mitterrand's Socialist Party won power in France. In August the French and Mexicans recognized the FMLN as "a representative political force." The two nations asked that the brutal Salvadoran armed forces be restructured and then "authentically free" elections held. Most important, the French and Mexicans disagreed with Reagan's assumption that the Salvadoran revolution could be decided on the battlefield; neither side seemed to have a chance at total victory. U.S. officials condemned the recognition of the FMLN. In December 1981, France signed a $15.8 million military deal giving Nicaragua several helicopters and coastal patrol boats, 45 trucks, and ammunition.

Haig told the French the deal was "a stab in the back." The French countered that it was disastrous to allow Nicaragua "to count entirely on Cuba and the Soviet Union to supply its defense needs." Apparently U.S. officials then tried to destroy other foreign markets for a French high-technology firm that had participated in the sale. After several months of such pressure, Mitterrand told Reagan in April 1982 that the delivery of the helicopters would be indefinitely delayed. Pressure was also applied elsewhere. Between 1981 and 1984 U.S. officials blocked about $200 million of development credits that Nicaragua badly needed, and also asked private bankers to stay out of Managua. At the Inter-American Development Bank, 41 members supported a road-building loan for Nicaragua in mid-1983, but the United States vetoed it. The British, knowing their place, kept quiet. A private British document concluded that London would support Washington "on technical grounds," to which a British official added, "If we can find them." The United States meanwhile did not bring in the Organization of American States at all; Reagan's policy violated the OAS charter's clause that prohibited "an armed attack by any state against another American state." Any public OAS consideration of U.S. policy would have brought overwhelming condemnation.[23]

The C.I.A., however, did hire Argentine military officers to train the Contras in Honduran camps. One Contra leader, Aristides Sanchez, later said the Argentines "knew nothing about a rural guerrilla war. The truth is, a lot of them were Nazis." N.S.C. Director Richard Allen called the Argentine President, General Leopold Galtieri, a "majestic personality." The usual pragmatic reasons were, however, of greater importance. As an intelligence officer explained, using Argentines allowed Washington to deflect embarrassing questions about C.I.A. involvement. The neat arrangement, however, collapsed on 2 April 1982 when Argentina attacked the British-held Falkland Islands. Despite strong pleas from Kirkpatrick and Enders, Reagan and Haig sided with London. After the British victory, Galtieri pulled out both his money and advisers from

Central America, although some mercenaries and arms aid went to the Contras as late as 1984. Now the C.I.A. had to do it all themselves. In April 1982 U.S. covert activities against Nicaragua were stepped up and $42.5 million allotted to expand C.I.A. operations with Guatemala's military regime.[24]

Honduran military leader General Gustavo Álvarez Martínez was quite confused. He had, for a price, cooperated with the Argentines and the C.I.A. only to find now that Washington had changed its mind. "Where is the Monroe Doctrine," Álvarez angrily asked U.S. Ambassador to Honduras John Negroponte, when Reagan supports British claims to islands in the Western hemisphere? "Is South America part of Europe?" Álvarez wondered aloud whether the United States would next betray Honduras. The General told friends of the old Latin American saying that the United States has "its mind in Washington, its heart in Great Britain, and its feet in Latin America." But he missed the point. The Monroe Doctrine had been first defined by an American President, and later Presidents (such as Theodore Roosevelt) reserved the right to change the Doctrine as they saw fit, and to do so unilaterally.

On 17 November 1984, Secretary of Defense Weinberger again updated the Doctrine. One of its "facets," he informed a national television audience, "was that there should be no interference, no sponsorship of any kind of military activity in this hemisphere by countries [from] other hemispheres." Monroe had actually said no such thing and, unlike Weinberger, had explicitly sided with Latin American revolutions. Weinberger, moreover, had already forgotten that Reagan had actually supported such "interference" when the British warred against the Argentines two years earlier. In any case, the Monroe Doctrine was to be whatever the United States declared it to be.[25]

Assumptions: Novak and Reaganomics for Latin Americans

By late 1981, then, the administration had developed a three-pronged approach. First, it stepped up military aid to El Salvador and reopened the pipeline for such aid to Guatemala.[26] Second, the President approved NSDD 17 to destabilize and overthrow the Nicaraguan government. Reagan and Haig tried to keep these two steps out of public debate. But they and Enders trumpeted their third set of policies: a large economic aid program capped by a Caribbean Basin Initiative (CBI). Reagan promised the CBI would revitalize friendly Central American and Caribbean countries through $350 million of U.S. aid and a major application of free-market principles.

No one doubted the need for a new approach. In 1980 the region's economic growth fell below its population growth. Unemployment shot upward as trade collapsed. Without major revolutionary problems, even Costa Rica endured a 60 percent inflation rate and a 200 percent devaluation of its currency.[27] Reagan offered $350 million, but gave $128 million of it to El Salvador. He also urged Latin Americans "to make use of the magic of the marketplace."

The best rationale for such an approach came from Michael Novak. A Roman Catholic and a Democrat, Novak had turned to neoconservatism in the late seventies. In his thoughtful essay, *The Spirit of Democratic Capitalism*, Novak rightly observed that Latin American growth rates since 1945 had risen at a pace seldom matched anywhere in the world. The southern nations, however, lacked "the political will and the economic techniques" to use the new wealth equitably. Novak understood that oligarchs and militarists were the guilty parties; he did not try to defend them. He instead called for business people to copy the North American example by developing a pluralistic, marketplace economy where capital could become "creative" and individual freedom prosper. If better times did not quickly appear, he worried, "Liberation Theology" could win the day.

Novak saved his sharpest knives for the radical priests and bishops who used dependency theory to explain the crisis, and who urged greater state involvement to break Latin American dependence on capitalist powers. He warned that their approach could lead to a "New union of Church and state (this time on the left)" that might well end in "economic decline" and the suppression of individual freedom. He countered by emphasizing "the role that business corporations—especially domestic ones—might play in building up structures of middle-class democracy." When that was accomplished, the three strong Latin American institutions—clergy, military, and large landowners—"may be checked by the growth of a new middle class based in commerce and industry." Novak thus justified the use of marketplace economics much as Kirkpatrick justified Reagan's support for Latin American dictators. Each policy rested on a certain reading of history.[28]

Novak's analysis, however, had little in common with Central American history after 1900. Contrary to his claim, "business corporations," including domestic firms, had been in the forefront of the region's development, but had never seen the need to build a "middle-class democracy." For their own reasons, they preferred cheap labor to an aggressive middle class. The foreign-owned banana and mining companies, the banks, and the huge agribusinesses that flourished in the sixties cared less about middle-class democracy than working with any government that held power. Wealthy and powerful Central Americans, not unnaturally, cooperated. Novak erred in believing that the majority of Central Americans bore major responsibility for their economic dilemmas. At nearly every opportunity, North American firms had tried to fix the marketplace instead of allowing it to operate freely. They had used their great political power in exactly the manner Novak condemned—that is, by controlling or eliminating political and economic competition. They often did so, moreover, with the help of the U.S. government.

Novak missed the main theme in post-1900 Central American history. The United States repeatedly used its political, economic, and military power to fix the marketplace. Thus the "magic of the marketplace" never worked. U.S. officials and business executives believed in *realpolitik*, not magic. Novak, moreover, failed to mention that Latin Americans repeatedly tried to break free of this system so they could indeed, in his words, "creatively . . . check clerical and military-power" and overcome "state tyranny." But each time they tried—in Nicaragua during the twenties or after 1977, in Guatemala during the early fifties, in El Salvador during the early eighties—they ran up against U.S. government power.

One cannot use force to prevent a people from controlling their own resources and political processes, then condemn that people for failing to do so. Novak emphasized that "liberty" was the "key" to having enough "bread." Neoconservatives in the United States raised that formula into an article of faith. The formula, however, had not worked in Central America. The people had the "liberty" only to starve until many concluded that control over "bread" might give them some "liberty."

The irony of Novak's position became apparent in 1982 when Reagan's Caribbean Basin proposal ran aground on North American—not Central American—refusals to play by marketplace rules. After intense lobbying by U.S. business and labor groups, Congress threw out the CBI's free-trade provisions for textiles, clothing, canned tuna, oil and oil products, watches, footwear, and leather goods imported from Latin America. The President then bowed to domestic pressure and imposed import quotas on sugar. The plan had little effect on other Central American exports because most (coffee, bananas) did not compete with U.S. products, so they already entered under favorable tariffs. Many Latin American executives also opposed key parts of the CBI, including tax breaks to foreign businesses and more rewards to foreign investors. These business people understood that once foreign investors entered their markets, U.S., Japanese, and Western European multinational corporations could control it.[29]

Novak's analysis did not recognize the role government would have to play in Central America before U.S. business virtues could be safely installed. But recognizing that problem would only have led Reagan and Novak into another sticky issue for free-marketeers: who would control the government? If Central American conservatives so favored by Reagan held power, the status quo would surely continue. To remove those conservatives, however, could require revolution.[30] Reaganomics could believe that the larger capitalists deserve favor because they create wealth, but in Central America that view continued to be a prescription for economic and political disaster. Reagan, Novak, and other neoconservatives could not have both a freer market in the Caribbean and also more equal distribution of wealth. Such a feat was impossible until a fundamental restructuring occurred, perhaps over decades and with revolutionary tactics. No one around Reagan advocated such a change. Novak did not even discuss the problem. Some business people understood the problem. One listened without enthusiasm to speeches by Enders, Clark, and other top officials who again blamed all problems on

Cubans and Soviets. The executive later commented, "So we're going to fight the Commies. What else is new?"[31]

Enders claimed that Canada, Mexico, and Venezuela "have almost precisely the same approach" to Central America.[32] These nations, however, pushed for political settlements before a region-wide armed conflict swept Central American economies back beyond their World War II stages.[33]

Meanwhile Latin Americans understood that Reaganomics aimed at tightening Central American dependence on the United States. Even before the CBI began, manufactured goods exported by Central Americans to U.S. markets jumped four times between 1979 and 1982 ($54.7 million to $216.5 million). CBI legislation tried to accelerate that trend, and entice U.S. investment, by requiring that Latin American governments had to accept Washington's rules when (and if) they expropriated U.S. property; accept arbitration judgments favorable to North American citizens and companies; and give Washington access to financial, tax, criminal, and legal information requested by U.S. officials. Reagan's "magic of the market" had pretty much disappeared by 1986. Two years after CBI began, U.S. imports from CBI nations had sunk 23 percent, while imports from the rest of the globe rose 36 percent.[34]

Dependency nevertheless tightened, however, because Central Americans came to rely on U.S. food for survival. Washington subsidized food aid to Guatemala, Honduras, El Salvador, and Costa Rica in the amount of about $10 million from 1954 to 1979, but $600 million from 1980 to 1988. The subsidies were designed to benefit U.S. farmers. The rising figures did not mean Central Americans received food equally. More than one-third of all Salvadorans received donated food, but little reached Nicaragua. In Honduras, one estimate calculated that the tiny class of Honduran wealthy in urban areas consumed 27 times more wheat than did the many rural poor. U.S. foodstuffs, moreover, were often distributed by the military, who had a keen sense of who were their friends and how the profits could buy arms. In some areas, pizza and sliced bread replaced tortillas. When an Honduran soldier was asked to identify the local dish, he replied, "Chow mein noodles."[35]

Traditional farmers thus suffered from both the ravages of war and the subsidized U.S. farm exports. They flooded for refuge into urban areas—

where they depended on imported food. Forests were stripped and soil bleached by overuse. "The rural areas no longer create jobs," an Inter-American Development Bank official noted in 1984. The bunching up in urban areas, however, only highlighted the larger problem of population growth: in the 22 years after 1961, from 1962–84, Central America's population doubled to nearly 22 million. Half the population was below the age of 20. U.S. aid worsened, not improved, these conditions. Reagan claimed that 77¢ of every dollar sent to the region from the Economic Support Fund (ESF) was spent on food and thus development. This was misleading. ESF dollars went only to nations of strategic importance. Their aim was to free the recipients' funds so they could create more military forces. By 1985, ESF accounted for $998 million (or 70 percent of all U.S. aid to the region); if, as the Congressional Research Service believed, "ESF in Central America is basically a security/military program undertaken to prop up the existing regimes and the elites who support them," there was a doubling, to over $2 billion, of the money that Reagan officials admitted spending on Central American militaries in 1985. With U.S. help, and amid widening poverty, El Salvador devoted more than half its government budget to the military, while Guatemala and Honduras devoted more than 25 percent.[36]

The 1983–84 Crisis (I): We Must "Persuade the American People the Communists Are Out to Get Us"

By 1985, the average U.S. cat ate more beef than the average person in Central America.[37] Such facts were the causes of the wars that ravaged the region. These were not the facts, however, that drove some Reagan officials to near-panic in the mid-1980s. They were more disturbed by the failure of U.S. policies and the rapidly growing resistance at home to those policies, especially as Reagan prepared to run for reelection.

In El Salvador, the President had refused to move toward negotiations to end the war after the FMLN's failed offensive in early 1981. He wanted a quick military knock-out. U.S. officials thus asked Congress to approve the sending of both money and military advisers. When Senator

Joseph Biden (Dem.-Del.) asked how long the advisers would remain, the answer was "months or at most one year." A year later, CNN and CBS television crews filmed five U.S. advisers in El Salvador carrying automatic rifles. In 1983 the advisers were widely reported to be with Salvadoran troops in a major offensive. U.S. pilots flew in combat situations, while military aid for the Salvadorans rose from $82 million in 1982 to $196 million in fiscal 1984. The FMLN nevertheless increased both their numbers and their hold over territory. In Nicaragua, the 500 Contras of 1981 multiplied to 12,000 by 1984. They were supported by $150 million and C.I.A. direction. The Sandinistas nevertheless consolidated their power. In Guatemala, one repressive regime gave way to another in 1983, and both mocked Reagan's attempts to reopen aid channels while declaring that he was fighting for a democratic Central America. In Honduras, the U.S. military buildup ($4 million of aid in 1980, $77.5 million in 1984) to provide bases for Contras threatened to capsize the economy and politics of the region's poorest country. In Costa Rica, the area's one democracy was proving fragile due to fears that the neighboring wars would spread and to U.S. demands (led by Jeane Kirkpatrick) that the Ticos create an army and join the crusade.[38]

This was not the way Reagan and Alexander Haig had promised in 1981 it would turn out. In June 1982 Haig had been replaced by George Shultz, former Nixon cabinet member, business school dean, and multinational corporation executive. Shultz had a sure sense of what he wanted to accomplish in Soviet and European affairs. He seemed to care much less about Central America, as long as he was involved in the decision-making. He grew to dislike Jeane Kirkpatrick. ("Shultz believes in professionalism and he won't put up with Mrs. Kirkpatrick," a former Republican cabinet secretary said in 1982). The new secretary of state, however, seemed willing to give way on Central America if she and other hardliners did not threaten his control of East-West relations. He was, moreover, a proud alumnus of the Marine Corps who believed that successful diplomacy often required the threat, if not the use, of force.[39]

On entering the State Department, Shultz found Enders putting together a two-track policy: tightening the military screws on the Sandinistas and FMLN, but also opening up negotiations. One track, the first, was enough for the White House, Kirkpatrick, and some congressional

Republicans. In May 1983, Enders was suddenly removed and appointed ambassador to Spain. Langhorne Motley, former ambassador to Brazil, replaced Enders. Shultz did not then realize it, but Enders's firing firmed the C.I.A.'s grip on Central American policy.

Regardless of the hardliners' success in Washington, they had no luck in changing either public opinion or strong congressional opposition. The danger went beyond domestic politics. Such heated opposition could threaten the core of Reagan's military policy: a long-term, so-called "low-intensity conflict" strategy that would slowly, quietly, and at little expense to North Americans, increase U.S. power in Central America until the revolutionaries disappeared. Another Vietnam could thus be avoided while, simultaneously, the United States proved its ability to destroy revolutions.[40] But low-intensity conflicts required time and patience, neither of which seemed to be in oversupply among North Americans and congressional critics in 1983–84.

Unable to devise a convincing foreign policy, Reagan officials devised a public relations campaign to make the policy appear to be convincing—and to make those who disagreed think twice before publicly opposing the policy. NSDD 77, approved in January 1983, created groups in the N.S.C. and State Department (the Office of Public Diplomacy), that aimed at "gluing black hats on the Sandinistas and white hats" on the Contras, to use an N.S.C. staff member's words. Stories were planted, journalists given carefully timed leaks, speakers dispatched nationwide. Lt. Colonel Oliver North of the N.S.C. helped decide which secret documents could be declassified to help the administration's case. Deputy Assistant Secretary of the Air Force, J. Michael Kelly, told a group studying low-intensity conflict in 1983, we must "persuade the American people that the communists are out to get us. . . . If we win the war of ideas, we will win everywhere else."[41]

It promised to be a tough war. Polls of early April 1983 revealed that fewer than one-third of those asked supported Reagan's "involvement in El Salvador." On April 27, the President countered with a nationally televised speech before Congress. He warned that Congress had to help him fight communism and "adventurism" in the Caribbean: "El Salvador is nearer to Texas than Texas is to Massachusetts. Nicaragua is just as close to Miami . . . and Tucson as those cities are to Washington." He then repeated, word-for-word, seven paragraphs of President Truman's 1947 Truman Doctrine speech that warned that the world was divided simply between "free peoples" and "armed minorities." Congress and the North American people had to decide which side they were on. Public opinion polls nevertheless showed little change. The *Washington Post* detected a "Reagan Doctrine" aimed at helping guerrilla fighters. The newspaper believed that undermining governments with which we were not at war was "dangerous business." Reagan's several attempts to dress the Contras up as "freedom fighters" and "the moral equal of our founding fathers" were derided. Mexican novelist and former diplomat Carlos Fuentes believed that the term "freedom fighters" only "provokes fits of laughter in Latin America. A 'freedom fighter' is one who fights for the independence of his country against the dependence induced on it by the major power. . . . The Contras are stooges of Washington."[42]

The 1983–84 Crisis (II): The Outside Threats

Reagan's use of the Truman Doctrine exemplified the attempt to blame the Central American crisis on Cuban and Soviet intrigues. Cuba "is not simply a Soviet surrogate," Enders told Congress in 1982, but, because of their success, Cuban leaders had developed "armed struggle" into a "way of life." A year later, a "Background Paper" released by the State and Defense Departments blamed Cuba for most ills in the region. As for the Soviets, the White House charged as early as 1981 that El Salvador was "a strikingly familiar case of Soviet . . . military involvement" in the third world. In 1983 the "Background Paper" charged that "The Soviets have played a major role in the militarization of the region."[43]

The Cuban-Soviet involvement, however, was both more complex and less dramatic. Cuba pursued, sometimes to Moscow's intense displeasure, an independent policy in the region. Castro had helped unify the Sandinista movement months before the triumph of 1979, and he tried to repeat that success in El Salvador. The Salvadorans, however, were less cooperative and less militarily efficient. Castro sent aid, but he was less confident about the FMLN. That confidence plummeted in

October 1983 when U.S. forces suddenly overthrew a pro-Castro regime on the Caribbean island of Grenada. More than forty Cubans died in the fighting. Castro wanted to keep the FMLN and Sandinistas alive, for reasons of both ideological affinity and mutual protection against the United States, but not at the expense of his own regime.[44]

The Soviets were also keeping the escape routes open. They had consistently misjudged Central America, not least in the 1970s when they underestimated the Sandinistas and overestimated the woeful Communist Party in Nicaragua. The Brezhnev regime, stumbling through economic and political decline to an unlamented end in 1983, wanted to keep the United States preoccupied in Central America, especially as the Kremlin became bogged down in the bitter Afghanistan war. The Sandinista economic problems, the U.S. invasion of Grenada, and simple geography indicated the limits of Moscow's reach. Besides, the Soviets could not pay for any more revolutions than the Cuban, which they were subsidizing with some $8 to $10 billion each year. (Even then, Cubans and Soviets did not see eye-to-eye; Haig was convinced in early 1982, after talks with top Soviet officials, that "Cuban activities in the Western Hemisphere were a matter between the U.S. and Cuba.") Between 1979 and 1982 the Communist bloc supplied about 20 percent of Nicaragua's credit, while Latin America provided 32 percent. Mexico alone gave almost twice as much economic aid as the Soviets.[45]

Moscow was more generous militarily. After Daniel Ortega's visit to Moscow in March 1983, the Kremlin declared that his government would have "sufficient means to defend its fatherland." At no time, however, did the Soviets call Nicaragua a "fundamental" interest (as the Eastern European regimes were considered), nor did they ever indicate they would defend Nicaragua. Moscow refused to send such major arms as MIG jet fighters, although the Sandinistas wanted such help. No high-level Soviet official even visited Managua until 1987 when, as Mikhail Gorbachev's reforms were rapidly improving East-West relations, Boris Yeltsin (then a candidate member of the Politburo) arrived as part of a "parliamentary exchange" program. Dimitri Simes, a respected U.S. analyst of Soviet policy, concluded in August 1983 that the Soviets were even denying sending military aid because they did not want to justify further U.S. involvement. In any case, Simes added, the Russians talk only of their "fraternal sympathy with the heroic people of the revolution," which was another way of saying the Sandinistas were on their own.[46]

Reagan thus had difficulty actually identifying a vital Soviet threat in Central America. Nor could he provide evidence that Cuban-supplied Nicaragua was the main channel for arms to the FMLN. U.S. intelligence bragged that it could detect even a "toilet flushing in Managua," but it could not gather the materials to convince Congress and the North American people that Sandinista aid to the FMLN justified a huge aid plan for the Contras. After Reagan officials presented their case to a House committee behind closed doors in June 1984, one congressman emerged to call it "amateurish," then observed: "to see three mules on a path with boxes on their backs doesn't confirm Nicaraguan involvement." A former C.I.A. analyst, David MacMichael, had quit the Agency and declared there was no significant arms flow. When a State Department official was asked about the lack of evidence in June 1984, he replied, "Don't ask us about any flood of arms. That comes from some White House speech writer, not from us."[47]

Kirkpatrick, however, never gave up. In March 1983 she warned of "the very large Soviet effort influencing the region. . . . The fact is," she charged, Nicaraguan military power "outstrips any other military establishment in the region." She failed to note an important exception: a single U.S. aircraft carrier had more fire power than all the Central American armies combined. By 1983–84, two such floating arsenals ploughed the seas along Central American coasts. The United States, moreover, had more men in its military than Nicaragua had in its total male population.[48]

The 1983–84 Crisis (III): The Inside Threats

A major threat to Reagan's policies emerged inside his own country. Especially in churches, some of which (most notably, the Roman Catholic) had long, intimate ties with Central America, opposition mobilized. The U.S. Catholic Bishops, never heretofore suspected as being soft on communism, spoke out against aid to the Salvadoran army and more arms to the Contras.[49] Not one of the 300 bishops urged aid to the Contras. Leading Protestant churches, even many Baptists and Presbyterians who usually supported presidential foreign policies, registered dissent. By the mid-1980s, at least 60,000 Americans had signed a pledge to disrupt cities and government operations through civil disobedience if U.S. forces invaded Nicaragua.

Reagan officials struck back. The North American Congress on Latin America (NACLA) was highly experienced in the region, influential, and deeply critical of U.S. policy. After Reagan mentioned NACLA twice and the conservative Heritage Foundation criticized it, the Internal Revenue Service forced NACLA to devote time and scarce resources to justifying its financial reports. The State Department meanwhile used the McCarran-Walter Act, which Congress had passed over Truman's veto in 1952 during the height of the anti-communist witchhunt conducted by Senator Joseph McCarthy (Rep.-Wisc.). The Reagan administration now interpreted the act as allowing it to exclude any foreigner it considered dangerous. In April 1984, U.S. officials barred Guillermo Ungo, a Salvadoran Social Democrat allied with the FMLN, from entering the United States. At the end of 1984 the State Department barred four Salvadoran women. They were human rights workers who had been invited to receive the first Robert F. Kennedy Human Rights Award at Georgetown University, a Roman Catholic school. The U.S. officials claimed that the women's organization, CO-MADRES (Committee of Mothers and Relatives of Political Prisoners Disappeared and Murdered in El Salvador), advocated violence. When asked for specifics, a State Department official said, "I can't be forthcoming with the information." On the other hand, Roberto D'Aubuisson, tied to death-squad murders in El Salvador, was allowed to enter the United States.[50]

In 1991, a former C.I.A. official, Alan D. Fiers, Jr., revealed that the Agency had regularly secretly monitored phone calls between the Sandanistas and Democrats in the U.S. Congress whom the C.I.A. suspected of not being sufficiently patriotic. But perhaps the Federal Bureau of Investigation (F.B.I.) was most active. Between 1981 and 1985, it conducted a secret, nationwide investigation of the Committee in Solidarity with the People of El Salvador (CISPES), that included photographing participants in peace rallies. The F.B.I. also investigated nuns, college students, and members of the United Automobile Workers. CISPES later claimed that the investigations lasted until 1988, and that more than 13,000 people and 11,000 organizations were targets. Tactics included breaking into offices and illegally searching files for evidence that CISPES was linked with terrorists. But not a single shred of wrongdoing on CISPES' part could be shown. FBI Director William S. Sessions finally apologized in 1988, condemned the investigation, and gave a two-week suspension from work to penalize three FBI employees who were involved. Critics called the penalty "outrageous." The hunt had occurred as President Reagan promised in his widely praised speeches "to get the government off the backs of the American people."[51] To the contrary, the wars were coming home.

The 1983–84 Crisis (IV): Unwanted Third Parties—Congress and Contadora

Even Congress was working up some anger over the administration's policies. In 1982, Reagan declared that the Contras' objective was to stop Nicaraguan arms flows to the FMLN. Few arms, however, were stopped. C.I.A. Director Casey bragged that Contra forces had grown from 500 to 4,000 as stories appeared that the Contras really intended to overthrow the Nicaraguan government. Led by Thomas Harkin (Dem.-Ia.), Democrats moved to cut off the covert funds for the Contras. They and Casey were saved, however, when the respected chair of the House Select Committee on Intelligence, Edward Boland (Dem.-Mass.), worked out a compromise. In December 1982 the first Boland Amendment (Boland I) prohibited the C.I.A. and Department of Defense from using funds for the purpose of overthrowing the Sandinistas or provoking a Nicaragua-Honduras military exchange. The law allowed the C.I.A. to continue to try to stop the arms flow. Reagan signed the measure with the words, "We are complying with the law."[52]

Congress had aroused itself, and the effects rippled beyond Capitol Hill. A Defense Department document of 1983 showed the military's growing concern: "The United States should not continue to pursue a policy in Central America that increases its commitment . . . unless Congress grants the means to succeed." In Latin America, a group of nations organized to stop the growing war before it spread over to neighboring states. In early 1982 Mexico had tried to mediate the growing U.S.-Nicaraguan-Salvadoran clash, but Haig killed the effort. The United States was determined to operate its own system its own way.[53]

In January 1983, Panama, Mexico, Venezuela, and Colombia met on the Panamanian island of Contadora to draft a peace plan. By September the Contadora group had a twenty-one-point Document of Objectives whose main points were (1) an end to external subversion, (2) a reduction of the number of foreign military advisers throughout the region, (3) arms reduction, and (4) democratization and respect for human rights. Secretary of State Shultz called it a "breakthrough," but complained that the Sandinistas refused to allow outsiders to monitor their internal political affairs. Actually, Nicaraguan officials offered to sign the treaty. They also met one U.S. demand by announcing that elections were to be held in 1985. Peace might have been at hand.

The United States set out to destroy the Contadora agreement. Reagan's first objective was not a settlement, but the destruction of the Sandinistas and the FMLN. With his reelection campaign beginning, however, and with a majority of the public opposed to his Central American policies, the destruction had to be artful. The United States demanded more negotiations, especially on the issue of democratization inside Nicaragua. At Contadora's request, the Reagan officials agreed to hold bilateral talks with the Sandinistas at Manzanillo, Mexico. The U.S. team demanded that Cuban and Soviet advisers be expelled and Nicaragua reduce its military; Washington did not offer to reduce its own military power in the region. As a U.S. official said, "The whole point was to get the Nicaraguans to accept the Contadora proposals. Now they have but we say we aren't satisfied. I'm not sure I would blame the Nicaraguans if they were confused." The United States, it seemed, would not take "yes" for an answer.[54]

The Manzanillo talks lasted until Reagan broke them off in January 1985. He was safely reelected and the Contadora nations' efforts were dead in the water. To ensure Contadora's death, Washington constantly accused Nicaragua of military provocations; meanwhile U.S. forces defied Contadora's request that the tension be reduced and instead launched major military maneuvers around Nicaragua. One, "Big Pine II," lasted 6 months and involved over 20,000 U.S. troops.[55]

Shultz wasted no love on the Sandinistas, but by mid-1983 he understood that Reagan's failed policies were poisoning relations with both Congress and Latin Americans. In May the State Department tried to regain control of decision-making by proposing that the administration distance itself from the inept Contras and talk seriously with the Sandinistas. Shultz not only lost the fight, but was stunned in July when U.S. warships, on N.S.C. orders, suddenly sailed for maneuvers in Central American waters. Later that month, N.S.C. officials left to negotiate in the Middle East without Shultz's knowledge. He offered Reagan his resignation "if this is the way things are going to be done." Faced with a reelection campaign and the unfruitful Central American approach, Reagan rejected Shultz's resignation. The President played for time. He established a bipartisan eleven-person commission headed by Henry Kissinger to investigate the mess and offer new policy proposals.[56]

During a quick trip to the region even Kissinger was reportedly "aghast" at the brutality of the Salvadoran government–associated death squads which had killed at least 1,300 people during the year without any convictions of murderers. In Nicaragua the commission endured such a tense, difficult meeting (perhaps in part because C.I.A.-directed planes had recently bombed Managua), that when Kissinger discovered that the highly able U.S. Ambassador, Anthony Quainton, was insufficiently tough on the Sandinistas, he reportedly pushed Reagan to fire Quainton. The President did so. The top Sandinista officials were without illusions. They had earlier believed that Kissinger would repeat his Vietnam policy of ten years before: sit at a "negotiating table while ordering bombs to rain on" the other side, as one top Sandinista phrased it. "We see in this commission the fundamental purpose of opening political space for Reagan . . . within the U.S.," he added.[57] Within two months, the C.I.A.-directed flights dropped bombs on Managua's airport and other targets.

In January 1984 the commission issued a 132-page report. It began with a historical overview arguing that the United States had given too little attention to Central Americans, an argument that Nicaraguans,

Hondurans, and Guatemalans must have found strange—and ominous. The report recommended an economic development aid program of about $8 billion over five years, and the creation of two new bilateral organizations and one multilateral body through which the United States would control the aid. The commission noted conditions which were so "miserable" that they "invite revolution," but then stressed as the most critical point the "hostile outside forces—Cuba backed by the Soviet Union and now working through Nicaragua." The report recommended more arms for Honduras and even Guatemala, but urged that the overwhelming amount be given to El Salvador. The majority of the commission believed those monies should be tied to the practice of human rights principles; Kissinger dissented. Yearning for governments that are "legitimized" (a key word in Kissinger's long fight against third-world revolutions), the commission urged only elections, not talks about power-sharing with the FMLN. A tough section on the Sandinistas warned that "we do not advocate a policy of static containment," and—in careful language—urged continued support of the Contras.[58]

The report combined ideas from Reagan's military policy, Kennedy's Alliance for Progress, and Eisenhower's use of the C.I.A. None of these policies had produced happy results. Specifically, the commission urged a huge aid program that Congress (facing an incredible $200 billion budget deficit) opposed; a large military package that Contadora and other regional nations opposed; and the linking of military aid to observing human rights practices—which Reagan opposed.

Seeking consensus, Reagan only intensified debate. Senator Daniel Patrick Moynihan (Dem.-N.Y.), known for his vocal anti-communism, said flatly that the commission had not produced any "facts" to show that the Soviet-Cuban bloc threatened U.S. interests in the region. A State Department–commissioned study conducted by the University of Miami concluded that Soviet influence in Central America had been falling—not because of Washington's actions, but because of aid from Western Europe and the Roman Catholic Church. The *Central America Report,* published in Guatemala, warned that the recommendations could only increase neodependency, or, as the newsletter phrased it, create "even more U.S. control of internal affairs than now exists and which is already a source of resentment in many sectors."[59]

As Congress moved to slash Reagan's aid requests, the President reiterated his charge that the Sandinistas "engaged in anti-Semitic acts"—a charge that Ambassador Quainton months before had warned lacked evidence. A frustrated Kissinger finally told friends that the best solution might be to drop the many unread copies of his report on Nicaragua.[60] The C.I.A.-N.S.C. militarization of U.S. policy accelerated, pushing aside congressional doubts, Contadora's efforts, and Shultz's objectives. In a tense June 1984 meeting Shultz again tried to revive the two-track policy of fighting and sincerely negotiating. Casey, Kirkpatrick, Weinberger, and N.S.C. Director McFarlane poured scorn on the idea. Shultz backed down. Fifteen thousand more Nicaraguans died before Oscar Arias Sánchez, President of Costa Rica, adapted Shultz's approach in 1987 and produced a workable peace plan.[61]

The 1983–84 Crisis (V): Reagan, the C.I.A., and the Origins of the Iran-Contra Scandal

Of course, the C.I.A.-N.S.C. policy had to be careful. A study by the Rand Corporation (a think-tank closely associated with the Pentagon), warned that a U.S. invasion of Nicaragua could require 100,000 troops and bog down the country in a long, bloody military occupation.[62] Meanwhile, U.S. cities could be paralyzed by anti-war protests.

C.I.A.-directed low-intensity conflict offered a safer alternative. Since Reagan had given Casey the green light in late 1981, the C.I.A. had built the Contras virtually from scratch. Some old-time "hairy necked paramilitary types" were needed to find, train, and direct the Contras, as one U.S. official phrased it. After the Argentinian instructors went home in 1982, Casey named Dewey Clarridge head of C.I.A.'s Latin American division. Long stationed in Europe, Clarridge knew little about Central America, but he and his colleagues soon told the Contras that Reagan "wants you to go to Managua," and to get there before the 1984 election. In late 1982, the Agency introduced as the new head of the Nicaragua Democratic Force (FDN) a former Managuan Coca-Cola bottling owner, Adolfo Calero. He was more presentable than most

FDN leaders, including the field commander, Enrique Bermúdez, who had been Somoza's military attaché in Washington. His closest adviser was Ricardo "Chino" Lau, once one of Somoza's most brutal National Guardsmen. North Americans provided some $300,000 monthly in large boxes filled with dollars for the 7,000 FDN training in Honduras. The Agency also recruited a former Sandinista hero, Edén Pastora (the fabled "Commandante Zero") who had been shut out of power in Managua. He had opened his own opposition front to the south along the Nicaraguan-Costa Rican border. Now the C.I.A. tried to bring him into its camp and coordinate the northern (Honduran) and southern fronts. Pastora, however, was his own man. He refused to be bought off.[63]

By November 1983, the C.I.A. concluded the Contras could not win a military victory. The FDN was too ineffective and unpopular inside Nicaragua, the Sandinistas too organized and battlefield-savvy. Nor had the C.I.A. covered itself in glory. In September 1983 Casey ordered that something dramatic be done, so the Agency bombed Managua airport— just as two U.S. Senators (William Cohen [Rep.-Me.] and Gary Hart [Dem.-Co.]) were landing. The furious Senators told Casey privately that the raid was idiotic and unproductive—especially, one imagines, in the Senate. Reagan then approved a C.I.A. request to escalate the violence in 1984 with the Agency doing the work itself. The State Department went along. C.I.A. operatives mined Nicaraguan harbors in clear violation of international law. Ships were damaged, lives endangered. A United Nations resolution formally condemning the mining was stopped only by a U.S. veto. Critics claimed the C.I.A. had become terrorists as measured by the State Department's own definition: "terrorism is premeditated violence perpetrated against noncombatant targets by subnational groups or clandestine state agents, usually intended to influence an audience." Nicaragua took its case to the International Court of Justice in The Hague. The Reagan administration refused to argue the merits of the case before the court; instead it defied international law by denying the court's jurisdiction. (The administration denounced the court at the same time the President proclaimed "Law Day" and intoned: "without law, there can be no freedom, only chaos and disorder.") In 1986 the court upheld Nicaragua's claim that the

United States had broken international law and violated Nicaraguan sovereignty. At home, the Sandinistas intensified a massive arms expansion in anticipation of a C.I.A.-Contra offensive.[64]

Congress, including Republican leaders, reacted angrily. Senator Barry Goldwater (Rep.-Az.), head of the Senate Select Intelligence Committee, fumed to Casey that he was "pissed off" about not being told about the plans to plant mines. In June 1984, Congress passed a second Boland Amendment (Boland II), that cut off all lethal aid to the Contras. Apparently, however, the C.I.A. had briefed Congress eleven times about the mining. The *Wall Street Journal* even published a story about the plans to mine the harbor. The House and Senate oversight committees did not so much regulate the Agency as agree with it during these years when covert activities more than doubled under Reagan to some forty operations worldwide.[65]

One covert action occurred on the night of 30 May 1984, although how deeply the C.I.A. was involved remains a topic of intense debate. Edén Pastora had accepted some Agency support, but adamantly refused to link his operations with the FDN's in the north. He hated the discredited *Somocistas* in the Contra command. On May 23, Pastora said the C.I.A. had "blocked all help to us." A week later he began a press conference. Suddenly a blinding blue flash wrecked the room. Eight people died. Pastora barely escaped with severe wounds. Two injured reporters, Tony Avirgan and Martha Honey, began intense investigations. They concluded that the plot had been laid by associates of the C.I.A. (especially with an Indiana-born rancher in Costa Rica, John Hull), and Oliver North. Hull, North, and the C.I.A. denied any connection with the bombing. Costa Rican authorities later indicted Hull for drug trafficking, with the profits going to support the Contras, and for violating Costa Rica's neutrality. Hull, at the demand of U.S. Congressmen, was released and jumped bail in 1989 to return to Indiana.[66] Pastora never returned to battle. He settled into the fishing business in Costa Rica. The C.I.A. now controlled all the anti-Sandinista operations.

But the Agency then suffered another embarrassment during the U.S. presidential election campaign. In October the C.I.A. admitted it had printed a manual instructing the Contras how to hire professional criminals for "selective jobs," and how to "neutralize" (kill) Nicaraguan judges and police. (In 1981 Reagan had ordered that no U.S. government employee "engage in or conspire to engage in assassination.") Congress again condemned the C.I.A. Despite the embarrassment, Reagan scored a landslide reelection victory in November. Then another C.I.A. publication was uncovered: the "Freedom Fighter's Manual" instructed Nicaraguans to "tie down the Marxist tyranny" by stopping up toilets, *"llegar tarde al trabajo"* (arrive late to work), and lighting a homemade Molotov cocktail explosive by using matchbooks. Near-tragedy had been followed by near-farce.[67]

But Casey was not to be stopped. Pressured by Congress to quit aiding the Contras, he (according to a later investigation) brought in South African money and advisers to help. Internationally condemned for its racial segregationist policy, the South Africans valued Casey's friendship. The Agency also apparently began sending mercenaries from a private Alabama-based group, the Civilian Military Assistance. Costa Rica captured and jailed five members of this group.[68]

Most important, with Boland II on the books, Casey and Reagan, with the support of Shultz, decided to ask foreign countries and rich, private North Americans to help. Lt. Colonel Oliver North of the N.S.C. staff headed the effort. Since 1983 the intensely ideological and energetic North had secretly guided privately funded public relations campaigns to help the Contras and drive from office such critics as Representative Michael Barnes (Dem.-Md.). (Barnes lost a Senate race in 1986.) In late spring 1984, North put Contra leader Adolfo Calero in touch with retired Air Force officer Richard V. Secord. Over the next eight months, Secord tapped rich Middle East governments for $32 million that went into offshore Contra bank accounts. Reagan himself appealed to wealthy private donors.[69]

Other U.S. officials tried to scare North Americans into joining the cause. The President warned "of hundreds of thousands of refugees fleeing Communist oppression" who would flood the United States. The biggest scare occurred on election night when television programs were suddenly interrupted for a report that eighteen to twenty-one Soviet MIG-21 jet fighters were heading for a Nicaraguan port. The United States had warned that such a shipment could trigger a military strike to destroy the planes. As tension built, U.S. jets' sonic booms rattled windows and nerves in Managua. Suddenly on the fourth day of the crisis, Washington officials said it had all been a mistake. Some State Department officials believed it had been a ploy by Pentagon civilian hardliners to ruin relations, if not precipitate a military attack. Shultz was blunt: whoever leaked the unverified intelligence "engaged in a criminal act, in my opinion."[70]

Nothing seemed to be working for Reagan as Central America became further immersed in a blood bath. From January 1984 until late 1986 his Nicaraguan policy never received more than 35-percent support in public opinion polls. "The two main alternatives to our policy—outright military intervention or a political solution—are both unacceptable," a State Department official said in late 1984, "but there's no agreement on what else to do."[71]

The despondency, indeed crisis, felt among U.S. officials was expressed by C.I.A. deputy director for intelligence, Robert Gates, in a secret memo to Casey on December 14, 1984. "The Contras, even with American support, cannot overthrow the Sandinista regime," Gates began. Nicaragua is becoming a consolidated, armed "ally of the Soviet Union and Cuba." Honduras and Guatemala are suddenly faced with "capital flight," and "political instability" could infect the entire region. Vietnam's is the history to study: "Half measures, half-heartedly applied will have the same result in Nicaragua. As in Vietnam, moreover, negotiations only allow communists further to entrench themselves." It is time "overtly to try to bring down the regime" through blockading Nicaragua economically and politically, increased military aid to the Contras, and "air strikes to destroy a considerable portion of Nicaragua's military buildup. . . . The fact is," Gates concluded, "that the Western Hemisphere is the sphere of influence of the United States"—either assume that or "abandon the Monroe Doctrine." The final question was how much of this proposal was "politically" possible given such strong opposition in the United States.[72]

Casey and North were meanwhile deciding how to ensure that North Americans did not know what was going on in Central America. Only Central Americans were to know, and to suffer.

Nicaragua: "The Epidemiology of Aggression"

The U.S. suspicion of revolution had originated in the 1790s and been articulated in the 1830s by Alexis de Tocqueville. Little changed in 150 years. A high Nicaraguan official remarked privately that if Carter had remained in office, "we would still be at loggerheads."[73] Reagan only turned the screws more rapidly and tightly. By late February 1981 economic aid was shut off. By November the President had flashed the "go" signal to the C.I.A. The combatants were not equal. People in the United States spent as much on digestive aids and shaving products as the Nicaraguan people had in total income. The smaller country needed the larger to open doors to international lending agencies. In the best of worlds, "We need 10 years to regain the 1977 gross national product." estimated one Nicaraguan official.[74]

Little help would be forthcoming, however, Haig announced in early 1981, until the Sandinistas stopped helping the Salvadoran revolutionaries. In early April, the State Department announced good news: "We have no hard evidence of arms movements through Nicaragua during the past few weeks, and propaganda and some other support activities have been curtailed." Then came the non sequitur: because "some arms traffic may [sic] be continuing and other support very probably continues," aid would be cancelled anyway.[75] Illogical on its face, the announcement made political sense because it fit into Reagan's world view and appeased the extreme right-wing of the Republican party led by Senator Jesse Helms of North Carolina, who had demanded an end to the assistance. With its economic leverage disappearing, the United States could no longer use it to discipline the Sandinistas, but only try to break them as they reopened the arms flow to El Salvador and imported Communist-bloc equipment and advisers to build a 25,000-man army and a 30,000-strong militia. They also sent seventy men to Bulgaria for jet fighter training. ("Yes, they are there," a high Nicaraguan official admitted privately, "but don't worry. They are flunking the course." His North American listeners were not amused.)[76]

To develop their country, the Sandinistas had to dismantle the

Somoza system and build light industry and agriculture for internal consumption as well as export. Without outside aid, that path would be difficult to follow. The revolution moved sharply to the left. Businessmen who criticized the government were arrested or exiled. (The regime carefully tried to maintain the appearance of balance by simultaneously jailing several Communist party members.) The Sandinistas looked to Western Europe, Mexico, and General Moammar Qaddafi's Libya, as well as to the Soviet bloc, for help. But it was not sufficient. "We have failed so far economically," a Nicaraguan official admitted in late 1981. Another official noted that the regime was caught in "a vicious circle": the more the government extended its control to protect itself, the more it alienated powerful groups. Business people let plants run down as they spirited money out to safe overseas accounts. A government economist told a U.S. visitor: "It's not as if there are just four or five of the big guys. If there were, you could round up one or two and make an example of them." Instead, the bourgeoisie was inflicting "death by a million cuts."[77]

Between 1979 and 1982 the Sandinistas received $42 million of foreign aid to stop the economic bleeding. It was not enough. They tried a balanced agrarian reform program that aimed to give land to peasant cooperatives; by 1984 less than 20 percent remained under state ownership. No limit was placed on the size of private holdings as long as they were productive. This was hardly Marxism-Leninism. Indeed, the emerging leader in the nine-person national directorate, Daniel Ortega, belonged to the most pragmatic, non-doctrinaire faction, the *Terceristas* (see p. 228). Ideological arguments broke out between Ortega and more radical leaders (Bayardo Arce, Tomás Borge, and Henry Ruiz Hernandez), a split worsened by the declining productivity and the government's determination to devote many of the declining resources to schools, health clinics, and adult education programs. By 1985, the Sandinistas had nearly doubled the number of hospitals to fifty-two, tripled the number of medical students to 550, and cut infant mortality in half. But the economy and the weakened political consensus could no longer support such ambitious programs.[78]

U.S. officials tried not only to break the Nicaraguan economy, but to appeal to the bourgeoisie, many of whom had long looked to Washington for timely protection. By killing the chances of loans from international agencies and banks, Washington aimed to make the Sandinistas' maintenance of the nation's infrastructure a mission impossible. Some New York City (Citibank) and West German banks did help, but most backed away. Nevertheless, at least forty-three other multinational corporations remained, including Texaco, IBM, Caterpillar, and Exxon which even agreed to refine Soviet oil. They provided some $87 million of investment and one-quarter of the nation's production, but it was insufficient to pay for the imports that were required for factory maintenance and food. The $1.6 billion debt left by Somoza ballooned to $3.5 billion. Shortages grew. Another blow fell in 1983 when floods caused $50 million of damage.[79]

Above all, there was the war. Defense soaked up 40 percent of the nation's budget by 1984 to pay for the now 75,000 active-duty army. Social programs suffered. Polio, once eliminated by vaccination programs, reappeared. One doctor called it "the epidemiology of aggression." The war turned as vicious as it was costly. Americas Watch, a nonpartisan human rights group, reported Contra "kidnappings, torture, and murder of unarmed civilians." One Contra testified to setting up a roadblock in 1983. A vehicle with thirteen people was stopped. Three nurses were raped and shot, then the men were executed. "We were happy" the Contra guerrilla reported, "and shouted again and again, 'With God and patriotism we will overthrow Communism.' "[80] By 1984 Washington had sent $150 million to the Contras, yet they did not control a single village. Soviet aid to Managua jumped from $7 million in 1980 to at least $250 million in 1984, including helicopter gunships. In 1984 alone between 4,000 and 5,000 Nicaraguans died; another 400,000 became displaced persons.[81]

In retaliation, the Sandinistas made a near-fatal error of imposing military control over some 50,000 Miskito Indians who lived along the distant Atlantic coastline. Never hispanicized, the Miskitos had fought all attempts to assimilate them. They became prime targets for C.I.A. recruiting. The Sandinistas burned eighty-one villages, relocated Miskitos in resettlement camps, and murdered at least twenty-five while another 250 disappeared. Some 10,000 Indians fled to Honduras where their leaders obtained C.I.A. weapons in early 1983. The Sandinistas then realized the dimensions of their mistake. They released 300 Indians and set up a special bureau to deal with the Miskitos' demands. By 1985, Indian leadership split into pro- and anti-Sandinista groups, but the Atlantic coast remained an Achilles heel of the revolution.[82]

So too was the Roman Catholic hierarchy led by Archbishop Miguel Obando y Bravo. He had supported liberation theology and the Sandinistas in the late 1970s, but as the new government moved to the left and the middle-classes became alienated, he ordered priests to return to their religious duties. Many refused. He charged that the government was imposing "Castroite textbooks based on materialism." A Sandinista official called him "the spiritual leader of the entire right wing," but as the economy declined Obando became a popular leader. The division sharpened in March 1983 when he welcomed Pope John Paul II to Nicaragua. The Pope condemned liberation theology, said nothing about the U.S. support of the Contras or the thousands killed in the war, and instead ordered priests to break with the government. He and Obando were furious when pro-Sandinista crowds disrupted a huge open-air Mass in Managua. The government's explanation was that the protesters were mothers of soldiers slain by the Contras who had grown angry because the Pope made no reference to their tragedies. Obando began raising money to support opposition groups. Tough Interior Minister Tomás Borge declared he would rather fight 10,000 Contras than several bishops, but his fight was made easier because the Church was so badly split. Many priests defied the hierarchy by working with the poor and espousing liberation theology. Into the division moved fundamentalist Protestant groups (many sponsored by conservative U.S. supporters), whose membership mushroomed in rural towns. These new sects strongly supported the Contras.[83]

Faced with these growing religious, economic, and military pressures, in September 1983 Daniel Ortega agreed to the Contadora group's peace proposals. He also offered to stop buying arms and expel all foreign military advisers if the other Central American nations (including El Salvador) would do the same. Reagan rejected the proposal and in early 1984 demanded that the Sandinistas "say 'uncle' to the rebels." The dramatic revelations of the C.I.A. activities, however, led to the cut-off of aid under Boland II. Ortega tried to maintain the initiative by an-

nouncing elections for November 1984 instead of 1985.[84]
The key question became whether either the Sandinistas or the U.S.
government would allow opposition candidates to participate fully in the
election. The Sandinistas used both their popularity and strong-arm tactics to keep the opposition as weak as possible. Washington had a different problem: if the Sandinistas won a fair election, the U.S.-supported
opposition would suffer a disastrous setback. Washington officials split.
Moderates, especially in the State Department, believed they had a
strong candidate in Arturo Cruz (a respected banker and former Sandinista ambassador to the United States before he resigned in 1981).
Hardliners in the N.S.C. and C.I.A. and among civilians in the Pentagon had no such faith. If Cruz did not participate, they argued, voting
would be meaningless. Before Cruz went to Nicaragua to campaign, he
privately told NBC television correspondent Fred Francis, "You know
I'm not really going to run." The two Nicaraguan sides met in Brazil to
negotiate terms. Cruz received assurances that he and his party, the
Coordinadora, could campaign freely. But talks broke down when he
demanded more time for debate on the terms and the Sandinistas refused to delay any longer. A State Department official, L. Craig John-
stone, said, "We did everything we could to support Cruz and get him
into the election." But an unidentified U.S. official told the *New York
Times* that the Reagan administration "never contemplated letting
Cruz stay in the race because then the Sandinistas could justifiably claim
that the elections were legitimate."[85]
Opposition candidates did run, but none with Cruz's stature. The
United States applied pressure by announcing ten days before the election that large military exercises were about to be held in the region. The
election nevertheless was held on 4 November 1984. Three-quarters of
registered Nicaraguans voted for seven parties. Ortega won the presidency with 63 percent of the vote; the Sandinistas obtained 61 of the 96
National Assembly seats. It was hardly a landslide of approval for the
Sandinistas. U.S. officials nevertheless termed the election a "sham,"
especially, they charged, because the winners had used *turbas* (mobs) to
silence opposition. Former Venezuelan President (and a leader of the
Socialist International), Carlos Andrés Perez, refused to attend Ortega's
inauguration because he charged the Sandinistas had gone back on their

pledges for "political pluralism, a mixed economy, and a non-aligned position" in foreign affairs. Others sharply disagreed. Western European delegations observed and approved the election process. Fifteen U.S. experts making up the Latin American Studies Association Observer Delegation reached unanimous agreement that (in the words of one leader), "the election was fair, clean, and competitive, and that the Reagan Administration and the U.S. mass media . . . had performed in a reprehensible manner" in judging the elections.[86]

Daniel Ortega was both tough and pragmatic. Reserved, soft-spoken, he had been jailed and tortured for seven years by Somoza. When denied water he had drunk his own urine to stay alive. With the election victory, he changed military tactics and began destroying Contra forces which no longer officially received arms from the U.S. Congress. Ortega placed more moderate colleagues in charge of the faltering economic institutions, but he also increased already tough government censorship of the major opposition daily, *La Prensa.* The new president intended to outlast the newly reelected Ronald Reagan.

Honduras: Refitting the Aircraft Carrier

Honduras had become so important for U.S. covert operations against Guatemala in 1954 and then Nicaragua in the 1980s that one expert called it "the USS Honduras, a [stationary] aircraft carrier of sorts." Washington's military aid jumped from $4 million in fiscal 1980 to $77.5 million in 1984. The money inundated the 4.5 million people whose average yearly income was $710. At least eleven airfields and base camps stretched out over 450 square miles. The flagship was the Palmerola Air Base where 132 U.S. army–built structures headquartered the officers who coordinated the Nicaraguan-Salvadoran operations. Some 12,000 Hondurans had been involuntarily removed from their land so the base could be built. No U.S. official seemed to know enough history to realize that one base site, Trujillo, was also the grave of William Walker, the 1850s U.S. freebooter who had tried to conquer Central America and was executed by Hondurans.[87]

By 1983 the U.S. operation was so large that the C.I.A. opened a press bureau in a Honduran Holiday Inn to brag about its exploits. Some 300 to 400 North American military personnel worked in the small country. The 116 members of the U.S. Embassy made it one of the largest in all Latin America. Honduras's main contribution was the chief of the armed forces, General Gustavo Álvarez Martínez. The Argentine-trained Álvarez was the choice of the C.I.A. and Pentagon to run the country. The weak front-man was Roberto Suazo Córdoba, who won the presidency in a 1981 election that, in the White House view, demonstrated that Honduras was democratic. More accurately, it was a "demonstration election," to use a term coined by authors Edward Herman and Frank Brodhead—that is, its purpose was not to elect fairly a person who held real power, but to give the illusion of such an election so that the North American people, and especially Congress, would think that increasing amounts of their money were supporting democracy. The army officer corps had become the most coherent native institution in an increasingly fragmented country.[88]

But then the U.S. presence was to be brief. In mid-1983 C.I.A. director Casey told Congress that the Contras could overthrow the Sandinistas by the end of the year. (Casey said this at the same time the White House was denying that the Contras' purpose was to overthrow a government with which the United States was not officially at war.) Similarly, the senior U.S. military adviser in El Salvador had said in 1982 that the FMLN would be reduced to being mere bandits within two years. But Álvarez fell first. He had begun questioning the overpowering U.S. pressure, and apparently feared that the United States might suddenly pull out and leave his country exposed to Nicaraguan anger. His main sin, however, seemed to be abusing the human rights of civilians and mistreating military colleagues who wanted to be cut in on deals that somehow had allowed him to own two $450,000 homes on his $30,000 annual officer's salary. In April 1984 he was replaced by Air Force Chief General Walter López Reyes, whom the Honduran Congress confirmed 78–0 as López's combat aircraft buzzed the Legislative Palace. López quickly demanded a guarantee of long-term U.S. protection (which was not given); he angrily told Washington that he most feared Salvadoran, not Nicaraguan, aggression (which was not understood); and actually prevented some Salvadorans from receiving U.S. training (which was not appreciated.)[89]

His attempts to modify the relationship were too late. Honduras was mired in its worst economic crisis in fifty years. After a good growth rate of 7 percent in 1979, per capita income fell over the next four years to zero. The trade balance did improve; unfortunately, for each dollar of banana exports generated, only 11¢ remained in Honduras. Capital fled the country, but because of U.S. military dollars, inflation ran as high as 45 percent annually. With 70 percent of Hondurans living in poverty, the nation also suddenly had to support 50,000 refugees, half of them Nicaraguan. The country became dependent on U.S. wheat shipments. Venereal disease and the AIDS virus spread among the growing number of prostitutes and their customers from military bases. "A lot of my buddies and me get confused because we don't sympathize with the system here," a U.S. soldier said in 1984. "All the poverty. The dogs and pigs and all the mud in those markets. This is a terrible place."[90]

Hondurans, who had displayed a capacity for unionizing and implementing reforms when they had a chance in the 1950s (see p. 135), went on strike, created protest groups, and held mass protests. A small land reform helped moderate some of the anger, but the military also moved. At least 290 people, mostly teachers, peasants, and labor leaders, disappeared between 1980–84. Eighty-nine died or disappeared at the hands of government forces in the first half of 1983. President Suazo carried out few investigations of these crimes; the United States exerted little pressure on him to do so. Two U.S. military advisers were shot and the Honduran Congress bombed, apparently by left-wing groups that had sprouted. One observer worried that Reagan's policy was pushing Honduras into "the early stages of 'Salvadorization' "—that is, the "radicalization and polarization of all sectors."[91]

El Salvador: "Plumping for Savagery"

If Honduras was becoming a U.S. fortress, El Salvador—long the most disciplined, productive, and (along with Costa Rica) independent nation in the region—was becoming a charnel house. Between 1979 and 1985 at least 50,000 civilians were slaughtered, or "disappeared," by death squads tied to the Salvadoran military. Meanwhile, despite U.S. officials pouring $2 million each day by the mid-1980s into this small nation of two million souls, the economy nearly collapsed under the weight of the war and corruption. By 1985, the national budget of this once productive country was, according to one estimate, less than half the annual revenues of the *New York Times*. An officer of the Salvadoran tourist industry noted the rapid decline of visitors and admitted, "We have an image problem."[92]

As Latin American analyst Adolfo Gilly noted, the war's purpose was not complex: it was to decide whether a very few could continue to dominate the many. When Reagan came to power, the Salvadoran revolutionaries' offensive had been destroyed by the military. The FMLN dwindled to no more than 2,000 troops. The rebels signaled a willingness to open talks, and they were supported by Cuba, Nicaragua, the Salvadoran Roman Catholic hierarchy, and European and Canadian social democratic leaders. Reagan and Haig, however, wanted none of it. Haig declared that the FMLN, "no question about it," was under the control of "Cuban, Nicaraguan, and, of course, indirectly Soviet" forces. In early 1982, a "senior official," clearly Haig, defined El Salvador as "a global problem." The United States insisted that only force could deal with this "problem." The four-man government junta, led by Christian Democrat José Napoleon Duarte, had little choice but to go along. The real power was held by the armed forces and their U.S. sponsors. As late as 1983, the commander of the U.S. advisers, Lt. Colonel John D. Waghelstein, looked back on Washington's aid and years of U.S. training of the Salvadorans and predicted that the FMLN threat could be ended in two years. Two years later the FMLN had extended its operations throughout the country and had even carried out raids in the capital of San Salvador that took the lives of U.S. military personnel.[93]

The Reagan-Haig policy rested on a series of flawed assumptions. Most important, they seemed ignorant of the deep historical roots of the revolution. One U.S. diplomat was more accurate in 1981: "Even if it were not for Cuba and the Soviet Union, we'd have a revolution here." Moreover, the rebels themselves were too divided, and too independent to be directed by outsiders. By 1981–82 the FMLN was made up of five different groups which disagreed over how to wage the war (see p. 253). Contrary to the Reagan-Haig claim, the groups that had the most soldiers had a history of opposing the Soviets and mistrusting Cuba. Or as one leader, Fermán Cienfuegos, put it, "We accumulated $60 million" through kidnappings and ransoms to buy arms. "We wouldn't have bothered if we were Soviet-Cuban proxies."[94]

According to one Soviet expert, Moscow did agree in 1980 to the pleas of Salvadoran Communist chief, Shafik Handal, to airlift arms through Cuba and Nicaragua. Handal, however, was mistrusted and isolated, as were other Communist party leaders, within the FMLN. In any case, the rebels could get a good supply of weapons from the international weapons market and from Salvadoran soldiers. The old men in the Kremlin rightly viewed the FMLN as independent, if not at times eccentric, revolutionaries who were insufficiently predictable. Nor did the Soviets and Cubans assume that a revolutionary victory was inevitable.[95] The major benefit was diverting and tying down U.S. resources.

Haig, Waghelstein, and other military experts believed they could win the war, decisively. Salvadoran officers were intensively trained in the United States and the Panama Canal Zone. The number of U.S. military advisers in-country doubled to over one hundred (with hundreds of other intelligence agents involved), although Congress continued to believe Reagan's claim that only fifty-five advisers were in El Salvador. After the United States helped bring about the firing of an incompetent Salvadoran defense minister in 1983, the top military command publicly complained of U.S. meddling. The command nevertheless continued to welcome thirty-five helicopters and C-47 rapid-firing gunships from Washington; these were used to bomb and machine-gun villages suspected of harboring the FMLN. Salvadoran officers' first allegiance was to protecting members of their *tanda* (their military school graduating class), rather than to the nation, and in many cases they were equally interested in getting rich. Salvadorans believed that their army's ranks were captain, major, colonel, and millionaire.[96]

The U.S.-trained military also opposed any meaningful economic reforms. Such changes were essential if mass support for the FMLN was to dry up, but the army officers had for fifty years worked hand-in-hand with the tiny, rich oligarchy, and now the officers were themselves becoming oligarchs. They especially opposed the proposed three-stage land reform, the centerpiece of any real program of change. But then, as Reagan had declared in 1981, winning the war came first, "then go forward with the reforms." The war and corruption so destroyed food production that El Salvador became dependent on U.S. supplies and soon became the largest per-capita recipient of government-supported U.S. food exports in the world. The military used much of the food to win the hearts and minds of villagers.[97]

Economic decline was devastating. The State Department admitted in 1983 that since 1979 the Salvadoran economy had sunk 25 percent. Unemployment approached 40 percent. The United States was underwriting the Salvadoran budget to nearly the same extent it had underwritten the sinking Vietnam government in the late 1960s. U.S. corporate investment dropped from $150 million in 1978 to $50 million in 1984, although some firms, especially in textiles and electronics, remained to use the cheap, disciplined labor force. Corporate executives rode to work in Cherokee Jeep vans, each equipped with $50,000 of armor plating.[98]

Executives were relatively safe, because the Salvadoran death squads were killing their own people—300 to 500 a week in 1981, and in quieter times, 120 each week in 1983. In 1981 Congress required Reagan to certify that human rights were improving before the President could send military aid. Reagan so certified every six months, and Congress professed to believe him. Both were trapped. To cut off aid could mean either the army's defeat or a bloodbath in which the military, free of U.S. control, would kill every suspect civilian it could find. Either way, the Reagan-Haig assumptions of 1981 were revealed as a disastrous set of errors. Either way, Reagan would blame the Democrat-controlled Congress for "losing" El Salvador. That political nightmare helped lead House Speaker Jim Wright (Dem.-Tex.) to support the President's request for ever-larger shipments of ever more lethal weapons.[99]

Reagan and other officials tried to muffle the embarrassment by claiming the Sandinistas had a bad human-rights record as well. A Salvadoran Roman Catholic bishop was puzzled: in Nicaragua "they don't shoot priests and workers, do they?" The Sandinistas heavily censored the opposition newspapers, but in El Salvador no opposition press had existed since 1981 when the editor and a photographer had been seized in a coffee shop and their bodies, hacked into pieces, found several days later. When the United States tried to track down the killers of the two

U.S. labor officials who were shot in the Sheraton Hotel in 1981, the largest Salvadoran business group condemned both the two labor organizers and the U.S. government for "open intervention in our internal affairs." The business group need not have worried. Reagan and Congress continued the massive military aid program. When U.S. Ambassador Deane Hinton condemned "the gorillas of the (Salvadoran) mafia" in 1981, the White House disavowed the remark.[100]

As FMLN power grew in December 1983, however, Vice President George Bush flew to El Salvador, demanded that the death-squad activity stop, and warned that U.S. aid might drop. Soon thereafter, officers arrested for killing the two U.S. labor advisers were freed. Roman Catholic Church officials showed that 2,600 civilians had been killed in the last half of 1984. Evidence built, moreover, that rich Salvadorans who had fled to Miami were financing some of the killings. The U.S. aid nevertheless continued. Roberto D'Aubuisson, a leader of death-squad activity, "is a chain smoker, as were many of the people I met in El Salvador," wrote Joan Didion, "perhaps because it is a country in which the possibility of achieving a death related to smoking remains remote."[101] (A decade later, however, D'Aubuisson had beaten those odds and had cancer. He died in February 1992.)

To support U.S. policies required a willing suspension of disbelief. Congress cooperated. Some journalists did not. Consequently when Raymond Bonner of the *New York Times* wrote of the slaughter of peasants, right-wing groups in the United States demanded that Bonner be fired. The U.S. Embassy in San Salvador and Lt. Colonel Waghelstein refused to talk with the correspondent. The *Times* finally removed him, and Bonner, after writing a highly respected book on the U.S. role in the Salvadoran tragedy, left the newspaper. One study showed that leading European newspapers, such as the French newspaper *Le Monde*, reported more fully and accurately on the sources of Salvadoran violence than did North American papers. Belief in reality also was suspended in the case of those among the 500,000 Salvadoran refugees in the United States who sought asylum. U.S. law allowed asylum to those who, if they had to return home, might face violence. In fiscal 1984, the State Department, and the U.S. Immigration and Naturalization Service, accepted 328 who sought asylum and rejected 13,045 on the grounds that they were really after jobs in the United States and faced no danger if they returned home.[102] Nicaraguan refugees meanwhile received asylum in nearly the reverse ratio.

The illusions shaped the Salvadoran presidency. In 1982, under strong U.S. pressure, the civilian junta and the military agreed to hold an election to legitimize the government. Reagan and his advisers desperately hoped that a moderate, elected regime could draw off support from both the extreme left and right. Moreover, as ABC television reporter Richard Threllkeld put it, the election was to be "a kind of final examination to see whether this place [El Salvador] is democratic enough to deserve our help." The Salvadorans could only pass that test, however, if they chose Duarte's Christian Democrats over D'Aubuisson's ARENA (Alianza Republicana Nacionalista) party in the vote to choose a constituent assembly. In turn, the assembly was to write a new constitution and choose an interim president until 1984 elections.[103]

The FMLN warned Salvadorans not to vote, but 1.2 million did so in March 1982. U.S. officials brandished the election turnout as if they were waving a talisman to drive off the forces of darkness. (They overlooked the absence of an opposition press, free speech, or freedom of assembly, not to mention the military's close watch on individual voting in the ballot places.) Darkness, however, won. The Salvadorans flunked the test—or, as *The Economist* of London put it, the "Salvadorans [were] apparently plumping for savagery." D'Aubuisson's alliance won thirty-six of the sixty assembly seats despite direct C.I.A. help to Duarte. D'Aubuisson's terrorist politics profited from a $200,000 campaign (paid for apparently by Miami's exiles), run by McCann-Erickson, the largest U.S. public relations firm. The C.I.A. proved no match for Madison Avenue.[104]

Having made the election the centerpiece of his policy, Reagan now tried to destroy its results. U.S. officials pressured the Salvadoran army to appoint a moderate as interim president. Alvaro Magana, a banker with close ties to Washington and the oligarchs, became a virtually unseen chief executive. More to the point, within four months after the election, a number of Christian Democrat leaders were murdered, including six mayors. A leading newspaper claimed that U.S. reform programs threatened the country with "total bankruptcy." The military moved even further to the right. U.S. Ambassador to the U.N. Jeane Kirkpatrick said in early 1983: "The guerrillas are not winning anything," and she applauded the country's "legitimate democratic government"—an apparent reference to D'Aubuisson's victory. Privately, however, she warned Reagan that U.S. military aid had to rise rapidly or the FMLN could win. Reagan began to warn Congress to pass more moneybills or Soviet-supported regimes would be on the U.S. doorstep.[105] ("As San Salvador goes so goes Nutley, New Jersey," as critics rephrased the Kirkpatrick-Reagan falling-domino theory.)

The 1984 presidential election had to have happier results. The United States sent $10 million to pay for expenses and another $1.4 million directly to Duarte. Not everyone in Washington was happy. Jesse Helms (Rep.-N.C.) warned that "Duarte is far to the left of George McGovern." D'Aubuisson tried to make the same point on the campaign trail. He told crowds that Duarte's party colors were green, then slashed open a watermelon to reveal the red inside. This time, however, Duarte won 54 percent of the vote in a May runoff. Congress quickly gave Duarte $6 million, but Senator Helms remained unhappy. He claimed that the C.I.A. and the State Department had "rigged" the vote for Duarte. Reagan denied this by saying that "taking sides in this election" was not "our place."[106]

Duarte's victory meant little outside the U.S. Congress. The army and death squads continued their work, meaningful land reform was dead, the economy declined, the FMLN grew. Duarte publicly complained that "The root of this problem" was that Americans were making the decisions—"how we spend our money, how many trucks we need . . . all of that." In October 1984 he dramatically tried to free himself of the war, the army, and the United States by offering in a U.N. speech to talk with the FMLN. Discussion began in late 1984 as the rebels offered a three-step peace plan. They demanded a new government and a reorganized army, two points that both the Salvadoran military and Secretary of State George Shultz warned Duarte not to accept. The talks collapsed. A Roman Catholic church spokesman in San Salvador had noted in mid-1984: "We see the [U.S.] military aid with very little optimism because it prolongs the conflict and will continue the pain and suffering of the people."[107]

Costa Rica: Hobson's Choice

The region's only democracy was being swept up into the maelstrom as well. By 1985 the question was not only whether Costa Rican democracy would survive, but whether the Ticos would have to make the Hobson's choice between saving their economy with anti-democratic austerity programs, or accepting U.S. pressure (sweetened with dollars) to create a full-fledged military and join the anti-Sandinista crusade.

Between 1980 and 1982, Costa Rica's web of welfare state, educational, and health programs that undergirded its democracy was torn by rapid economic decline and mismanagement. A severe recession (related to the U.S. downturn), oil-price shocks, falling trade—all exhausted treasury reserves and jacked up unemployment and inflation. In 1981 the Ticos became the first Latin Americans in modern times to default technically on their burgeoning foreign debt of $4 billion, one of the world's highest per-capita debts. Coffee exports slid nearly one-third during the early 1980s, in part because of a blight that killed entire trees. The other leading export, bananas, increased about 25 percent, but sharply lower prices, labor problems, and mismanagement finally forced the last remnant of United Brand's (formerly United Fruit Company) operation to close. One person found some consolation: "I breathed a sigh of relief," U.S. Ambassador Francis McNeil recalled, when UFCO ceased to be "a banana plantation overlord."[108]

In 1982, the new and hardpressed president, Luis Alberto Monge, worked out an economic relief package with the United States and the International Monetary Fund. At U.S. and IMF demand, Monge imposed a tough austerity program that cut government spending, devalued the currency, eliminated subsidies, and raised prices of fuel and utilities. The program also cut back aid to small farmers and promoted exports of new and large agribusinesses. U.S. aid shot up from $15 million in 1981 to $214 million in 1983 and $220 million in 1985. During the 1980s only El Salvador received more among Central American nations. Washington also made a major exception and increased the Ticos's share of the rich U.S. sugar market. The austerity nevertheless extracted a heavy price. Labor and lower-income earners suffered. Social tensions rose. Leftist terrorism broke out. Small farmers, the backbone of the socio-economy, organized and fought back; for example, they forced the government to stop importing certain U.S. food products (especially powdered milk) on which Ticos were unnecessarily becoming dependent.[109]

Reagan also exacted a price in foreign policy. He demanded that Costa Rica join the anti-Sandinista war. The temptation was great. Besides U.S. dollars, the Ticos were moved by their traditional dislike of Nicaragua. They said there were three seasons in a Costa Rican year: rainy, dry, and a season for trouble with Nicaraguans. In 1982 the C.I.A. began working with Edén Pastora's forces that used Costa Rican bases for forays into Nicaragua. Monge secretly approved that link, and also accepted U.S. assistance to build the 8,000-member Civil Guard and Rural Guard into a more formidable military force. By 1985 Green Beret Special Forces trained these units. U.S. military aid, virtually nothing in 1980, jumped to $11 million in 1985. Monge tried to cover his slide toward militarism by saying that Costa Rica was "permanently neutral." Then came the revelations that the C.I.A. and Contras had used the nation's territory for attacks on the Sandinistas. Public opinion polls showed that Ticos now disliked North Americans more than Nicaraguans. Some 30,000 went into the streets to demand real neutrality. Monge responded by arresting some Contra sympathizers. Hardline U.S. Ambassador Curtin Winsor bitterly complained that Ticos were "overzealous in interpreting . . . Monge's policy of neutrality." Washington suddenly held back $58 million in aid with the claim that Costa Rica was spending too much on state-run businesses. To some Ticos this appeared to be blackmail.[110]

The United States and the region's only democracy seemed to be on a collision course. The collision finally occurred in 1987. U.S.-Central American relations were to be transformed.

Guatemala: "Totally Dedicated to Democracy"

In Costa Rica, the United States worried less about democracy than about destroying the Sandinistas. In Guatemala, Washington worried less about cooperation with the hemisphere's worst human rights record-holder than it did about destroying the Sandinistas. Democratic Costa Rica and militaristic Guatemala seemed to appear much the same to the Reagan administration as long as they cooperated in destroying the Sandinistas.

Washington's problem, however, was that Guatemalans valued their independence. They had little hatred for Nicaragua (unlike Costa Ricans), and they cared little about economic democracy (four-fifths of Guatemalans lived below the poverty line, and the Indians, who comprised half the population, ranked among the hemisphere's poorest people.) Guatemalan leaders cared most about exterminating the four revolutionary guerrilla groups that in 1981–82 merged into the Guatemalan National Revolutionary Union (URNG). The rebels especially grew among the Indians and in Guatemala City's rapidly expanding slums where no houses, sewers, or jobs existed.[111]

In March 1982 elections, an army candidate won the fraudulent presidential election. He lasted two weeks before junior army officers overthrew him and installed General Efraín Ríos Montt. A graduate of the Dale Carnegie School and a born-again evangelical Christian, Ríos Montt wrote one of the most brutal chapters in post-1954 Guatemala's violent history. With a *"fusiles y frijoles"* ("guns and beans") campaign, Ríos Montt's forces butchered as many as 15,000 Indians on the suspicion they had cooperated—or might cooperate—with URNG. During these 1982–83 months of *"La Violencia"* ("the violence"), entire villages were leveled. The army then set up "Civilian Self-Defense Patrols" (PACS) that forced 900,000 villagers "voluntarily" to help police the area and track down suspects. Military rule destroyed and replaced centuries-old Indian communities and welfare systems. As 40,000 survivors sought refuge in Mexico, Guatemalan helicopters machine-gunned the camps.[112]

The Reagan administration saw Ríos Montt as an opportunity to pull Guatemala back fully into the anti-Sandinista campaign. The President himself announced to a surprised press conference that Ríos Montt "is totally dedicated to democracy in Guatemala," whose regimes, Reagan added, have "been getting a bum rap." U.S. officials moved to send $4 million of military aid, including helicopter parts, and break the post-1977 arms embargo. U.S. Ambassador Frederic Chapin welcomed Ríos Montt with the words, "The killings have stopped. . . . The Guatemalan government has come out of the darkness and into the light." In 1983 Vice President George Bush could not understand why priests insisted on helping URNG sympathizers: "I'm puzzled," he told a Washington audience. "I just don't understand it." In the audience, Father Theodore Hesburgh, President of Notre Dame University, tried to educate Bush by noting that helping the poor does not necessarily make one Marxist. Bush remained puzzled. Meanwhile, Congress stopped Reagan from sending military aid. U.S. economic assistance, however, rose from $13 million in 1980 to $38.8 million in 1983. Two close U.S. allies, Israel and Taiwan, sent Ríos Montt the military supplies he needed. And the C.I.A. secretly helped the Guatemalan army.[113]

By August 1983 Ríos Montt's brutal, unpredictable Christianity, and his failure to placate some military factions, undid him. Nor was he helped by his refusal to enter wholeheartedly into the anti-Sandinista war. On 6 August, U.S. military officers met with General Oscar Mejía Víctores. The next day Mejía Víctores overthrew Ríos Montt. (The State Department announced that absolutely no links existed between the two events.) The brutality continued. In one village, the army herded the entire population into the courthouse, raped the women, beheaded the men, and took the children outside to smash them to death against rocks. The U.S. Agency for International Development (AID) meanwhile sent at least a million dollars to help the army create their "model villages." Again Reagan tried to send helicopters. The military almost went too far, however, when it killed Guatemalans involved with AID projects. Aid stopped, temporarily. Civilians killed by death squads doubled in number to 220 a month by late 1983. *The Economist* of London noted that "Knocking off your wife's lover or business rival cost no more than $100" in Guatemala City.[114]

It was perhaps one of the few growing businesses. Per capita income fell four years in a row between 1980 and 1984 until it barely reached 1971 levels. Capital fled the country and government budgets were written in red ink. But the military prospered. It enjoyed its own bank, real estate business, and numerous other enterprises including the national airline. One officer owned 100,000 acres of good land in an area known as the "Zone of the Generals." The army was becoming independent of both the once all-powerful oligarchs and the government's civilians. By 1985 the military force of thirty thousand claimed it had reduced the 4,000 URNG guerrillas of 1982 by nearly half. But the army leaders began to realize they could use even more U.S. aid for both fighting and profit. In 1985, they allowed a civilian, Vinicio Cerezo Arevalo, to become president. As Cerezo explained, "They need a president who can obtain money for the country." Reagan meanwhile planned to increase economic aid by 40 percent and, again, to try to open the overt military aid channel.[115]

Conclusion: Beyond Neodependence

It all sounded like mid-1954. The cycle in Central America seemed never-ending. Since at least the 1890s, U.S. economic power (which played a less important role in government policy-making after the 1960s) and pressures for political stability at all costs had produced widespread revolution. The Reagan administration could have chosen negotiated settlements, international supervision, and multilaterally shared responsibilities. It chose unilateral escalation of the C.I.A.-military effort to win supposed final victories. Instead of victories, however, the policy only made much of Central America a blood-soaked battlefield that was evermore dependent on the United States. Whether North Americans had the patience, knowledge, or resources to deal with such responsibility was doubtful given the past century's history. Meanwhile as North Americans debated and escalated, Central Americans grew poorer and died.

VI

REARRANGING THE REMAINS OF THE SYSTEM

Ronald Reagan rode triumphantly into 1985 on the wave of one of the great election victories in modern U.S. history. He reassured happy voters that "it was morning in America." In months Mikhail Gorbachev assumed power in Moscow and began dismantling the Soviet "evil empire," as Reagan had called it. Within a year the forty-year-long Cold War began winding down. The United States, Reagan could claim, had won. Nevertheless, even with his best smile and shoeshine, the President could not sell his argument that he had won in Central America.

Congress had cut off lethal aid for the Contras in October 1984. In Honduras terrorism, corruption, and political disintegration accelerated as Washington used the poorest of the region's nations to overthrow the Sandinistas. In El Salvador, the revolution continued, even as the United States poured in $2 million each day to support a brutal, increasingly wealthy military, and to prop up the weakening civilian government. In Guatemala, a new civilian presidency, trumpeted as a victory for democracy by U.S. officials, turned out to be only a cover for intensified military control and human rights abuses. Costa Rica meanwhile staggered under the burdens of a shattered economy, spreading regional war, and tremendous U.S. pressures to help overthrow the Sandinistas. Ever-darker political storm clouds seemed to gather over the region's only real democracy. Out of these Costa Rican clouds, however, a bolt of lightning suddenly flashed in 1987 that transformed the Central American landscape and short-circuited Reagan's attempts to destroy the San-

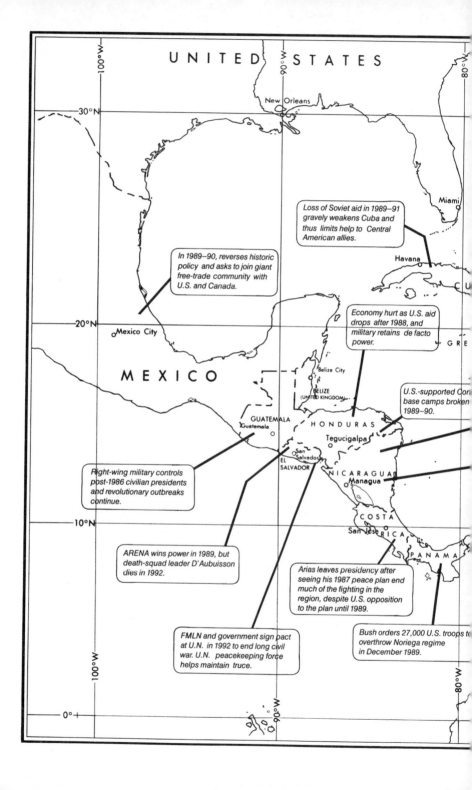

UNITED STATES

New Orleans

Miami

Loss of Soviet aid in 1989–91 gravely weakens Cuba and thus limits help to Central American allies.

Havana

In 1989–90, reverses historic policy and asks to join giant free-trade community with U.S. and Canada.

Mexico City

Economy hurt as U.S. aid drops after 1988, and military retains de facto power.

GRE

MEXICO

Belize City

BELIZE
(UNITED KINGDOM)

U.S.-supported Con base camps broken 1989–90.

GUATEMALA
Guatemala

HONDURAS

Tegucigalpa

San
Salvador

EL
SALVADOR

NICARAGUA
Managua

Right-wing military controls post-1986 civilian presidents and revolutionary outbreaks continue.

COSTA

San José RICA

PANAMA

ARENA wins power in 1989, but death-squad leader D'Aubuisson dies in 1992.

Arias leaves presidency after seeing his 1987 peace plan end much of the fighting in the region, despite U.S. opposition to the plan until 1989.

FMLN and government sign pact at U.N. in 1992 to end long civil war. U.N. peacekeeping force helps maintain truce.

Bush orders 27,000 U.S. troops t overthrow Noriega regime in December 1989.

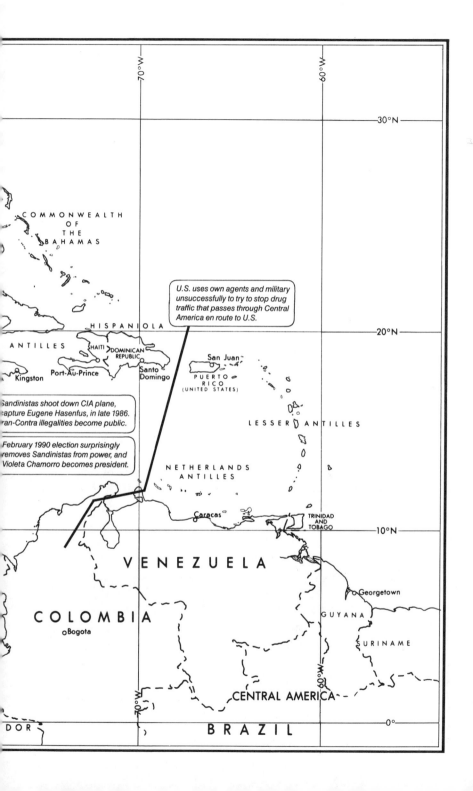

COMMONWEALTH
OF
THE
BAHAMAS

HISPANIOLA

ANTILLES

HAITI DOMINICAN
REPUBLIC

Kingston   Port-Au-Prince   Santo
Domingo

San Juan

PUERTO
RICO
(UNITED STATES)

U.S. uses own agents and military
unsuccessfully to try to stop drug
traffic that passes through Central
America en route to U.S.

Sandinistas shoot down CIA plane,
capture Eugene Hasenfus, in late 1986.
Iran-Contra illegalities become public.

February 1990 election surprisingly
removes Sandinistas from power, and
Violeta Chamorro becomes president.

LESSER ANTILLES

NETHERLANDS
ANTILLES

Caracas

TRINIDAD
AND
TOBAGO

VENEZUELA

COLOMBIA
o Bogota

Georgetown

GUYANA

SURINAME

CENTRAL AMERICA

DOR

BRAZIL

30°N

20°N

10°N

0°

W.°07

W.°06

dinistas forever through military force. By 1989, as the President retired to California, his policies had indeed succeeded only in corrupting his own government and undermining the century-old U.S. system in Central America. It was left to his successor, George Bush, and to Central Americans (many of whom the Reagan administration had despised) to try to pick up, and then rearrange, the pieces of twentieth-century U.S. foreign policy in the region.[1]

1985–86: Trying to Create Consensus

With the C.I.A.-Contra ties discredited in Washington, Reagan turned to his favorite weapon of diplomacy, the podium. In speeches and press conferences "The Great Communicator" (as the former baseball broadcaster–Hollywood actor was now known) delivered dire warnings and threats. "If other policy alternatives fail," he told Congress, "direct application of U.S. military force" could be a real option. Soon thereafter, the Commander of Army and Air Force combat forces in the United States, General Wallace H. Nutting, publicly opposed a U.S. invasion of Nicaragua. Stressing that Central America's problems were political and economic, Nutting reflected the uniformed military's growing belief that "we are going to have to learn to live with Nicaragua." Reagan then claimed that Pope John Paul II was "urging us to continue our efforts in Central America," only to have the Vatican in Rome flatly deny that the Pope had endorsed any policy that had "military aspects." The President and Secretary of State George Shultz next tried to play on North Americans' fears of communism by warning that the Soviets were bent on establishing a new Cuba in the region, only to have a strongly pro-Reagan newspaper, the *Wall Street Journal*, run a story that contradicted Reagan under the headline, "Despite Fears of the U.S., Soviet Aid to Nicaragua Regime Appears to Be Rather Limited."[2]

The propaganda machine nevertheless ran full speed. Lt. Colonel Oliver North of the National Security Council helped arrange congressional testimony by Tom Dowling about Sandinista atrocities. Dowling appeared dressed as a Roman Catholic priest, but it was soon discovered that he worked for North and was not an ordained Roman Catholic priest. In September 1985 the State Department published a White Paper claiming that Nicaragua's radical Interior Minister, Tomás Borge, had bragged that the Sandinista revolution "goes beyond our borders." Investigation revealed that Borge had actually said that the Sandinistas were part of a larger "current of the revolution of our time" that went "beyond our borders." And, Borge added, "This does not mean that we export our revolution." In 1986 Reagan's officials suddenly announced that the 800 to 1,200 Cuban advisers in Nicaragua had burgeoned to nearly 3,500. Critics soon noted a lack of evidence. As a State Department official recalled, it was only "an esoteric exercise in extrapolation," with the numbers "seized upon because it was convenient for policy."[3] The Great Communicator was having his problems.

On the urgent advice of his National Security Adviser, Robert McFarlane, Reagan finally acted so others could not contradict (and correct) him. Declaring that Nicaragua posed "an unusual and extraordinary threat" to U.S. security, he used powers, given the Executive under a 1977 congressional act, to impose economic sanctions on Nicaragua. These sanctions ended most U.S.-Nicaraguan trade. The United Nations General Assembly condemned the sanctions 91–6. The other four Central American nations either condemned and/or simply ignored the President's attempt to isolate the Sandinistas. Even some Contras opposed the embargo because it hurt their families living in Nicaragua. Most notably, Secretary of State Shultz, who as an economist understood the ineffectiveness of such sanctions, opposed them, but lost to White House hardliners who argued—correctly—that after four years the administration had no better, more usable policy.[4]

The hardliners also outgunned Shultz when they forced the resignation of his Assistant Secretary of State for Inter-American Affairs, Langhorne Motley. He was replaced by thirty-seven-year-old Elliott Abrams. A former Democrat turned neoconservative, Abrams had been head of the department's human rights bureau where he consistently produced the facts and figures that were necessary to allow continued aid to the Salvadoran military. On the day of his appointment, Abrams was welcomed, with relief, at a private party attended by Otto Reich (the head of the administration's propaganda office for Central America), Alan Fiers (director of the C.I.A.'s task force in Central America), and Shirley

Christian, a *New York Times* correspondent. Shortly afterwards Abrams declared that no negotiated agreement with Nicaragua was possible because "the Sandinistas are communists," and so "such agreements are lies." When he discovered that a top Latin American expert, Francis McNeil, convincingly contradicted Abrams's report to Shultz that the Contras were doing well, Abrams forced McNeil out of the State Department. "The situation," McNeil declared, "reeks of McCarthyism." He further warned that Abrams and other true-believers were bullying intelligence officers to tell Shultz and Reagan what Abrams wanted them to hear, not what was true.[5]

The USS Honduras *to the Rescue*

Fortunately for his collapsing policy, Abrams had at least one trustworthy ally. "Honduras is the [sic] key player in U.S. and regional efforts to promote democracy and economic development in Central America," Abrams declared in early 1987. If so, there was still a ways to go: the people of Mesa, Arizona, had five times more telephones than all the people in Honduras, and the average American's liquor expenses each year alone would cover six months of living expenses for the average Honduran. Fifty percent of Honduras's population was illiterate, perhaps as many as 80 percent lived below the officially defined poverty line. The Reagan administration sent an average of $750,000 in aid daily, but most went into arms or the military's many corrupt businesses.[6]

The region's poorest country nevertheless cooperated fully with Washington. Guatemala's cynical army officers claimed, "There are expensive prostitutes, there are cheap prostitutes—and there are Hondurans who give it for nothing." Not that Honduras had much choice, given its integration into the U.S. system and the presence of 7,000 U.S. military personnel. The Guatemalan claim, moreover, was untrue: Honduras bargained hard to obtain help in return for its territory. In 1986, President José Azcona Hoyo even dissented from Washington's version of Central American events, only to have the White House (in an act the *Miami Herald* termed "extortion"), threaten to stop most aid. Azcona quieted, and the U.S. Agency for International Development

(AID) again was "calling the shots," as one U.S. expert phrased it. The C.I.A. and State Department took over hundreds of square miles, expelled at least 12,000 peasants, invited in 40,000 Contras and their dependents (including some 20,000 Miskito Indians), and created a "New Nicaragua" in Honduras. Most important, in 1985–86, after the U.S. Congress cut off lethal aid to the Contras, Washington secretly increased funds to Honduras by $110 million with the understanding the Hondurans would send the money on to the Contras. This plan to circumvent Congress was sufficiently important that Vice President George Bush personally carried the policy guidelines to the Hondurans.[7]

The country meanwhile became one huge military base. In 1988 the two nations agreed that the United States could build permanent air and port facilities. The deal was struck after U.S. officials had declared for seven years that their presence was only temporary. Some Honduran military officers greatly benefited. In 1984 U.S. intelligence discovered that a former Honduran Army Chief of Staff, General José Bueso Rosa, was busy planning to kill the nation's president and move $40 million of cocaine into the United States. When the ambitious general was captured in Florida, a major break in disrupting drug traffickers seemed to be imminent. By 1986–87, however, U.S. officials—including, some observers claimed, Abrams—worked to get Bueso Rosa off scot-free because they wanted him and his colleagues to help fight the Sandinistas. The U.S. Ambassador to Honduras, John Ferche, was not as lucky. Abrams fired this Foreign Service professional of twenty-seven years when Ferche warned that U.S. policy was becoming too militarized and, hence, ineffective.[8]

As Honduras slid toward possible conflict with Nicaragua (or with a turbulent El Salvador—historically its enemy in the region), its economy slid as well until it was totally dependent on U.S. aid. Because their agricultural production dropped nearly 23 percent between 1975 and 1990, Hondurans even depended on imported beans and corn for staple food. The social fabric ripped apart. Human rights violations rose as the economy and society declined. In September 1985 a prominent critic of U.S. policy in Honduras was found with a steel file driven into his heart. In 1986–87, Honduran peasants, with their long history of organized protests, staged mass demonstrations to reclaim land that had been taken from them. In early 1988, several leading peasant and labor organizers were murdered. In the first case tried by the Inter-American Court on Human Rights in which a government was the defendant, Honduras was accused of having death squads of U.S.-trained personnel who killed or "disappeared" suspected leftists. "I have never seen a case in which the United States Government is so deeply linked to the human rights abuses of a Government as in Honduras," declared Aryeh Neier of Americas Watch. The attacks hit closer to home in 1987 when six American and six Honduran soldiers were wounded in a bombing of a restaurant. In April 1988 mobs firebombed the U.S. Embassy after North American agents violated Honduran law by seizing and flying to the United States a drug trafficker. Five people were killed. "The reason this is taking place," a Latin American ambassador remarked, "is not because of a drug trafficker but as a popular response to six years of American impositions."[9]

Washington officials bragged that the three presidential elections between 1981 and 1990 displayed Honduran democracy. The United States even spent $900,000 to ensure that the 1985 balloting would appear to be fair. In truth, power was held by hardline colonels who did as they pleased. With U.S. training, and aid that paid for more than 50 percent of their budget, the Honduran military copied their counterparts in El Salvador and Guatemala: they skimmed off U.S. aid to set up their own bank, insurance company, investment firm, and other profitable businesses that made them both rich and independent of civilian control. In 1990 when U.S. Ambassador Crescio Arcos demanded an investigation of atrocities and urged civilians to stand up to the military, the civilians told him to mind his own business. Meanwhile, after the Sandinistas lost power in Nicaragua, the new George Bush team cut aid to Honduras during 1990. The reduction nearly left the small nation, which depended on the $2 billion in U.S. aid during the 1980s, to go cold turkey economically. Suffering spread among already desperate laborers and peasants. The army prospered. Conditions breeding revolt and revolution spread.[10]

Iran-Contra: "General Custer in Diplomatic Drag"

In October 1986 the Reagan administration's continued pressure paid off when Congress approved $70 million of military, and $30 million of nonmilitary, aid for the Contras. Public opinion polls showed that by as much as 2–1 U.S. citizens opposed sending such aid. Congress, with the Republican leadership and conservative Democrats at the fore, listened to the "Great Communicator" instead of the hundreds of groups (especially from churches) who opposed the measure. Congress believed Reagan when he claimed that it was Nicaragua that had killed the Contadora nations' peace initiative in 1986—although the Sandinistas had actually twice accepted, and Reagan had twice rejected, the Contadora proposals. Congress also believed State Department officials who said that during the previous two years the administration had obeyed congressional wishes and sneaked no illegal aid to the Contras; "None of it ever got past chitchat over lunch," one official assured reporters.[11]

On the other hand, Congress paid little attention to its own General Accounting Office which reported in early 1986 that more than half of $12 million earlier given the Contras had found its way into private Miami bank accounts of Contra leaders who were living good lives while their soldiers complained of shortages. Nor did Congress agree with resolutions passed by leading churches that (in the words of the Presbyterian Church U.S.A.), "In Central America, the specter of communism is being used to justify terrible acts of brutality and inhumanity." Nor was Congress extending sympathy to the hundreds of sanctuary churches (at least eight of which were in the Washington, D.C. area), which defied U.S. law by shielding Salvadoran and Guatemalan refugees who faced death, possibly, if the Reagan administration returned them home. When Abrams said in 1985 that reports about such returned Salvadorans dying were "not true . . . it isn't happening," *The National Catholic Reporter* published a series of graphic examples to prove that Abrams was wrong. In 1988, for the first time, a U.S. Circuit Court ruled in favor of the refugees and the sanctuary movement, and found Abrams's version of the facts to be incorrect.[12]

In late 1986 the Contras predicted victory within a year. The Sandinistas reacted to Congress's aid measure by preparing for full-scale conflict. They closed a chief critic, the newspaper *La Prensa;* moved against another powerful critical voice, the Roman Catholic church hierarchy in Managua; and accelerated their military buildup. The buildup paid off more stunningly than the Sandinistas could have expected. On 5 October 1986, they shot down a C.I.A. supply plane. Two U.S. pilots died in the crash, but a third crew member, Eugene Hasenfus, was captured. Congress again believed Abrams when a House Committee asked if the U.S. government was involved with Hasenfus: "Absolutely not," the Assistant Secretary of State lied. The Sandinistas sentenced Hasenfus to thirty years in jail, but having a keen recollection of the bad things that had happened to José Santos Zelaya in 1910 when he mistreated U.S. prisoners (see p. 48), they freed the prisoner during the Christmas holiday season. In early November, Attorney General Edwin Meese dramatically announced that investigations had revealed that for several years U.S. officials had been selling arms to Iran (a nation that most Americans thought was one of their bitterest enemies), and used the profits to buy arms for the Contras in direct defiance of Congress's laws that prohibited such aid.[13]

The Iran-Contra debacle had begun. Reagan, his closest advisers feared in late 1986, could be impeached if it were proven that he had authorized his officials to break U.S. law by arming the Contras with funds obtained from the arms sales in 1984–86. That charge was not proven, however. Reagan was apparently kept uninformed by his own advisers about his administration's policies, and he was too lazy and uninterested to discover the telling details for himself. The ringleaders in the arms-diversion-and-coverup scheme were Lt. Colonel Oliver North of the N.S.C. staff; Robert McFarlane and Admiral John Poindexter, the President's N.S.C. advisers between 1984 and 1987; and Elliott Abrams. C.I.A. officials, led by director William Casey, were also deeply involved, although it remains unclear whether the scheme began with Casey or with North and Poindexter in the White House. It did become clear that these men, along with Alan Fiers, who headed the C.I.A. operations with the Contras, did not know "a damned thing about Latin America," in the words of one experienced Foreign Service officer. Their chief qualifications for running this illegal policy was (as one official said of Fiers) "total loyalty, total dedication, 'true believerhood,' " especially in waging the anti-Sandinista crusade.[14]

The intensity of "true believerhood," of course, was especially hot at the top. On the Nicaraguan issue, one key U.S. official observed, the White House "has been more like the papacy than a presidency. To . . . talk to the President about the nuances of the Contras was like going to the Pope to discuss a few dissident points on the Virgin birth—you couldn't do it." Lower-level officials were well positioned to act on such intense beliefs. Under Casey, the intelligence budget grew even faster than the bloated defense budget. Covert-action capabilities especially mushroomed. Casey, moreover, served one further purpose: a true believer himself, he repeatedly told Reagan that the Contras were about to win. "He carried that garbage straight to the President, who believed him," one U.S. Ambassador declared. The N.S.C., for its part, had been enlarged and transformed under John F. Kennedy into a personal Department of State which did not have to go before the press or congressional committees to tell the public what it was doing. As historian Garry Wills observed, the C.I.A.-N.S.C. operators who concocted the disastrous Bay of Pigs invasion in 1961 and foolishly mined Nicaraguan harbors in 1984 "may have been a bit less loony than Oliver North (who is not?), but they prepared the way for North. They made him possible."[15] The Iran-Contra roots ran back far beyond Reagan; they were embedded in U.S.-Central American history.

The Reagan chapter had begun with the President's 1981 order that the C.I.A. create a new Contra force. By 1983 that force numbered 10,000. When Congress cut back funds in 1984, top U.S. officials heatedly disagreed on 25 June 1984 over how to respond. Vice President Bush saw nothing wrong in "encouraging third parties to help." But Shultz warned that such an end-run around Congress "is an impeachable offense." Reagan urged that nothing be said publicly, and he gave the green light for Oliver North to organize a drive to flush money out of conservative North Americans and foreign allies. Singer Pat Boone, Texas oil billionaire Nelson Bunker Hunt, beer producer Joseph Coors, and wealthy Cuban-Americans in Miami, among others, contributed to campaigns that netted $10 to $20 million. Saudi Arabia meanwhile contributed $32 million at White House urging. In August 1986, North assured a congressional committee that he was not raising this money. He later admitted he had lied on this and similar occasions. So did Abrams. This top State Department official, representing the world's greatest democracy, finally begged for money from Brunei, an oil-rich monarchy whose sultan gave $10 million so Reagan would better like him. When Congress checked rumors of the money flow, the administration blocked it by invoking executive privilege (and thus kept White House documents secret), or simply by lying repeatedly to Congress and the press.[16]

All this was not enough, so in April 1986 North helped devise the plan to use profits from arms sales to Iran for the Contras' benefit. North and Abrams also found other ways to ignore laws. Since at least 1983 Panamanian dictator Manuel Antonio Noriega had secretly helped the C.I.A. and the Contras. When it turned out in 1986, however, that Noriega had been a double agent who passed U.S. secrets to Fidel Castro, and that he was a drug trafficker who helped smuggle tens-of-millions-of-dollars of cocaine into the United States, the Reagan administration grew uneasy. According to Francis McNeil, Abrams privately made it clear that the administration had decided nothing was to be done to Noriega until after the Sandinistas were removed. (In 1991, a Colombian drug kingpin told a Florida court that his drug cartel gave the Contras $10 million in the 1980s, with the Reagan administration's knowledge.) North and Abrams meanwhile supported private U.S. mercenaries who fought with the Contras. Among the more notable was former U.S. Army Major General John Singlaub. Asked to resign from the military after he demanded production of the neutron bomb (a device that obliterated people but spared property), Singlaub headed the World Anti-Communist League, a group tied to neo-Nazis and Latin American death squads—although Singlaub vowed that the League had cleaned up this part of its act. Reagan publicly welcomed Singlaub's group to the fight.[17] The President was choosing interesting ways to teach Central Americans the virtues of democracy.

But even with all their busyness, North, Poindexter, and Abrams could not bring a single Nicaraguan village under Contra control. And there were other problems. The Contra leaders, according to North's aide, Robert Owen, were corrupt: "The war has become a business to many of them," Owen secretly cabled North in 1986, and if another $100 million is given "it will be like pouring money down a sinkhole." Another problem was Secretary of State Shultz. He had vigorously fought (and lost) sending arms to Iran; he failed to see how this would woo supposed "moderates" of the Iranian revolution toward the United States. North and Poindexter simply refused to tell Shultz about diverting profits from these arms sales to help the Contras, although both Shultz and Abrams knew of North's network that funneled private funds and mercenaries into Central America. That network broke in October 1986 when Eugene Hasenfus was captured, and again several weeks later when a journal in the Middle East hinted at the Iran arms deals. Then on 25 November 1986, Meese announced the discovery of the illegal relationship between the arms sales and aid sent to the Contras (or, at least, to their leaders living well in Miami, if Owen is to be believed).[18]

Events then moved as rapidly as the Contras' fortunes sank. Poindexter and North were immediately forced to resign. In mid-1987 Congress held nationally televised hearings in which North declared that he thought Reagan knew nothing about the diversion of the funds; that Casey (now dead of a brain tumor) had devised the plan; and that he was personally unrepentant about having worked nights to destroy, contrary to law, U.S. government documents that contained the damning evidence. Poindexter, known for his photographic memory, replied 184 times "I don't recall," or "I don't remember" when confronted with evidence of his role in the affair. He was more direct in declaring that he had not kept Reagan informed, and again when he said he had run the Contra operation secretly because "I simply didn't want any outside interference"—that is, he did not want to be accountable to Congress, the press, Secretary of State Shultz, or the law. Poindexter and North argued that as bureaucrats they could do virtually anything they thought proper, regardless of the law. They were (as were many of their aides in the operations) also professional military men. Other, wiser, military officers condemned them: "They were held in contempt as uniformed yuppies on a power and ego trip," as Retired Colonel Harry Summers wrote. But the militarization of U.S. policy in Central America was not, of course, new. Its lineage ran back to the 1850s at least.[19]

North, Poindexter, and several aides were found guilty of various charges. North faced twelve felony counts, including lying under oath to Congress and destroying government documents. In 1990–91, however, charges against both North and Poindexter had to be dropped on technicalities: their testifying under immunity before Congress and the television audience made it legally impossible to use the evidence, with which they had publicly condemned themselves, to convict them in a court of law.

Abrams, investigations revealed, not only had secretly begged Brunei's Sultan for a handout, but had helped build a secret airstrip in Costa Rica for the Contras' use, then pressured the Costa Rican government not to reveal the field's existence. The Assistant Secretary misled Congress about the U.S. role. Representative Jack Brooks (Dem.-Tx.) called him "a lying son-of-a-bitch." Senator David Durenberger (Rep.-Min.) emerged from an Intelligence Committee hearing to say, "I would not trust Elliott Abrams any further than I could throw Ollie North." But Shultz refused to fire him, and Abrams lasted out his term until January 1989. Two years later he escaped felony charges by plea bargaining with Special Prosecutor Lawrence Walsh, and received a light fine on two misdemeanor counts of withholding information from Congress.[20]

The Iran-Contra scandal posed a dangerous threat to the United States. Unelected and unaccountable military officers in the N.S.C. worked with key State Department personnel to defy U.S. laws. They did so for the sole reason that they thought their case was right and that all opposition, even from Congress and Shultz, was wrong. They dragged the Constitution, U.S. policies in Central America, Americans' reputations and credibility around the world through the mud. They were headed, even before they were discovered, for total failure. "What a joke," former Contra commander Edén Pastora remarked. "What lousy imperialists you are." One of the State Department's most experienced officers on Latin America called Abrams "a General Custer in diplomatic drag." But that description fit all of Reagan's advisers who pushed the nation into this embarrassment. The congressional Iran-Contra committees concluded that the President himself had failed to uphold his sworn oath to "take care that the laws be faithfully executed." Reagan was asked in 1987 whether the late C.I.A. director Casey had carried out covert operations without him, the President, knowing about them. "Not that I know of," Reagan seriously replied.[21]

The Beginning of the End: Costa Rica and the Arias Peace Plan

After eight years and at least 43,000 Nicaraguan casualties, one of Reagan's critics observed in 1988, "the only town the Contra mercenaries ever held was Washington." Even that objective was slipping away. Contra supporters admitted their troops were losing 400 dead and wounded each month as Sandinista operations and Soviet-supplied equipment became more efficient. The Contras' problem was not lack of equipment. They had so much ammunition that they lacked room to store it, and by mid-1987 the C.I.A. had given them deadly "Red-Eye" missiles to shoot down helicopters. They also used advanced communications to foretell when the helicopters were coming. But the Contras still could not fight effectively. Even such supporters as N.S.C. adviser Robert McFarlane called the Contra leaders "well-meaning, patriotic but inept Coca-Cola bottlers," a reference to Adolfo Calero's former business in Managua. In February 1987, the C.I.A. and Abrams forced Calero out and reorganized the United Nicaraguan Opposition (the UNO) which led the Contras. "This shake-up proves two things," Senator Christopher Dodd (Dem.-Conn.) observed; "one, the situation is a mess; two, this is not what you'd call an indigenous [Nicaraguan] uprising when you pick rebel leaders in the State Department." Within two months the new leadership also quit. In April 1987 the top commander of the Miskito Indians who were fighting the Sandinistas, Steadman Fagoth Muller, stopped cooperating because of the UNO's and the Contras' "incompetence." When asked why the FMLN revolutionaries in El Salvador kept fighting, even though they were only one-third the number of the Contras, Fagoth replied, "It is because the military and political strategy of the United States in Nicaragua has failed."[22]

Central America nevertheless continued to resemble a huge, bloody battleground. The FMLN went on the offensive in a stalemated war that by 1989 had killed 70,000 Salvadorans and driven out perhaps a million more. The C.I.A. accelerated its training of Contra troops in the United States. By late 1986, the multinational effort to find peace through the three-year-old Contadora Plan (see p. 297) was dead, the victim of militant U.S. opposition and internal Central American division. Mexico, which had tried for years to broker a settlement, retreated to care for a shattered economy at home. That care had been made more difficult by repeated U.S. demands that before Mexico could get needed financial help from Washington, the Mexicans had to stop supporting any peace plans that left the Sandinistas in power. The tragedy was that peace prospects had brightened in 1987 because Mikhail Gorbachev's government in the Soviet Union was slowly but surely cutting its support to Central American allies. It was now estimated that in 1980 the U.S.S.R. had sent 1.7 tons of arms to Managua, but as the C.I.A.-Contra effort built, a record 24,250 tons of Soviet arms had arrived in 1986. In 1987 and 1988, however, the aid fell by nearly 4,000 tons. The essential Soviet oil shipments to Nicaragua dropped sharply. More importantly, Gorbachev, faced with economic disasters at home, transformed Soviet policy toward Latin America: instead of sending billions of rubles worth of aid to revolutionaries in Cuba and Central America, he devoted his scarce resources to creating new ties with the large nations, such as Argentina and Brazil, who could send food and other aid to the U.S.S.R.[23] The time was ripening for a peace settlement. But no one in Washington seemed interested.

And in Costa Rica, the need for peace was especially pressing. The declining economy (only 1.2 percent annual per capita income growth during 1980 to 1986, or less than one-third the growth in the late 1970s) had saddled Ticos with both a huge $4 billion foreign debt and spreading doubts about whether they would be able to remain the region's only democracy. The Reagan administration showed little sensitivity; it demanded that Costa Rica pay off U.S. banks before qualifying for continued aid from the International Monetary Fund. Japanese and European objections forced Washington to back off from this demand in 1988–89, but the problems ramified. Some 60 percent of Costa Rica's exports went to pay off debts (not help the poorer people or increase productivity) in 1986. But even those exports were threatened when

Standard Fruit Company (a U.S. subsidiary of Castle and Cook Inc.) and other banana companies slid toward bankruptcy. Reports appeared of the companies firing labor union leaders and trying to hire cheap, non-organized labor. Violence erupted in the banana plantations and also in San José, the capital, where in 1986 the Civil Guard tear-gassed crowds protesting the slashing of food subsidies.[24] Such things were not supposed to happen in Costa Rica.

The Central American wars were a key cause of the Ticos' growing tragedy. The small country of about three million people suddenly had to care for 200,000 refugees fleeing from Nicaragua and El Salvador. The devastation in the region made it impossible for Costa Rica to sell goods in other Central American markets. Something else, however, was far more ominous. Since the early 1980s the Reagan administration had pressured the Ticos to forget their 1949 pledge not to create a military force. U.S. officials, led by Jeane Kirkpatrick, urged that the Pentagon and C.I.A. be allowed to train a force that could become part of the spreading conflagration. In 1985 twenty U.S. Green Beret Special Forces arrived to turn the Civil Guard into a different kind of police. In 1986, Abrams and U.S. Ambassador Lewis Tambs pressured Costa Rica to support a secret supply network for the Contras. It was clear that continued U.S. aid depended on the Ticos welcoming the Green Berets and Tambs's demand. What was most frightening, however, was the speed with which some Costa Ricans responded. Their dislike of Nicaraguans ran back to the nineteenth century, and it only intensified in the 1980s. Right-wing paramilitary groups, moreover, arose to welcome U.S. arms and training. With such names as "Country and Truth," these small private armies forcefully broke up strikes and protests against large landowners and businesses. "For us," one right-wing militant observed in 1986, "having Reagan as U.S. President was great luck." Costa Rican democracy and the neutrality which that democracy required were under siege.[25]

In 1986 the seige began to be lifted by a short, wealthy (from coffee growing), newly elected president who idolized John F. Kennedy as a political role model. Oscar Arias Sánchez of the National Liberation Party had studied at Boston University and the London School of Economics. His wife, Margarita, had graduated from Vassar. They knew the

United States well, and they also understood the growing Costa Rican right-wing movement which, indeed, Arias had defeated in an all-out intraparty fight to obtain the presidential nomination. Most importantly, the new President understood that U.S. policies had hit a deadend; that Reagan and Congress apparently did not want to recognize this; and that unless the Central American wars were stopped, Costa Rica's democracy could be wiped out. "We had to choose," Arias later remarked, "between rationality and madness."[26]

In February 1987 President Arias proposed a fresh peace plan. In August the proposals, to the surprise of apparently everyone but Arias, were agreed to in principle by all the Central American nations meeting in Guatemala City. The "Guatemala Plan's" provisions included (1) immediate cease-fires throughout the region and talks between opposing forces; (2) each nation's pledge to hold free elections under the country's existing schedule (in Nicaragua this would be 1990); (3) the requirement that all outsiders, including the United States, terminate military aid to "irregular insurrections and forces," including the Contras, by early November 1987; and (4) a Sandinista pledge to strive for a cease-fire with, and to declare an amnesty for, the Contras. All five nations would then discuss reducing their armed forces. Throughout the peace process, nations would not allow their land to be used as a base for attacks against neighbors—that is, Honduras and Costa Rica would no longer be obliged to host the Contras.[27]

Like most of his countrymen, Arias had little love for the Sandinistas. He understood, however, that the use of force had only led them to tighten their grip over Nicaragua. His plan differed from the now-dead Contadora proposals by requiring democratic reforms within both Nicaragua and El Salvador. (The Sandinistas were already moving away from their long-held position that they would deal only with the United States and never directly with the Contras: "We want to talk to the owner of the circus," they had claimed, "not to the clowns.") Arias was convinced these reforms could peacefully topple the Sandinistas from power, or force them to rest their power on a thoroughly democratized Nicaragua. The Sandinistas apparently disagreed that they would be toppled. In any case, they bowed to the growing pressures from their neighbors, from their disastrous economy, and, it must be added, from Gorbachev. In

August 1987 the Managua government agreed to Arias's plan.[28] Reagan and Abrams were furious. They had humored Arias in the belief that the Nicaraguans would never accept the plan; after the plan failed Reagan could then push Congress to grant massive aid to the Contras. Now, however, Arias's stunning success meant, in Reagan's eyes, that the Sandinistas would enjoy power indefinitely. In June 1987 Reagan and Arias had met at the White House. It was not pleasant. The U.S. president talked as if the Arias plan was already dead because Sandinistas could not be trusted and Contras could never be abandoned. Arias told Reagan that no respectable nation supported the Contras except the United States, and it was isolated on this issue. One participant later recalled that "Reagan kept looking over at his advisers as if to ask, who let this *midget* in here?" By August 1987 Reagan had grown concerned; he said publicly that Arias's plan was "fatally flawed." Then he offered one of his own that aimed to keep open full U.S. aid to the Contras (and the Salvadoran regime), while the Sandinistas were pushed from power well before the scheduled Nicaraguan elections in 1990. The plan was modified by House Speaker Jim Wright (Dem.-Tex.) to give the Arias plan some time to work before the United States renewed Contra aid. A week later the Central Americans accepted Arias's proposals. All of this occurred as the deadly revelations of the Iran-Contra scandal were televised daily throughout the world. One U.S. official tried to make the best of it: he noted that Reagan's special ambassador to Central America, Philip Habib (a distinguished and experienced diplomat) had worked hard for Arias's success. But then, in late August 1987, Habib rocked Washington by suddenly resigning because, he indicated, Reagan and Abrams had ordered him to have no further talks with the Sandinistas. The President next urged Congress to send $270 million of aid to the Contras. If Congress had accepted this request it could have killed the Arias plan. But the Contras were finished. In Managua, President Daniel Ortega recalled an old Nicaraguan bird-hunting phrase: "You're wasting gunpowder on vultures."[29]

During October 1987, Arias won the Nobel Prize for Peace. A leading Reagan supporter in Congress, Newt Gingrich (Rep.-Ga.) called the award "premature and saddening." One of Abrams's top aides in the State Department told reporters that "All of us . . . reacted with disgust, unbridled disgust." Speaker Wright declared that the award insured no more congressional approvals for Contra arms. Reagan's team nevertheless refused to give up. The C.I.A. continued to pour hundreds of thousands of dollars into the Contras in a desperate effort to keep them afloat. The money kept flowing even after the Contras executed Benjamin Linder, a U.S. engineer who was helping build governmental projects in Nicaraguan villages. U.S. officials also showed their anger by suspending $85 million to $160 million of promised aid that Costa Rica desperately needed. They further turned up the pressure on the Ticos to pay their debts to private foreign banks. A Costa Rican economic expert drew the conclusion: "They want our economy to get out of hand." In early 1988, General Colin Powell, Reagan's new National Security Adviser, bluntly told Central American leaders that they would be made to suffer if they did not help the Contras—and, by implication, kill Arias's plan. A month later Congress rejected Reagan's Contra-aid plan, but, sent non-lethal help that aimed at sending home the 40,000 Contras and their dependents in Honduras.[30]

The Reagan policy began to change, but only in tactics, not in its determination to destroy the Sandinistas. A new weapon was the National Endowment for Democracy (NED), a private but congressionally funded nonprofit group of Democrats and Republicans that had been created in 1983. Its publicly stated purpose was to funnel money to support free and fair elections in foreign countries. Such efforts, of course, were touchy subjects. When the U.S. Congress had discovered that the Somoza dictatorship contributed large sums to help Richard Nixon's presidential run in 1972, it condemned foreigners who interfered in U.S. elections, then passed a measure in 1974 to outlaw such outside interference. When Secretary of State Shultz pushed for the NED's creation in 1983, he assured Congress it would not "support this or that party in a given government." But in Nicaragua during 1987–88, the NED sent $1 million to help anti-Sandinista trade unions, political parties, and newspapers. Central Americans soon called the results *"democracies de fachada,"* or "facade democracies." Congress said nothing. Nicaragua claimed the NED and C.I.A. worked in tandem, which the NED denied. The Sandinistas nevertheless forcefully broke up opposition rallies, closed the Catholic Church's radio station, and shut down the newspaper *La Prensa* in mid-1988. Speaker Jim Wright suspected the C.I.A. had organized the rallies to provoke the crackdown. If so, it worked. Arias and other Central American leaders criticized the Sandinistas for breaking promises to allow opposition parties and other reforms. Congress appropriated $2 million more for the NED's use in Nicaragua during 1988–89.[31]

The Sandinistas were becoming trapped, but so were Reagan's policies. They had failed to destroy either the Sandinistas or the FMLN in El Salvador. Nine years after the President refused negotiations and sought all-out military victory, General Maxwell Thurman, the top U.S. Army commander in the region, said the Salvadoran rebels could not be beaten; the war could only be ended by negotiations. Between 100,000 and 200,000 Central Americans had been killed in fighting or by death squads after 1979. Another 4 million (15 percent of the region's population), were refugees or displaced persons. The policies had brought the United States into alliance with two of the world's most brutal regimes, the Guatemalan and Salvadoran. The policies had led Washington to disavow international law in 1984–85. They had even nearly destroyed Reagan's own government in the Iran-Contra scandal. They had helped bring Costa Rica, a real democracy, and Honduras, with its streak of post-1950 liberal reforms, to the brink of bankruptcy and disorder. By 1990 the former 9,000 Costa Rican Civil Guard and rural Guard had become an army of 27,000 accused of killing 13 people during detention. Perhaps the unkindest cut of all occurred when the Salvadoran and Honduran Presidents, despite almost total dependence on the United States, demonstrated their fear of continued war by ignoring U.S. demands and signing the Arias peace plan.[32]

The Reagan era was rooted in Theodore Roosevelt's traditional policy of bringing "order" to Central America by unilaterally using U.S. force. Eighty years of that policy had increased, not lessened, the inevitability of revolution in the region. The 1980s, however, closed with the Central Americans themselves, for the first time in the century, cooperating to control their own region's affairs in defiance of U.S. wishes. It was a historic turn. It put a new twist on T.R.'s famous remark, with which Reagan could sympathize as he left office in 1989: "These wretched republics cause me a great deal of trouble."

The Bush Years: Coming to Terms with a Rearranged System

The new President, George Bush, and his Secretary of State, fellow Texan James Baker, understood firsthand about such "trouble." Bush had been Vice President for eight years, and Baker had served as White House Chief of Staff and then Secretary of the Treasury. Baker's political instincts were widely admired. He had managed Bush's presidential campaign to victory in 1988, and throughout his years in Washington had understood the need to get along with Congress and the press. It was rumored that Baker's instinct was due to his ambition to follow Bush with a Baker presidency. Others noted that Baker (and Bush) were more pragmatic and much less ideological than the other Reaganites. Both men knew that a March 1989 report, written by a congressional agency, told the truth when it concluded that U.S. policy in Central America had led to "unintentional negative consequences" by building local military forces that had little use for democracy, and that "large-scale poverty and economic inequities exist at levels worse than a decade ago." But Bush and Baker also had problems on their right. *Sante Fe II: A Strategy for Latin America in the Nineties* was written in 1988 by conservative area experts and a military officer who warned darkly of the "communist subversive and terrorist network" sneaking from Mexico through Central America into South America. Correctly identifying the backbreaking debt problem as a central villain, the Sante Fe authors condemned "statism" as a response, and urged free-market forces as the cure-all.[33]

The Bush administration reflected this left-right split. The new Assistant Secretary of State for Inter-American Affairs, Bernard W. Aronson, had once worked for Democratic Party and labor union leaders, but as a militant anti-communist he had also written a speech for President Reagan that urged more Contra aid. By 1989 he agreed with his boss, Baker, that the Contras were a lost cause and a diplomatic settlement was needed—not least so Baker could get the no-win problem behind him and move on to other issues (such as U.S.-Soviet relations), where the diplomatic and personal political payoffs would be more grand. The National Security Council's new Latin American expert, however, was Everett Ellis Briggs, former hardline ambassador to Honduras from 1986–89, where he worked long hours to earn his title of "Ambassador to the Contras." Briggs and Vice President Dan Quayle teamed up as the true believers who thought that only the Reagan-Abrams military approach could settle the region—at least on terms acceptable to them, that is, the elimination of the Sandinistas and the FMLN.[34] Quayle's motives were partly his right-wing ideology that had been shaped since his Indiana childhood, and partly, no doubt, by his belief that he and Baker were already competing to be Bush's successor in the White House.

Just a month before they settled into their new jobs, both factions in the administration were badly shaken. In February 1989 the five Central American Presidents pushed the Arias plan one giant step farther when Nicaragua agreed to reforms and elections during February 1990. In return, the Sandinistas were given a pledge by the other four countries that the Contras would finally be disbanded within ninety days. White House officials admitted they had been blindsided by the sudden agreement. They put enormous pressure on the Hondurans to back out of the pact. But Baker and Aronson seized the opportunity to cut another deal with Congress; leaders on Capitol Hill agreed to send $50 million of non-lethal aid to the Contras in return for tight congressional control over its spending. The deal's clear purpose was to use the money to stop the fighting by breaking up the Contra camps in Honduras and moving their inhabitants back to Nicaragua. The agreement marked a turn. Baker and Aronson had put down a high-stakes wager that Arias was correct: by taking the military pressure off the Sandinistas, they would be more willing to hold an election, and that election, the U.S. officials bet, would peacefully remove the Sandinistas from power.[35]

Baker and Aronson then revealed another string on their policy bow. They had serious talks with Soviet leaders about Central America. These talks began in 1983–84, during some of the most tense moments of the Cold War, when younger State Department officials argued that explosive regional issues (Central America, Afghanistan, the Middle East) had to be discussed before they got out of hand. These officials were opposed by the true-believers (such as Kirkpatrick and the N.S.C. staff), who assumed that talking with Communists was, by definition, neither productive nor moral. The talks, however, proved to be quite productive, especially by 1987 when Gorbachev searched for quiet, face-saving agreements for reducing Soviet commitments abroad. Despite the critics' claims that by discussing Central America with the Kremlin he was profaning the Monroe Doctrine, Baker said "we ought to recognize facts." Gorbachev was ready to deal. In late 1988 the two superpowers struck an agreement: in return for the U.S. willingness to wind down the war against Nicaragua and go along with Arias, Gorbachev promised to cut off arms shipments to Managua and to pressure the Sandinistas to accept the results of an election.[36]

The road to the balloting was not smooth. The Bush administration dragged its feet in disbanding the Contras in the belief that the Sandinistas had to be pressured until the election. The Sandinistas responded by breaking the nineteen-month-long ceasefire and attacking Contra units. In November 1989, when missiles were found in a plane that had crashed in El Salvador, the Sandinistas did not deny they had been sending weapons to the FMLN. In December 1989, the deadline for the Contras' disbanding passed with the camps still in existence and living on $200,000 of U.S. monthly aid.[37] The Contras, however, were no longer as grateful. In late 1989 a younger group pushed aside the older, English-speaking, ineffective Contra leaders whom they accused of caring more about obtaining dollars than fighting. The new leaders used C.I.A. supplies but refused to listen to U.S. orders. Right-wing observers in the United States, such as the Heritage Foundation, were delighted—not least because the younger Contras did not feel bound by the Arias plan.[38]

Nicaragua's February Surprise of 1990

The Sandinistas believed they could handle the new Contras as long as the struggle was on the battlefield. The real problem could be the ballot box, and that problem loomed ever larger as the Nicaraguan economy spun out of control. Suffering spread. Some 40 percent of the government's budget went to military expenditures rather than investment in agriculture or industry. Meanwhile the Sandinistas desperately tried to maintain support, and to carry out the revolution's promises, by continuing the remarkably successful programs that increased literacy and provided health care for all. Government spending thus skyrocketed as income from production and exports plummeted. "We tried to do too much, too fast," Sandinista economist Xabier Gorostiaga observed in 1989. The year before, Nicaragua's per-capita production had reached only $300; the country was therefore ranked as one of the world's poorest. Overall production had been sliced in half since 1979. War had devastated sugar- and coffee-producing lands. In 1978 Nicaraguans had exported $660 million of goods; a decade later the amount was little more than $200 million and dropping. The government tried to pay for its ever-larger expenses by begging for aid from abroad and printing more money. As the printing presses rolled, inflation turned red hot. Too much money chased too few goods: inflation accelerated rapidly toward an unbelievable 14,000 percent annual rate by 1988. This meant in turn that each Nicaraguan's real wages (the money needed, for example, to buy beans or flour), fell an equally incredible 93 percent between 1981 and 1989. As early as mid-1986 food was in short supply and reports circulated that some were living on iguana meat. "We are like dogs," one Nicaraguan complained. "We eat when we find something."³⁹

The Sandinistas tried to control inflation by slashing government expenditures and laying off 30,000 public employees in 1988. The winding down of the war and drastic currency devaluation helped. Inflation dropped to a still-incredible 800 percent in 1989. But it was too late. Since 1979 per capita private consumption had dropped 70 percent. As unemployment spread, peasants left their land to swell the Managua slums, and the government lacked resources to turn the economy around. At Managua's Tona Beer plant, one of the nation's key industries, communist labor leaders convinced 480 hard-pressed workers in 1988 to quit the Sandinista union and join theirs. The communists promptly obtained a new contract increasing workers' pay. But the Sandinistas determined to hold the line, especially against communists. They used workers armed with clubs, as well as Army reserve battalions, to expel the communists. Strikes nevertheless spread through many industries. One Sandinista claimed that the United States used the communists to overthrow the revolution. Such an alliance was doubtful, but no doubt existed that with the U.S.-supported Contra war, the communist internal operations, and their own mismanagement, the Sandinistas could no longer help poorer Nicaraguans as the revolution once did.[40]

President Daniel Ortega refused to deal with the problems by following Castro: "For geopolitical reasons we have not taken profound steps like those taken in Cuba, where private property has been abolished." Nicaragua's traditions, Ortega's own more moderate ideology, the inability of the Soviet bloc to help—all worked against the possibility of following the Cuban model. But neither could he find help to construct a mixed economy. When Ortega visited ten West European nations in April 1989 to ask for $250 million from such former good friends as West Germany and France, he received only $20 million. The Europeans believed that the Sandinista economy was a bad investment. Secretary of State Baker, moreover, "burned up the telephone wires" to Europe (according to a U.S. official) with requests that Ortega receive nothing. As early as 1986 even the Soviets had criticized the failure of the Sandinistas' economic planning and the unwillingness of laborers to work to meet production targets. Henry Ruiz, one of the nine ruling Sandinista commanders, considered such complaints "legitimate."[41]

Daniel Ortega's more pragmatic policies had guided the nation since at least 1986 when he bested the hardline, ideological Interior Minister, Tomás Borge, in a power struggle. Ortega tightened his grasp on power by elevating his brother, Humberto, to a new rank, General of the Army. The Ortegas were in a political position to guide the nation out of the economic wilderness, but they could not find the path. Some 60 percent of the country's production remained in private hands. The Sandinistas knew that the peasant-owned farms were less efficient than large agribusinesses, but the government believed it had to sacrifice efficiency for the not-always-reliable allegiance of the peasants during the Contra war. The Sandinistas even committed themselves to a free market for staple grains. Communist-bloc diplomats understood that "This is hardly what we would call socialism," as one remarked. "It is much too undisciplined, much too chaotic." When the economy did appear to improve, as in 1982–83, it was undermined by the need to pay for the war. Reagan's policy aimed at overthrowing the Sandinistas by force, once and for all. The policy instead helped lead to "the depletion of the economy and undermining of the social foundation," as a British economist in Nicaragua phrased it. By 1987–88, the Sandinistas received important aid from some 500 private U.S. groups who sent more than $30 million, and also from such U.S. multinationals as IBM, Xerox, and Exxon, which tried to remain in Nicaragua despite multiplying problems of nearly worthless currency and lack of spare parts.[42] But such help was far from enough.

As economic discontent spread, and as the Contras continued to exist with swelling C.I.A. aid, the Sandinistas cracked down with arrests of political suspects. The numbers, not to mention the violence, never faintly resembled the scale and brutality of the Salvadoran or Guatemalan death squads. Americas Watch believed, however, that the Sandinistas held over 4,000 political prisoners in 1986, and other human rights observers put the number as high as 7,000. The government was also deeply, and correctly, suspicious of the Roman Catholic hierarchy's opposition. The Sandinistas did receive support from a majority of the country's 320 priests; most of them worked in rural areas where liberation theology continued to take hold. In 1988 President Ortega welcomed U.S. television evangelist Jimmy Swaggart for a three-day crusade that drew crowds of up to 40,000. Ortega said the visit demonstrated religious freedom. The Catholic hierarchy, frightened by the rapid spread of fundamentalist Christianity throughout Central America, believed that Swaggart and Ortega were actually declaring religious war on Roman Catholicism.[43]

Neither crackdowns nor televangelists, however, could halt the spreading economic woes. Nor, with the Arias plan winding down the war, could the Sandinistas as effectively blame Washington for their problems. In 1989, as the nation sunk toward the economic level of Haiti, the U.S. Congress gave the National Endowment for Democracy another $9 million to take advantage of the Sandinistas' problems in the upcoming election. The Nicaraguan government used half the funds to pay for the balloting expenses, but at least $4 million went to Violeta Barrios de Chamorro's National Opposition Union (UNO), and related groups that opposed Ortega and the Sandinistas. The widow of the martyred journalist, Pedro Joaquín Chamorro (see p. 230), Violeta had once been a member of the Sandinista government. After quitting in 1980, she remained in Managua to make the family newspaper, *La Prensa*, the focal point for anti-government opposition. By 1990 she was in a wheelchair because of a broken knee and advanced osteoporosis, so she could not campaign full-time. Her UNO, moreover, was a hastily cobbled-together coalition of fourteen parties, some of which hated the others. But on 25 February, 1990, as 2,500 international observers monitored the balloting, Chamorro's name provided enough charisma, and the economy provided enough misery, to enable her to defeat Ortega in a stunning upset. Arias was one of the few who were not surprised; he had bet his peace plan against Reagan's war plan that the Sandinistas could not win in fair balloting.[44]

The Sandinistas' loss, however, did not seem to be fatal. Ortega won 40 percent of the vote. The FSLN remained by far the nation's strongest single party. Unlike Chamorro, Ortega received no last-minute help from foreign friends. When he asked the Soviets to fund a quick stocking of stores with goods, they turned him down and later explained the decision with the words, "We didn't think it was a good investment." The Sandinistas made the best of it: they "privatized" state property and gave it to themselves. They also passed laws, in the final moments before Chamorro gained power, exempting themselves from any future prosecution of crimes committed while they held office. Of most importance, Daniel Ortega and his colleagues retained the political leverage to persuade Chamorro to keep Humberto Ortega as head of the nation's military. U.S. officials were furious. Chamorro refused to budge. She understood the extent of Sandinista influence in the military and trade unions, and she was not about to push the country back toward civil war by overtly challenging that power. The Sandinistas were positioning themselves to win back the presidency in 1996.[45]

Nicaraguans had thrown out Ortega in the hope (a hope they had nurtured since the 1840s), that the Giant of the North might help them if the Giant's enemies were out of the way. In the past, such hope had usually been dashed. Now Washington's ability and willingness to help was at least doubtful. President Bush lifted the economic embargo in March 1990, sent in $30 million of emergency aid, and cooperated with

Congress in finding another $300 million. These amounts were far less than Chamorro expected. Bush begged Japan and the Europeans to help pay for a joint economic effort in Central America. Little aid appeared. Of much greater importance, private right-wing groups, such as televangelist Pat Robertson's organization, the National Endowment for Democracy, and a vastly expanded U.S. Embassy and AID staff, worked to turn state enterprises into private businesses. Nicaraguan trade was again to be integrated into, and made dependent on, the U.S. market (especially in sugar). AIFLD battled to destroy the Sandinista unions. By early 1991, unemployment since the election had increased by one-third to about 40 percent. Living standards had retreated to 1930s levels. The Sandinistas meanwhile went through severe self-examination and reformulated their program so that ties to the Soviet Union and the need to centralize power were deemphasized. The victors of 1979 did not believe their revolution was over.[46]

The Contras meanwhile threatened to reopen the guerrilla war, but this time against Chamorro's government. Sandinistas, former Sandinistas, and U.S.-armed Contras fought with each other as they seized farms and other property. As Chamorro's personal power declined, and without the money needed from the United States, in the early 1990s Nicaragua threatened to fragment into many small civil wars. The Reagan-C.I.A. policy was casting long shadows. As he prepared to leave office in 1988, George Shultz was asked whether the United States should have been involved in the Contadora-Arias peace processes earlier. "You could argue," the Secretary of State replied, "that it might have been a good idea."[47]

El Salvador: Expanding the Killing Fields

While the U.S.-opposed Sandinistas accepted the election results and surrendered government power, in El Salvador the U.S.-supported government fixed elections and refused to convict a single army officer of the thousands of civilian murders the officer corps had committed. Not even Arias could change the U.S.-Salvadoran policy of fighting what one Central American observer called *"guerra total"* against the FMLN revolutionaries. The killings stretched toward 75,000 in number as the 1980s passed. A corrupt army and the right-wing ARENA party, led by death-squad organizer Roberto D'Aubuisson, consolidated themselves in power as the United States poured in so much aid that by the late 1980s it approached 100 percent of the Salvadoran government budget. Not since it had underwritten South Vietnam at the high point of the 1960s war had the United States so fully funded a regime. El Salvador became the third-largest recipient of U.S. aid, just behind Israel and Egypt. As the army and ARENA fattened, some 75 percent of the people lived in poverty. In 1988 basic exports were half those of 1979. Despite nearly $3 billion of overall U.S. aid in the 1980s (or about $800,000 each day of the entire decade), per-capita income dropped by one-third. If the U.S. aid given in 1985 alone had been handed to the poorest 20 percent of Salvadorans, their annual income would have quadrupled.[48]

Land reform, loudly trumpeted as the savior of the peasants in 1981, had not only been stopped by 1987. It had been used by the wealthy oligarchs to enrich themselves through simple devices: the government, which they controlled, paid them for giving up some land; the oligarchs then invested the money in profitable businesses (often overseas), and frequently took back the land when the peasants went bankrupt because they could not obtain the credit needed to buy seeds and fertilizers. In 1989, 1 percent of the landowners owned 41 percent of the arable land, while 60 percent of rural households had none. "The wealth of the country is now concentrated in fewer hands than before agrarian reform," the dean of the University of El Salvador declared in 1987. "The rich have more control than before."[49]

This was not the result the Reagan administration had planned. The plan was to have José Napoleon Duarte elected over the ARENA candidate in 1984; use U.S. aid to smash the FMLN militarily; and then, through Duarte, carry out enough reform to dry up support for the revolutionaries. At the same time, the economy was to be reoriented toward new, labor-intense exports (such as textiles and clothing) that would create a more democratic and enlightened elite to replace the old fourteen-family oligarchy and its longtime allies in the army's death squads. That was the plan.

It began well. Duarte won the presidency in 1984 with massive U.S.

help. In 1985, peace talks between Duarte and the FMLN broke off as the top Salvadoran military leader, General Adolfo Blandon, grandly announced the guerrillas would be crushed within the year. Special U.S. military trainers, he added, were to help. The war instead raged into 1986 when a C.I.A. report stated that the FMLN no longer had "the capacity to launch and sustain major offensives." In the spring of 1987, the guerrillas attacked the garrison at El Paraiso. They killed forty-three soldiers and a U.S. military adviser while Salvadoran officers hid in a bunker. The adviser was the eighteenth U.S. soldier or C.I.A. employee to die in the war since 1983. By late 1987, the FMLN force of about nine thousand operated in all fourteen of the country's provinces, despite the 50,000 government troops.[50]

Duarte was hit from both sides. The oligarch-army coalition opposed reforms, especially any that might endanger the military's ability to grow richer from its insurance, banking, real estate, and ocean-side resort businesses. For the first time, the army was becoming independent of the oligarchs. U.S. officials knew of the corruption, but they feared that cracking down on the military would only drive it to more anti-Duarte and death-squad activity. In a gruesome twist of the usual dependency relationship, the United States was becoming dependent on the brutal Salvadoran army. Duarte, however, also lost the support of unions, which before the 1980s had been among the region's strongest. When he tried to save the economy in 1986 with a severe austerity program that targeted the lower classes, the unions gained strength as they protested. Open warfare then erupted between the left-wing National Union of Salvadoran Workers (UNTS) and a right-wing union that was backed by the American Institute for Free Labor Development (AIFLD).[51]

By 1988 Duarte was dying of cancer. Washington nevertheless clung to him and the army. Nor did this policy change even after Salvadoran death squads appeared in southern California to attack critics. Again the Committee in Solidarity with the People of El Salvador (CISPES) was targeted. One of its leaders, a Salvadoran, was kidnapped in Los Angeles. She told police that she was burned with cigarettes and sexually assaulted by men who had Salvadoran accents, and who freed her with orders to warn others that "we are here." Probably more worrisome to U.S. officials was a 1988 report written by four U.S. Army Lieutenant Colonels who had been in El Salvador. They were shocked by what they had seen. Their report bluntly concluded that the FMLN, "tough, competent, highly motivated," could fight indefinitely; that U.S. policy had failed; and that the Salvadoran military fought only from "nine-to-five" and grew rich as the conditions that spawned revolution multiplied. The officers worried that the U.S.-built military would someday fight its historic enemy, Honduras, and the region erupt in flames. The report concluded that Washington must do more to remove the socioeconomic causes of the upheaval. It had no suggestion about how to create a Salvadoran government that could effectively deal with those causes.[52]

Nor did the Reagan administration have such a suggestion. It struck with its incredible (and unprovable) belief of 1986 that "the military in El Salvador has supported establishment of a democratic political system and a more equitable economic system." For good measure, the State Department added that the armed forces were "subject to a civilian authority" in San Salvador that had been "elected . . . through a democratic system." The appropriate comment on such statements was made by writer Larry Gelbart. In his 1989 Broadway show, "Mastergate," Gelbart described the pro-U.S. country, "San Elvador," as having "a democratic form of government that has been run by its army for the past forty years."[53]

Salvadorans tried to help themselves. In 1988 Duarte used the Arias plan as a lever to open talks with the FMLN. They went nowhere. The FMLN demanded both disbanding the death squads and bringing the murderers to justice. The opposite occurred: in 1987 the National Assembly responded to Arias's plan by giving amnesty to hundreds of guerrillas—and then outlawing any prosecution of death-squad members. The law meant that the murderers of the two U.S. labor organizers in 1981, as well as other North Americans, could never be brought to justice.[54]

In 1988 and again in 1989, Salvadorans gave smashing election victories to the ARENA party of death-squad leader Roberto D'Aubuisson. ARENA, however, had not named D'Aubuisson as its presidential candidate. The party's more moderate businessmen realized that he would not be the most attractive figure to bring in more U.S. aid. They instead turned to Alfredo Cristiani. Wealthy, U.S.-educated (Georgetown University, 1968), married to Margaret Llach (a daughter of one of the fourteen oligarch families), Cristiani's main claim to fame had been winning the Salvadoran squash championship. But he spoke perfect English and had a velvet touch in keeping ARENA's factions together. He won the presidency in 1989. The FMLN declared a truce during the elections, but as *The Economist* of London recorded, the "army frightened the voters, [ARENA] fixed the results, and its electoral commission delayed announcing them" until the result was satisfactory. D'Aubuisson had put it directly: it was time, he told audiences, to "get rid of the blond-heads [from the United States] who . . . got us into this mess." President Bush congratulated ARENA for its commitment to democracy. D'Aubuisson was again welcomed at the U.S. Embassy. Washington's money kept flowing.[55]

Cristiani kept the Bush administration reassured. In 1989 he cautiously opened talks with the FMLN. Death squads quickly reacted. Three leading liberal politicians and a labor organizer were gunned down. The FMLN responded with a massive, surprising offensive that included mortar attacks on the Defense Ministry's building in San Salvador. Then, in November 1989, killers later identified as Salvadoran military slaughtered six Jesuit priests, a housekeeper, and her daughter in cold blood with high-powered rifles at Central American University. The priests were widely known and admired in both El Salvador and the United States. U.S. and Roman Catholic officials demanded justice. But Cristiani announced that key evidence had mysteriously disappeared. His government moved slowly to follow leads uncovered by North American investigators. A bipartisan group of the U.S. Congress reported that of the fifteen highest-ranking Salvadoran military officers, fourteen had commanded troops accused of death-squad activities. Not a single officer had been convicted through 1991. U.S. Ambassador William Walker privately demanded justice, but publicly called D'Aubuisson "the best politician in the country" and—shocking friends who knew him well—seemed to agree with the Salvadoran military's claim that the FMLN, not death-squads, had killed the six Jesuits and two women. No evidence existed to support Walker's claim. Meanwhile in 1989–90 nearly a half-billion-dollars of overall U.S. aid flowed to the army and Cristiani's government.[56]

In late 1990, the FMLN began effectively using Soviet SA-14 surface-to-air missiles to shoot down army helicopters. "This all means a significant change in the balance of power," a foreign military expert concluded. The FMLN's senior military commander, Joaquín Villalobos, announced the rebels' "Marxist phase" was to give way to a cease-fire and unarmed political organizing. Realizing that his forces' 1989–90 offensive had made its point, but that neither side could win total victory, he declared, "There will be a negotiated solution." This was helped by D'Aubuisson's lingering illness and death from cancer in early 1992. Negotiations slowed down as army officers refused to be held accountable for corruption and death-squad activity. At two minutes before New Year's Day of 1992, however, the two sides agreed to a United Nations–brokered settlement. The FMLN did not gain an immediate share of power, but the rebels did obtain equal numbers with the right-wing in a new civilian police force; the reduction of the armed forces in half; and a rebel-approved panel set up to purge brutal and corrupt army officers. A key U.N. official declared, "This is the closest that any process has ever come to a negotiated revolution." In return for stopping the fighting, the FMLN's demands were to be institutionalized and accepted by Cristiani. Notably, and appropriately, the United Nations (not the United States) prepared to send more than 1,000 peacekeepers to monitor and help enforce the cease-fire in early 1992.

Even if the delicate deal held (and this was problematical given continued shooting and many military officers' hatred of it), El Salvador would never finish paying for the revolution. "This is a site of retching foulness where cows, children, and vultures stand side by side, wrenching survival from a mountain of rotting animal corpses and human waste." *Los Angeles Times* reporter Kenneth Freed wrote from Cutumay Camones, El Salvador in mid-1991. This poison-waste dump was only a tiny part of the nation's disaster. Once lush and productive, El Salvador has lost 94 percent of its original forests, 80 percent of its natural vegetation, 77 percent of its arable soil (due to erosion), and at least 75,000 people dead with another 1,000,000 displaced.[57]

Guatemala: "They're Poor Here . . . , They'll Be Better Off in Heaven"

In the region's oldest civil war, the human devastation was equally horrifying. The thirty-year Guatemalan blood bath, one count estimated, had killed 150,000 and left another 40,000 missing. In 1985, however, Vinicio Cerezo Arevalo's presidential victory caused celebration. A critic of social injustice, he was welcomed in Washington. The Guatemalan military, its autonomous power protected by the country's constitution, was also pleased. "Vinicio is a project of ours," a top army officer observed. U.S. aid was needed, so "this civilian project is really a military project." Or, as a Roman Catholic priest in Guatemala City declared, "Elections are merely a note in the song of democracy. Washington keeps playing the note and expecting us to hear the tune."[58]

Many Guatemalans, especially the military, were tone deaf. When Cerezo attempted low-key land and tax reforms, the oligarchs stopped both while the army killed peasant leaders. Per capita income levels fell to those of 1970. Cerezo tried to impose an austerity program that, as usual, squeezed the masses, especially urban labor and government employees. Although only 10 percent of the workers were unionized, massive strikes erupted. In early 1988 Cerezo agreed to push for higher wages, lower prices, and recognition of the militant labor union that organized sugar-cane cutters. The right-wing was not pleased. In May, and again in August, 1988, the President barely escaped the army's attempts to overthrow his government. The high command finally protected him (it still could use Cerezo in Washington), but in return he retreated from his reforms, broke off talks with the rebels, and gave the military new powers over internal security. Cerezo spent the last three years of his presidency womanizing, sailing on his yacht, and accumulating wealth.[59]

Frustrated with Cerezo, U.S. officials moved closer to the army. Washington's military aid of $9.4 million, and $146 million of economic help, kept flowing even as evidence piled up in 1989–90 that the forces were growing rich from drug trafficking. The trafficking produced such huge profits that the military, long known anyway for its independence, would be less dependent on U.S. supplies and advice. Nor would it be dependent on the oligarchs. "You people," the Guatemalan Defense Minister told wealthy civilians, "have been using us to kill your Marxists for the past 400 years." The military would now do that on its own. But by 1990, despite the army's scorched-earth policy, rebels operated in fourteen of the twenty-two provinces. The three factions that made up the Guatemalan National Revolutionary Union (URNG) also had sophisticated arms bought in part, western diplomats believed, from drug profits.[60]

U.S. military support had long been intimate. In 1987 North American helicopter crews even flew Guatemalan troops into battle against the URNG. Green Berets and other U.S. military specialists helped develop anti-URNG projects. Now, faced with the threats posed by growing rebel strength and the Arias peace plan, the army went on a killing spree. In 1989–90, five members of the University of San Carlos were killed and another five "disappeared." U.S. citizen Michael Devine, who owned a hotel and restaurant, was beaten and beheaded. A world-renowned anthropologist, Myrna Mack, who had worked closely with peasants, was stabbed to death just outside her classroom. A U.S. nun, Diana Ortiz, was kidnapped, raped, and thrown in with corpses before she managed to escape. Salvadoran FMLN leader, Hector Oqueli, was murdered. In addition, unarmed Indians and street children were gunned down by police and army units. In late 1990, President Bush finally cut military aid and froze arms sales.[61]

A new Guatemalan President, Jorge Serrano Elías, replaced Cerezo and had to face the United States' displeasure. A right-wing businessman with a Stanford University degree, Serrano became the first Protestant elected to head Guatemala. He had won in a stunning upset because the rapidly growing Christian fundamentalists, who now accounted for about one of every three Guatemalans, had joined with voters tired of Cerezo's inaction. Anyway, as a reporter noted, the candidates "ranged from the right to the extreme right." Serrano had been a high government official in 1982–83 when the army scotched the rebels by murdering tens-of-thousands of Indians. Enjoying personal ties to conservative Senator Jesse Helms (Rep.-N.C.), and to U.S. fundamentalist sects, Serrano knew that his religion had spread rapidly among the growing poor. As one Guatemalan fundamentalist leader declared, "The poor get the message that while they're poor here on earth, they'll be better off in heaven." Such placid acceptance of the status quo was exactly what the army and oligarchs wanted—not least because it undercut Roman Catholic liberation theology that aimed to improve peasant's lives in this world. Serrano won despite vigorous Roman Catholic opposition.[62]

Guatemala's army had made it plain that it did not believe Arias's peace plan had anything to do with Guatemala. But in the face of Washington's pressure, Serrano opened talks with the URNG. The army did not have to fear a sellout by this President. The talks broke down in 1991 over URNG's demands for both human-rights monitors to protect all Guatemalans and the government's penance for past atrocities. Meanwhile the economy continued to slide as prices of the two key exports, coffee and cotton, fell worldwide. Los Angeles, California had offered to help in 1987 by paying Guatemala for taking 10,000 tons of sewage, but Cerezo's spokesmen said his nation would not allow the entry of "processed human excrement." By 1991, one observer reported that each day at Guatemala City's garbage dump, "mangy dogs and clouds of vultures compete with hundreds of people to survive off the trash. A whole shantytown has grown up at the dump." One Guatemalan living there explained, "They have to leave their land when the landlords want to grow sugar cane."[63]

This was probably not what the U.S. Embassy in Guatemala City had in mind when it declared in 1985 that Cerezo's election was "the final step in the reestablishment of democracy in Guatemala." More to the point was Philip Roettinger's view. He had been a C.I.A. agent in the 1954 operation. "Our 'success,' " he wrote thirty-two years later, led to "repressive military rule and the deaths of more than 100,000 Guatemalans. Furthermore, the overthrow . . . destroyed vital social and economic reforms, including land distribution, social security, and trade union rights. Thirty years later, Nicaraguans finally have such benefits; Guatemalans and Hondurans are still waiting."[64]

Conclusion

The two chapters on the 1980s have taken up a disproportionate amount of this book. They demanded such detail and space for four reasons. First, the years from 1979 to 1991 turned out to be the bloodiest, most violent, and most destructive era in Central America's post-1820 history. The number of dead and "disappeared" varies according to different sources. The minimum is 200,000 (40,000 in Nicaragua, 75,000 in El Salvador, 75,000 in Guatemala, 10,000 in Honduras and the frontier fighting in Costa Rica), but this is only an estimate. Millions have been displaced or made refugees. If a similar catastrophe struck the United States in proportion, 2½ million North Americans would die and 10 to 20 million would be driven from their homes. Disasters on this scale deserve more attention than one-minute sound-bites. The million Central Americans who flooded into U.S. cities have affected schools, labor markets, city budgets, race relations, and law. The U.S. government's legal challenges, and secret scrutiny, of North Americans involved in the sanctuary movement have aroused great concern among those who have followed these episodes.[65]

The FBI and other federal agencies, including possibly the C.I.A., have investigated, and allegedly raided and harassed, U.S. groups involved in working with those Central Americans who were not in favor with the Reagan administration. The FBI was aided by right-wing groups, allegedly including the Reverend Sun Myung-Moon's "Moonies," whose college groups infiltrated CISPES and fed raw information to the FBI. The disasters in Central America became, on a much smaller scale, disasters for individual rights in the United States.[66]

A second reason for such detailed attention is the wars' economic devastation of Central America, and the effect they have on the historic U.S.-Central American relationship. The Center for Latin American Monetary Studies, located in Guatemala City, estimated that the region suffered $30 billion in economic losses between 1980 and 1987. Joao Baena Soarez, Secretary General of the Organization of American States, declared in 1986, on the twenty-fifth anniversary of the Alliance for Progress: "On the whole, the region is worse off now than it was twenty-five years ago." The gap between rich and poor widened. In the mid-1980s the amount spent by people in the United States on cosmetics, hair care, and disposable diapers equalled the combined gross domestic product of Costa Rica, El Salvador, Nicaragua, and Honduras. And the gap widened within individual nations. In El Salvador the rich spent $10 for a box of imported raisin bran cereal, while the poor were landless and suffered 40 percent unemployment. In Guatemala an economist warned that it might be only a matter of time before food riots occurred: "What's stopping raids on supermarkets?" he asked in 1990. The answer was, very little except the army.[67]

The region's armies profited most from these catastrophes. As billions of U.S. dollars flooded into the area, the militaries of every nation except Costa Rica grew fat on banking, insurance, real estate, and drug-running, among other occupations. That enterprise created an economic and political independence from the rich civilians with whom the military had worked, and had protected against the angry poor. Army leaders tolerated elections that produced civilian presidents because they pleased U.S. officials, and especially pleased Congress where foreign aid was handed out. When the Honduran President requested an important favor in 1990, a Colonel turned him down then explained to a visitor: "He's only the President." In every country in Central America, U.S. policy during the 1980s had helped create military monsters. As these armies doubled in size between 1981 to 1986, one senior Honduran official spoke for many Central American civilian leaders when he said that the military officers "don't overthrow us because it's not in their interest right now and because the United States has told them not to. But what the United States is basically doing here is paying our army not to have a coup. Who knows what will happen when you [North Americans] are no longer here to stop them?"[68]

U.S. officials sought economic answers. The failure of the Alliance for Progress had been key in triggering the 1980s disasters. Reagan's Caribbean Basin Initiative (CBI) tried to encourage new industries by opening U.S. markets. By the late 1980s, CBI was widely regarded as a failure. U.S. imports from the area indeed increased, but these were largely fruit, flowers, and (as Elliott Abrams pointed to with pride in

1988) Guatemalan fly-fishing lures made by 300 people. But Congress more than offset these gains by slashing import quotas of sugar to protect U.S. beet-sugar producers—and force the North American consumer to pay nearly four times the world market price for the sweetener. Moreover, not even the most enlightened economic policy could remedy the devastation caused by war. To pay for the damages, while keeping the wars going, Reagan sent in about $1 billion of Economic Support Funds (ESF) each year. "Thanks to our policies, the countries of the region have become ESF junkies," a U.S. congressional staff expert said in 1988.[69]

In 1990, President George Bush outlined an "Enterprise for the Americas Initiative" to bolster trade and investment by creating "a hemisphere-wide free trade zone." It was to replace the failed CBI. Bush's program would require much time. Meanwhile, U.S. economic aid to the Central American-Caribbean region was slashed 40 percent between 1989–91 because of Washington's growing financial troubles and less attention being paid to Central America now that the Sandinistas no longer held power. Costa Rica's democracy lost 47 percent of its aid in one year. The region's infrastructure, devastated by war, had little chance for rebuilding. Bush hoped that Western Europe and Japan would help. Between 1985 and 1990 the Japanese had become Latin America's key financial source; they provided 50 percent more funds for the southern hemisphere than did the United States. Wrapped in war, however, Central America was not attractive to Japan. The region seemed to be recycling back to the 1970s and 1960s economically.[70]

A third reason for paying special attention to the 1980s is that the decade revealed so much about how key North Americans viewed their own history and constitutional system. Reagan campaigned successfully as a man who held the deepest faith in his own country. Ironically, he and his advisers had little faith in the U.S.-Central American system as it had evolved in the half-century since F.D.R.'s Good Neighbor policy. Reagan, of all people, concluded that North American cultural, economic, and political attractiveness was impotent to isolate and, over time, neutralize revolutionary movements. He believed that only military force could work.

The objective of not merely defeating and isolating, but destroying the Sandinistas, the FMLN, and Guatemala's URNG has not been realized. Instead, both Central and North American politics were corrupted. Most notably this corruption occurred in the 1982 and 1989 Salvadoran elections, and in the Guatemalan and Honduran elections in the 1980s, when Washington officials cheered them as a sign of democracy. These were *"democracias de fachada"* of the first order—façade democracies to show Congressional leaders and their constituents that they could now safely send billions of dollars to these new "democratic" regimes. Certain words, such as "democracy," George Orwell wrote, "are often used in a consciously dishonest way. That is, the person who uses them has his own private definition, but allows his hearer to think he means something quite different." The corruption climaxed with the Iran-Contra scandal. It marked the logical conclusion of the post-1890 development of imperial presidential powers, the post-1945 fear of "communism," the post-1947 growth of a national security apparatus that was accountable to no one but the President, and a post-1973 determination to rewrite the history of the Vietnam experience. It also culminated the post-1823 belief that the United States alone should define the principles of an American system.[71]

U.S. policy largely failed because it rested on a contradiction: the stated belief was that the region's stability and prosperity depended on attaining democracy under U.S. guidance, while, at the same time, Washington officials helped right-wing militarists fight wars that were not for democratic objectives, but instead aimed at perpetuating the wide class differences between rich and poor that had triggered the revolutions originally. When the contradiction surfaced, it was pushed down again by other false beliefs—that (as Kirkpatrick argued), authoritarians were preferable to totalitarians because totalitarians were impossible to change peacefully; that U.S. security was at risk; that U.S. credibility worldwide was on the line; or that democracy could be created on the cheap through mass voting. Octavio Paz placed the last belief in proper perspective: "Democracy is not a superstructure, but a popular creation." The ultimate test of a democracy is the protection of individual life and liberty. During the Reagan administration not a single military officer in El Salvador, Guatemala, or Honduras was convicted for the tens-of-thousands of death-squad crimes. In El Salvador and Guatemala laws were even passed to protect officers who perpetrated such crimes against future prosecution.[72]

The fourth reason for noting the 1980s is that they marked a historic watershed in twentieth-century international relations. The nearly seventy-year East-West Cold War ended. Military priorities began to give way to economic needs. In Central America the United States, at least as early as 1987, could no longer justify aiding right-wing militarists with the claim that they were the only alternative to Soviet-dominated governments. In reality, of course, the overwhelming number of Central Americans had not seen their countries' struggles in Cold War terms at all.[73] The military regimes, however, knew how to turn on Washington's aid faucets by warning about possible Soviet control of the region.

Two dangers emerged in the 1990s as the Cold War became history. The first was that the United States would pay little attention to helping solve Central American socioeconomic problems and instead devote its resources to those regions that had traditionally drawn Washington's attention, especially Europe, Russia, and Eastern Asia. News correspondent Mark A. Uhlig described the Central American view: "Like a train roaring through a rural town, United States foreign policy burst through Central America at full speed and has now disappeared into the night." The second danger was integral with the first: when crises arose in Central America (or Panama), Washington officials would go for the quick fix of unilateral military intervention. U.S. military forces, no longer needed to fight nuclear or massive conventional wars with the Soviet Union, were reorganizing—and justifying—themselves by creating light- and medium-force units for third-world combat. As Senator William Cohen (Rep.-Me.) put it in 1990, the need now was to "project power into other regions and maintain access to distant markets and resources." The probable opponent was not identified. Cohen's remark resembled those of Mahan and McKinley a century earlier. The Arias peace plan was the most hopeful sign in the past century of U.S.-Central American relations that neither of the two dangers would materialize. The plan demonstrated how, if the United States cooperated instead of opposed, Central Americans might handle their own affairs—and do so through negotiations instead of military force.[74]

The fundamental problem was posed by former Colombian President

Belisario Betancur: "Without peace there can be no development, and without development there can be no peace. We must break this vicious circle."[75] Arias started to make that break, albeit over strenuous U.S. opposition. (In 1989 it was revealed that the Republican Party's Institute for International Affairs, possibly working with the National Endowment for Democracy, secretly funneled a half-million dollars between 1986 and 1989 into Costa Rica to defeat Arias. This illegal use of U.S. taxpayers' funds stopped only when Congressional Democrats raised questions, and then the *Wall Street Journal* and Richard Gonzales of National Public Radio made the information public.) The problem became how to find ways to break the century-old system whose cornerstone had become U.S. hegemony. As a respected Costa Rican historian notes, with the exception of his own nation, Central American rulers were unable to transform late nineteenth-century agrarian capitalism. Economic growth was therefore not matched by the necessary social change. The 1980s explosions resulted. Future explosions are inevitable unless economic growth is more equitably distributed among one of the most rapidly growing populations on earth. The Latin American sociologist, Edelberto Torres-Rivas, placed the 1980s upheaval in the necessary context: "Central American countries . . . have in common . . . a history as undeveloped societies within a particular geographic region of the U.S. sphere of influence."[76]

The system had a long, interconnected history. As one Latin American acidly phrased it, "Yesterday tranquil banana republics, today a 'convulsed region' *(convulsionada región)*" Throughout the post-1890 era, the United States had dominated the area at will. Even in El Salvador, whose oligarchs had a proud history of keeping foreigners at bay, North American influence developed until by the 1920s, in the words of one horrified diplomat, the U.S. Minister bragged "that he made the native police kneel down when he passed." When neither kowtowing nor the U.S. Marines could assure Central American stability, Washington officials used the Good Neighbor approach, the C.I.A., and the Alliance for Progress. They did not work either. As poverty accelerated, revolution erupted. In 1983, Secretary of State Shultz told Congress that the United States would not tolerate "people shooting their way into power." But other U.S. officials had not taken that view when oligarchs and generals shot their way into power in El Salvador in 1932, Nicaragua in 1934–36, Guatemala in 1954, or Honduras in 1963. (And fortunately, Shultz's rule was not applied in 1776 when George Washington and Thomas Jefferson shot their way into power against an imperial British system.)[77]

Unable to deal with the products of its own system, reconcile the contradiction between its professed ideals and its century-old foreign policy, or work with other nations to resolve these dilemmas, the United States, from Eisenhower to Bush, has resorted to force. The result has been more revolution. If the future is to be different, the past must be confronted. That past is the history of how the class-ridden remains of the Spanish empire turned into the revolution-ridden parts of the North American system.

Notes

███████████████

INTRODUCTION

1. U.S. Department of State, Bureau of Public Affairs, *GIST; A Quick Reference Aid on U.S. Foreign Relations* (May 1982), 1. Most of the statistics in the tables are from John Paxton, ed., *The Statesman's Yearbook . . . 1982–1983* (London, 1982). See especially President Ronald Reagan's speech to Congress, text in *New York Times*, 28 April 1983, A12.
2. Franklin D. Parker, *The Central American Republics* (London, 1964), 1.
3. Eduardo Frei Montalva, "The Second Latin American Revolution," *Foreign Affairs* 50 (Oct. 1971): 83.
4. Alan Riding, "Guatemala: State of Siege," *New York Times Magazine*, 24 Aug. 1980, 66–67.
5. Juan José Arévalo, *The Shark and the Sardines* (N.Y., 1961).
6. Quoted in "Caribbean Pie," *The Nation*, 13 June 1981, 716.
7. This is argued in Eldon Kenworthy, "Reagan Rediscovers Monroe," *democracy* 2 (July 1982): 80–90.
8. Robert Freeman Smith, "The American Revolution and Latin America," *Journal of Interamerican Studies and World Affairs* 20 (Nov. 1978): 437–39.
9. Tom J. Farer, "Reagan's Latin America," *The New York Review of Books*, 19 March 1981, 13.
10. Minutes of cabinet meeting of 6 Nov. 1959, Dwight D. Eisenhower Library, Abilene, Kansas (microfilm), 2.
11. Princeton Seminar, May 15–16, 1954, Dean Acheson Papers, Harry S. Truman Library, Independence, Missouri (microfilm).
12. A discussion of this point is in Eldon Kenworthy, "U.S. and Latin America . . . ," *democracy* 1 (July 1981): 86–97.
13. Quoted by Viron Vaky in U.S. Congress, House Committee on Foreign Affairs,

Subcommittee on Inter-American Affairs, *Central America at the Crossroads, Hearings of September 11–12, 1979*, 96th Cong., 1st sess., 11. (Hereafter cited as House, *Central America at the Crossroads.*)

14. Among the vast literature on dependency theory, the following have been especially useful: Theotonio Dos Santos, "The Structure of Dependence," in K.T. Fann and Donald C. Hodges, eds., *Readings in U.S. Imperialism* (Boston, 1971); Osvaldo Sunkel, "Big Business and 'Dependencia': A Latin American View," *Foreign Affairs* 50 (April 1972); Edelberto Torres-Rivas, *Procesos y estructuras de una sociedad dependiente (centroamerica)* (Santiago, Chile, 1969), a Latin American perspective especially interesting for the interwar period; Richard R. Fagen, "A Funny Thing Happened on the Way to the Market: Thoughts on Extending Dependency Ideas," *International Organization* 32 (Winter 1978): 287–300. A useful critique is David Ray, "The Dependency Model of Latin American Development: Three Basic Fallacies," *Journal of Interamerican Studies and World Affairs* 15 (Feb. 1973): 4–20.

CHAPTER I

1. Quoted in Robert A. Nisbet, *The Social Impact of the Revolution* (Washington, D.C., 1974), 23.

2. Jefferson to Stuart, 25 Jan. 1786, in *The Papers of Thomas Jefferson*, Julian P. Boyd, ed. (Princeton, 1950), 9: 218; Hamilton's interest can be found in Robert Hendrickson, *Hamilton . . . (1789–1804)* (N.Y., 1976), 462–64.

3. Quoted in Arthur P. Whitaker, *The Western Hemisphere Idea* (Ithaca, N.Y., 1954), 29.

4. Arthur Schlesinger, Sr., "America's Ten Gifts to Civilization," *The Atlantic* 204 (March 1959): 65–69.

5. Charles Francis Adams, ed., *The Memoirs of John Quincy Adams* (Philadelphia, 1874–77), 5: 323–26.

6. Lester D. Langley, *Struggle for the American Mediterranean . . . 1776–1904* (Athens, Ga., 1976), 46–48, 52.

7. Alastair White, *El Salvador* (N.Y., 1973), 62 provides good background. This is one of the best volumes on Salvadoran history.

8. Graham H. Stuart, and James L. Tigner, *Latin America and the United States*, 6th ed. (Englewood Cliffs, N.J., 1975), 484, footnote.

9. Parker, *Central American Republics*, 57, 72; William S. Stokes, *Honduras: An Area Study in Government* (Madison, Wi., 1950), 33.

10. Arturo Humberto Montes, *Morazán y la Federacíon Centroamericano* (Mexico, 1958), 85–140 on the confederacy and counterrevolution; a good brief account is Lionel King, "Francisco Morazán and Central American Unity," *Contemporary Review* 223 (Nov. 1973): 225–29.

11. This discussion is taken from a small classic, Robert C. West and John P. Augelli,

Middle America: Its Lands and Peoples, 2nd ed. (Englewood Cliffs, N.J., 1976), 378–79; Thomas L. Karnes, *The Failure of Union: Central America, 1824–1975* (Tempe, Ariz., 1976), 248.

12. J. Fred Rippy, *British Investments in Latin America, 1822–1949* (Minneapolis, Minn., 1959), 105–09.

13. Stokes, *Honduras*, 5–7, 11.

14. Karnes, *Failure of Union*, 177–78.

15. Stuart and Tigner, *Latin America and the U.S.*, 482–84.

16. Ibid. 484–87; William O. Scroggs, *Filibusterers and Financiers; The Story of William Walker*. (N.Y., 1916), esp. 280–85.

17. Charles S. Campbell's standard work, *The Transformation of American Foreign Relations, 1865–1900* (N.Y., 1976) aptly subtitles its chapter on the Venezuelan crisis, "A Turning Point in Anglo-American Relations."

18. Robert A. Friedlander, "A Reassessment of Roosevelt's Role in the Panamanian Revolution of 1903," *Western Political Quarterly* 14 (June 1961): 538–39.

19. Quoted in David Pletcher, *The Awkward Years: American Foreign Relations Under Garfield and Arthur* (Columbia, Mo., 1962), 105.

20. Kenneth Hagan, *American Gun-Boat Diplomacy . . . 1877–1889* (Westport, Conn., 1973), 171.

21. David S. Muzzey, *James G. Blaine* (N.Y., 1935), 365; James G. Blaine, *Political Discussions, Legislative, Diplomatic and Popular, 1856–1886* (Norwich, Conn., 1887), 411; *New York Tribune*, 30 August 1890, 1.

22. Quoted, with a good analysis, in Pletcher, *Awkward Years*, 35–36.

23. *International American Conference. Reports of Committees.* (Washington, D.C., 1890), esp. volume 1; Whitaker, *Western Hemisphere Idea*, 76–79.

24. Howard K. Beale, *Theodore Roosevelt and the Rise of America to World Power* (N.Y., 1962), 43.

25. Cleona Lewis, *America's Stake in International Investments* (Washington, D.C., 1938), esp. 590, 606; Rippy, *British Investments in Latin America*, 68; Thomas Schoonover, "Costa Rican Trade and Ties . . . ," *Jahrbuch Für Geschichte von Staat, Wirtschaft und Gesselschaft Lateinamerikas* 14 (1977): 269–307; also Schoonover's *The U.S. in Central America, 1860–1911* (Durham, 1991), 39–45, 69–76, 84–86.

26. Speech of 20 Nov. 1906, *Foreign Relations of the United States* (cited hereafter as *FRUS*), *1906*, Part 2 (Washington, D.C., 1909), 1457–61. This view of Root, and indeed the entire section on the Progressive Era, has been informed by Robert N. Seidel, *Progressive Pan Americanism . . . 1906–1931* (Ithaca, N.Y., 1973).

27. Quoted in William Everett Kane, *Civil Strife in Latin America: A Legal History of U.S. Involvement* (Baltimore, 1972), 66–67; Schoonover, *U.S. in Central America*, 111–48, 168–71.

28. James D. Richardson, ed., *Messages and Papers of the Presidents* (N.Y., 1897–1914), 16: 7375–76.

29. Roosevelt to Cecil Arthur Spring Rice, 24 July 1905, in *The Letters of Theodore*

Roosevelt, 6 vols., ed. Elting E. Morison (Cambridge, Mass., 1952), 4: 1286; Richard D. Challener, *Admirals, Generals and American Foreign Policy, 1898–1914* (Princeton, 1973), 20.

30. Raymond Leslie Buell, "The United States and Central American Stability," *Foreign Policy Reports* 7 (8 July 1931): 174–75.

31. A discussion of this point is in Challener, *Admirals, Generals, and American Foreign Policy*, 288–89.

32. Dana G. Munro, *Intervention and Dollar Diplomacy in the Caribbean, 1900–1921* (Princeton, 1964), 534–35; Schoonover, *U.S. in Central America*, 150–65.

33. Quoted in Daniel Aaron, *Men of Good Hope* (N.Y., 1951), 268.

34. Thomas L. Karnes, *Tropical Enterprise; The Standard Fruit and Steamship Company in Latin America* (Baton Rouge, La., 1978), 38; Buell, "U.S. and Central American Stability," (8 July 1931), 162–64.

35. Quoted and discussed in Stuart and Tigner, *Latin America and the U.S.*, 496–98.

36. Germán Arciniegas, *Caribbean: Sea of the New World* (N.Y., 1954), 444–45.

37. The best account is Karnes, *Tropical Enterprise*, well-written and based on rich company records of Standard Fruit; a good description of Zemurray's start is in Thomas P. McCann, *An American Company, The Tragedy of United Fruit* (N.Y., 1976), 18–24.

38. The figures are from Pan American Union, *The Foreign Trade of Latin America Since 1913* (Washington, 1952).

39. Stokes, *Honduras*, 27.

40. Robert T. Aubey, "Entrepreneurial Formation in El Salvador," *Explorations in Entrepreneurial History* 6 (Spring 1969): 279.

41. Challener, *Admirals, Generals, and American Foreign Policy*, 309.

42. Buell, "U.S. and Central American Stability," (8 July 1931), 175–76 has a good discussion of the revolution and its background; Challener, *Admirals, Generals, and American Foreign Policy*, 309; Charles D. Kepner, Jr., and Jay H. Soothill, *The Banana Empire . . .* (N.Y., 1935), 104–12.

43. This UFCO-Zemurray story is well told in an extraordinary book, William H. Durham, *Scarcity and Survival in Central America . . .* (Stanford, 1979), 115–18; also Kepner and Soothill, *The Banana Empire*, 110–12; Charles D. Kepner, Jr., *Social Aspects of the Banana Industry* (N.Y., 1936), 53–54; Christmas is quoted in Joanne Omang and Aryeh Neier, *Psychological Operations in Guerrilla Warfare* (New York, 1985), 3.

44. Vice-consul Caldera to Knox, 20 Nov. 1909, *FRUS, 1909* (Washington, 1914), 448–49; Buell, "U.S. and Central American Stability," (8 July 1931), 168–70.

45. Knox to Nicaraguan chargé, 1 Dec. 1909, in *FRUS, 1909*, 455.

46. Hans Schmidt, *Maverick Marine: General Smedley D. Butler* (Lexington, Ky, 1987), 40–42; John Weeks, *The Economics of Central America* (New York, 1985), 23–24.

47. Elliott Northcott to Knox, 25 Feb. 1911, in *FRUS, 1911* (Washington, D.C., 1915), 655–56.

48. Buell, "U.S. and Central American Stability," (8 July 1931): 172–73; Anna I. Powell, "Relations Between the U.S. and Nicaragua . . . ," *Hispanic American Historical Review* 8 (Feb. 1928): 43–64.
49. Quoted in Donald F. Anderson, *William Howard Taft . . .* (Ithaca, N.Y., 1968), 263.
50. The story is well told in Schmidt, *Maverick Marine*, 43–57; quoted in Buell, "U.S. and Central American Stability," (8 July 1931), 163.
51. Challener, *Admirals, Generals, and American Foreign Policy*, 329.
52. T.R. to Root, 3 Aug. 1908, in *Letters of Roosevelt*, ed. Morison, 6: 1150.
53. "From the Diary of Colonel House," 25 Nov. 1914, in *The Papers of Woodrow Wilson*, ed. Arthur S. Link (Princeton, N.J., 1966) 31: 355.
54. Arthur S. Link, *Wilson, Vol. III, The Struggle for Neutrality, 1914–1915*, (Princeton, 1960), 495–98; John Weeks, *The Economies of Central America* (New York, 1985), 119–20.
55. Edward Lowry, "What the President is Trying to Do for Mexico," in *Papers of Wilson*, ed. Link, 29: 92–94; "Declaration of Policy with Regard to Latin America," *FRUS, 1913* (Washington, D.C., 1920), 7, has the March 1913 statement.
56. Wilson to Count Johann Heinrich von Bernstorff, 16 Sept. 1914, in *Papers of Wilson*, ed. Link, 31: 35.
57. British Embassy to Sir Edward Grey, 14 Nov. 1913, in Ibid. 28: 543–44.
58. Quoted in Frederick Pike, *Chile and the United States, 1880–1962* (Notre Dame, Indiana, 1963), 144–45.
59. Bryan to Wilson, 20 July 1913, in *Papers of Wilson*, ed. Link, 28: 48; William Diamond, *The Economic Thought of Woodrow Wilson*, (Baltimore, 1943), 153; Bryan to Wilson, 12 June 1914, in *Papers of Wilson*, ed. Link, 30: 174–75; Selig Adler, "Bryan and Wilsonian Caribbean Penetration," *Hispanic American Historical Review* 20 (May 1940): 206–10.
60. Bryan to Wilson, 12 June 1914, in *Papers of Wilson*, ed. Link, 30: 174–75.
61. Karnes, *Failure of Union*, 200–2.
62. Diamond, *The Economic Thought of Wilson*, 154.
63. Rippy, *British Investment in Latin America*, 108; Mitchell A. Seligson, "Agrarian Policies in Dependent Societies: Costa Rica," *Journal of Interamerican Studies and World Affairs* 19 (May 1977): 212–30.
64. Ibid. 218–20, 222–24; McCann, *An American Company*, 15–30; John Findling, *Close Neighbors, Distant Friends* (Westport, CN, 1987), 46–48.
65. Ulrich Fanger, "Costa Rica," in *Latin America and the Caribbean, A Handbook*, ed. Claudio Veliz (N.Y., 1968), 176.
66. George W. Baker, Jr., "Woodrow Wilson's Use of the Non-Recognition Policy in Costa Rica," *The Americas* 22 (July 1965): 3–4.
67. The story is best told in *FRUS, 1919* (Washington, D.C., 1934), 1: 865, 870, 872–74, 876 on oil; 1: 847–61 on political affairs; and *FRUS, 1920* (Washington, D.C., 1935), 1: 833–42; also useful is Joseph S. Tulchin, *The Aftermath of War: World War I and U.S. Policy Toward Latin America* (N.Y., 1971), 136–40. An

important Costa Rican view of Tinoco (but little on the U.S.) is Carlos Monge Alfaro, *Historiá de Costa Rica* (San José, Costa Rica, 1960), 258–76. This popular textbook is also important for its discussion of the Esquivel presidency and its relationship to Costa Rican democracy, 232–36.

68. Quoted and analyzed in Herbert Feis, *Diplomacy of the Dollar . . . 1919–1932* (Baltimore, 1950), 29.

69. Karnes, *Failure of Union,* 223–24; Lester D. Langley, *The United States and the Caribbean, 1900–1970* (Athens, Ga., 1980), 106–7.

70. Kane, *Civil Strife in Latin America,* 129–30.

71. Quoted in Brenda Gayle Plummer, "Black and White in the Caribbean: Haitian-American Relations, 1902–1934," (Ph.D. diss., Cornell University, 1981), "Epilogue."

72. Pan American Union, *Foreign Trade of Latin America Since 1913,* esp. 37–48, 95–98, 123–40, 149–56, 169–72.

73. Ibid.

74. Robert W. Dunn, *American Foreign Investments* (N.Y., 1926), 107–18.

75. James A. Morris, and Steve C. Ropp, "Corporatism and Dependent Developments: A Honduran Case Study," *Latin American Research Review,* 12 (No. 2, 1977): 31–32; Langley, *U.S. and the Caribbean, 1900–1970,* 108–10.

76. Laurence Duggan, *The Americas; The Search for Hemisphere Security* (N.Y., 1949), 52.

77. Herbert Hoover, *American Individualism* (Washington, D.C., 1922), 31.

78. See the discussion in Dana C. Munro (a key U.S. official in Central America during the twenties), *The United States and the Caribbean Republics, 1921–1933* (Princeton, 1974), esp. "Introduction," and Chapter 11.

79. Quoted in Lloyd C. Gardner, *Economic Aspects of New Deal Diplomacy* (Madison, Wisc., 1964), 35–36.

80. Quoted in Munro, *U.S. and Caribbean Republics, 1921–1933,* 378.

81. Bryce Wood, *The Making of the Good Neighbor Policy* (N.Y., 1961), 14–15; Stuart and Tigner, *Latin America and the U.S.,* 511–12.

82. Raymond L. Buell, "Reconstruction in Nicaragua," *Foreign Policy Association Information Service,* 6 (12 Nov. 1930): 339–45; Wood, *Making of the Good Neighbor Policy,* 37.

83. Donald Dozer, *Are We Good Neighbors? . . . 1930–1960* (Gainesville, Fla., 1959), 11–12.

84. Wood, *Making of the Good Neighbor Policy,* 42–45.

85. Bernard Diederich, *Somoza and the Legacy of U.S. Involvement in Central America* (N.Y., 1981), 18–19; Wood, *Making of the Good Neighbor Policy,* 140–41. The classic account is now Neill Macaulay, *The Sandino Affair* (Chicago, 1967), especially for the Nicaraguan context.

86. Sacasa, Chamorro, Diaz to Hull, 30 Nov. 1936, *FRUS, 1936* (Washington, 1954), 5: 844–46; Somoza's background is well-discussed in Diederich, *Somoza,* 8–12.

87. Dozer, *Are We Good Neighbors?*, 50–51 has the quote.
88. Aubey, "Entrepreneurial Formation in El Salvador," 281. A good working definition of the term was given by an oligarch: "It's an oligarchy because these families own and run almost everything that makes money in El Salvador. Coffee gave birth to the oligarchy in the late 19th century, and economic growth has evolved around them ever since." Quoted in Paul H. Hoeffel, "The Eclipse of the Oligarchs," *New York Times Magazine*, 6 Sept. 1981, 23; Adolfo Gilly, *Guerra y politica en El Salvador* (Mexico, 1981), 29–31.
89. There is a superb account in Durham, *Scarcity and Survival*, 33–36, 40–43, 57–59.
90. Quoted in Kenneth J. Grieb, "The United States and the Rise of General Maximiliano Hernández Martínez," *Journal of Latin American Studies* 3 (November 1971): 152.
91. Wallace Thompson, *The Rainbow Countries of Central America* (N.Y., 1926), 106–8.
92. White, *El Salvador*, 96–97.
93. Ibid. 98, 101, 113–14; Thomas P. Anderson, *Matanza* (Lincoln, Neb., 1971); see also Stephen Kinzer, "Central America," in *Boston Globe Magazine*, 16 Aug. 1981, 38.
94. Secretary of State to the Minister in Guatemala, 9 Feb. 1932, *FRUS, 1932* (Washington, D.C., 1948), 5: 575.
95. Grieb, "U.S. and Rise of Martínez," 165–67.
96. Alfred Joachim Fischer, "Agrarian Policy in Central America," *Contemporary Review* 224 (April 1974): 187 has the quote.
97. A good discussion is in John D. Martz, "Guatemala: The Search for Political Identity," in *Political Systems of Latin America* ed. Martin C. Needler (Princeton, 1964), 38–45.
98. Kenneth J. Grieb, *Guatemalan Caudillo; The Regime of Jorge Ubico. . . .* (Athens, Ohio, 1979), 69–73, 180. This is an important work on Guatemalan development as well as Ubico's standard biography. Also see Ronald M. Schneider, *Communism in Guatemala, 1944–1954* (N.Y., 1959), 48–49; Feis, *Diplomacy of the Dollar*, 28; Tulchin, *Aftermath of War*, 143–46, 190–98.
99. The best analysis is Grieb, *Guatemalan Caudillo*, 2–21.
100. Piero Gleijeses, "La aldea de Ubico . . . ," *Mesoamérica*, 17 (junio de 1989), esp. 38–59. Schneider, *Communism in Guatemala*, 8–9; Grieb, *Guatemalan Caudillo*, 133–37, 282–83.
101. Edgar B. Nixon, ed., *Franklin D. Roosevelt and Foreign Affairs*, 3 vols. (Cambridge, Mass., 1969), 3: 315; Langley, *U.S. and Caribbean, 1900–1970*, 164–65; Alton Frye, *Nazi Germany and the American Hemisphere, 1931–1941* (New Haven, 1967), 67.
102. Grieb, *Guatemalan Caudillo*, 74–77, 148, 186–88, 236.
103. Wood, *Making of the Good Neighbor Policy*, 5.
104. Butler's quote is in Schmidt, *Maverick Marine*, 231; Dexter Perkins, *The Monroe Doctrine, 1867–1907* (Baltimore, 1937), 426.

105. Munro, *U.S. and Caribbean Republics, 1921–1933,* 378 has a good discussion with a different focus on the issue of the memorandum.
106. Memorandum, 10 Oct. 1941, Diary, Papers of Adolf Berle, Box 213, Franklin D. Roosevelt Presidential Library, Hyde Park, N.Y.; the broad context for the development of military dictators in the thirties is described in brief in Edwin Lieuwen, "The Latin American Military," in U.S. Congress, Senate Committee on Foreign Relations, *Survey of the Alliance for Progress,* 91st Cong., 1st sess., 94.
107. Frederick C. Adams, *Economic Diplomacy: The Export-Import Bank and American Foreign Policy, 1934–1939* (Columbia, Mo., 1976), 214–17.
108. A good discussion of the treaties' effects on Central America can be found in Dick Steward, *Trade and Hemisphere. The Good Neighbor Policy and Reciprocal Trade* (Columbia, Mo., 1975), 208–20.
109. Ernest May, "The Alliance for Progress in Historical Perspective," *Foreign Affairs* 41 (July 1963): 759–60.
110. Cordell Hull, *The Memoirs of Cordell Hull,* 2 vols. (N.Y., 1948), 1: 365.

CHAPTER II

1. Entry of 19 Aug. 1944, Morgenthau Presidential Diaries, Book no. 6, 1386–88, F. D. Roosevelt Library, Hyde Park, New York; Gardner, *Economic Aspects of New Deal Diplomacy,* 67–68.
2. The best account of the war's effect on the Good Neighbor policy is David Green, *The Containment of Latin America* (Chicago, 1971) especially chapters 2, 4; see also Dozer, *Are We Good Neighbors,* 70–77; and Irwin F. Gellman, *Good Neighbor Diplomacy . . . 1933–1945* (Baltimore, 1979), 166–70, which contains the Commerce Department official's quote.
3. Memorandum, 18 Oct. 1945, Box 4, Charles Bohlen Papers, National Archives, Washington, D. C. I am indebted to Professor Lloyd Gardner for calling my attention to this document.
4. Quoted in Green, *Containment of Latin America,* 38.
5. Edward G. Miller, Jr., "Economic Aspects of Inter-American Relations," *Department of State Bulletin* 23 (25 Dec. 1950): 1014; Duggan, *The Americas,* 123–26.
6. Pan American Union, *Foreign Trade of Latin America Since 1913,* especially the final set of tables.
7. Raymond Dennett and Robert K. Turner, eds., *Documents on American Foreign Relations* 8 (1945–1946), (Princeton, 1948): 607–8.
8. "Political Developments and Trends in the Other American Republics in the Twentieth Century," Office of Intelligence Research Report, No. 4780, 1 Oct. 1949, 5, National Archives, Record Group 59 (hereafter cited, NA, RG 59).
9. R. Harold Smith to J. Stanton Robbins, 19 July 1945, 611.1815/7–345, NA, RG 59.
10. James F. Schnable, *The Joint Chiefs of Staff and National Policy, 1945–1947* (Wil-

mington, 1979), chapter 8; F. Parkinson, *Latin America, Cold War, and World Powers, 1945–1973* (Beverly Hills, 1974), 11–12; Joint Chiefs of Staff, "Estimate of World Situation to 1957," 11 Dec. 1947, JSPC 814/3, *Declassified Documents Quarterly* (henceforth *DDQ*), 1975, 75B.

11. Memorandum on discussion between State and War-Navy, General File, Box 112, President's Secretary's File, Harry S. Truman Papers, Harry S. Truman Library, Independence, Missouri.

12. Edward G. Miller, Jr., "Nonintervention and Collective Responsibility in the Americas," *Department of State Bulletin* 23 (15 May 1950): 768–70.

13. Dean Acheson Oral History Interview, 18 Feb. 1955, Harry S. Truman Post-Presidential Papers, Truman Library.

14. U.S. Department of State, *Fortnightly Survey of American Opinion on International Affairs* (4 Sept. 1946), 2–3.

15. Will Clayton to Douglas H. Allen, 30 Nov. 1945, Chronological File, 1945, Will Clayton Papers, Truman Library.

16. "Political Developments and Trends . . . ," Office of Intelligence Research Report, No. 4780, 1 Oct. 1949, 3, NA, RG 59.

17. The Bogotá Charter and a useful introduction to the Economic Agreement is in Raymond Dennett and Robert K. Turner, eds., *Documents on Foreign Relations* 10 (1948): (Princeton, 1950), 484–532.

18. J. Fred Rippy, *Globe and Hemisphere* (Chicago, 1958), 75–76.

19. Enclosure in Secretary of State to Diplomatic Representatives in the American Republics, 21 June 1948; *FRUS, 1948,* 9: 193–201.

20. John Patrick Bell, *Crisis in Costa Rica: The 1948 Revolution* (Austin, Texas, 1971), 25.

21. The State Department understood these developments, e.g., "Political Developments and Trends . . . ," Office of Intelligence Research Report, No. 4780, 1 Oct. 1949, 1–2, NA, RG 59.

22. Bell, *Crisis in Costa Rica,* 19–27.

23. Charles Ameringer, *Don Pepe. . . .* (Albuquerque, N.M., 1978), 4–5.

24. Memorandum by Mr. William Tapley Bennett, Jr., of the Division of Central America and Panama Affairs, based on San José ambassador's dispatch, 26 March 1948, *FRUS, 1948,* 9: 502–3.

25. Bell, *Crisis in Costa Rica,* 150.

26. Davis to Secretary of State, 6 April 1948, *FRUS, 1948,* 9: 504–5; Memorandum of conversation, 13 April 1948, Ibid. 508–9.

27. See also Memorandum of telephone conversation, 22 March 1948, Ibid. 499–500; Ibid. 517–21, for the U.S. handling of Somoza's attempted invasion.

28. "Current U.S. Policy Toward Nicaragua," 27 Feb. 1946, R&A no. 3573, NA, RG 59; "Political Developments and Trends . . . ," Office of Intelligence Research Report, No. 4780, 1 Oct. 1949, 80, NA, RG 59; John Morton Blum, ed., *The Price of Vision: The Diary of Henry A. Wallace, 1942–1946* (Boston, 1973), 165–66. In

April 1954, Somoza again tried to take advantage of the growing U.S. concern over communism in Guatemala by alleging that Figueres's agents were planning to kill him. Again exiles tried to invade Costa Rica. This time the United States flew air force bombers into San José and fighter planes to the Canal Zone as warnings that Somoza should reconsider his plans. He did, and settled for challenging Figueres to a personal duel at the border. It was a comic opera act that the Costa Rican disdained.

29. Memorandum of Conversation, 27 May 1948, *FRUS, 1948*, 9: 167–68.

30. "Study Group Reports, Inter-American Affairs," 7 Feb. 1949, Record of Groups, Vol. XVI-D, Council on Foreign Relations, New York City. Jeane Kirkpatrick's essay was first published in *Commentary* 68 (Nov. 1979).

31. Willard F. Barber and G. Neale Ronning, *Internal Security and Military Power: Counterinsurgency and Civic Action in Latin America* (Columbus, Ohio, 1966), 36, 145.

32. James L. Busey, "Foundations of Political Contrast: Costa Rica and Nicaragua," *Western Political Quarterly* 11 (Sept. 1958): 640.

33. "The Probable Position of José Figueres with Respect to Costa Rica's Domestic and Foreign Policies," Office of Intelligence Research, Intelligence Report No. 6238, 21 Aug. 1953, NA, RG 59.

34. Mann to Charles S. Murphy, "Latin America and U.S. Policy," 11 Dec. 1952, *DDQ* (1977): 336B.

35. "Political Developments and Trends . . . ," Office of Intelligence Research Report, No. 4780, 1 Oct. 1949, 4–5, NA, RG 59; Central Intelligence Agency, "Review of World Situation," 17 Aug. 1949, *DDQ* (1977): 282A; Central Intelligence Agency, "Review of World Situation," 19 April 1950, *DDQ* (1977): 283D.

36. "2nd Regional Conference of U.S. Chiefs of Mission, Rio . . . 1950," Inter-American Economic Affairs Committee, 1945–1950, Box 5, National Archives, Record Group 353; An interesting later Latin American view of Kennan is in Robert Bardini, "Centroamerica," *Nueva Sociedad* 99 (Jan.–Feb., 1989), 13.

37. Edward G. Miller, Jr., "Economic Aspects of Inter-American Relations," *Department of State Bulletin* 23 (25 Dec. 1950): 1015.

38. Marshall to Acheson, 10 Jan. 1951, Annex to ISAC D-5, 13 Feb. 1951, *FRUS, 1951* (Washington, 1979): 2: 990–91; John M. Baines, "U.S. Military Assistance to Latin America: An Assessment," *Journal of Interamerican Studies and World Affairs* 14 (Nov. 1972): 471–72.

39. U.S. Congress, Senate Committee on Foreign Relations, *Nomination of John Foster Dulles . . .* , 83d Cong., 1st sess., 1953, 31.

40. Minutes of cabinet meeting, 3 July 1953, Dwight D. Eisenhower Library, Abilene, Kansas (microfilm), 2; American Assembly, *The U.S. and Latin America* (N.Y., 1959), 176, has the Dulles quote.

41. John J. Johnson, *The Military and Society in Latin America* (Stanford, 1964), 5.

42. Minutes of meeting of 12 Jan. 1953, Eisenhower Library (microfilm), b5–b6.

43. Blanche Weissen Cook's two important chapters, based on newly available

Guatemalan and State Department documents, in *The Declassified Eisenhower* (Garden City, N.Y., 1981); Richard Immerman, *The CIA in Guatemala* (Austin, Texas, 1982), important for the entire period of 1953 through 1961; Stephen Schlesinger and Stephen Kinzer, *Bitter Fruit: The Untold Story* . . . (N.Y., 1982), a detailed, well-told account.

44. "Political Developments and Trends . . . ," Office of Intelligence Research Report, No. 4780, 1 Oct. 1949, 59, NA, RG 59.

45. Ron Seckinger, "The Central American Militaries: A Survey of the Literature," *Latin American Research Review* 16 (No. 2, 1981): 249; Kenneth J. Grieb, *Guatemalan Caudillo; The Regime of Jorge Ubico.* . . . (Athens, Ohio, 1979), 284.

46. Ronald Schneider, *Communism in Guatemala* (N.Y., 1958), 18–21.

47. Memorandum from R. Wilson to Wise and Newbegin, 6 May 1948, 814.00B/5–648, NA, RG 59.

48. Richard H. Immerman, "Guatemala as Cold War History," *Political Science Quarterly* 95 (Winter, 1980–81): 633; Langley, *U.S. and the Caribbean, 1900–1970,* 206.

49. Mr. Wise to Mr. Barber and Mr. Miller, 1 Aug. 1949, 814.00/8–149, NA, RG 59; and Miller to Patterson, 27 July 1949, 814.5045/7–2749, NA, RG 59; the "duck test" is well analyzed in Immerman, *The CIA in Guatemala,* 102–3; Memorandum of conversation between Mann and Guatemalan ambassador, 24 March 1950, *DDQ* (1975): 179C; "Political Developments and Trends . . . ," Office of Intelligence Research Report, No. 4780, 1 Oct. 1949, 60, NA, RG 59.

50. U.S. Congress, Senate, *Executive Sessions of the Senate Foreign Relations Committee (Historical Series),* 8, Part 1, 82d Cong., 1st sess., 1951, 345; the Embassy statement is in Chargé to the Secretary of State, 15 Nov. 1950, *FRUS, 1950* (Washington, 1976), 922–25.

51. Notes of the Undersecretary's Meeting, 15 June 1951, *FRUS, 1951,* 2: 1440–43, 1445.

52. Mann is quoted in Cook, *Declassified Eisenhower,* 222.

53. Neale J. Pearson, "Guatemala: The Peasant Union Movement, 1944–1954," in *Latin American Peasant Movements* ed. Henry A. Landsberger (Ithaca, 1969), 324, 335; John A. Booth, "A Guatemalan Nightmare; Levels of Political Violence, 1966–1972," *Journal of Interamerican Studies and World Affairs* 22 (May 1980), 195–96.

54. Pearson, "Guatemala: The Peasant Union Movement," 338–41; Cook, *Declassified Eisenhower,* 224.

55. Ibid., 326–27, 344; *New York Times,* 5 Aug. 1960, 27.

56. Pearson, "Guatemala," 365–68.

57. "Agrarian Reform in Guatemala," Office of Intelligence Research, Intelligence Report No. 6001, 5 March 1953, NA, RG 59.

58. Dozer, *Are We Good Neighbors?,* 264.

59. McCann, *An American Company,* 139–40.

60. Stuart and Tigner, *Latin America and the United States,* 519–20; Cook, *Declassified Eisenhower,* 221–25.

61. This point is well analyzed in Ronald Radosh's review of Schlesinger and Kinzer, *Untold Story,* in *The New Republic,* 19 May 1982, 32–33. The "Disney" reference is in McCann, *An American Company,* 58–60, 177.

62. Immerman, "Guatemala as Cold War History," 638–39.

63. Cook, *Declassified Eisenhower,* 234.

64. Quoted in Ibid. 242–43.

65. Cabinet minutes, 14 May 1954, Eisenhower Library, (microfilm), 2.

66. The text is in C. Neale Ronning, *Intervention in Latin America* (N.Y., 1970), 76–78.

67. U.S. Congress, Senate Committee on Foreign Relations, *Statements of Secretary John Foster Dulles and Admiral Arthur Radford . . . ,* 83d Cong., 2d sess., March 9 and April 14, 1954, 18.

68. Cook, *Declassified Eisenhower,* 269–70.

69. "Guatemalan Support of Subversion and Communist Objectives (1950–1953)," Office of Intelligence Research, Intelligence Report No. 6185, 18–19, NA, RG 59.

70. Schneider, *Communism in Guatemala,* 44–49, 308.

71. The Toriello speech is in Ronning, *Intervention in Latin America,* 71–79.

72. Diederich, *Somoza,* 45.

73. For a good survey of the literature on this crucial point, see Seckinger, "The Central American Militaries," esp. 249; also Pearson, "Guatemala: The Peasant Union Movement," 369–70; Langley, *U.S. and the Caribbean, 1900–1970,* 209; Cook, *Declassified Eisenhower,* 263–64, 282–84.

74. Langley, *U.S. and the Caribbean,* 210.

75. Radio and television address, 30 June 1954, U.S. Department of State, *American Foreign Policy, 1950–1955. Basic Documents,* 2 vols. (Washington, 1957), 1: 1311–15; Immerman, *CIA in Guatemala,* 141 has the Peurifoy quote.

76. Pearson, "Guatemala: The Peasant Union Movement," 327.

77. David Graham, "Has Intervention in Guatemala Paid Off?" *The New Republic* (16 Sept. 1957): 9; Stuart and Tigner, *Latin America and the United States,* 522–23.

78. Congressional meeting at White House, 17 Nov. 1954, "Meetings with the President, 1954" (1), White House Memoranda Series, John Foster Dulles Papers, Eisenhower Library.

79. Cabinet minutes, 3 Dec. 1954, Eisenhower Library (microfilm), 4; Dozer, *Are We Good Neighbors?,* 369–70.

80. Cabinet minutes, 11 March 1955, Eisenhower Library (microfilm), 1–3; Ibid., 25 March 1955, 1.

81. U.S. Department of Commerce, *U.S. Business Investments in Foreign Countries* (Washington, D.C., 1960), esp. 91–92, 137.

82. Ronald James Clark, "Latin-American Economic Relations With the Soviet Bloc, 1954–1961," (Ph.D. diss., University of Indiana, 1963); Admiral Edwin T. Layton to JCS, "Sino-Soviet Bloc Thrust into Latin America," 7 Dec. 1955, *DDQ* (1980): 159C.

83. "Discussion at the 296th Meeting of the NSC," 6 Sept. 1956, Ann Whitman File, Eisenhower Library, 6 Sept. 1956, 3.

84. Ibid. 7–13.
85. Hugh B. Stinson and James D. Cochrane, "The Movement for Regional Arms Control in Latin America," *Journal of Interamerican Studies and World Affairs* 13 (Jan., 1971): 2.
86. U.S. Congress, Senate Special Committee to Study the Foreign Aid Program, *Foreign Aid Program: Compilation of Studies and Surveys,* 85th Cong., 1st sess., 1957, especially James Minotto, "Survey No. 9, Central America and the Caribbean Area," 1511–14, 1530–31.
87. "Discussion at the 299th Meeting of the NSC," Ann Whitman File, Eisenhower Library 4 Oct. 1956; Diederich, *Somoza,* 48.
88. Mitchell A. Seligson, "Agrarian Policies in Dependent Societies; Costa Rica," *Journal of Interamerican Studies and World Affairs* 19 (May 1977): 223; John P. Powelson, *Latin America. Today's Economic and Social Revolution* (N.Y., 1964), 155–56.
89. Duggan, *The Americas,* 27.
90. Albert F. Nufer to Robert A. Lovett, 17 Nov. 1948, 711.00/11–1748, NA, RG 59.
91. Charles W. Anderson, et al., *Issues of Political Development* (Englewood Cliffs, N.J., 1967), 158; Stuart and Tigner, *Latin America and the United States,* 529.
92. An especially useful analysis is Karnes, *Tropical Enterprise;* 279–81; James A. Morris and Steve C. Ropp, "Corporatism and Dependent Development: A Honduran Case Study," *Latin American Research Review,* 12 (No. 2, 1977): 42–43 is a superb brief account of the causes of the new Honduran pluralism.
93. Durham, *Scarcity and Survival,* 117–19, 126.
94. Guillermo Molino Chocano, "Dependencia y cambio social en la sociedad hondureña," *Estudios Sociales Centroamericanos* 1 (Enero–Abril, 1972): 17–19, especially; Senate Foreign Relations Committee, Subcommittee on American Republic Affairs, Executive Session, "Briefing on the Cuban Situation," 15 May 1961, 92–93, Legislative Division, National Archives, Record Group 46.
95. Graham, "Has Intervention in Guatemala Paid Off?," 9.
96. U.S. Congress, *Foreign Aid Program* (1957), 1537; *New York Times,* 6 Sept. 1959, sec. 3, 7.
97. *Time,* 16 Feb. 1959, 40–42.
98. Robert M. Macy, Summary Report of Latin America Trip, Bureau of the Budget, Jan.–Feb. 1955, *DDQ* (1980): 338A.
99. "Political Change and Probable Trends in Guatemala," 1 April 1958, Office of Intelligence Research, Intelligence Report No. 7680, NA, RG 59.
100. *New York Times,* 1 Nov. 1959, 12; Ibid. 27 Sept. 1959, 23; Ibid. 20 July 1960, 5; Schneider, *Communism in Guatemala,* 321.
101. John Gillin and K. H. Silvert, "Ambiguities in Guatemala," *Foreign Affairs* 24 (April 1956): 482.
102. Minutes of cabinet meeting, 16 May 1958, Eisenhower Library (microfilm), 1–2; U.S. Congress, Senate, *Executive Sessions of the Senate Foreign Relations Committee (Historical Series),* 85th Cong., 2nd sess., 10: 201.
103. Milton Eisenhower, *The Wine is Bitter* (Garden City, N.Y., 1963), 206–44, 229–30.

The state of U.S.-Central American relations can perhaps best be gleaned from Milton Eisenhower's account of the end of the trip: "My associates and I were completely worn out. Our nerves were shot from tension, anticipating Nixon-like incidents. So when we were well in the air [after leaving Guatemala, the last stop], we all burst into hearty cheering, and had a few drinks, and sat back to breathe." Ibid. 221.

104. The most recent and well-researched account is Burton I. Kaufman, *Trade and Aid: Eisenhower's Foreign Economic Policy, 1953–1961* (Baltimore, 1982), especially 161–65 on Latin American policy; also Harold G. Vatter, *The U.S. Economy in the 1950s* (N.Y., 1963), a small classic, 19–20, 259–64; Rendigs Fels, *Challenge to the American Economy* (Boston, 1961), 453; Walt Whitman Rostow, *The Diffusion of Power, 1957–1972* (N.Y., 1972) 61–62, notes the change in the auto industry.

105. Fels, *Challenge to the American Economy,* chapter I; the Dulles quotes are from *Department of State Bulletin* 38 (3 March 1958), and Ibid. 40 (14 Dec. 1959): esp. 874; John Foster Dulles is quoted in *Washington Post,* 28 July 1974, A7.

106. For another view, see the useful analysis by Benjamin Rowland, "Economic Policy and Development: The Case of Latin America," in *Retreat from Empire? The First Nixon Administration* ed. Robert Osgood (Baltimore, 1973), 241–77, esp. 249.

107. Kaufman, *Trade and Aid,* 164–66. Milton Eisenhower, *The Wine is Bitter,* 230 notes the advantages of attaching conditions to loans through the IADB.

108. "Comments on Interamerican Economic Problems," a paper for the cabinet, 27 Feb. 1959, Cabinet Meetings of President Eisenhower, Eisenhower Library, (microfilm).

109. Senate Foreign Relations Committee, Executive Session Manuscripts, 18 Feb. 1960, "Cuban and Caribbean Affairs," 17–21, Legislative Division, National Archives, Record Group 46.

110. *Department of State Bulletin* 43 (1 Aug. 1960): 170–171.

111. Minutes of cabinet meeting, 6 Nov. 1959, Eisenhower Library, (microfilm), 2.

CHAPTER III

1. U.S. Congress, Senate Committee on Foreign Relations, *Interamerican Development Bank Fund for Special Operations,* 92d Cong., 1st sess., 1971, 55–56; Bruck essay in *Latin American-U.S. Economic Interactions: Conflict, Accommodation, and Policies for the Future* eds. Robert B. Williamson et al. (Washington, 1974), 172, 174; for per capita figures, see Raymond F. Mikesell, "Inflation in Latin America," in U.S. Congress, Senate Committee on Foreign Relations, *Survey of the Alliance for Progress* 91st Cong., 1st sess., 45.

2. *Public Papers of the Presidents . . . John F. Kennedy . . . 1961* (Washington, 1962), 175.

3. U.S. Congress, Senate Committee on Foreign Relations, Executive Session, 28 Feb. 1961, "Briefing by . . . Rusk," 6–10, NA, RG 46.

4. Arthur M. Schlesinger, Jr., *A Thousand Days. John F. Kennedy in the White House* (Boston, 1965), 790.

5. U.S. Congress, Senate Committee on Foreign Relations, Executive Session, 2 May 1961, "Briefing on the Cuban Situation," 58–59, NA, RG 46.

6. Ibid. 1 May 1961, 9–10; Secretary of State to all ARA diplomatic posts, 30 Aug. 1963, John F. Kennedy Library, copies in author's possession; the Dulles remark is in U.S. Congress, Senate Committee on Foreign Relations, Executive Session, 2 May 1961, "Briefing on the Cuban Situation," 4, NA, RG 46.

7. Gordon Chase to McGeorge Bundy, 24 July 1963, NSC, Countries, Cuba, General, Box 39, Kennedy Library.

8. Robert Kennedy to the President, 11 Sept. 1961, NSC files, Meetings and Memoranda, NSAM 88, "Training for Latin American Armed Forces," Kennedy Library.

9. John M. Baines, "U.S. Military Assistance to Latin America: An Assessment," *Journal of Interamerican Studies and World Affairs* 14 (Nov. 1972): 481.

10. Ibid. 474–75; Edwin Lieuwen, "The Latin American Military," in U.S. Congress, Senate Committee on Foreign Relations, *Survey of the Alliance for Progress*, 91st Cong., 1st sess., (1969), 115, is an especially useful contemporary critique; Alfred Stepan, "The New Professionalism of Internal Warfare and Military Role Expansion," in *Armies and Politics in Latin America* ed. Abraham F. Lowenthal (N.Y., 1976), 248; James Petras, "Revolution and Guerrilla Movements in Latin America . . . Guatemala," in *Latin America: Reform or Revolution* eds. James Petras and M. Zeitlin (N.Y., 1968), 350–51; Arthur Schlesinger, Jr., "The Alliance for Progress," *Latin America, The Search . . .* eds. R.C. Hellman and H.J. Rosenblum (N.Y., 1975), 74–75; Etchison, *Militarism in Central America,* 64–66. A good discussion of civic action in Central America is in Willard F. Barber and C. Neale Ronning, *Internal Security and Military Power* (Columbus, Ohio, 1966), 130–34.

11. Lieuwen, "The Latin American Military," in *Survey of the Alliance for Progress*, 95–98; Etchison, *Militarism in Central America,* 107; Benjamin M. Rowland, "Economic Policy and Development: The Case of Latin America," in *Retreat From Empire? The First Nixon Administration* ed. Robert Osgood (Baltimore, 1973), 258, quotes the Mexican ambassador.

12. Quoted in Cynthia Arnson, *El Salvador; A Revolution Confronts the United States* (Washington, 1982), 19; Theodore Sorensen, *Kennedy* (N.Y., 1965), 535–36.

13. James D. Cochrane, "U.S. Policy Towards Recognition of Governments . . . Since 1963," *Journal of Latin American Studies* 4 (Nov. 1972): 276, footnote; Schlesinger, *Thousand Days,* 768.

14. Sorensen, *Kennedy,* 535.

15. C. T. Goodsell, "Diplomatic Protection of U.S. Business in Peru," in *U.S. Foreign Policy and Peru* ed. D. A. Sharp (Austin, 1972), 247.

16. A discussion of AID support for U.S. firms and exports is in Penny Lernoux, *Cry of the People . . .* (N.Y., 1980), 206–9.

17. U.S. Congress, Executive Session, 2 May 1961, "Briefing on the Cuban Situation," 82–83, NA, RG 46.

18. See, for example, Robert T. Aubey, "Private Sector Capital Mobilization and Industrialization in Latin America," *Journal of Interamerican Studies and World Affairs* 12 (Oct. 1970): 588.

19. *New York Times,* 7 April 1963, 24.

20. *Public Papers of the Presidents . . . John F. Kennedy . . . 1962* (Washington, 1963), 223.

21. Oral History Interview, Thomas Mann, 9, John F. Kennedy Library.

22. Central Intelligence Agency, "Survey of Latin America," 1 April 1964, enclosed in Cline to Bundy, 17 April 1964, NSC Country File, Latin America, Container no. 1, Lyndon B. Johnson Library.

23. Oral History Interview, Harry McPherson, Tape no. 4, 13, Lyndon B. Johnson Library.

24. CIA, "Survey of Latin America," 1 April 1964, LBJ Library.

25. Ibid.

26. A good discussion is in Robert A. Packenham, *Liberal America and the Third World* (Princeton, 1973), 95–96; and Samuel Baily, *U.S. and South America* (N.Y., 1975), 106; see also McNamara to Bundy, 11 June 1965, enclosures, NSC Country File, Latin America, LBJ Library.

27. *New York Times,* 3 May 1965, 10 has the text of Johnson's speech.

28. Ibid. 9 May 1965, 13; Philip Geyelin, *Lyndon B. Johnson and the World* (N.Y., 1966), 254.

29. J. I. Dominguez, "United States and Its Regional Security Interests: The Caribbean, Central, and South America," *Daedalus,* 109 (Fall 1980): 116.

30. "Agenda for OAS Summit Meeting," 26 Feb. 1967, OAS Summit file, Box 3, George Christian Papers, LBJ Library.

31. Lyndon B. Johnson, *The Vantage Point . . . 1963–1969* (N.Y., 1971), 350–51.

32. *Department of State Bulletin,* 19 Feb. 1968, 230; an excellent and key study of the Alliance's problems is Robert G. Williams, *Export Agriculture and the Crisis in Central America* (Chapel Hill, 1986).

33. U.S. Cong., Senate Committee on Foreign Relations, *Latin American Summit Conference* 90th Cong., 1st sess., 1967, 126–27.

34. *New York Times,* 10 May 1966, 1.

35. Busey, "Foundations of Political Contrast: Costa Rica and Nicaragua," 642; Langley, *U.S. and Caribbean, 1900–1970,* 203; Harvey K. Meyer, *Historical Dictionary of Nicaragua* (Metuchan, N.J., 1972), 425–426.

36. Ryan, ed., *Area Handbook for Nicaragua,* 78–82.

37. Ibid. 308; CIA, "Survey of Latin America," 1 April 1964, LBJ Library; Table in Williamson, ed., *Latin American-U.S. Economic Interactions,* 174.

38. Peter Dorner and Rodolfo Quiros, "Institutional Dualism in Central America's Agricultural Development," *Journal of Latin American Studies* 5 (Nov. 1973): 226–29; Ryan, ed., *Area Handbook for Nicaragua,* 295–97.

39. Etchison, *Militarism in Central America,* 37.

40. Lieuwen, "The Latin American Military," 125; CIA, "Survey of Latin America," 1 April 1964, LBJ Library; David C. Burks, "Insurgency in Latin America," in U.S. Congress, Senate Committee on Foreign Relations, *Survey of the Alliance for Progress* 91st Cong., 1st sess., (1969), 233; Etchison, *Militarism is Central America*, 105–6.
41. *New York Times*, 28 Feb. 1960, 35.
42. Oral History Interview, John Muccio, 3–6, John F. Kennedy Library.
43. Richard N. Adams, "The Development of the Guatemalan Military," *Studies in Comparative International Development* 4 (1968–1969): 103; Etchison, *Militarism in Central America*, 13.
44. U.S. Congress, Senate Committee on Foreign Relations, *Guatemala and Dominican Republic . . . 30 Dec. 1971* (Washington, 1971).
45. John R. Hildebrand, "Latin-American Economic Development, Land Reform, and U.S. Aid with Special Reference to Guatemala," *Journal of Interamerican Studies* 4 (July 1962): 357–59, has the quotation and statistics.
46. Senate, *Guatemala and the Dominican Republic*, 5.
47. Roger Plant, *Guatemala, Unnatural Disaster* (London, 1978), 74–75; Pearson, "Guatemala," 371–72; *New York Times*, 15 Oct. 1966, 8.
48. "Statement of David D. Burks," 1 March 1968, U.S. Congress, Senate Committee on Foreign Relations, *Survey of the Alliance for Progress*, 413. José A. Villamil, "Situación demográfica de Guatemala y sus efectos socio-económicos," *Journal of Interamerican Studies and World Affairs* 13 (April 1971): 212–13.
49. Constantine V. Vaitsos, "The Changing Policies of Latin American Governments Toward Economic Development and Direct Foreign Investments," in *Latin American-U.S. Economic Interactions*, Robert B. Williamson, et al. (Washington, 1974), 105.
50. John P. Powelson, *Latin America; Today's Economic and Social Revolution* (N.Y., 1964), 83.
51. Stuart and Tigner, *Latin America and U.S.*, 525–26.
52. Burks, "Insurgency in Latin America," 225; Petras, "Revolution and Guerrilla Movements . . . Guatemala," 331–33, 364–65.
53. Burks, "Insurgency in Latin America," 224; John A. Booth, "A Guatemalan Nightmare; Levels of Political Violence, 1966–1972," *Journal of Interamerican Studies and World Affairs* 22 (May 1980): 210.
54. Adams, "Development of the Guatemalan Military," 102–6; Brian Jenkins and Caesar D. Sereseres, "U.S. Military Assistance and the Guatemalan Armed Forces," *Armed Forces and Society* 3 (Summer 1977): 576–82, 588; Jerry L. Weaver, "Political Style of the Guatemalan Military Elite," *Studies in Comparative International Development* 5 (1969–1970): 78–79. These are three most important surveys.
55. Stuart and Tigner, *Latin America and U.S.*, 527; Lernoux, *Cry of the People*, 186.
56. Henry Ginger, "Guatemala is a Battleground," *New York Times Magazine*, 16 June 1968, 14.

57. Differing views of the Maryknoll episode are in "Violence," *The Nation*, 4 March 1968, 290–92; F. X. Gannon, "Catholicism, Revolution, and Violence in Latin America," *Orbis* 12 (Winter 1969): 1204–25.

58. David F. Ross, "Death in Guatemala," *The New Republic*, 21 Sept. 1968, 14; the Fuentes Mohr quote is in Ginger, "Guatemala is a Battleground," 22.

59. CIA, "Survey of Latin America," 1 April 1964.

60. Senate, *Guatemala and Dominican Republic*, 1–7 has a good analysis.

61. CIA, "Survey of Latin America," 1 April 1964.

62. Lieuwen, "Latin American Military," 99–100.

63. Ronald H. McDonald, "Electoral Behavior and Political Development in El Salvador," *Journal of Politics* 31 (May 1969): 402–5; John Gerassi, *The Great Fear . . .* (N.Y., 1963), 160–61; Tommie Sue Montgomery, *Revolution in El Salvador* (Boulder, 1982), 71–75, a fine analysis.

64. Quoted in Stuart and Tigner, *Latin America and U.S.*, 530–31; Arnson, *El Salvador*, 20.

65. Speech of Murat Williams (U.S. Ambassador, Ret.), reprinted in 16 Nov. 1981, *Congressional Record*, 97th Cong., 1st sess.; Etchison, *Militarism in Central America*, 54, recounts the television episode; on redistribution of wealth, see letter of Joseph P. Mooney to the Editor, *Foreign Affairs* 59 (Fall 1980): 182.

66. Aubey, "Private Sector Capital Mobilization," 586–88; Robert T. Aubey, "Entrepreneurial Formation in El Salvador," *Explorations in Entrepreneurial History* 6 (Spring 1969): 272–73.

67. CIA, "Survey of Latin America," 1 April 1964.

68. A superb account is Durham, *Scarcity and Survival in Central America*, 30–35, 44; Dorner and Quiros, "Institutional Dualism in Central America," 231–32; Robert C. West and John P. Augelli, *Middle America: Its Lands and Peoples* (Englewood Cliffs, N.J., 1966), 407, 410.

69. Durham, *Scarcity and Survival*, 1–2; Edelberto Torres-Rivas, *Repression and Resistance* (Boulder, Co., 1989), 35–36.

70. Quoted in Alfred Joachim Fischer, "Agrarian Policy in Central America," *Contemporary Review* 224 (April 1974): 182.

71. CIA, "Survey of Latin America," 1 April 1964.

72. Alan Riding in *New York Times*, 11 March 1981, A2.

73. Letter from Murat W. Williams to Editor, *New York Times*, 22 July 1969; U.S. Congress, Senate Committee on Foreign Relations, *U.S. Military Policies and Programs in Latin America. . . .* 91st Cong., 1st sess., (1969), 76; Johnson, *Military and Society in Latin America*, 107.

74. Gerassi, *The Great Fear*, 158–59; Guillermo Molina Chocano, "Dependencia y cambio social en la sociedad hondureña," *Estudios Sociales Centroamericanos* 1 (Enero-Abril 1972): esp. 11–19.

75. Oral History Interview, Charles R. Burrows, John F. Kennedy Library, 8–9.

76. Ibid. 14–17.

77. Ibid. 49.
78. H. I. Blutstein, et al., *Area Handbook for Honduras* (Washington, 1971), 121.
79. Oral History Interview, Charles R. Burrows, 45–46.
80. Schlesinger, *Thousand Days*, 1001.
81. Oral History Interview, Charles R. Burrows, 35.
82. This discussion is based on the superb analysis in Steve C. Ropp, "The Honduran Army in the Socio-Political Evolution of the Honduran State," *The Americas* 30 (April 1974): 504–28.
83. The text of the agreement is in Gerassi, *The Great Fear*, 413–14.
84. Etchison, *Militarism in Central America*, 21–22.
85. Figures are from the table in the Bruck essay in Williamson, *Latin American-U.S. Economic Interactions*, 174; Blutstein, *Area Handbook for Honduras*, 167–68.
86. David Rockefeller, "What Private Enterprise Means to Latin America," *Foreign Affairs* 44 (April 1966): 408.
87. Oral History Interview, Charles R. Burrows, 18.
88. Durham, *Scarcity and Survival*, 122; Tom Barry et al., *Dollars and Dictators, A Guide to Central America* (Albuquerque, N.M., 1982), 105.
89. Blutstein, *Area Handbook for Honduras*, 155. Durham, *Scarcity and Survival* is the best analysis of the 1969 crisis.
90. Molina Chocano, "Dependencia y cambio social en la sociedad hondureña," 12–16.
91. Daniel Goldrich, *Sons of the Establishment: Elite Youth in Panama and Costa Rica* (Chicago, 1966), 54–55, 56.
92. Secretary of State to Tolles, in Costa Rica, 30 Dec. 1961, NSC Files, Countries, Costa Rica, Box 35, John F. Kennedy Library. JFK speech incident is in Memorandum for the President from Rusk, 15 April 1961, NSC, Countries, Costa Rica, Box 35, John F. Kennedy Library.
93. U.S. Congress, Senate Committee on Foreign Relations, *Latin American Summit Conference*, 90th Cong., 1st sess., 17 and 21 March 1967, 111.
94. Kennedy to Robert L. Searle, Mayor of Coral Gables, Florida, undated, but probably 23 March 1962, NSC Files, Countries, Costa Rica, Box 35, John F. Kennedy Library.
95. Dorner and Quiros, "Institutional Dualism in Central America," 227; West and Augelli, *Middle America*, 444.
96. The quotation is from Charles F. Denton and Preston Lee Lawrence, *Latin American Politics; A Functional Approach* (San Francisco, 1972), 138; the agricultural sector is well analyzed in Mitchell A. Seligson, "Agrarian Policies in Dependent Societies: Costa Rica," *Journal of Interamerican Studies and World Affairs* 19 (May 1977): 212–30.
97. Gary W. Wynia, *Politics and Planners: Economic Development Policy in Central America* (Madison, Wisc., 1972), 100–3.
98. Dwight B. Heath, "Costa Rica and Her Neighbors," *Current History* 58 (Feb. 1970): 96–99.

99. The background is briefly and well discussed in W. Andrew Axline, "Latin American Regional Integration: Alternative Perspectives on a Changing Reality," *Latin American Research Review* 16 (1981): 167–86.
100. James D. Theberge and Roger W. Fontaine, *Latin America: Struggle for Progress.* . . . (Lexington, Mass., 1977), 50–51, 53.
101. Durham, *Scarcity and Survival*, 1–2; William R. Cline and Enrique Delgado, eds., *Economic Integration in Central America* (Washington, 1978), 394; Gary W. Wynia, "Central American Integration: The Paradox of Success," *International Organization* 24 (Spring 1970): 324–25.
102. Miguel S. Wionczek has written two important essays from which this discussion is drawn: "U.S. Investment and the Development of Middle America," *Studies in Comparative International Development* 5 (1969–1970): 4–5 that has the percentages; and "Latin American Integration and U.S. Economic Policies," in *International Organization in the Western Hemisphere* ed. Robert W. Gregg (Syracuse, 1968), 129–30; also Cline and Delgado, *Economic Integration in Central America*, 409.
103. Wionczek, "U.S. Investment and the Development of Middle America," 8–11; Wionczek, "Latin American Integration and U.S. Economic Policies," 126–31; Cline and Delgado, *Economic Integration in Central America*, 396.
104. Wionczek, "Latin American Integration and U.S. Economic Policies," 104–5.
105. Cline and Delgado, *Economic Integration in Central America*, 396–99; for a good study of El Salvador in this context, see Gerald E. Karush, "Plantations, Population, and Poverty. . . ." *Studies in Comparative International Development* 13 (Fall 1978): 69.
106. Wynia, "Central American Integration," 325–30.
107. Cline and Delgado, *Economic Integration in Central America*, 410; Wionczek, "Latin American Integration," 91–92.
108. "Statement of Prof. Ernest Halperin," in U.S. Congress, Senate Committee on Foreign Relations, *Survey of the Alliance for Progress*, 1 March 1968, 417.
109. A good analysis is David Green, "Paternalism and Profits: The Ideology of U.S. Aid to Latin America, 1943–1971," in *Historical Papers, 1972*, ed. J. Atherton (Ottawa, 1973), 351.
110. The Strasma essay in Sharp, *United States Foreign Policy in Peru*, 164–66, tells this story.
111. *New York Times*, 24 Feb. 1967, 2 has an account of Rostow's speech; for a good discussion of the "stages of growth" theory in Latin American policy, see Rowland, "Economic Policy and Development," 250–51.
112. See Rollie E. Poppino, *International Communism in Latin America* (London, 1964), 16.
113. "Statement of Richard N. Adams," in U.S. Congress, Senate Committee on Foreign Relations, *Survey of the Alliance for Progress*, 448–49.
114. Eduardo Frei Montalva, "The Second Latin American Revolution," *Foreign Affairs* 50 (Oct. 1971): 87.

CHAPTER IV

1. Diederich, *Somoza*, 56.
2. R. Judson Mitchell and Robert H. Donaldson, "USSR," *Yearbook on International Communist Affairs, 1973* (Stanford, 1974), 95; the Theberge essay in *Latin America's New Internationalism* eds. Roger W. Fontaine and James D. Theberge (N.Y. 1976), 158; Herbert Dinerstein, "Soviet Policy in Latin America," *American Political Science Review* 61 (March 1967): 80–90.
3. U.S. Congress, Senate Committee on Foreign Relations, *U.S. Military Policies and Programs in Latin America. Hearings. . . .* 91st Cong., 1st sess., 57–59; Jiri Valenta, "The USSR, Cuba, and the Crisis in Central America," *Orbis* 25 (Fall 1981): 718.
4. U.S. Congress, House Committee on Foreign Affairs, *Governor Rockefeller's Report on Latin America* 91st Cong., 1st sess., (1970), 16, 44.
5. Ibid. 10–12; Lernoux, *Cry of the People*, 164.
6. Nixon's speech is in "Appendix" of House, *Rockefeller Report; Latin America Digest* 4 (Nov. 1969): 9.
7. J. I. Dominguez, "U.S. and Its Regional Security Interests . . . ," *Daedalus* 109 (Fall 1980): 126; Etchison, *U.S. and Militarism*, 99–100, 109–10; on the MAP rate, see Francis P. Kessler, "Kissinger's Legacy: A Latin American Policy," *Current History* 72 (Feb. 1977): 77–78.
8. Lernoux, *Cry of the People*, 69.
9. Etchison, *U.S. and Militarism*, 67–68.
10. The earliest and still a significant account is James Petras and Morris Morley, *U.S. and Chile* (N.Y., 1975).
11. James H. Street, "The Internal Frontier and Technological Progress in Latin America," *Latin American Research Review* 12 (1977): 28–29; William Bowdler, "Latin America and the Caribbean," in U.S. Department of State, *Current Policy*, 16 April 1980, No. 166.
12. Alan Riding in *New York Times*, 1 Feb. 1982, A6.
13. Shoshana B. Tancer, *Economic Nationalism in Latin America* (N.Y., 1976), 213–14; *Latin America* 8 (12 July 1974), 213–14; McCann, *American Company*, 215–17, 232–34; Barry, *Dollars and Dictators*, 18–19.
14. John S. Odell, "Latin American Trade Negotiations with the United States," *International Organization* 34 (Spring 1980): 228; Bowdler, "Latin America and the Caribbean;" Vaky testimony in House, *Central America at the Crossroads*, 20.
15. Alexis de Tocqueville, *Democracy in America*, 2 vols., trans. Henry Reeve (Cambridge, Mass., 1862), 2: 308–23.
16. For Brzezinski's earlier view of Latin America, see his *Between Two Ages* (N.Y., 1970), 288.
17. The administration's view is briefly and usefully presented in U.S. Department of State, "U.S.-Cuban Relations," *GIST,* November 1979.

18. *Public Papers of the Presidents . . . Carter . . . 1977* (Washington, 1978), 1: 3, 958.
19. A most recent and excellent analysis is Lars Schoultz, *Human Rights and U.S. Policy Towards Latin America* (Princeton, 1981); Sandy Vogelgesang, *American Dream, Global Nightmare* (N.Y., 1980) is important on El Salvador; see especially U.S. Congress, Senate Committee on Foreign Relations, *Human Rights and U.S. Foreign Assistance . . . , (1977–78)* 96th Cong., 1st sess., 105–6.
20. Richard Cooper, "North-South Dialogue," in U.S. Department of State, *Current Policy*, 15 May 1980, No. 182.
21. Pat M. Holt testimony in Senate, *Survey of the Alliance for Progress*, 14–24. Two useful essays are Olga Pellicer de Brody and Bruce M. Bagley in *Mexican-American Relations* ed. Susan Kaufman Purcell (N.Y., 1981); and Susan Kaufman Purcell, "Mexico-U.S. Relations . . . ," *Foreign Affairs* 60 (Winter 1981/82): 379–92.
22. Wolf Grabendorff, "Mexico's Foreign Policy. . . ." *Journal of Interamerican Studies* 20 (Feb. 1978): 86–90.
23. George W. Grayson, "Oil and U.S.-Mexican Relations," Ibid. 21 (Nov. 1979): 427–30.
24. Viron P. Vaky, "Hemispheric Relations . . . ," *Foreign Affairs* 69 (No. 3): 634; Robert D. Bond, "Regionalism in Latin America . . . ," *International Organization* 32 (Spring 1978): 417–23.
25. Alan Riding in *New York Times*, 8 May 1981, 46.
26. Purcell, "Mexico-U.S. Relations," 380–82, 388–90; Grayson, "Oil and U.S.-Mexican Relations," 445–50.
27. Sheldon Liss, *Diplomacy and Dependency: Venezuela, the U.S. . . .* (Salisbury, N.C., 1978), 204–5, 207–8.
28. William Smith in *New York Times*, 27 Oct. 1973, 41; Taylor essay in *Latin America's New Internationalism*, eds., Fontaine and Theberge, 151.
29. Ibid. 177; this Cuban problem went back to the sixties: Memorandum for DeVier Pierson from W. G. Bowdler, 24 July 1968, White House, Confidential File, Box 8, LBJ Library.
30. Taylor essay in *Latin America's New Internationalism*, eds., Fontaine and Theberge, 179; James A. Morris and Steve C. Ropp, "Corporatism and Dependent Development: A Honduran Case Study," *Latin American Research Review* 12 (1977): 64.
31. An overview is in J.I. Dominguez, "Mice that Do Not Roar . . . ," *International Organization* 27 (Spring 1971): 175–208.
32. Michael Dodson, "The Christian Left in Latin American Politics," *Journal of Interamerican Studies* 21 (Feb. 1979): 52–54.
33. Levine essay in *Churches and Politics in Latin America* ed. Daniel H. Levine (Beverly Hills, Calif., 1980), 21–24.
34. Charles F. Denton and Preston Lee Lawrence, *Latin American Politics . . .* (San Francisco, 1972), 146–47.
35. Quoted by Poblete in *Churches and Politics*, 46, and also see 24–25, 29–30.
36. Marcos G. McGrath, "Ariel or Caliban?" *Foreign Affairs* 52 (Oct. 1973): 86.
37. Eldon Kenworthy, "Reagan Rediscovers Monroe," *democracy* 2 (July 1982): 88–89.

38. *Latin American Digest* 4 (Jan. 1970): 3; Lernoux, *Cry of the People*, 65.
39. Durham, *Scarcity and Survival*, 167; Lernoux, *Cry of the People*, 75–76.
40. Berryman essay in *Churches and Politics*, 57.
41. Ibid. 66–67, 68–69, 73–78.
42. Alan Riding, "Sword and Cross," *New York Review of Books*, 28 May 1981, 6, 8; Alma Guillermoprieto in *Washington Post*, 10 June 1981, A24; Lernoux, *Cry of the People*, 101.
43. Arnson, *El Salvador*, 64–67.
44. Clifford Krauss, "Their Bible is the Bible," *The Nation*, 3 July 1982, 7.
45. Lernoux, *Cry of the People*, 13.
46. Raymond Bonner in *New York Times*, 18 July 1982, 3 has the quote.
47. Diederich, *Somoza*, 88–89.
48. Quoted in Etchison, *U.S. and Militarism*, 41.
49. Plant, *Guatemala*, 78; *Central America Report* 8 (21 April 1980): 114.
50. The banker is Arturo Cruz, quoted by Warren Hoge in *New York Times*, 26 July 1979, A3; Diederich, *Somoza*, 115.
51. *Wall Street Journal*, 13 August 1970, 21; Ibid. 10 Feb. 1972, 6.
52. Diederich, *Somoza*, 88–89.
53. Ibid. 97–100.
54. Duncan testimony in House, *Central America at the Crossroads*, 52–53; important background is in Edelberto Torres-Rivas, *Repression and Resistance* (Boulder, CO., 1989), 125–31.
55. A good overview is in Dwight B. Heath, "Current Trends in Central America," *Current History* 68 (Jan. 1975): 29–35; Etchison, *U.S. and Militarism*, 40; and see especially Richard L. Millett, *Guardians of the Dynasty* (Maryknoll, N.Y., 1977), 253.
56. Diederich, *Somoza*, 106–14.
57. Ibid. 119, 120–24.
58. Ibid. 125, 130–31.
59. Ibid. 148–51.
60. The best-known attack on Carter is Jeane J. Kirkpatrick's, reprinted in her *Dictatorships and Double Standards* (N.Y., 1982), 23–52.
61. Thomas W. Walker, "The Sandinist Victory in Nicaragua," *Current History* 78 (Feb. 1980): 58; *New York Times*, 19 Feb. 1978, 1; *Washington Post*, 4 March 1978, A14; Karl Berman, *Under the Big Stick* (Boston, 1986), 262.
62. Thomas Walker, *Nicaragua: Land of Sandino* (Boulder, Colo., 1981), 109–10; Lernoux, *Cry of the People*, 104–6.
63. *New York Times*, 30 July 1978, VI: 12; *Washington Post*, 3 Aug. 1978, A22.
64. *Washington Post*, 1 Aug. 1978, 6; Diederich, *Somoza*, 172.
65. Organization of American States, Inter-American Commission on Human Rights, *Report on the Situation of Human Rights in Nicaragua* (Washington, 1978); Lernoux, *Cry of the People*, 98–99.
66. Quoted in Diederich, *Somoza*, 236.

67. Ibid. 216, 229–30; Arnold Levinson, "Nicaraguan Showdown," *Inquiry*, 11 and 25 June 1979, 13.

68. Richard R. Fagen, "Dateline Nicaragua: The End of the Affair," *Foreign Policy* (Fall 1979): 178–91.

69. Quoted in Dominguez, "U.S. and Its Regional Security Interests," 116; Merilee Grindle, "Armed Intervention and U.S.-Latin American Relations," *Latin American Research Review* 16 (1981): 207–17.

70. Alan Riding in *New York Times*, 21 May 1981, A3; Diederich, *Somoza*, 282–83; Levinson, "Nicaraguan Showdown," 14; Berman, *Under the Big Stick*, 271.

71. Alan Riding in *New York Times*, 10 July 1979, A3.

72. Ibid. 15 July 1979, 1.

73. Diederich, *Somoza*, 296–98; Warren Hoge in *New York Times*, 12 July 1979, A14.

74. Diederich, *Somoza*, 311; U.S. Congress, Senate Committee on Foreign Relations, *Human Rights and . . . Assistance (1977–78)*, 96th Cong., 1st sess., 187–94.

75. Stephen Kinzer, "Central America: In Search of Its Destiny," *Boston Globe Magazine*, 16 Aug. 1981, 52, is a good analysis.

76. NBC "Meet the Press," quoted in *New York Times*, 26 Aug. 1979, E3.

77. Differences between the early Nicaraguan and Cuban revolutions are outlined by Tad Szulc in *New York Times*, 7 Aug. 1979, op-ed column.

78. A good brief Nicaraguan view is the Bendaña essay in *Nicaragua in Revolution*, ed. Thomas A. Walker (N.Y., 1982), 325; on Castro, see *New York Times*, 9 July 1980, 10; author's interview, 29 Oct. 1981.

79. Walker, "Sandinist Victory," 59–60.

80. House, *Central America at the Crossroads*, 40–41, also 22–23, 32–33.

81. Ibid. 28–29.

82. *Latin American Digest* 14 (Fall 1980): 15.

83. *Central America Report* 7 (14 April 1980): 109; Susan Jonas, "The Nicaraguan Revolution in the Emerging Cold War," in *Nicaragua in Revolution*, 380–81; *Washington Post*, 12 Sept. 1979, A20; Walker, *Nicaragua: Land of Sandino*, 119–20.

84. *Central America Report* 7 (28 April 1980), 123; *New York Times*, 23 March 1980, 8.

85. Vaky, "Hemispheric Relations," 621; Jonas, "Nicaraguan Revolution," 380–83.

86. *New York Times*, 13 Nov. 1980, 19; Peter Kornbluh, *Nicaragua, The Price of Intervention* (Washington, 1987), 18–19 on the CIA.

87. Gerald E. Karush, "Plantations, Population, and Poverty . . . El Salvador," *Studies in Comparative International Development* 13 (Fall 1978): 59–75.

88. Durham, *Scarcity and Survival*, 22–24, 51–52, 173.

89. Karush, "Plantations, Population, and Poverty," 59.

90. Stephen Webre, *José Napoléon Duarte and the Christian Democratic Party in Salvadoran Politics, 1960–1972* (Baton Rouge, 1974), is the best analysis; also Arnson, *El Salvador*, 22–24; Edward Schumacher in *New York Times*, 15 March 1981, 4E.

91. Kinzer, "Central America," 50; Etchison, *U.S. and Militarism*, 32–33; Lernoux, *Cry of the People*, 185.

92. Paul H. Hoeffel, "The Eclipse of the Oligarchs," *New York Times Magazine*, 6 Sept. 1981, 23.

93. A good summary of the various sides can be found in *Washington Post*, 9 March 1981, A19; Arnson, *El Salvador*, 29–31; Krauss, "Their Bible Is the Bible," 10.

94. U.S. Congress, House Committee on International Relations, *Arms Trade in the Western Hemisphere*, 95th Cong., 2nd sess., 1978, 197; Arnson, *El Salvador*, 30–33.

95. U.S. Congress, House Committee on International Relations, *The Recent Presidential Elections in El Salvador*, 95th Cong., 1st sess., 1977, 1–2, 22–24.

96. *Washington Post*, 11 March 1981, A18.

97. Vogelgesang, *American Dream, Global Nightmare*, 173.

98. Ibid. 174–75; Frank J. Devine, *El Salvador: Embassy Under Attack* (N.Y., 1981), 46–47, 56–58.

99. Ibid. 120–21; Arnson, *El Salvador*, 38–41; OAS, *Report on the Situation*, 137.

100. *New York Times*, 17 Oct. 1979, 10; John Womack, Jr., "El Salvador and the Central American War: Interview with John Womack, Jr.," *Socialist Review* 12 (March–April 1982): 12–13. A good analysis is Dermot Keogh, "The Myth of the Liberal Coup," manuscript in possession of the author (1985).

101. Devine, *El Salvador*, 142–43, 144–46.

102. Ibid. 21; *New York Times*, 30 and 31 Oct. 1979, 1.

103. Devine, *El Salvador*, 149–50; Arnson, *El Salvador*, 45.

104. Ibid. 48–49.

105. Letter of Joseph P. Mooney to editor, and LeoGrande and Robbins reply, *Foreign Affairs* 59 (Fall 1980): 182–83; Penny Lernoux, "El Salvador's Christian Democrat Junta," *The Nation*, 13 Dec. 1980, 632–36; for a slightly different version of Cheek's statement, see Tommie Sue Montgomery, *Revolution in El Salvador* (Boulder, Colo., 1982), 165.

106. Quoted by Warren Hoge, *New York Times*, 8 June 1981, A8.

107. Riding, "Sword and Cross," 6, 8.

108. Adolfo Gilly, *Guerra y politica en El Salvador* (Mexico, 1981), 77–84; Kinzer, "Central America," 59, 64; Hoeffel, "Eclipse of the Oligarchs," 30; Robert E. White, "Central America: The Problem That Won't Go Away," *New York Times Magazine*, 18 July 1982, 24.

109. Speech of Murat Williams, reprinted in *Congressional Record*, 97th Cong., 1st sess., 16 Nov. 1981; *Central America Report* 7 (14 April 1980): 106.

110. Quoted in Arnson, *El Salvador*, 50; on AIFLD see Robert Lubar, "No Easy Choices in El Salvador," *Fortune*, 4 May 1981, 226; U.S. Department of State, "El Salvador: US Policy," *Gist*, Nov. 1980.

111. James Petras, "The Junta's War Against the People," *The Nation*, 20 Dec. 1980, 675.

112. Hoeffel, "Eclipse of the Oligarchs," 26, 28.

113. Ibid. 23.

114. Quoted in Arnson, *El Salvador*, 61.

115. White, "Central America," 21.

116. *Washington Post*, 9 March 1981, A18; *New York Times*, 28 Dec. 1980, 4.
117. Karen DeYoung in *Washington Post*, 10 Jan. 1981, A12; Tommie Sue Montgomery's fine essay, "Fighting Guerrillas . . ." *New Political Science*, 18/19 (Fall/Winter 1990), 28–29 has the KISSSS reference.
118. Quoted by Alan Riding in *New York Times*, 23 March 1980, 8.
119. House, *Arms Trade in the Western Hemisphere*, 229; "Good Neighbor," *New Republic*, 24 April 1971, 9.
120. John A. Booth, "A Guatemalan Nightmare: Levels of Political Violence, 1966–1972," *Journal of Interamerican Studies* 22 (May 1980): 199–200, 218–20; Victor Perera, "Guatemala . . . ," *New York Times Magazine*, 13 June 1971, 12; *Latin American Digest* 5 (Oct. 1970): 3; Etchison, *U.S. and Militarism*, 16–18.
121. Brian Jenkins and Caesar D. Sereseres, "U.S. Military Assistance and the Guatemalan Armed Forces," *Armed Forces and Society* 3 (Summer 1977): 585–92.
122. Alfred J. Fischer, "Agrarian Policy in Central America," *Contemporary Review* 224 (April 1974): 185–86.
123. Clark Reynolds essay in *Latin America and World Economy*, ed. Joseph Grunwald (Beverly Hills, Calif., 1978), 208–10; Plant, *Guatemala*, 1, 8, 90–91.
124. Blanche Wiesen Cook, *The Declassified Eisenhower* (Garden City, N.Y., 1981), 291–92; Jerry Stilkind, "Guatemala's Unstable and Uncertain Future," *Country Notes* published by Center For Development Policy (Washington, 1982), 6.
125. J. C. Louis and Harvey Z. Yazizian, *The Cola Wars* (N.Y., 1980), 186–90; *Central America Report* 7 (14 April 1980): 106.
126. Stilkind, "Guatemala's Unstable and Uncertain Future," 7 quotes the vice-president; *Economist*, 6 Sept. 1980, 32.
127. Roland H. Ebel, "Political Instability in Central America," *Current History* 81 (Feb. 1982): 58.
128. Riding, "Guatemala," 66–67.
129. Morris and Ropp, "Corporatism and Dependent Development," 32–33; Molina Chocano, "Dependencia y cambio social en la sociedad hondureña," 14–17, 21–22.
130. Steve C. Ropp, "The Honduran Army in the Socio-Political Evolution of the Honduran State," *The Americas* 30 (April 1974): 528; Morris and Ropp, "Corporatism and Dependent Development," 41, 46–47; Etchison, *U.S. and Militarism*, 24–28.
131. Durham, *Scarcity and Survival*, 167–71; Heath, "Current Trends," 32; Lernoux, *Cry of the People*, 107–9, 118–19.
132. Ibid. 117, 120–23; Durham, *Scarcity and Survival*, 169–71.
133. For Panzós, see Robert G. Williams's superb *Export Agriculture and the Crisis in Central America* (Chapel Hill, 1986), 147–51; Alan Riding in *New York Times*, 23 Dec. 1980, A2.
134. House, *Central America at the Crossroads*, 88–89, has Vaky's quote; Karen deYoung and Jim Hoagland in *Washington Post*, 9 March 1981, A18; Kornbluh, *Nicaragua*, 136.
135. Alan Riding in *New York Times*, 9 Dec. 1981, D6.

136. See, for example, *Wall Street Journal,* 11 Feb. 1972, 5; 18 Feb. 1972, 3; and on the U.S.S.R. 29 March 1972, 1.

137. Ibid. 22 Oct. 1975, 1; Heath, "Current Trends," 34–35.

138. See tables in *New York Times,* 9 Dec. 1981, D6.

139. Mitchell Seligson, "Agrarian Policies in Dependent Societies: Costa Rica," *Journal of Interamerican Studies* 19 (May 1977): 212–30.

140. Ebel, "Political Instability in Central America," 59; Stone essay in *Contemporary Cultures and Societies of Latin America* ed. Dwight Heath (N.Y., 1973), esp. 409–10, 418–19.

141. Interview by Don Oberdorfer, *Washington Post,* 18 Feb. 1979, C4.

CHAPTER V

1. The document's text is in *New York Times,* 7 April 1983, A16; also Lt. Colonel Alden M. Cunningham to Editor of *New York Times,* 20 August 1984, A22; Adolfo Gilly, *Guerra y politica en El Salvador* (Mexico, 1981), 187–96.

2. *The Inter-Hemispheric Education Resource Center Bulletin,* II (Fall, 1985): 1; a different view is in "Nicaragua," *Wilson Quarterly* (New Year's, 1988), 97.

3. Text is conveniently found in *New York Times,* 13 July 1980, 14.

4. Richard Millett, "An Unclear Menace: U.S. perceptions of Soviet Strategy in Latin America," Eusebio Mujal-Leon, ed.; *The USSR and Latin America: A Developing Relationship* (Winchester, Ma., 1989), 102–3; the Allen quotes are in *Latin America Weekly Report,* 4 Dec. 1981, 1; and Penny Lernoux, "El Salvador's Christian Democrat Junta," *The Nation,* 13 Dec. 1980, 633; *Washington Post,* 7 Oct. 1977, A20.

5. Committee of Santa Fe, *A New Inter-American Policy for the Eighties,* Lewis Tambs, ed. (Washington, D. C., 1980); Abraham F. Lowenthal, *Partners in Conflict: The U.S. and Latin America* (Baltimore, 1987), esp. chapter II, has a good perspective.

6. Carla Anne Robbins, "A State Dept. Purge," *New York Times,* 3 Nov. 1981, A19; *Boston Sunday Globe,* 6 Sept. 1981, 44; Roy Gutman, *Banana Diplomacy: The Making of American Policy in Nicaragua, 1981–1987* (N.Y., 1988), 32–33, 60–61, 58–59.

7. This and other Kirkpatrick essays can be found in her *Dictatorships and Double Standards* (N.Y., 1982), especially 23–90; Haig's speech is excerpted in *New York Times,* 21 April 1981, A6.

8. Critiques can be found in Theodore Draper, "The Ambassador's Theories," *New York Times Book Review,* 25 July 1982, 1; Thomas J. Farer, "Reagan's Latin America," *The New York Review of Books,* 19 March 1981, 12–13; Robert E. White, "Central America: The Problem that Won't Go Away," *New York Times Magazine,* 18 July 1982, 22.

9. Bernard Diederich, *Somoza and the Legacy of U.S. Involvement . . .* (N.Y., 1981), 327.

10. William Deane Stanley, "Economic Migrants or Refugees from Violence? A Time-Series Analysis of Salvadoran Migration to the United States," *Latin American Research Review*, XXII (No. 1, 1987), 148; George Black, *The Good Neighbor* (N.Y., 1988), 158 (galley); Timothy Garton Ash, "Back Yards," *The New York Review of Books*, 22 Nov. 1984, especially 8.

11. Text is in *New York Times*, 21 Feb. 1981, 6; also quotes in *Washington Post*, 9 March 1981, 1; *New York Times*, 14 March 1982, 1; U.S. Department of State, "Cuban Support for Terrorism and Insurgency," *Current Policy*, 12 March 1982, 376, 3; The first time the "go to the source" phrase was used was probably by William Clark, and is given in *Washington Post*, 9 March 1981, A18; *Latin America Weekly Report*, 18 Dec. 1981, 12.

12. Jiri Valenta, "The U.S.S.R., Cuba, and the Crisis in Central America," *Orbis* 25 (Fall 1981): 736–38; Wayne Smith, "Dateline Havana . . . " *Foreign Policy*, 48 (Fall 1982); Enders's statement is in U.S. Department of State, "Cuban Support for Terrorism and Insurgency," 1; and in Enders's essay in Howard J. Wiarda, ed., "The Crisis in Central America," *AEI Foreign Policy and Defense Review* 4 (1982).

13. Mark Falcoff, "The El Salvador White Paper and Its Critics," Ibid. 18–24 is a good defense of the "White Paper," and gives some of the criticisms offered by James Petras in *The Nation*, 28 March 1981; John Dinges in *Los Angeles Times*, 17 March 1981; and Jonathan Kwitny, *Wall Street Journal*, 8 June 1981. The original "White Paper," was *Communist Interference in El Salvador; Documents Demonstrating Communist Support of the Salvadoran Insurgency*, issued by the Department of State, 23 Feb. 1981 (author's possession).

14. A good summary is in Cynthia Arnson, *El Salvador* (Washington, 1982), 73; Bernard Gwertzman has an analysis in *New York Times*, 14 March 1981, 1.

15. *Latin America Weekly Report*, 26 March 1982, 10–11; the Reagan quote is in text, *Washington Post*, 29 March 1981, A6.

16. Gutman, *Banana Diplomacy*, 82–83.

17. Excellent discussions are Eldon Kenworthy, "The Selling of a Policy," in Thomas W. Walker, ed., *Reagan Versus the Sandinistas* (Boulder, 1987); and George Herring, "Vietnam, Central America, and the Uses of History," in Kenneth M. Coleman and George Herring, eds., *Understanding the Central American Crisis* (Washington, 1991), 181–91; Garry Wills, *Reagan's America* (N.Y., 1987), 347; Dennis Gilbert, "Nicaragua," in Morris J. Blachman, William M. Leogrande, Kenneth Sharpe, eds., *Confronting Revolution* (N.Y., 1986), 102; the Motley quote is in Joanne Omang and Aryeh Neier, *Psychological Operations in Guerrilla Warfare* (N.Y., 1985), 17.

18. Sidney Blumenthal, "Marketing the President," *New York Times Magazine*, 13 Sept. 1981, 112; Gutman, *Banana Diplomacy*, 28–30, 93; Raymond Bonner, "The Thousand Small Escalations of Our Latin Wars," *Washington Post*, 16 Sept. 1984, Bl; U.S. Government, *Public Papers of the Presidents. Ronald Reagan. 1982* (Washington, 1983), 181–85.

19. Bob Woodward, *Veil: The Secret Wars of the CIA, 1981–1987* (N.Y., 1987); Eve Pell, "The Backbone of Hidden Government," *The Nation*, 19 June 1989, 850.
20. Ibid.; *New York Times*, 24 Dec. 1981, A14; ibid., 28 Dec. 1981 has quote; ibid., 2 May 1981, 3.
21. The text is in *New York Times*, 7 April 1983, A16.
22. U.S. Department of State, *Current Policy*, 576 (9 May 1984): 3; Louis Hartz, *The Liberal Tradition in America* (N.Y., 1955), 288.
23. *New York Times*, 29 Aug. 1981, A1; *Latin America Weekly Report*, 18 Sept. 1981, 2; Ibid., 16 July 1982, 11; George Black and Robert Matthews, "Arms from the U.S.S.R.—Or From Nobody," *The Nation*, 31 Aug. 1985, 148–49; Gilbert, "Nicaragua," 105; Bradford Burns, *At War in Nicaragua* (N.Y., 1987), 107–8, 133; Kai Bird and Max Holland, "Capitol Letter," *The Nation*, 15 March 1986, 296 has the British quote; *Washington Post*, 30 July 1983, D8; *New York Times*, 7 April 1983, A16 has the N.S.C. document showing U.S. concern.
24. James LeMoyne, "Can . . ." *New York Times Magazine*, 4 Oct. 1987, 65; *Newsweek*, 20 May 1985, 40 has the Allen quote; NACLA, *Report on the Americas* 21 (July/Aug. 1987): 25–26; *New York Times*, 8 April 1982, A10.
25. Gutman, *Banana Diplomacy*, 105; Transcript of CNN "Newsmaker Saturday," 17 Nov. 1984, 2–3 (author's possession); Walter LaFeber, "The Evolution of the Monroe Doctrine" in Lloyd C. Gardner, ed., *Redefining the Past: Essays in Diplomatic History in Honor of William Appleman Williams* (Corvallis, 1986), 125, 139.
26. *Latin America Weekly Report*, 13 Nov. 1981, 11.
27. Enders essay in Wiarda, ed., "Crisis in Central America"; Alan Riding's analysis in *New York Times*, 1 Feb. 1982, A1.
28. Michael Novak, *The Spirit of Democratic Capitalism* (N.Y., 1982), especially 287–314.
29. *Latin America Weekly Report*, 28 May 1982, 4; Michael Kryzanek, "President Reagan's Caribbean Basin Formula," in Wiarda, ed., "Crisis in Central America"; Economist Intelligence Unit, *Quarterly Economic Review of Nicaragua, Costa Rica, Panama. Annual Supplement, 1985* (London, 1985), 7.
30. Especially important is Richard R. Fagen, "A Funny Thing Happened on the Way to the Market . . . ," *International Organization* 32 (Winter 1978): 292–93.
31. *Latin America Weekly Report*, 2 July 1982, 6.
32. Ibid., 18 Sept. 1981, 5 has the Enders quotation
33. Ibid., 13 Aug. 1982, 5; *New York Times*, 11 March 1981, A2.
34. Secretary Shultz, "Caribbean Basin Economic Recovery Act," U.S. Department of State *Current Policy* 477, 13 April 1983, outlines the program; *Central America Report*, XI, 20 Jan. 1984, published a special insert to critique it; also *Washington Post*, 20 Feb. 1986, A1;
35. Rachel Garst and Tom Barry, *Feeding the Crisis* (Lincoln, Neb., 1990), 1–2, 17–18, 45, 59, 87, 148–49.

36. Joshua Cohen and Joel Rogers, *Inequality and Intervention* (Washington, D.C., 1986), 44; *Central America Report*, 3 Oct. 1986, 302–3.

37. *The Inter-Hemispheric Education Resource Center Bulletin* II (Fall 1985): 1

38. A good summary at this time is Bonner, "The Thousand Small Escalations of Our Latin Wars," B1.

39. John E. Findling, *Close Neighbors, Distant Friends* (Westport, Conn., 1987), 152; *Wall Street Journal*, 28 June 1982, 11; *Washington Post*, 12 June 1983, A1, A21.

40. Michael T. Klare and Peter Kornbluh, eds., *Low Intensity Warfare* (N.Y., 1988), especially Kornbluh and Siegel-Hackel essays; D. Michael Shafer, *Deadly Paradigms* (Princeton, 1988), 283–88.

41. Robert Parry and Peter Kornbluh, "Iran-Contra's Untold Story," *Foreign Policy* 72 (Fall 1988): 10, 18; Eve Pell, "The Backbone of Hidden Government," 850; Reagan officials' views are in *Washington Post*, 1 Oct. 1988, A17

42. "President Reagan: U.S. Interests in Central America," 9 May 1984, in U.S. Department of State, *Current Policy* 576: 3; Burns, *At War With Nicaragua*, 79; text in *New York Times*, 28 April 1983, A11; *Washington Post*, 7 May 1983, A22; John Mueller, "Bloodbaths and Dominoes," 21 April 1985, 21 (manuscript in author's possession).

43. U.S. Department of State, "Cuban Support for Terrorism and Insurgency. . . ." *Current Policy* 376 (12 March 1982): 3; text of "Background Paper" in *New York Times*, 28 May 1983, 7.

44. E. D. Reyes, "Soviet Relations with Central America . . . ," *The Annals* 481 (Sept. 1985): 157–58.

45. Mary Desjeans and Peter Clement, "Soviet Policy Toward Central America," in Robbin F. Laird, ed., *Soviet Foreign Policy* (N.Y., 1987), 229; Reyes, "Soviet Relations with Central America," 151; Peter Shearman, "The Soviet Challenge in Central America," in Laird, ed., *Soviet Foreign Policy*, 213; Dimitri K. Simes, "The New Soviet Challenge," *Foreign Policy* 55 (Summer 1984): 118.

46. Reyes, "Soviet Relations with Central America," 151; Desjeans and Clement, "Soviet Policy Toward Central America," 224; *New York Times*, 7 Aug. 1983, E1; Simes, "The New Soviet Challenge," *Passim*.

47. *Wall Street Journal*, 15 June 1984, 34.

48. Kirkpatrick is quoted in *New York Times*, 6 March 1983, 1; William Pfaff, "Reflections. Manifest Destiny," *The New Yorker*, 27 May 1985, 94; *Wall Street Journal*, 17 Aug. 1983, 15 on the carriers.

49. Robert F. Drinan, SJ, "Is It Premature to Celebrate Peace in Central America," *National Catholic Reporter*, 4 Sept. 1987, 4.

50. David Burnham, *A Law Unto Itself; Power, Politics, and the IRS* (N.Y., 1989), 259–60; *New York Times*, 6 April 1984, 4; Colman McCarthy, "Four Empty Chairs," *Washington Post*, 1 Dec. 1984, A17.

51. Fiers is noted in *New York Times*, 20 Sept. 1991, A20; Ross Gelbspan, *Break-ins,*

Death Threats and the FBI (Boston, 1991), 41–45, 154–64, 226–28; *Washington Post*, 30 Jan. 1988, A18; Ibid., 15 Sept. 1988, A1; Ibid., 27 July 1989, A22.

52. Theodore Draper, *A Very Thin Line; The Iran-Contra Affairs* (N.Y., 1991), 17–18; Cynthia Arnson, "Congress and Central America," 9, 22–25 (Manuscript in author's possession).

53. Good background and analysis of 1982–86 is in Mary B. Vanderlaan, *Revolution and Foreign Policy in Nicaragua* (Boulder, Co., 1986), 239–48; Terry Karl, "Mexico, Venezuela, and the Contadora Initiative," in Blachman, et al., *Confronting Revolution*, 276; *New York Times*, 24 July 1983, 1E.

54. Karl, "Mexico, Venezuela," 286–89; Secretary of State Shultz, "U.S. Efforts to Achieve Peace in Central America," 15 March 1984, U.S. Department of State, *Special Report No. 115; New York Times*, 24 Sept. 1984, A12.

55. Cohen and Rogers, *Inequality and Intervention*, 45; William I. Robinson and Kent Norsworthy, *David and Goliath* (London, 1987), 110–11.

56. Emilio Pantojas García, "La política exterior norteamericana en la decada del ochenta y los procesos electorales," *Homines* 11 (1–2, 1987–88): 288–90; Gutman, *Banana Diplomacy*, 132–34, 146–48, letter to author, 23 July 1984.

57. Interview with Sergio Ramírez by author and Professor Thomas Holloway, 19 Aug. 1983, in Managua, Nicaragua.

58. *Report of the National Bipartisan Commission on Central America*, January 1984, manuscript copy, especially 4, 10, 12, 110–12, 115.

59. *New York Times*, 13 Jan. 1984, A5; Ibid., 13 March 1984, A12; *Central America Report*, 27 Jan. 1984, 25–26; a good analysis is in PACCA, *Changing Course* (Washington, 1984), 105–12; an important analysis is Anibal Romero, "The Kissinger Commission—A Latin American Perspective," in Dermot Keogh, ed., *Central America: Human Rights and U.S. Foreign Policy* (Cork, Ireland, 1985), 127–42.

60. U.S. Department of State, "President Reagan: U.S. Interests in Central America," 2; *Washington Post*, 29 Aug. 1983, A14; Ibid., 24 Sept. 1983, A5 for White House publicity attempts; *New York Times*, 27 Sept. 1983, A18; Ibid., 1 Feb. 1985, 5; John Weeks, *The Economies of Central America* (N.Y., 1985), 199–200.

61. A fuller account of the 1984 debate and its context is in John Prados, *Keepers of the Keys* (N.Y., 1991), 496–97; Clifford Krauss, *Inside Central America* (N.Y., 1991), 11–12.

62. Gutman, *Banana Diplomacy*, 277.

63. *Wall Street Journal*, 5 March 1985, 24; Robinson and Norsworthy, *David and Goliath*, 47; Edgar Chamorro with Jefferson Morley, "Confessions of a 'Contra' ", *The New Republic*, 5 Aug. 1985, 18–23.

64. Woodward, *Veil*, 270–75; *The Nation*, 30 April 1990, 609 has the Reagan quote on Law Day; *Washington Post*, 25 Nov. 1983, 1; Gutman, *Banana Diplomacy*, 199, 202; Burns, *At War with Nicaragua*, 149, 151 has the State Department definition of terrorism; *New York Times*, 2 July 1986, A31.

65. *Wall Street Journal*, 7 April 1988, editorial, "Remember Corinto"; *New York Times*, 2 July 1986, A1.

66. Dennis Bernstein and Janet King, "Hostile Acts," *The Progressive*, March 1989, 25–26; *New York Times*, 8 April 1983, A11.

67. The manual's text is helpfully introduced by Omang and Neier, *Psychological Operations in Guerrilla Warfare; New York Times*, 15 Oct. 1984, A7; *The Boston Sunday Globe*, 16 Dec. 1984, 26.

68. *Newsweek*, 15 Feb. 1988, 36; *Boston Globe*, 22 Aug. 1986, 5.

69. *Washington Post*, 19 Sept. 1987, A18; Ibid., 4 May 1987, A1.

70. Ibid., 18 Nov. 1984, A34.

71. Morris J. Blachman and Kenneth E. Sharpe, "Central American Traps," *World Policy Journal* 5 (Winter, 1987–88): 25; Eldon Kenworthy, "Seeing Central America Without Blinders," *New York Times*, 17 Jan. 1985, A23 has the State Department official's quote.

72. Text in *New York Times*, 20 Sept. 1991, A20.

73. Author's interview with Ambassador Cruz, 29 Oct. 1981.

74. Ibid.; *The Inter-Hemispheric Education Resource Center Bulletin* 2 (Fall 1985): 1.

75. *New York Times*, 2 April 1981, 3.

76. Ibid., 14 Jan. 1982, A2; author's interview, 29 Oct. 1981; *Washington Post*, 31 Jan. 1981, 1, 14; Alan Riding analysis in *New York Times*, 12 Feb. 1981, A11.

77. A good brief discussion is in *Latin America Weekly Report*, 25 June 1982, 9; the first quote is from author's interview; see also *New York Times*, 8 May 1981, A6, and Thomas W. Walker, "The Sandinist Victory in Nicaragua," *Current History* 78 (Feb. 1980): 61; *New York Times*, 28 Dec. 1981, A16; Ibid., 2 May 1981, 3; Gilbert, "Nicaragua," 100–1; Dennis Gilbert, "The Bourgeoisie and the Nicaraguan Revolution," in Thomas Walker, ed., *Nicaragua: The First Five Years* (N.Y., 1985).

78. A superb analysis of the bourgoisie runs throughout Dennis Gilbert, *Sandinistas* (N.Y., 1988), especially 117–20; Gilbert, "Nicaragua," 78, 112–14; Laura J. Enriquez, "Half a Decade of Sandinista Policy-Making," *Latin American Research Review* 22 (no. 3, 1987): 209–22; Piero Gleijeses, "Resist Romanticism," *Foreign Policy* 54 (Spring 1984): 122–23, 128–30; *New York Times*, 12 Feb. 1981, A11; Colman McCarthy, editorial page, *Los Angeles Times*, 5 March 1985, quantifies medical services.

79. *Business Week*, 10 Jan. 1983, 43; Burns, *At War With Nicaragua*, 33–34; *New York Times*, 22 Oct. 1984, A10; *The Economist*, 29 Oct. 1983, 33–37; *Christian Science Monitor*, 30 Jan. 1985, 7.

80. Gilbert, "Nicaragua," 113; *New York Times*, 9 July 1984, A19; Dieter Eich and Carlos Rincon, *The Contras: Interviews with Anti-Sandinists* (San Francisco, 1984), 64.

81. *New York Times*, 11 Nov. 1984, 16; Alma Guillermoprieto, "Letter from Managua," *The New Yorker*, 26 March 1990, 86; Gilbert, "Nicaragua," 116–17; *Los Angeles Times*, 18 Jan. 1985, I, 10.

82. Gutman, *Banana Diplomacy*, 150–51, 158; *New York Times*, 9 July 1984, A19.

83. Gilbert, *Sandinistas*, 142–52; Vanderlaan, *Revolution and Foreign Policy*, 108–21; Stephen Kinzer, "Nicaragua's Combative Archbishop," *New York Times Magazine*, 18 Nov. 1984, 90–96; *New York Times*, 6 March 1983, 1; *Central America Report*, 17 Aug. 1984, 251–52; Alison Rooper, *Fragile Victory: A Nicaraguan Community at War* (London, 1987), 119; *New York Times* 22 May 1984, A8 on Obando as the key opposition leader.

84. Gilbert, "Nicaragua," 119; Burns, *At War With Nicaragua*, 26; Republica de Nicaragua, *Consejo de estado; segunda legislatura* (Managua, 1981), 5.

85. Vanderlaan, *Revolution and Foreign Policy*, 91–94; Thomas W. Walker, *Nicaragua*, 3rd ed. (Boulder, Co., 1991), 135–38; Gutman, *Banana Diplomacy*, 232–40, 241; *New York Times*, 4 Oct. 1984, A5; Ibid., 21 Oct. 1984, 12.

86. *Wall Street Journal*, 11 Jan. 1985, 19 has Andrés Perez comments; *Latin America Regional Reports, Mexico & Central America*, 11 Jan. 1985, 4; *Washington Post*, 26 Oct. 1984, A1 on U.S. maneuvers; Thomas W. Walker to Scholars, 21 Nov. 1984 (manuscript in author's possession), gives the LASA Observer Delegation view.

87. This is drawn from a fine analysis by Philip L. Shepherd, "The USS Honduras: U.S. Foreign Policy and the Destabilization of Honduras" (manuscript in author's possession), March 1984; Central Intelligence Agency, *The World Factbook* (Washington, 1984), 99; Bonner, "The Thousand Small Escalations," B5; Lucy Komisar, "Honduran Anger at the U.S." *New York Times*, 11 Oct. 1984, A27.

88. Loren Jenkins, "Honduras on the Edge," *Atlantic Monthly* 250 (Aug. 1982): 18; *New York Times*, 10 Feb. 1983, 3; Edward S. Herman and Frank Brodhead, *Demonstration Elections* (Boston, 1984); a different Honduran view is Mario Posas, "El proceso de democratización en Honduras," *Estudios Sociales Centroamericanos* 47 (May–Aug. 1988): esp. 66–71.

89. Bonner, "A Thousand Small Escalations," B1; *Newsweek*, 16 April 1984, 44; *Central America Report*, 17 Aug. 1984, 255; *New York Times*, 9 Oct. 1984, A10; Ibid., 20 Nov. 1984, A9 on anti-El Salvador feeling.

90. The background of the "structural" Honduran agricultural crisis is in Mario Ponce Cámbar, "Honduras: politica agricola y perspectivas," in Centro de Documentación de Honduras y Universidad Internacional de La Florida, *Honduras: realidad nacional y crisis regional* (Tegucigalpa, 1986), 249–78; John Weeks, "The Central American Economies in 1983 and 1984," *Latin America and Caribbean Contemporary Record* 3 (N.Y., 1985): 64–65; *New York Times*, 14 Jan. 1985, A19; *Central America Report*, 10 Aug. 1984, 247 on spread of diseases; *Central America Report*, special insert, Jan. 1984, 14 on banana economy.

91. Background and breakdown of figures is in Ramon Custodio López, "Derechos humanos en Honduras," in Centro de Documentación, *Honduras: realidad nacional*, 107–31; Weeks, "The Central American Economies in 1983 and 1984," 65; *Honduras Update* 3 (Nov./Dec. 1984): 8–9, 16; Cynthia Brown, ed., *With Friends Like These. The Americas Watch Report . . .* (N.Y., 1985), 149–50; Shepherd, "USS

Honduras," 26, 43; *New York Times,* 14 June 1984, A5; Honduran officer quoted by Christopher Dickey in *Washington Post,* 5 May 1981, A20; *New York Times,* 25 Sept. 1981, A9; *The Economist,* 4 Sept. 1982, 33–34.

92. *Boston Globe,* 14 Jan. 1985, 5; *The Inter-Hemispheric Education Resource Center Bulletin* 2 (Fall 1985): 1; *Latin America Weekly Report,* 26 Feb. 1982, 3 on "image problem."

93. Adolfo Gilly, *Guerra y politica en El Salvador* (Mexico, 1981), 13–15; *New York Times,* 25 July 1983, A13; Ibid., 24 Feb. 1981, A7 on rebel request for talks; Diskin and Sharpe, "El Salvador," in Blachman, et al., *Confronting Revolution,* 60–61 on Reagan refusal to negotiate; "Interview on 'Meet the Press,' " 29 March 1981; U.S. Department of State, *Current Policy* 271, for Haig quote; also text of remarks in *New York Times,* 21 Feb. 1981, 6; Ibid., 14 March 1982, 1 on "global problem" view; *Washington Post,* 29 June 1983, A21 for Waghelstein quote; *New York Times,* 28 May 1983, 3 on U.S. personnel killed.

94. Raymond Bonner, "The Agony of El Salvador," *New York Times Magazine,* 22 Feb. 1981, 31 has diplomat's quote; Robert Leiken, "Anatomy of Resistance," *Worldview* 26 (June 1983): 5, 7–8 on the rebel groups; also *Washington Post,* 8 July 1983, A13.

95. Vladimir I. Stanchenko, "The Soviet Role in Central America," *The Washington Quarterly* 13 (Summer 1990): 197; *New York Times,* 1 March 1981, 14; Reyes, "Soviet Relations with Central America," 154.

96. Murat W. Williams, "Limits in Aiding Salvador," *New York Times,* 17 June 1983, 17; Ibid., 3 May 1983, A10 on ouster of Defense Minister; Ibid., 24 Sept. 1984, A12 on training; Ibid., 7 Oct. 1984, 15 on optimism; Ibid., 9 Jan. 1985, 3 on use against civilians; *Detroit Free Press,* 27 Sept. 1984, 6A on anti-U.S. feelings; Diskin & Sharpe, "El Salvador," 78–79; *New York Times,* 19 Aug. 1983, A2 on corruption.

97. Garst and Barry, *Feeding the Crisis,* 12, 186; Gutman, *Banana Diplomacy,* 22–23; *New York Times,* 15 Dec. 1983, A3.

98. U.S. Department of State, *Current Policy* 467: 6; *New York Times,* 25 March 1984, 6F on corporations; Arms Control and Foreign Policy Caucus, *U.S. Aid to El Salvador* (February 1985).

99. Arnson, "Congress and Central America," 13–15; *New York Times,* 27 July 1982, A3; Department of State, "El Salvador: Certification Process," *Gist* (Feb. 1983).

100. Raymond Bonner, "Sandinistas Aren't The Worst," *New York Times,* 14 Sept. 1984, A31; *Boston Globe,* 30 Nov. 1984, 3; Julia Preston, "What Duarte Won," *The New York Review of Books,* 15 Aug. 1985, 30–35.

101. Diskin and Sharpe, "El Salvador," 68; *New York Times,* 17 Jan. 1984, A6; Bonner, "The Agony of El Salvador," 28–30 on the Miami connection; Joan Didion, "In El Salvador," *The New York Review of Books,* 4 Nov. 1982, 14.

102. Joel Millman, "Reagan's Reporters," *The Progressive,* 20 Oct. 1984, 22; William Deane Stanley, "Economic Migrants or Refugees from Violence?" *Latin American Research Review* 22 (no. 1, 1987): 133–34, 148.

103. Black, *Good Neighbor,* 151; *New York Times,* 28 Jan. 1982, A10.

104. *Wall Street Journal,* 16 July 1982, 16; *Latin America Weekly Report,* 6 Aug. 1982, 3; *New York Times,* 30 July 1982, A6; Wayne Biddle, "The Selling of D'Aubuisson," *The Nation,* July 1982, 24–31, 72–73; *The Economist,* 1 May 1982, 14.

105. *New York Times,* 20 June 1982, 9; Ibid., 10 Feb. 1983, A3; especially the analysis by John M. Goshko and Don Oberdorfer in *Washington Post,* 6 March 1983, A1, A10; Ibid., 11 March 1983, A14 about Reagan's speech.

106. Findling, *Close Neighbors,* 159; I.M. Destler and Patricia Cohen, "Congress Swings," *Foreign Service Journal,* July/Aug. 1982, 19–21, 38; U.S. Government, *Public Papers of the Presidents. Ronald Reagan. 1984* (Washington, D.C., 1984), 388 (interview of 20 March 1984); *Wall Street Journal,* 27 Feb. 1984, 1, 16 on watermelon story; Arnson, "Congress and Central America," on Helms.

107. "Playboy Interview: José Napoleon Duarte," *Playboy,* Nov. 1984, 108 has the Duarte quote; *New York Times,* 1 Dec. 1984, 3 on rebel peace plan; Diskin and Sharpe, "El Salvador," 83 on Shultz and army; *Boston Sunday Globe,* 14 Oct. 1984, A19; *Washington Post,* 12 Aug. 1984, A13 for Church view.

108. Weeks, "The Central American Economies in 1983 and 1984," 56, 61–62; *U.S. News and World Report,* 17 Sept. 1984, 41 on the foreign debt; Frank McNeil, *War and Peace in Central America* (N.Y., 1988), 53; *Central America Report,* 18 Jan. 1985, 12–13.

109. Sylvia Saborio, "Central America," in John Williamson, ed., *Latin American Adjustment* (Washington, D.C., 1990), 292–97; Thomas Carothers, *In the Name of Democracy* (Berkeley, Ca., 1991), 72–74; Garst and Barry, *Feeding the Crisis,* 77–81; *Central America Report,* 15 Feb. 1985, 45–46.

110. Findling, *Close Neighbors,* 177; *Time,* 16 July 1984, 40; Vanderlaan, *Revolution and Foreign Policy in Nicaragua,* 226–34; *U.S. News and World Report,* 17 Sept. 1984, 40 on anti-U.S. views.

111. Susanne Jonas, "Whose Transition? Whose Guatemala?: An Exchange," *World Policy Journal* 5 (Winter 1987–88): 177; the "culture of fear" is coined by Piero Gleijesis, *Politics and Culture in Guatemala* (Ann Arbor, 1988), 4–16;

112. Sheldon Annis, *God and Production in a Guatemalan Town* (Austin, Tx., 1987), 3–11 is context for key case study; Jonas, "Whose Transition," 176 on PACS; *Christian Science Monitor,* 18 Jan. 1985, 12; Aryeh Neier to Editor, *Washington Post,* 7 Dec. 1985, A21.

113. *Papers of the Presidents. Ronald Reagan. 1982,* 1562–66; *Washington Post,* 13 March 1983, G6 for the Bush story; Carothers, *In the Name of Democracy,* 62, has Chapin quote; *Boston Globe,* 5 Feb. 1984, B1 has aid figures; *Wall Street Journal,* 15 Oct. 1984, 22 on Israel and Taiwan; *New York Times,* 10 Aug. 1983, A9 on C.I.A. help.

114. *New York Times,* 13 Aug. 1983, 115 on U.S.-Mejía Víctores; Trudeau and Schoultz, "Guatemala," in Blachman, et al., *Confronting Revolution,* 39, 45; *The Economist,* 5 Nov. 1983, 35.

115. *Central America Report,* "Special Document," 19 July 1985; Trudeau and Schoultz,

"Guatemala," 32–33, 42–43; *Time*, 16 July 1984, 40; *Washington Post*, 14 Dec. 1984, A35.

CHAPTER VI

1. An ordering and sorting of the region's various conflicts can be found in Gabriel Aguilera, "Las Fuerzas Armadas y la democracia en Centroamerica," *Homines* 11 (1–2, 1987–88): esp. 208–15.
2. A key essay on the topic is Eldon Kenworthy, "The Permanent Campaign's Impact on U.S. Central American Policy," in Kenneth M. Coleman and George Herring, eds., *Understanding the Central American Crisis* (Wilmington, De., 1992), 193–218; Reagan on possible use of troops is in *New York Times*, 17 April 1985, quoted in Cynthia Arnson, "Congress and Central America," 30 (manuscript in author's possession); *New York Times*, 30 June 1985, 3; *National Catholic Reporter*, 26 April 1985, 1 on Reagan and Pope's denial; Department of State and Department of Defense, *The Soviet-Cuban Connection in Central America and the Caribbean* (Washington, D.C., 1985) is the administration's case; *Wall Street Journal*, 3 April 1985, 1, 22 is a balanced refutation of that case.
3. Robert Parry and Peter Kornbluh, "Iran-Contra's Untold Story," *Foreign Policy* 72 (Fall 1988): 14–15; Eldon Kenworthy, "The Selling of a Policy," in Thomas W. Walker, ed., *Reagan Versus the Sandinistas* (Boulder, Co., 1987); Frank McNeil, *War and Peace in Central America* (N.Y., 1988), 162.
4. "Recommended Telephone Call," 25 April 1985, in "Memorandum for the President," from Robert C. McFarlane (document in author's possession); E. Bradford Burns, *At War in Nicaragua* (N.Y., 1987), 32; Peter Shearman, "The Soviet Challenge in Central America," in Robbin F. Laird, ed., *Soviet Foreign Policy* (N.Y., 1987), 217–18.
5. Eric Alterman and Peter Kornbluh, "The Washington Animal: The Escape Artist," *Regardie's* 9 (March 1989): 86–96; Wayne Smith, "Lies about Nicaragua," *Foreign Policy* 67 (Summer 1987): 88–89; Elliott Abrams, "U.S. Interests and Resource Needs in Latin America and the Caribbean," *Current Policy* 932.
6. Abrams, "U.S. Interests and Resource Needs," especially 4; *The Inter-Hemispheric Education Resource Center Bulletin* II (Fall 1985): 1; *Christian Science Monitor*, 9 March 1989, 1, in *Central America NewsPak*, 27 Feb.–12 March 1989, 7; reports by *Excelsior* (Mexico City), 22 Oct. 1991 and 17 Oct. 1991 in *Central America NewsPak*, 26 Oct.–3 Nov. 1991, 5.
7. The expert quoted is Philip L. Shepherd, "The Case of the Invisible Aid," *NACLA: Report on the Americas* 22 (Jan./Feb. 1988): 31–40; Piero Gleijeses, "The Guatemalan Silence," *The New Republic*, 10 June 1985, 23; *New York Times*, 19 April 1985, A1; Ibid., 4 June 1989, 30; *United States of America v. Oliver L. North*, Defendant, document introduced by Brendan Sullivan in regard to Bush's role (manuscript in author's possession; I am grateful to Max Miller for a copy of this document).

8. *Washington Post,* 13 Sept. 1988, A20; Richard Millet, "The Honduran Dilemma," *Current History* 86 (Dec. 1987): 412; McNeil, *War and Peace,* 137 on Bueso Rosa; *Central America Report,* 1 Aug. 1986, 226;

9. *New York Times,* 4 June 1990, A17 letter from Paul R. Epstein, M.D. on diseases in Honduras; Sylvia Saborio, "Central America," in John Williamson, ed., *Latin American Adjustment* (Washington, D.C., 1990), 300; *Excelsior,* 27 Oct. 1990, 1 in *Central America NewsPak* 22 Oct.–Nov. 4 1990, 7; *New York Times,* 29 Sept. 1985, 7; Millet, "The Honduran Dilemma," 410; *Honduras Update* 5 (June/July 1987): 1–2; *Honduras Information Center,* 15 Jan. 1988, special release; *New York Times,* 19 Jan. 1988, A1; Ibid., 9 April 1988, 1; Ibid., 13 April 1988, A10 on anti-U.S. feelings; CODEH, *Annual Report on the situation of Human Rights in Honduras* (Tegucigalpa, 1990), especially 13–14.

10. John A. Booth, "Socioeconomic and Political Roots of National Revolution in Central America," *Latin American Research Review* 26 (No. 1, 1991): 52–55, 62; Millet, "Honduran Dilemma," 409; *New York Times,* 24 Nov. 1985, 3 on U.S. support of elections; Ibid., 12 Feb. 1988, 1 on drug trade; *Miami Herald,* 16 Aug. 1991, 18A in *Central America NewsPak,* 12 Aug.–25 Aug. 1991, 9; *Excelsior,* 30 Aug. 1991, 2A in *Central America NewsPak,* 26 Aug.–8 Sept. 1991, 8 on army corruption; an alternative Honduran view is Mario Posas, "El proceso de democratización en Honduras," *Estudios Sociales Centroamericanos,* 47 (May–Aug. 1988): 61–78.

11. *Washington Post,* 26 March 1986, A12 for polls; Ibid., 12 March 1985, A8 on Reagan's assurance on no illegal aid; Clifford Krauss, "Democracia," *Wilson Quarterly* (New Year's 1988), 131; Smith, "Lies," 101 on Contadora.

12. Burns, *At War,* 75–76; "Resolution on U.S. Policy in Central America," adopted by Presbyterian Church (U.S.A.), June 1985, 3 (author's possession); *Washington Post,* 22 March 1986, C20 on "Church Groups Help Fight Aid to Contras"; Ibid., 25 March 1985, B7; *National Catholic Reporter,* 31 May 1985, 10 on Abrams's denial; *Washington Post,* 13 Oct. 1988, A13.

13. Eldon Kenworthy, "U.S. Policy in Central America," *Current History* 86 (Dec. 1987): 401–2; *Central America Report,* 25 July 1986, 217; Theodore Draper, *A Very Thin Line: The Iran-Contra Affair* (N.Y., 1991), 354–59, 537–45; *New York Times,* 30 Nov. 1986, 10 on Hasenfus-Zelaya relationship.

14. McNeil, *War and Peace,* 33; Casey's problematical role is discussed in Draper, *A Very Thin Line,* 530–34; *New York Times,* 30 July 1991, A12.

15. *New York Times Magazine,* 4 Oct. 1987, 65; Roy Gutman, *Banana Diplomacy* (N.Y., 1988), 183, 314; Garry Wills, "The Man Who Wasn't There," *The New York Review of Books,* 13 June 1991, 7; *Washington Post,* 31 March 1986, A14 on C.I.A. buildup.

16. John Prados, *Keepers of the Keys* (N.Y., 1991), 497; "Contras get increasing private aid," in *Miami Herald,* 21 Jan. 1985, 5; *New York Times,* 7 Feb. 1987, 3 on advertising campaign; Alterman and Kornbluh, "The Washington Animal," 93–98.

17. *Washington Post,* 27 Dec. 1991, A16 on drug cartel; Alterman and Kornbluh, "The Washington Animal," 95 on Abrams-Noriega; Senator John Kerry, " 'Private Assist-

ance' and the Contras. A Staff Report," 14 Oct. 1986 (manuscript in author's possession) on Singlaub; also *Time*, 27 May 1985, 35.

18. James Chace, "The End of the Affair," *The New York Review of Books* 8 Oct. 1987, 30.

19. *New York Times*, 17 Sept. 1991, A19 for helpful chronology; *Washington Post*, 27 July 1987, A2 on Poindexter; also Ibid., 18 July 1987, A1; U.S. House and Senate Select Committees, *Report of the Congressional Committees Investigating the Iran-Contra Affair . . .*, 100th Congress, 1st Session (Washington, D.C., 13 Nov. 1987), especially chapters 18–20 (I am indebted to Max Miller for a copy of this document); *Los Angeles Times*, "Opinion," of 7 Dec. 1986 has Summers's condemnation.

20. *New York Times*, 4 March 1987, A15; Eric Alterman, "The Best and the Brightest," *Tikkun* II (July–Aug. 1987): 23 for Durenberger quote; *Washington Post*, 16 Nov. 1991, A20 on Abrams's sentencing.

21. *New York Times Magazine*, 4 Oct. 1987, 66 for Pastora quote, noted by James LeMoyne; McNeil, *War and Peace*, 19 for General Custer reference; *Washington Post*, 28 Dec. 1987, A2 for Reagan quote.

22. Gutman, *Banana Diplomacy*, 341 on McFarlane quote; *Newsweek*, 2 March 1987, 32; *New York Times*, 2 April 1987, 11 for Fagoth quote; Ibid., 28 June 1987, E3; Blase Bonpane to Editor, Ibid., 5 Oct. 1988, A32; *New York Times Magazine*, 4 Oct. 1987, 66.

23. *New York Times*, 9 Jan. 1989, A1; Ibid., 24 Oct. 1986, A1 on Mexico; Mary Desjeans and Peter Clement, "Soviet Policy toward Central America," in Robbin F. Laird, ed., *Soviet Foreign Policy* (N.Y., 1987), 226–27, 231–32; Neil MacFarlane, "The USSR and the Third World," *The Harriman Institute Forum* I (no. 3): 3; author's interview at Department of State, 9 April 1985; *Washington Post*, 19 Oct. 1988, A11.

24. Oscar Arias Sanchez, "El futuro de la democracia en Centroamerica," *Penamiento Centroamericano* 42 (July–Sept. 1987): 63–66 especially for the broad economic motives; *New York Times*, 1 Feb. 1989, D2; The Economist Intelligence Unit, *Quarterly Economic Review of Nicaragua, Costa Rica, Panama 2* (London, 1985): 16; *Central America Report*, 6 Feb. 1987, 38 is on labor problems.

25. McNeil, *War and Peace*, 250–51; Arias Sanchez, "El Futuro de la democracia," 66 for broad criticism of these developments; *National Catholic Reporter*, 31 May 1985, 10; Richard J. Walton, "How the U.S. is Changing Costa Rica," *The Nation*, 5 Oct. 1985, 297; Jean Hopfensperger, "Costa Rica, Seeds of Terror," *The Progressive*, Sept. 1986, 24–27 is important.

26. *New York Times*, 4 Feb. 1986, A3; James Chace, "The End of the Affair?" *The New York Review of Books*, 8 Oct. 1987, 26.

27. *New York Times*, 4 Oct. 1987, 16 compares U.S. and Arias plans.

28. Chace, "The End of the Affair?" 24; *New York Times*, 26 March 1988, A1; a well-known Latin American's view of Gorbachev's reforms and their effect on Nicaragua is Octavio Paz, "Plan de paz: punto de viato de un latinamericano," *Pensamiento Centroamericano* 42 (Oct.–Dec. 1987): 25.

29. Chace, "The End of the Affair?" 26; James LeMoyne, "Arias: Whom Can He Trust?" *New York Times Magazine*, 10 Jan. 1988, 69; Julia Preston, "Oscar Arias," *Washington Post*, 30 Oct. 1987, D9 for Reagan quote and excellent background; *Washington Post*, 14 Sept. 1987, A21 for Ortega quote; Martha Doggett, "Taking Note," *NACLA: Report on the Americas* 21 (May/June 1987): 3.

30. *New York Times*, 14 Oct. 1987, 30; and Ibid., 14 Oct. 1987, A14 for U.S. criticisms of Arias; Arthur C. Hicks letter to Editor, Ibid., 12 Nov. 1987, A30; Ibid., 14 Jan. 1988, A30 on Powell.

31. The "democracies de fachada" is in Emilio Pantojas García, "La politica exterior norteamericana en la decada del ochenta . . . ," *Homines* 11 (1–2, 1987–88): 285; John Spicer Nichols, "Get the N.E.D. Out of Nicaragua," *The Nation*, 26 Feb. 1990, 266–67; *Washington Post*, 29 Aug. 1988, A19 on the funding: U.S. Department of State, *Central America. Regional Brief*, July 1988, 7 on press and speech freedoms in Nicaragua.

32. *Excelsior*, 25 May 1989, 2A in *Central America NewsPak*, 22 May–4 June 1989, 11; *New York Times*, 9 Feb. 1990, 9A has Thurman quote; *Miami Herald*, 26 July 1990, 4A in *Central America NewsPak* 30 July–12 Aug. 1990, p. 1 (index) for the Costa Rican army.

33. *New York Times*, 9 March 1989, A13; *Sante Fe II*, 13 Aug. 1988 (manuscript in author's possession), especially 5–6 on "statism."

34. *New York Times*, 24 Aug. 1989, B10.

35. Ibid., 16 Feb. 1989, A1; Ibid., 25 March 1989, A1 on Contra deal with Congress; Nina M. Serafino and CRS Issue Brief, *Central American Peace Prospects: U.S. Interests and Response* (22 March 1989), is a fine overview.

36. *Washington Post*, 16 May 1989, A1; author's interviews with State Department officials, May 1983, March 1989, Feb. 1990.

37. *New York Times*, 3 Nov. 1989, A8; Ibid., 27 Feb. 1990, A12

38. Ibid., 5 Nov. 1989, 16.

39. Mary B. Vanderlaan, *Revolution and Foreign Policy in Nicaragua* (Boulder, Co., 1986), 202–9; Saborio, "Central America," 300–1; *New York Times*, 6 July 1989, A6; Ibid., 12 July 1989, D2; *Washington Post*, 25 July 1986, A24.

40. *Washington Post*, 3 Sept. 1988, A19; *New York Times*, 7 Nov. 1989, A10; *Miami Herald*, 4 March 1988, 16 in *Central America NewsPak*, 29 Feb.–13 March 1988, 6.

41. *New York Times*, 17 June 1988, A13 for Ortega's quote; *Washington Post*, 28 Feb. 1990, A1, A18; Peter Clement and W. Raymond Duncan, "The Soviet Union and Central America," in Eusebio Mujal-Leon, ed., *The USSR and Latin America* (Winchester, Mass. 1989), 286; Chace, "The End of the Affair?" 26.

42. A good discussion on the economy is in Dennis Gilbert, *Sandinistas* (N.Y., 1988), 98–103; *New York Times*, 23 March 1985, 3; Ibid., 2 March 1987, 1 on the power struggle; *Central America Report*, 29 Aug. 1986, 260 quotes the British economist; *Ithaca Journal*, 15 Oct. 1987, 12A has Associated Press story on multinationals; *Washington Post*, 19 April 1987, A20 on U.S. groups.

43. Chace, "The End of the Affair?" 28; *Washington Post*, 8 April 1986, A16; Ibid., 15 Feb. 1988, A29 on Swaggart.

44. A good overview is Olga Alexandrova and Uwe Halbach, "The Change of Government in Nicaragua: Its Regional and Global Significance," *Aussenpolitik* 41 (3rd quarter 1990): especially 280–88; Octavio Paz, "Plan de paz: punto de vista de un latinamericano," *Pensamiento Centroamericano* 42 (Oct.–Dec. 1987): 25; *New York Times*, 18 Oct. 1989, A8, and John Spicer Nichols, "Get the N.E.D. Out of Nicaragua," *The Nation*, 26 Feb. 1990, 226 for the NED funds; Alma Guillermoprieto, "Letter from Managua," *The New Yorker*, 26 March 1990, 92.

45. Alexandrova and Halbach, "The Change of Government in Nicaragua," 287–88; *Washington Post*, 30 May 1990, A22 on Soviet refusal; Larry Birns and Christa D'Alimonte, "Already, Bush Weakens Chamorro," *New York Times*, 27 April 1990, A15.

46. Nicaragua's hope for U.S. aid is in Alexandrova and Helbach, "The Change of Government in Nicaragua," 282; *New York Times*, 10 Aug. 1990, A14 on Sandinista rethinking; *Miami Herald*, 18 March 1991, 1A in *Central America NewsPak*, 11 March–24 March 1991, 9–10; *National Journal*, 18 Aug. 1990, 200 on Japan and EEC; *Resource Center Bulletin* 21 (Fall 1990): 1–6 on U.S. activity.

47. *New York Times*, 3 July 1988, 8.

48. The Central American quoted is Lic. Francisco Alvarez, "Notas de trabajo sobre la democratización y la contrainsurgencia en El Salvador," *Estudios Sociales Centroamericanos* 47 (May–Aug. 1988): 52–53; Saborio, "Central America," 297–98; *The Inter-Hemispheric Education Resource Center Bulletin* 2 (Fall 1985): 1; *Excelsior*, 22 March 1989, 1, in *Central America NewsPak*, 24 March–9 April 1989, 2–3; *Washington Post*, 7 July 1987, A1.

49. *New York Times*, 26 March 1989, 2E; Ibid., 28 Sept. 1987, A1; *Washington Post*, 27 March 1989, A17; *Excelsior*, 22 March 1989, 1, in *Central America NewsPak*, 27 March–9 April 1989, 2–3.

50. "Duarte: Prisoner of War," *NACLA: Report on the Americas* 20 (Jan./March 1986): 13–21; Terry Lynn Karl, "U.S. Aid to El Salvador," *Memo on Central America* (1985); McNeil, *War and Peace*, 162; *New York Times*, 5 April 1987, 2E; *Los Angeles Times*, 3 Jan. 1985, 17; *Washington Post*, 4 Jan. 1991, A12.

51. *Washington Post*, 3 Jan. 1990, A25 for military corruption; Ibid., 16 July 1987, A21 for union opposition; Martin Diskin and Kenneth E. Sharpe, "El Salvador," in Morris Blachman, William M. Leogrande, Kenneth Sharpe, eds., *Confronting Revolution* (N.Y., 1986), 73–74; Frank Smyth, "El Salvador's Forgotten War," *The Progressive*, Aug. 1987, 22–24.

52. Lt. Colonel A. J. Bacevich, et al., *American Military Policy in Small Wars: The Case of El Salvador* (March 1988), (manuscript in author's possession; the author is indebted to Gabriel Kolko for a copy of this paper). Note especially 6–8, 91–94. *Time*, 3 Aug. 1987, 20–21 tells of the California death squads.

53. U.S. Department of State, "The Situation in El Salvador," *Special Report No. 144* (April 1986), especially p. 5; *New York Times*, 14 Feb. 1989, 15 on Larry Gelbart.

54. Morris J. Blachman and Kenneth E. Sharpe, "Central American Traps: Challenging the Reagan Agenda," *World Policy Journal* 5 (Winter 1987–88): 17–18; Enrique A. Baloyra, "The Seven Plagues of El Salvador," *Current History* 86 (Dec. 1987): 415; *New York Times*, 29 Oct. 1987, A16.

55. Katherine Ellison, "Why Peace is Elusive," in *San Jose Mercury News*, 17 Nov. 1989, 1A has overview after election; *The Economist*, 23 March 1991, 62; *Washington Post*, 16 March 1989, A55; *New York Times*, 24 March 1988, A7; Ibid., 21 March 1989, A8 on Cristiani.

56. *The Guardian* (London), 27 March 1991, 13; *New York Times*, 7 May 1990, A1; Staff of the Arms Control and Foreign Policy Caucus, *Barriers to Reform; A Profile of El Salvador's Military Leaders* (Washington, D.C., 21 May 1990); *Washington Post*, 19 Dec. 1989, C1 on Walker; Ibid., 24 May 1990, A49.

57. *Los Angeles Times*, 15 June 1991, 1A in *Central America NewsPak* 17 June–30 June 1991, 1–2; *New York Times*, 24 July 1991, A2; Ibid., 10 March 1991, E2 has Villalobos quotes; Ibid., 5 Jan. 1992 has the peace terms.

58. Stephen Kinzer, "Walking the Tightrope in Guatemala," *New York Times Magazine*, 9 Nov. 1986, especially 38; *Washington Post*, 18 Dec. 1985, A28; *New York Times*, 5 Dec. 1985, A30; Robert H. Trudeau, "The Guatemalan Election of 1985," in John A. Booth and Mitchell A. Seligson, eds., *Elections and Democracy in Central America* (Chapel Hill, 1989), 98–107.

59. Susanne Jonas, "Whose Transition? Whose Guatemala?: An Exchange," *World Policy Journal* 5 (Winter 1987–88), 178; Saborio, "Central America," 298–300; *Central America Report*, 5 June 1987, 163; *New York Times*, 26 March 1989, 2E; *Christian Science Monitor*, 14 March 1989, 1 in *Central America NewsPak*, 13 March–26 March 1989, 6.

60. *Miami Herald*, 3 Oct. 1988, 11A in *Central America NewsPak*, 26 Sept.–9 Oct. 1988, 6; *Washington Post*, 30 June 1989, A25 on drug corruption; *New York Times*, 3 June 1990, 18; Ibid., 5 July 1990, A6; Penny Lernoux, "Guatemala's New Military Order," *The Nation*, 28 Nov. 1988, 556–58.

61. *Washington Post*, 6 May 1987, A16 on helicoptering; Ibid., 18 Aug. 1989, A25; Ibid., 22 Dec. 1990, A9; Beatriz Manz, "In Guatemala, No One is Safe," *New York Times*, 27 Oct. 1990, 23 on Myrna Mack; *San Francisco Chronicle*, 18 March 1991, 13A, in *Central America NewsPak*, 11 March–24 March 1991, 8.

62. Lindsey Gruson is quoted from a column in *New York Times*, 8 Jan. 1991, A3; Ibid., 17 Oct. 1990, A15; *Washington Post*, 13 Nov. 1990, A12; Ibid., 8 Jan. 1991, A8; Phillip Berryman, *Liberation Theology* (N.Y., 1987), 108–15.

63. The observer quoted is Tom Gibb in *Washington Post*, 8 Jan. 1991, A8; *Latin America Regional Reports*, 24 Sept. 1987, 8.

64. Robert Trudeau and Lars Schoultz, "Guatemala," in Morris J. Blachman, William M. Leogrande, Kenneth Sharpe, eds., *Confronting Revolution* (N.Y., 1986), 48 has Embassy quote; Philip Roettinger, "For a CIA Man . . ." *Los Angeles Times*, 16 March 1986, pt. V, 5 (with thanks to Max Miller for this reference).

65. *Washington Post*, 20 Dec. 1990, A1.

66. Ross Gelbspan, *Break-ins, Death Threats and the FBI* (Boston, 1991), 74–75, 209–31.

67. *Excelsior*, 15 Dec. 1987, 2 in *Central America NewsPak*, 21 Dec. 1987–3 Jan. 1988, 1–2; *Washington Post*, 19 March 1986, A30 for Baena Soares quote; *New York Times*, 18 June 1990, A11.

68. Gabriel Aguilera, "Las Fuerzas Armadas y la democracia en Centroamerica," *Homines* 11 (1–2, 1987–88): especially 215–19 discusses avenues to democracy; *New York Times*, 24 June 1990, E3; Ibid., 19 April 1987, 1.

69. The relationship between the Alliance for Progress approach and the revolutions has been superbly analyzed in Robert G. Williams's important *Export Agriculture and the Crisis in Central America* (Chapel Hill, 1986); Elliott Abrams, "Caribbean Basin," *Current Policy No. 1137* (Dec. 2, 1988); *New York Times*, 1 March 1990, D1; *Miami Herald*, 20 March 1988, 1 in *Central America NewsPak*, 14 March–27 March 1988, 1.

70. President Bush, "Enterprise for the Americas Initiative," *Current Policy No. 1288*, 27 June 1990; *Miami Herald*, 8 Feb. 1991, 6A in *Central America NewsPak*, 11 Feb.–24 Feb. 1991, 1; Institute of the Americas, *Hemisfile* (March 1990), 1–2 on Japanese investment.

71. Pantojas García, "La politica exterior norteamericana," 285–86, 289–95; George Orwell, *Shooting an Elephant and Other Essays* (London, 1950), 91; Draper, *A Very Thin Line*, 553–98; Francisco Alvarez, "Notes de trabajo sobre la democratización," 51–58.

72. A good discussion on "credibility" is Eldon Kenworthy, "Central America: Beyond the Credibility Trap," in Kenneth M. Coleman and George Herring, eds., *The Central American Crisis* (Wilmington, 1985), 111–35; Octavio Paz, *One Earth, Four or Five Worlds. Reflections on Contemporary History*. Translated by Helen R. Lane (San Diego, 1985), 168; Jerome Slater, "Dominoes . . ." *International Security* 12 (Fall 1987): 123–24; Howard J. Wiarda, "Transitions to Democracy in Comparative Perspective," *PAWSS Perspectives* 1 (Dec. 1990): especially 25–29; *New York Times*, 7 Jan. 1989, 3.

73. Arias Sánchez, "El futuro de la democracia," 63–64; Laurence Whitehead, "The Imposition of Democracy," in Abraham Lowenthal, ed., *Exporting Democracy* (Baltimore, 1991), 356–60, 371–81. The entire Lowenthal volume is important in this context.

74. *New York Times*, 3 Feb. 1991, 4E has Uhlig quote; Michael T. Klare, "The U.S. Military Faces South," *The Nation*, 18 June 1990, 861 has Cohen quote.

75. Blachman and Sharpe, "Central American Traps," 23.

76. Hector Pérez Brignola, *A Brief History of Central America*, Translated by Ricardo Sawrey A. and Susana Stettri de Sawrey (Berkeley, 1989), 179–83; Edelberto Torres-Rivas, *Repression and Resistance* (Boulder, 1989), 2; a key overview of the causes for the failure to transform the system is Victor Bulwer-Thomas, *Studies in the Economies of Central America* (N.Y., 1988), especially chapters 2 and 8; Richard Gonzales

reporting on National Public Radio "Morning Edition" of 19 Oct. 1989 (transcript in author's possession; I am indebted to Max Miller for this transcript).

77. Roberto Bardini, "Centroamerica, otro año de esperanzas frustradas," *Nueva Sociedad* 99 (Jan–Feb. 1989): 13; Francis White to Joseph Grew, 11 Oct. 1924, 121.4/12, NA, RG 59; "Testimony of Secretary of State . . . Shultz Before the Subcommittee on Foreign Operations, Senate Appropriations Committee, March 22, 1983," typescript in author's possession, H32.

Bibliography

_____

Lester Langley has estimated that some 700 publications on Central America's upheavals appeared during the 1980s. Other estimates are as high as 900. The following, therefore, is (to understate considerably) a selective bibliography. Also check the items in this book's footnotes; I have not repeated most of them here for reasons of space. A number of the references in the "General" section and those listed at the beginnings of the following sections, moreover, usually have good bibliographies for further reading. For pre-1981 annotated references to U.S. policy, start with the superb volume edited by Richard Dean Burns, _Guide to American Foreign Relations Since 1700_ (1983). Important materials are issued regularly by Central America Resource Center, National Security Archive, Amnesty International, Council on Hemispheric Affairs, NACLA, Americas Watch, and American Enterprise Institute, among other organizations.

GENERAL

The Franklin D. Roosevelt Library at Hyde Park, New York; the Harry S. Truman Library at Independence, Missouri; the Dwight D. Eisenhower Library at Abilene, Kansas; the John F. Kennedy Library at Boston; and the Lyndon B. Johnson Library at Austin, Texas have primary documents open for researchers, although accessibility and importance vary. The Roosevelt, Truman, Eisenhower, and Johnson libraries are most useful. The newly opened presidential libraries built by the friends of Richard Nixon and Ronald Reagan have only recently opened relatively few files to researchers. The Classification/Declassification Division of the Department of State, an office manned unfortunately not by professional scholars but by older Foreign Service Officers who could have a personal stake in the question of releasing records, has established overly restrictive guidelines that are sometimes even silly (as when it tries to lock up documents that have been in the public domain for years). Legislation passed by Congress in 1991 will, one can only hope, more intelligently and systematically open State Department, C.I.A., and other relevant agencies' files, although it is to be noted that the Bush administration fought the legislation in an attempt to keep executive papers locked up for longer periods of time. The Council on Foreign Relations archives in New York City are important; they are open with twenty-five years limit. The key documentary source is the State Department's *Foreign Relations of the United States,* although again its publication rate has slowed to a crawl for the post-1957 volumes because of the Carter-Reagan-Bush policies on declassification.

For general works, note Ralph Lee Woodward, Jr., *Central America, a Nation Divided* (1985), the standard account; Ralph Lee Woodward, Jr., *Central America: Historical Perspectives on the Contemporary Scene* (1988), valuable essays; Robert C. West and John P. Augelli, *Middle America: Its Lands and Peoples,* 2nd ed. (1976), a small classic; James W. Wilkie, et. al., *Statistical Abstract of Latin America,* an annual with vol. 28 published in 1990; Central America Resource Center, *Directory of Central America Organizations* (1984–), also an annual; Edelberto Torres-Rivas, *Procesos y estructuras de una sociedad dependiente (Centroamérica)* (1969), especially on pre-1945 era; Martin C. Needler, ed., *Political Systems of Latin America* (1964), with important essays; Thomas P. Anderson, *Politics in Central America,* revised edition (1988), excellent overview of 1980s placed in historical context; Jan Flora and Edelberto Torres-Rivas, eds., *Central America* (1989), especially for pre-1980 comparative studies; Tom Barry, *Central America Inside Out* (1991), an encyclopedic guide; Phillip Berryman, *Inside Central America* (1985), especially for the military's role; Héctor Pérez Brignoli, *A Brief History of Central America,* translated by Ricardo Sawrey A. and Susana Stettri de Sawrey (1989), notably on Costa Rica and Nicaragua; Abraham F. Lowenthal, *Partners in Conflict* (1987), excellent for placing the Central American debate in hemispheric context; Abraham F. Lowenthal, ed., *Exporting Democracy* (1991), especially the Tulchin-Walter, Lowenthal, and Whitehead essays on the region; and Roland H. Ebel, "Governing the City-State: Notes on the Politics of the Small Latin American Countries," *Journal of Interamerican Studies* 14 (Aug. 1972): 325–46 deserves special attention.

Additional accounts providing overviews of the U.S.-Central American relationship include Lester Langley's two surveys, *Struggle for the American Mediterranean . . . 1776–1904* (1976), and *The United States and the Caribbean, 1900–1970* (1980), as well as his *The Banana Wars* noted below; Kenneth Coleman and George Herring, eds., *Understanding the Central American Crisis* (1991), the new edition of a well-received book for classroom use that has fresh essays in this edition; John H. Findling, *Close Neighbors, Distant Friends* (1987), a well-guided scholarly journey back into time; Guy Poitras, *The Ordeal of Hegemony* (1990), which has good sections on Central America; Thomas M. Leonard, *Central America and the United States* (1991), by a widely published scholar of the relationship; Robert Leiken, ed., *Central America: Anatomy of Conflict* (1984); and see post-1960 section as well as footnotes of this book.

On economic aspects of the U.S.-Central American relationship, William H. Durham, *Scarcity and Survival in Central America* (1979) is the model; John Weeks, *The Economies of Central America* (1985), a superb narrative history; Tom Barry, *Roots of Rebellion* (1987), key on the imbalances; Charles D. Brockett, *Land, Power, and Poverty* (1990), especially for the political results; Eva Paus, ed., *Struggle Against Dependence* (1988), especially the Zimbalist, Karp, Heffernan, and Paus essays; Thomas L. Karnes, *The Failure of Union: Central America, 1824–1975* (1976), which can be read as a political companion to Karnes's important *Tropical Enterprise: The Standard Fruit and Steamship Company* (1978); José Roberto López, *La Economía del Banano en Centroamérica* (1986); Thomas P. McCann, *An American Company* (1976), and Stacy May and Golo Plaza, *The United Fruit Company in Latin America*, all of which are useful for information on "The Octupus."

Additional works on individual nations include on GUATEMALA: Peter Calvert, *Guatemala* (1985); Jim Handy's readable *Gift of the Devil* (1984); and Carol A. Smith, ed., *Guatemalan Indians and the State, 1540–1988* (1990). On HONDURAS: James A. Morris, *Honduras* (1984), especially on the military; Alison Acker, *Honduras: The Making of a Banana Republic* (1988); and Colin Danby and Richard Swedberg, *Honduras Bibliography and Research Guide* (1984). On EL SALVADOR: Marvin Gettleman, et al., *El Salvador* (1981), key documents and secondary sources; Federal Research Division, Library of Congress, *El Salvador, A Country Study*, 2nd edition, Richard A. Haggerty, ed., (1990); Alastair White, *El Salvador* (1973); and the key work of Tommie Sue Montgomery, *Revolution in El Salvador* (1982), detailed with a suggestive model for understanding Salvadoran history. On NICARAGUA: John A. Booth, *The End and the Beginning*, revised edition (1985), which is a standard account along with Thomas Walker's volumes, cited frequently in the footnotes; Peter Kornbluh, *Nicaragua* (1987); Karl Bermann, *Under the Big Stick* (1986), valuable for its research especially of the pre-1956 years; David Close, *Nicaragua* (1988), especially on rural developments; and two annotated bibliographies that have analytical introductions, both of which are produced by Neil Snarr and Associates: *Sandinista Nicaragua. Part 1: Revolution, Religion and Social Policy* (1989), and *Sandinista Nicaragua. Part 2: Economy, Politics, and Foreign Policy* (1990). Recent accounts on COSTA RICA include Marc Edelman and Joanne Kenen, eds., *The Costa Rica Reader* (1989), invaluable for its perpsectives and depth; Edward J. Heubel, "Costa Rican Interpretations of Costa Rican Politics," *Latin American Research Review* 25 (No. 2, 1990): 217–25, a review essay; and Mitchell A. Seligson' standard account, *Peasants of Costa Rica and the Development of Agrarian Capitalism* (1980).

THE 1820s TO 1945

The starting point is now Thomas Schoonover, *The United States in Central America, 1860–1911* (1991), a superb multinational, multiarchival study. Richard V. Salisbury, *Anti-Imperialism and International Competition in Central America, 1920–1929* (1989), is equally important for the next era. Lester D. Langley, *The Banana Wars* (1983), and Thomas Leonard, *Central America and U.S. Policies, 1820s–1980s* (1985) are good, different perspectives on the United States especially; while Warren G. Kneer, *Great Britain and the Caribbean, 1901–1913* (1975), provides yet another perspective. Victor Bulmer-Thomas's two books are standard on the economics: *The Political Economies of Central America Since 1920* (1987), and *Studies in the Economics of Central America* (1988), especially on the interwar era. Again consult footnotes, especially the Schmidt work on

Smedley Butler, and the volumes by Challener, Tulchin, Seidel, and Raymond Leslie Buell's two articles of 1931: "The United States and Central American Stability," *Foreign Policy Reports* 7 (8 July 1931): 161–86, and "The United States and Central American Revolutions," Ibid., (22 July 1931): 187–204. Also useful are David Haglund, *Latin America and the Transformation of U.S. Strategic Thought, 1936–1941* (1984), and Kenneth A. Jennings, "Sandino Against the Marines: The Development of Air Power for Conducting Counterinsurgency Operations in Central America," *Air University Review* 37 (July–Aug. 1986): 85–95.

On COSTA RICA, besides sources in the footnotes, consult Watt Stewart, *Keith and Costa Rica* (1964); and Carlos Calvo Gamboa, *Costa Rica en las segunda mundial, 1939–1945* (1985). On HONDURAS, besides the footnotes and works cited above in the "General" section, note Mario Argueta, *Tiburcio Carías* (1989), and Argueta's *Historia de Honduras*, 3rd ed. (1983). On GUATEMALA: books noted above and Julio Castellanos Cambranes, *Coffee and Peasants in Guatemala . . . 1853–1897* (1985). On NICARAGUA, the following among many important accounts: Ephraim G. Squier, *Nicaragua* (1860), a classic still; E. Bradford Burns, *Patriarch and Folk* (1989) on 1798–1858 anti-U.S. feeling; Craig L. Dozier, *Nicaragua's Mosquito Shore* (1985); Jaime Biderman, "The Development of Capitalism in Nicaragua: A Political Economic History," *Latin American Perspectives* 36 (Winter 1983); Henry L. Stimson, *Conservatives, Liberals, and Sandinistas: American Policy in Nicaragua*, introduction and commentary by Paul H. Boeker, a needed reissue of Stimson's account; Augusto C. Sandino, *Sandino: The Testimony of a Nicaraguan Patriot*, edited and translated . . . by Robert Edgar Conrad (1990), which should be a companion volume to the important Macaulay and Millett books noted in the text; Harold N. Denny, *Dollars for Bullets* (1929), a contemporary exposé; William Kamman, *A Search for Stability*, standard for the 1925–33 years. On EL SALVADOR the key event's model treatment is Thomas P. Anderson, *Matanza: El Salvador's Communist Revolt of 1932* (1971); E. Bradford Burns, "The Modernization of Underdevelopment: El Salvador, 1858–1931," *The Journal of Developing Areas* 18 (April 1984), explains superbly why *Matanza* climaxed the era.

1945–1960

Standard accounts on the relationships are Donald Dozer, *Are We Good Neighbors? . . . 1930–1960* (1959); Laurence Duggan, *The Americas* (1949), by a key State Department policymaker who became disillusioned; David Green, *The Containment of Latin America*, especially for the 1940s context; Milton Eisenhower, *The Wine is Bitter* (1963), important for the 1957–59 turn; and of special note, Gabriel Kolko's provocative, *Confronting the Third World* (1988), which puts U.S.-Central American policy in the 1945–80 global context. Edelberto Torres-Rivas, *Repression and Resistance* (1989) is five essays especially important for post-1945 class development; while the U.S. perspective is in Thomas M. Leonard, "Nationalism or Communism: The Truman Administration and Guatemala, 1945–1952," *Journal of Third World Studies* 7 (Spring 1990): 34–51. Other recent, key works on Guatemala include Susanne Jonas, *Test Case for the Hemisphere* (1974), on

1950–74; Piero Gleijeses, *Shattered Hope* (1991), unsurpassed for analyzing the Guatemalan side of the 1944–54 developments; Gleijeses's *Politics and Culture in Guatemala* (1988); and the Immerman, Schlesinger-Kinzer, and Wiesen Cook volumes cited in the footnotes. Two books by Charles D. Ameringer are of special note here as well as in the footnotes: *The Democratic Left in Exile* (1974), key on post-1945 Central American politics as a whole, and *Don Pepé* (1978), a life-and-times treatment of Figueres.

SINCE 1960

For further reading, start with the references cited in the footnotes, especially of Chapters IV, V, and VI, as well as material noted in the "General" section above. Many of those references and materials are not repeated here. An extraordinary work that links the 1960s to the 1980s is Robert G. Williams, *Export Agriculture and the Crisis in Central America* (1986), a starting point for future research; also Richard Fagen, *Forging Peace* (1987), which suggestively links economic growth and political results; Morris J. Blachman, William M. Leogrande, and Kenneth Sharpe, eds., *Confronting Revolution* (1986), outstanding essays on individual countries and regional and foreign powers involved; Bonne Szumski, et al., *Central America: Opposing Viewpoints* (1984) a convenient compendium of the arguments; John A. Booth and Mitchell Seligson, *Elections and Democracy in Central America* (1989), another set of excellent essays on individual episodes; Stan Persky, *America, The Last Domino* (1984), Canadian journalist's firsthand account, especially interesting on El Salvador; Clifford Krauss, *Inside Central America* (1991), revealing work on the 1980s by *New York Times* correspondent; John M. Kirk and George W. Schuyler, *Central America* (1988); diverse essays placing 1980s events in social context especially; Howard Jones, ed., *The Foreign and Domestic Dimensions of Modern Warfare* (1988), conference papers especially useful because of Woodward and Leonard essays; Roger W. Fontaine and James D. Theberge, *Latin America's New Internationalism* (1976), for the Fontaine, Smith, and Theberge essays.

On special topics, the indispensable volumes on human rights are Lars Schoultz, *Human Rights and U.S. Policy Towards Latin America* (1981); Sandy Vogelgesang, *American Dream, Global Nightmare* (1980); Dermot Keogh, ed., *Central America: Human Rights and U.S. Foreign Policy* (1985), a multinational view; Ann Crittenden, *Sanctuary* (1989), a critique of the 1986 U.S. Immigration Act; Barbara M. Yarnold, *Refugees Without Refuge* (1990), important on U.S. asylum policies. On the church, the starting place can be Edward L. Cleary, OP, *Crisis and Change* (1985), especially on liberation theology; Dermot Keogh, ed., *Church and Politics in Latin America* (1990). Peter Dale Scott and Jonathan Marshall, *Cocaine Politics* (1991) reveals U.S. involvement with the drug traffickers in Central America. Jonathan Feldman, *Universities in the Business of Repression* (1989) tells a tragic regional story. Bruce M. Bagley, *Contadora and the Diplomacy of Peace in Central America* (1988) is a multinational perspective. On economic relationships, besides the Robert Williams and the Durham volumes noted above, note Richard E. Feinberg and Bruce M. Bagley, *Development Postponed* (1986); SELA (Sistema Economico Latinoamericano), *América Latina/Estados Unidos* (1986), part of a series on economics during the debt crisis; William R. Cline and Enrique Delgado, eds., *Economic Integration in Central America* (1978), invaluable; and the Clark W. Reynolds essay in Joseph Grunwald, ed., *Latin America and World Economy* (1978); as well as Gary W. Wynia, *Politics and Planners: Economic Development Policy in Central America* (1972), and the important Weeks's volume noted above under "General."

Some of the works that are helpful on U.S. policy include Cynthia J. Arnson, *Crossroads* (1989), a firsthand account of the congressional-executive struggle; Edward Best, *U.S. Policy and Regional Security in Central America* (1987); Nora Hamilton, et al., editors, *Crisis in Central America* (1988), especially the essays on case studies; Robert A. Pastor, *Condemned to Repetition* (1987), an N.S.C. official's account of why the Carter policies failed; Luis Maira, ed., *La Politica de Reagan y la crisis en Centroamerica* (1982), papers from 1980–82; U.S. Congress, House, Committee on Foreign Affairs, Subcommittee on Western Hemisphere Affairs, *Central America: The Ends and Means of U.S. Policy* (Washington, 1984), one of many revealing congressional hearings by this subcommittee; Morris Morley and James Petras, *The Reagan Administration and Nicaragua* (1987), which ranges beyond Nicaragua; and Morley's and Petras's essay in Morley, ed., *Crisis and Confrontation* (1988); Karl Grossman, *Nicaragua: America's New Vietnam?* (1984), especially on Reagan's larger policies toward Contras; Joshua Cohen and Joel Rogers, *Rules of the Game: American Politics and the Central America Movement* (1986); John Womack, Jr., "El Salvador and the Central American War: Interview with John Womack, Jr.," *Socialist Review* 12 (March–April 1982): 9–30, which again goes far beyond El Salvador.

For regional and extra-American involvement, in addition to the footnote citations, the following are useful: James Petras and Morris Morley, *U.S. Hegemony Under Siege* (1991), especially for Germany and Japan; Jorge I. Domínguez, *To Make a World Safe for Revolution: Cuba's Foreign Policy* (1989); Francisco López Segrera, *El conflicto Cuba-Estados Unidos y la crisis Centroamericana* (1985); Wolf Grabendorff and Riordan Roett, eds., *Latin America, Western Europe, and the U.S.* (1985). For the Soviet policies: Nicola Miller, *Soviet Relations with Latin America, 1959–1987* (1989); Cole Blasier, *The Giant's Rival: The USSR and Latin America* (1983); Timothy Asby, *Bear in the Backyard* (1987); Augusto Varas, *Soviet-Latin American Relations in the 1980s* (1987); Robert Wesson, ed., *Communism in Central America and the Caribbean* (1982).

There are numerous important works on Nicaragua and the Contras, but besides the footnote citations the places to start are Dennis Gilbert, *Sandinistas* (1988), which is invaluable for both its argument and coverage; Thomas W. Walker's books, including *Nicaragua, The Land of Sandino*, 3rd ed. (1991); his editing of *Revolution and Counterrevolution in Nicaragua* (1991), which has post-February 1990 material; and his other works noted in footnotes; Mary B. Vanderlaan, *Revolution and Foreign Policy in Nicaragua* (1986), a detailed, comprehensive view; Shirley Christian, *Nicaragua* (1985), a critical view of the Sandinistas by a correspondent; Forrest D. Colburn, *Post-Revolutionary Nicaragua* (1986), which keys on the land-politics relationships; Gary Ruchwarger, *People in Power* (1987), a study of grass-roots organizations and especially useful for its analysis of women's role in the revolution; Alejandro Martínez Cuenca, *Sandinista Economics in*

Practice (1991), by a top Sandinista economic official; Martin Diskin, et all, *Peace and Autonomy on the Atlantic Coast of Nicaragua* (1986), a LASA report on treatment of the Miskitos; Michael Dodson and Laura Nuzzi O'Shaughnessy, *Nicaragua's Other Revolution: Religious Faith and Political Struggle* (1990), highly important. John Booth's *The End and the Beginning*, noted above in "General," is standard.

For El Salvador, in addition to Tommie Sue Montgomery's work noted above, the following are important: Enrique A. Baloyra, *El Salvador in Transition* (1982); Raymond Bonner's superb firsthand account (buttressed with newly declassified documents), *Weakness and Deceit* (1984); Martin Diskin and Kenneth Sharpe, *The Impact of U.S. Policy in El Salvador, 1979–1986* (1986), succinct and important; Adolfo Gilly, *Guerra y politica en El Salvador* (1981), by an analyst who obviously knows the regional context; Philip Russell, *El Salvador in Crisis* (1983); Martha Doggett's *Underwriting Injustice: AID and El Salvador's Judicial Reform System* (1989); America's Watch, *El Salvador's Decade of Terror* (1991), horror authoritatively; Stephen Webre, *José Napoleon Duarte and the Christian Democratic Party in Salvadoran Politics, 1960–1972* (1974) is the necessary background of the 1960s and 1970s.

On Honduras, in addition to footnote citations, an important place to begin is Cornell Capa and J. Mayone Stycos, *Margin of Life* (1974), also important for El Salvador; Mark B. Rosenberg and Philip L. Shepherd, eds., *Honduras Confronts Its Future* (1986); Philip L. Shepherd, *The Honduran Crisis and U.S. Economic Assistance* (1988); Steve C. Ropp, "The Honduran Army in the Socio-Political Evolution of the Honduran State," *The Americas* 30 (April 1974): 504–28, definitive; Nancy Peckenham and Annie Street, eds., *Honduras* (1985); and James A. Morris and Steve C. Ropp, "Corporatism and Dependent Development: A Honduran Case Study, *Latin American Research Review* 12 (No. 2, 1977): 27–68, essential for the post-1932 era.

On Guatemala, begin with footnote citations and "General," then: Susanne Jonas, *The Battle for Guatemala* (1991), especially for Indian degradations and U.S. policy; Michael McClintock's two-volume *The American Connection*, with Volume II, *State Terror and Popular Resistance in Guatemala* complementing the first volume, *State Terror and Popular Resistance in El Salvador* (1985); George Black, et al., *Garrison Guatemala* (1985), especially on 1981–83 slaughter; Beatriz Munz, *Refugees of a Hidden War* (1988) on effects of counterinsurgency on Indians; Henry J. Frunt, *Refreshing Pauses: Coca-Cola and Human Rights in Guatemala* (1987), on union, Catholic Church involvement; Ligia Mercedes García Alburez, *El proceso de industrialization y el desarrollo del mercado interno en Guatemala* (1978), important for its discussion of Alliance for Progress impact.

For Costa Rica, in addition to footnote references, Mitchell Seligson's work, noted in "General" above, is the starting point; also Victor Brajer, "An Analysis of Inflation in the Small, Open Economy of Costa Rica," Research Paper #18 University of Mexico Latin American Institute (June 1986).

Acknowledgments

(First Edition)

This book attempts to turn the vast amount of material available on U.S. relations with five Central American nations into a coherent and, it is hoped, instructive story. In a sense, this is a companion (but much longer) volume to *The Panama Canal; The Crisis in Historical Perspective* (N.Y., 1978, 1979). Both books try to move beyond the usual diplomatic history—that is, what we said to them, they to us, and we to ourselves—to analyze the impact of U.S. policies on the peoples and institutions of Central America. This account necessarily only sketches the multiple aspects of that relationship, but it tries to offer several frameworks and an historical outline that others can fill in, prove, or disprove.

I owe debts, both personal and scholarly, to friends who read the drafts and raised questions about this account: Thomas Holloway, Dick Polenberg, and Joel Silbey of Cornell; Lloyd Gardner of Rutgers; and Thomas McCormick of the University of Wisconsin. Others have been generous in providing important materials; these friends include Max Miller, Eric Edelman, Virginia Harrington, Katherine Harris, Susan Horn, Stephen Arbogast, and Richard Mandel. Professor John Booth of the University of Texas-San Antonio graciously sent me galleys of his important work on the Nicaraguan revolution. I am grateful to Ambassador (Ret.) Murat W. Williams for materials relating to U.S. policy in El Salvador. Students in my senior seminar from 1981 to 1983 were not only delightful to work with, but helped me understand U.S.-Central

American relations far more than their grades indicated. Coraleen Rooney handled the typing with patience and care.

The Cornell Library staff, particularly Carolyn Spicer and Dan Hazen, provided, as always, indispensable help. I am also indebted to the staffs of Presidential Libraries: John Wickman and Martin Teasley of the Eisenhower Library; Linda Hanson, David C. Humphrey, and Martin Elzy of the Johnson Library; and the professionals at the Kennedy and Truman libraries. David Langbart, of the diplomatic division of the National Archives in Washington, went far beyond his duty in locating sources. Mr. Gary L. Fitzpatrick and Mr. Thomas G. DeClaire of the Library of Congress Map Division provided important help with the maps.

The idea for this book came from Michael Curtis of *The Atlantic*. He published part of its main argument in *The Atlantic* and kept me at the project even after it grew far beyond what he or I had envisioned. I am grateful to him; Edwin Barber, vice-president (and tactful editor) at W. W. Norton; Kathy Kornovich and the Norton staff; and Gerry McCauley, whose handling of this manuscript was that of a friend as well as a professional.

Once again, I am indebted to Marie Underhill Noll, to whom this book is dedicated, for her long commitment to Cornell and her friendship and encouragement to my family and me. As always, I am most indebted to Sandy—and to Scott and Suzanne who may most benefit from this book.

Acknowledgments

(Second Edition)

For this edition, new material has been added to the first four chapters, Chapter V has been completely rewritten, and Chapter VI has added the 1985 to 1992 years. Besides those mentioned in the first edition's acknowledgments, I owe special thanks to many for advice and materials that shaped this new edition, including Max Miller, Dan Weill, Mary Vanderlaan, Cynthia Arnson, Tommie Sue Montgomery, Jim Siekmeier, Tom Walker, Dennis Gilbert, Gabriel Kolko, Dermot Keogh, Eric Alterman, Eric Patterson, David Maisel, David Langbart, Karl Meacham, Alan Lepp, Dr. Peter Mott, Gail Mott, Ms. Winnie Jordan, Michael Kammen, Joel Silbey, Dick Polenberg, Bill Brownfield, Eric Edelman, and, of course, Tom Holloway and Bud Kenworthy. I especially appreciate the help, interest, and friendship of several on the list because they disagree with many of the arguments offered in this book. In addition, I am most grateful to Leslie Hilgeman, Kerry Chase, Agnes Sagan, and Lizann Rogovoy who as Cornell undergrads provided important research help over some four years; to Steve Gimber of American University; to the Cornell Libraries' staff, especially David Corson and Caroline Spicer, for help over many years; and to Amy Loyd and Juli Goldfein of W. W. Norton.

Above all, I am indebted to the general readers who obtained this book on their own and often reacted to it; and to the many students who did not always obtain it voluntarily, but sometimes reacted to the argument by joining one side or the other in the public debate. All of these readers made the possibilities of a second edition attractive to Ed Barber of W. W. Norton and Gerry McCauley, two friends who have been unfailingly patient and encouraging.

—February 1992

Index